FETHULLAH GÜLEN

&

THE GÜLEN MOVEMENT

IN 100 QUESTIONS

FETHULLAH GÜLEN

&

THE GÜLEN MOVEMENT

IN 100 QUESTIONS

Doğu Ergil

Translated by Bekir Aksoy

Published by Blue Dome Press
535 Fifth Avenue, Ste.601
New York, NY 10017-8019

www.bluedomepress.com

Library of Congress Cataloging-in-Publication Data Available

ISBN: 978-1-935295-15-0

Printed by
Çağlayan A.Ş., Izmir - Turkey

CONTENTS

INTRODUCTION FOR THE ENGLISH TRANSLATION

The Gülen Movement was born at a time when a rapid social change was taking place in Turkey. However, at the same time a parallel movement was taking place in the world: emergence of political Islam or politization of Islam, in response of globalization. What was transpiring in Turkey at the time? As rapid urbanization, class differentiation, and cultural shifts from village and small towns were flocking to the cities, alternative frames of reference were needed. A balance had to be struck between the traditional values that people were socialized in and modern values; these new behavioral patterns would help them to navigate through the challenges of modern city life.

Fethullah Gülen offered them this balance, neither praising traditionalism nor condemning modernity as many Islamic currents do. Gülen always was reluctant in being adopted in dimensional approaches to the understanding of social reality and management of social life.

For example, he rejected uncontrolled power of the state over the society, as well as the individual. He was a firm believer in human volition and individual choice. This meant empowerment of the individual, as well as the civil society.

The Gülen Community started and developed as a civic movement. The reason why it has grown so rapidly and so large is its civic and voluntary character. Additionally, it empowers its adherents through a system of solidarity and collaboration. This is a social-psychological haven in which individuals meet their soul mates and future partners. They grow a sense of belonging to a worthy group that protects and supports them through mutual economic enterprise; they help each other by engaging in common venture. Through education, not only do they rise on the social ladder but they also become international actors, through international activities and networks they form or partake in. The members of the Gülen Movement try to influence international affairs. They try to mitigate between beliefs and belief groups, helping to reduce tensions. They try to emphasize common values and principles among religions, thus bringing out human similarities rather than differences. They believe that by emphasizing what is human, the universal triumphs over the particular.

Many in countries populated by Muslims see modernity and the West as the main culprits of their colonization, underdevelopment and victimization. In order to dry out this infectious swamp of negative feelings, Gülen proposes two things:

1. A healthy blend of religion and science that would meet the needs of mind and soul.
2. Simultaneously, reifying Islam from the historical and cultural baggage full of superstition, anger, and violence, because it has been infested with politics and has become an instrument of power struggles.

Political Islam denies the apolitical character of religion. For Gülen, politicized Islam is a political project rather than faith. It is totalistic and it has an antidemocratic program of its own in shaping all aspects of social life. He does not accept this totalitarian understanding of religion. To his understanding, Islam's statements about politics and the state do not exceed 3–5% of its teachings. And these are general principles about good governance.

According to Gülen, if there is to be an Islamic identity, it has to be constructive and based on achievement, adaptive creativity, and peacefulness. However, in most Muslim countries the Islamic identity is based on the rejection of modernity and western values and institutions including democracy, pluralism, and rule of law. This rupture with Western civilization and failure to create its own civilization in modern times not only has brought clash of values, but also prevented the amalgamation or blending of civilizations which Islam, especially its Turkish version (as Islam is perceived and is practiced in Turkey), could contribute a lot.

Gülen sees this amalgamation as the dawning of an Islamic renaissance, as well as a world built on interfaith peace.

Now a few sentences on Turkey:

Turkey is claimed to be a nation state; however, it resembles a state nation, where the state controls all vestiges of life and behavior of its citizens. That is why all opposition to this totalistic control of individuality and collectivity has been directed to over throwing the authoritarian system, rather than democratizing it and reinstructing a new one. The leftist movements and the Kurds are clear examples.

Only Gülen has chosen a peaceful way to transform the authoritarian system: dialog, deliberation, education, economic enterprise, civic organization, and building solidarity and networks. Empowering the civil society is the means of this peaceful transformation. If the definition of revolution is to alter the social and economic infrastructure of a political system, it may be done forcefully, as before, or peacefully as Gülen suggests. It begins with people changing themselves, a change from below as opposed to the other version of change or modernization. This is a revolution which has never been witnessed in Turkish history. Let us see whether his spark ignites the whole society or not.

Doğu Ergil
November 2011

INTRODUCTION

*Fethullah Gülen: The Phenomenon of an Opinion Leader in a
Rapidly Modernizing Turkey*

S
ocieties need ideologies of solidarity to hold them together. In underdeveloped societies, family and blood relationships are far more important. Living with people whom one has known for one's entire life provides a sense of security. Strangers are not trusted and are generally little more than a source of anxiety for locals. For this reason, communities that live together and cooperate extensively obtain the mutual trust they are seeking by establishing blood relations among themselves.

Kinship of this sort can be achieved in two rather ritualistic ways. The first method is through the intermarrying of two groups. The second is the literal mixing of blood through self-inflicted wounds. By this method, the two members become blood brothers. Either method ensures that the next generation is blood relatives. Tribes that were historically influential, but did not have the population necessary to establish hegemony, developed their strength by these methods. For example, the Quraysh, the Prophet Muhammad's tribe, increased its population and influence by these means. Similarly, this is how the original Ottoman tribe was able to spread its influence in such a short time.

The spread and growth of communities based solely on blood relations has always been limited, however. Sooner or later, many groups are brought together either by necessity, (either for defense or cooperation) or by force. The feudal system of Europe and the empires in Asia came into existence as a result of such an evolution. The emperor or central authority may be able to maintain the unity of numerous ethnic and religious communities for a long time. Once this oppressive unifying power is weakened, however, a process of fragmentation takes place. The largest empire that the world had ever known at the time was the

Mongolian Empire of Genghis Khan. As soon as Genghis Khan died, this large nation divided into smaller, more manageable states.

After the fall of the Roman Empire, feudalism was the dominant political system in Europe. Feudalism generates a deeply fragmented world and has three attributes: local administration, local production, and local consumption. Even the kingdoms established from time to time arose from this structure. In this fragmented world, it was unavoidable to feel the need for a common culture and a common vision of the world and an understanding of humanity's place in it. There was a need for a system of ethics and values which would guide social relations among them, at least within the ruling class.

This need was satisfied by an institution which would at least unite the fragmented political setting, as well as add a more sophisticated cultural dimension to medieval life. That institution was Christianity. If someone were to ask what idea had the greatest influence on medieval Europe, the answer would incontestably be Christianity. In pre-national Europe, which was divided by groups of peoples and kingdoms, religion comprised the primordial material of European culture. Religion and its agents acted above political and social groups and above the jurisdiction of feudal lords. If we were to read history backwards, the foundations of the European Union could be traced back to this common culture.

If today's Europe is saying, "The foundation of our political unity lies not in religion, but in democratic culture and ideals like equality and pluralism," we cannot deny this. At the same time, though, can we ignore the role of the faith-based infrastructure which prepared Europe for this unity?

This is because religion served as a chest that carried Europe's common cultural heritage from the past to the present. The keys to this chest are in the cultural consciousness and memory of all of the Christian nations. Why then do the leaders of the European Union refer more often to their secular and democratic values rather than to Christianity?

They do so because they know that humanity has values other than religious ones and these values are epitomized in a libertarian legal system, shaped by the supremacy of the law, democracy, human rights, and equality. It could not be otherwise, because in addition to numerous different sects of Christianity, the European continent also contains 20 million Muslims and several million Jews. In such a diverse Europe, it is no longer possible to establish a political system based completely on religion.

Additionally, it does not seem possible to have healthy and peaceful relations with the adherents of other religions in a Europe based purely on religious foundations. For all of these reasons, Christianity has to a great extent become a purely spiritual practice, moved from the worldly sphere to an exclusively cultural one. Politics and the administration of worldly life are based on the foundation of democracy, the rule of law, individual rights and freedoms, and cultural plurality.

Democratic culture is open to all societies because it is independent of religious and ethnic bonds, but is on good terms with them at the same time. This message also attracts Turkey, the population of which is predominantly Muslim, to the European Union. Two questions prevent this attraction from reaching a happy union. First, to what extent and in what future timeframe, will Turkey be able to internalize the culture of democracy, disposing of the statist, authoritarian, and ethnic reflexes that have been living in its collective consciousness? Second, when will Europe look at Turkey with a measure of political, economic, and legal development, rather than from the angle of her religious and cultural differences?

Returning to the idea of an ideology based on cultural solidarity, nationalism fits perfectly in history as a unifying ideology, which is based neither on blood nor on faith. Nationalism is an ideology of solidarity for people seeking political unity or for those privileged few who would like to establish a group of nations by use of the power of the state. Nationalism represents the ideal of unity based on political partnerships among groups based on different ethnic, religious, or cultural backgrounds.

There are two requirements for nationalism to be successful. First, the state must be successful in the goals which are the reasons for its establishment. It must provide welfare, dignity, security, freedom, and justice to its subjects. It must be loyal to the ideal of the supremacy of law and stay away from capricious actions and decisions which can slip so easily into degeneration. In other words, it has to display an effective administrative system and direct that system in an ethical and fair manner. This is the balance between the material and the moral.

Second, there should be no discrimination among the groups within a nation that come from different ethnic, religious, and cultural backgrounds. The state must stand an equal distance from all and provide absolute and unquestionable legal guarantees, along with full rights to participate in the political system. Implementation of a nationalism based only on one element of this plural structure would be a source of division, trouble, and confrontation rather than a source of unity.

In fact, many nations have failed to establish this balance. In the end, civil wars take place and the sense of national unity is forever scarred. People who lose their security and hope in this sort of internal fighting often seek refuge in mental and spiritual shelters. Many of them turn to religion. Across the world, people of all ethnicities and cultures seek in religion the same security and solidarity that nationalism ultimately failed to provide.

Nevertheless, the "metanarratives" of the three great religions are too large and comprehensive for modern society, which corresponds with the dissolution of tradition and traditional societies. For this reason, people feel the need for new interpretations to accommodate them and their new worlds, as long as that new interpretation is loyal to the roots of their faith and the value system established by it.

These communities, composed of people who share a vision, are not the kind into which one is born, but those which one voluntarily joins. In these communities religion is less rule-based and more spiritual, which is more adaptable to a secular lifestyle. Many signs exist indicating that the world is entering into an age of secular spirituality. This process is causing a rapprochement between differing belief systems and shows a tendency to bring together adherents of different belief systems at a point with humanity itself at the center. It is observed that the act of praying to the Supreme Being, the act of following the rules that govern interpersonal relationships, and the process of seeking the self, begin to resemble each other.

The great religions receive enriched interpretations from the diversification of worldly life, and from these new interpretations worldly life becomes subsequently more enjoyable by way of the same progress which it provoked. In this opened space, many spiritual realms previously closed are opening, and these enriched civil societies are, through new groupings, coming together to make up many different s (communities).

This new born pluralistic structure is creating a new field, a blend of the traditional and the modern, between the religious and the worldly. In this space, individuals are able to find appropriate answers and relationships corresponding to their desires and needs that they could not find in other spaces and relations. They finally reach the motivation, the opportunity for personal development, to act together, and from this togetherness the possibility to manufacture a culture of peace. All these prepare the required foundation of solidarity on which democracy can be constructed.

These changes bring all aspects of life closer to middle. On one hand, they pull the great religions towards the significance of the human individual and on the other hand, they provide a soul and a conscious to the cruel, selfish, market economy. Even if not at the structural level, at least within the framework of a spiritual community, it provides a solution to the loneliness and powerlessness of the individual. Within this group, the individual feels more powerful and protected.

The more secure one feels, the more bonds he forms with the community. If a thought system cannot accommodate these communities, which are so significant to the individual, it will be difficult for it to evolve from a community into a society, and from a society into a nation. If parallel communities are unable or unwilling to produce a common culture through political ideologies, then spirituality would fill the vacuum that politics had left.

Market economics are often divisive for societies and they give priority to the community's material concerns. To bring into it an altruistic and compassionate spirit without disrupting its core requires a religious perspective. By this token, there is a need for the sense of spirituality that comes from a community. Such a unity keeps in check the divisive and materialistic practices of the market economy, which already encompasses the entire globe.

It is no accident that these practices are replacing the entirely secular state, from which we are increasingly distancing ourselves as a people. The two major trains of secular spirituality, one sustained entirely by religion and the other related to worldly conditions, present themselves as an urban phenomenon and correspond to the post-modern world.

It seems that Gülen is acutely aware of this process. Since his name first became known in 1970s, the number of his followers has increased over the past 35 years. This period corresponds with high inflation (at times 100% annually), internal civil turmoil, and military interventions. All of these issues lead to an absence of a feeling of security and solidarity. Gülen and his teachings provided a remedy for this ailment and his ideas were sought out and heard with ever-increasing enthusiasm.

With his religious message, Gülen has worked to fill a social gap which pure nationalism failed to do. With words that show that the salvation of the people and the nation lay in the hands of the people and the nation, he has worked to lift the spirits of the masses and to initiate a communal mobilization. Initially, this was a flame which at the time seemed completely extinguished, yet he sought to reactivate the masses that had been long starved for a route to national solidarity.

Gülen offers his followers a Turkish renaissance. The caveat for this renaissance, however, is that it can only happen in a society which has achieved peace and tranquility. Most people are attracted to the idea of civil law based on agreement and consensus rather than on imposition, a conception of ethics and morality based on acceptance not force, and an understanding of solidarity, not based on favor but working hard, producing, and sharing and before everything else, the suggestion that the individual being responsible for the entire society as well as for himself. What is offered is not a nation built on the state in the Turkish sense of the word, but the idea of an order and a nation based on the partnership of the citizens.

The message and the work of Gülen should be assessed within this framework. And from this perspective, what is the secret of his success? This book will provide the answers to this question. The answers are taken from sociological analysis which he expressed in interviews, as well as in writings he provided to the author which had already been published.

1. Who is Fethullah Gülen?

Fethullah Gülen, "Hocaefendi" (pronounced as "Hodjaefendi") in the words of those who respect and love him, was born in the village of Korucuk, Pasinler, Erzurum in Turkey, in 1938. Due to the slow pace of life in villages, he was registered later in the official ledger. For this reason, the official entry in the ledger states 27th of April 1941. His father was Ramiz Efendi and his mother Refia Hanım. With the encouragement of the family and pious acquaintances, he read the Qur'an and became a *hafiz* (a person who knows the entire Qur'an from memory). His family, who detected a tendency toward the religious disciplines in him, made sure that he obtained good religious education from renowned scholars in Erzurum, beginning with Osman Bektaş Hoca after completing the Qur'an memorization. He enriched his knowledge by participating in the teaching circles of leading Sufis. After finishing his studies, Gülen began his official career (being a civil servant of the Republic of Turkey) as an *imam* (prayer leader) at Edirne Üç Şerefeli Mosque.

Before and after mandatory military service (he served in Mamak, Ankara, and İskenderun), he worked in this mosque as an *imam* and preacher for a total of four years. After Edirne, he was appointed to a mosque in Kırklareli province, where he served as *imam* for one year. He was transferred to İzmir in 1966 as a preacher. He served first at Kestanepazarı mosque and later at Bornova mosque. In addition to giving religious sermons, he also governed the Kestanepazarı Boarding Qur'anic Course (which is also owned and operated by the Turkish government). He was already on his way to becoming an opinion leader who was deferred to and respected through his public and private teaching circles. From about 1969 to 1971, he traveled to different cities and towns, giving religious sermons and providing religious education. His activities were not limited to only the province of İzmir. Until 1980, he provided his services in Edremit, Balıkesir and the province of Manisa. By this time, his reputation went beyond the Aegean Sea region of the country and reached the largest metropolitan center in Turkey, İstanbul. In 1989, at the insistence of the citizens of İstanbul, he began acting as a volunteer *imam* in the largest mosques of İstanbul. He maintained this work until 1992.

It was during this time that he improved on the Arabic and Persian languages he had learned during his childhood, and he became capable of reading religious documents firsthand. The Aegean and Marmara regions and especially İzmir and İstanbul had received a massive wave of immigrants from the interior of Turkey. These immigrants came from traditional backgrounds in Anatolia and had difficulty adapting to an urban lifestyle. They acutely felt the need for a new interpretation of lifestyle to reconcile their traditional values with the expectations of this new urban environment. But this interpretation had to be provided by an *alim*, a religious scholar who was trained in classical learning, whose learning and character they trusted. They found this person in Gülen. They had been waiting to see sacred texts purified of the past social residues—namely, from the experiences of other nations and societies. They sought an authentic understanding, loyal to the core of the Islamic message and able to answer the real needs of the day. In fact, this need was felt by Muslims throughout Turkey. Gülen's ability to meet this need made him a sought-after opinion leader and "Hocaefendi," a respectful title, which means "a man of high education" or "scholar" (out of extreme modesty, Gülen feels embarrassed to be subject to such a respect).

Learning circles started around him, consisting of those who sought his leadership and who saw his interpretation of Islam as a compass by which they could orient their lives. Gülen, who was drawing larger and larger crowds, was forced to make a critical decision. Would he be a civic leader? Was he going to govern daily lives of people? And probably most important of all, was he going to play a political role in his community? Or, would he take another path and preach solely a message of spirituality and inspire others to make their own choices in the religious and ethical fields of daily life? Gülen chose the second option. He committed his life to addressing the problem of how people were to establish a direct relationship with their Creator and based his philosophy on that foundation. He taught that true faith was the key to discovering one's true self in interpersonal relationships. When he said that loving your fellow human being was the other side of the coin of loving the Creator, he was suggesting that through the bridge of love, it is possible to reach other human beings. He emphasized that by using tolerance and dialog it was possible to make the "other" closer. He believed that anyone who could achieve this was the beloved servant of God.

In his teachings and suggestions he always reiterated that the local and the global did not contradict each other, neither could be dispensed with. Rather than they being in opposition and exclusive of each other, they had to be in harmony. His ideas, which are compatible with the modern life, resonated with the urban middle class. They used to see themselves as part of the modern world. They had respectful lives and professions; they had no problems earning their livelihoods. Nevertheless, they were acutely aware that their spiritual lives were not rich enough to make their lives meaningful. They wanted to see moral and ethical degeneration eradicated; they wanted the sense of trust and solidarity strengthened, which had been increasingly weakened. They also were looking for a way to connect with other people who felt the same way that they did. Much of the urban middle class was gathering around Gülen to have these needs fulfilled.

2. What is Gülen's education, both official and unofficial?

Gülen's only official education is elementary school. Gülen explains some interesting episodes in the process of his own education:

> In those days there was no school in our village. The school that exists there today was not opened until much later. They used the *madrasah* [school of religious education] next to the mosque that still stands today as a classroom. They used to teach reading and writing to the children during the day and to the older men and women at night. As I observed the state in which those old men and women found themselves, I used to laugh at them. They seemed to me funny. They did not let me into the school the first year because I was not old enough. When I attended, I still was not old enough; but I attended anyway. I attended two or three years. One of the teachers was an ardent enemy of religion. He could not even stand that I was praying during the breaks. But I used to climb up one of the desks and pray there. He named me *mullah* [Islamic scholar] just because I did my ritual prayers.[1]

His mother Refia Hanım had a great impact on him. It could even be said that she was his first teacher. She would teach the Qur'an to her

---

[1]   Erdoğan 2006, 35.

daughters during the day and to him during the night. According to his mother, "Fethullah had finished reading the entire Qur'an at the age of four, in one month. Since then he never skipped his prayers."[2]

Gülen recalls some of his memories belonging to his childhood:

> Sibgatullah, my brother, is three years younger than me. That means if I was 9, he had to be around 6. So, all the foot service was left to me. Shepherding our cows and sheep was my responsibility.
>
> I used to pass my free time by reading. I do not know how I learned it, but I have been able to read Ottoman Turkish fluently for as long as I can remember. In those days I read all the books that my father owned. I inherited his admiration for the Prophet and his Companions. I had almost memorized their life-stories.
>
> My father was also my first Arabic teacher. He taught me some portions of the classical books *Amsila* and *Bina*. But later, some people suggested to my father that he should have me memorize the Qur'an. My father hesitated at first, but later he decided to send me away for that purpose with couple of other children.
>
> I used to do memorization whenever I had time left over from doing chores and shepherding. Despite the distractions, I put in as much extra effort as I could in those days. I could memorize as much as half a *juz*, that is to say 10 pages. During the summer it was difficult to find time for memorization, but I finished it during the winter.[3]

The foundation of Gülen's unofficial education was his education in the *madrasah* in Erzurum. Gülen completed his memorization of the Qur'an at the age of fourteen. His father wanted him to go to Hasankale, a village 5 miles away, to take *tajwid* (refined technique of reciting the Qur'an) courses with Hacı Sıdkı Efendi. The problem was that he did not have a place to stay in Hasankale. Therefore, every morning he would have to walk five miles to participate in Hacı Sıdkı Efendi's study circle. And every evening he would have to walk the same distance back home.

Gülen's father was not ready to allow him to walk this distance back and forth alone, as he was still a child. But at the same time, he did not want to deprive him of this important religious education. So, Gülen was sent to the religious scholar Sadi Efendi in Erzurum. His *madrasah* education in the Molla Mosque became the foundation of the love of learning and discovery that continues to this day.

---

2   *Ibid.*, 28.
3   *Ibid.*, 36.

In summary, a religious family environment and parents who made efforts for their son to have a good religious education determined the future of Gülen. Since his childhood, Gülen looked at life through the window of faith. This outlook allowed him to dedicate his life to thinking about how the needs of the modern human could be reconciled with the requirements of faith, without breaking away from the realities and richness of life and without fear or worry. Gülen considers every day of his life to be a continuation of his never-ending education; the world is his classroom. This perspective has become the most salient feature of his personality.

3. What are the primary teachings—religious, historical, political, and social—which have greatly impacted Gülen's worldview?

In my opinion, though a person must know the importance of religious introspection and the training of the soul, he must also see the value of the sciences, literature, history, and philosophy. He should learn from physics to chemistry, from biology to astronomy, their fundamental principles at least. He may also read from the existential philosophers, and primary sources from both the East and the West, like Camus, Sartre and Marcuse. With this aim in mind, I have kept my range of reading a little bit wider than it might have been otherwise.

As for my religious development, it would be safe to say that it came mostly from the Qur'an and Islamic sources. In order to reach the depths of Islamic civilization, I have benefited from the classics, Imam Rabbani, Ghazzali, Rumi, Abu Hanifa and the other thinkers in the fields of *Kalam* [Islamic Philosophy] and *Tafsir* [Exegesis]. From among the contemporary thinkers, I read Elmalılı Muhammad Hamdi, Mustafa Sabri, Ahmet Hamdi Aksekili, Babanzade Ahmet Naim, İzmirli İsmail Hakkı, İsmail Fenni Ertuğrul, M. Şemseddin Günaltay, M. Ali Ayni. These teachers and a number of others have contributed new dimensions to my accumulation of knowledge.

Over the course of one Ramadan, with some friends, I studied the largest of the *hadith* [Prophetic saying] collections, 16 volumes of *Kanzu'l Ummal* of Muttaki'l Hindi, which contains more than 46,000 *hadiths*, from cover to cover. Likewise, even if not with the same intensity, I have studied some important works in the fields of Islamic *Fiqh* [Islamic Jurisprudence], *Tafsir*, *Tasawwuf* [Sufism], and *Balaghat* [Rhetoric] collections, and some of them several times. I have loved reading since I was a kid.

My love of reading began in my childhood with *siyar*, namely the biography of our dear Prophet, and the stories of the Companions. In later years, it continued with scholarly works of intellectual and philosophical books. Meanwhile in addition to the Eastern classics, with the advice of one of my superiors in the army, I read almost all of the Western classics. As I tried to get to know the masters of the Eastern classics like Rumi, Sadi, Hafiz, Molla Jami, Firdawsi, Anwari, I tried to know, through their works, Shakespeare, Balzac, Voltaire, Rousseau, Kant, Zola, Goethe, Camus, Sartre. Besides those I also read Bertrand Russell, Pushkin, Tolstoy and some others. I have researched many different subjects from Bacon's logic to Russell's theoretical logic, from Pascal to Hegel's dialectic from Dante's Divine Comedy to the relationship between subject and object in Picasso.

As I read, I discovered the subtle relationships between thought and the art and I took great pleasure in it. Alongside giants of our classical literature, like Fuzuli, Baki, Sheikh Galib and Leyla Hanım, I also read with passion the most significant writers of Turkish prose and poetry, like Yahya Kemal, Necip Fazıl, Mehmet Akif Ersoy, Sezai Karakoç, and also Namık Kemal, Şinasi, Tevfik Fikret.[4]

From the explanations of Gülen about the sources that shaped him, two ideas become clear:

The life of a human being does not consist of two separate compartments, the material and the spiritual. This is impossible. For this reason, one should have access to both of them and benefit from each. This is the path to becoming an ideal human being.

The second is that if the mental equipment of a man of religion is limited to religious sources that man cannot benefit from the fruits of all the ideas of human civilization. He will never be a true guide for the people of our time and for the complex problems of modern life.

3a. What is Gülen's understanding of history? Where does he place himself in the flow of time?

For as long as I can remember, I have always felt a yearning for the Golden Age of Ottoman history which was taught to me. I imagined and felt this time not only in my mind but in my heart.

I am unable to know what role I will play in history, or at what point I am entering. When we talk about history, as the late Turkish poet Akif reminds us,

If I had seen His rose period,
I would be nightingale.

---

[4]   Ünal 2002, 509.

O my Lord, I wish you had brought me
to this world a little earlier!

... my heart always roams around the Golden Age and looks for him. I sincerely believe that a time such as that can be brought onto our country again. I am grateful and thankful to God that we are living on the eve of such an age.

The way I see things we are new fresh shoots of our national roots. By thinking this way, if we anchor ourselves mentally and spiritually to the better periods of our society, we could purify ourselves of our deviations and faults. We could renew ourselves. We could find in our history the goodness and kindness that we have lost. We could discover ourselves once again to be in the ocean of meaning, we could release ourselves from the loss of identity. By virtue of creating a continuity, we establish in our minds and souls, to the extent that we could comprehend the depth that our history submits to us, we could find the strength to reconstruct it, according to the needs and the new circumstances of the new world. This would make us a part of the history as well as makers of it. What a great privilege it is to feel this way![5]

3b. Who has influenced him the most in history?

Each one of the Four Rightly Guided Caliphs [Abu Bakr, Umar, Uthman, and Ali] with their particular merits seems very striking to me. For instance, Caliph Abu Bakr squeezed so much good work into only two years that it is difficult for me to imagine such industry. In order to understand him, I am thinking that it is necessary to investigate the time period he was living in under a microscope. Umar brings in me a feeling of deep admiration because he opened, over a larger period, many gates into different areas of life. And yet despite all of this work, the true greatness that he achieved was in his modesty, through which he nearly erased himself. He said: "Whenever I go, I will go a happy man, for I have come into this world, and that alone is good enough for me." He had no desire for worldly wealth and temporary power, he sought only to deepen his own piety and not refused to recognize the authority of any other than God. It is often stated that Marx was also fond of him.

When I remember Umar bin Abdul-Aziz, my eyes are filled with tears. Again I admire Fatih and especially Osman Ghazi. Compared to the acts of Fatih like the conquest of İstanbul, the things Osman Ghazi accomplished might seem to be smaller, but he is the architect of a nation. While laying the foundation of a great formation, he had employed all of his intellectual, spiritual, and physical energy onto his work and using the military and

---

[5]   Gündem 2005, 73.

political genius which he displayed during difficult times, he accomplished great things. In short, there are certain men of action and thinkers who influenced me. This is normal but I would like to explain my views about cultural transactions: Different cultures mutually influence each other. The continuity of thought is maintained this way across generations of humans. But culture, just like garments, cannot simply be taken off of someone else's back and given to another to wear. What happens when we try to do that? New, hybrid cultures are born. They are no longer the pure form of what they were in a previous time or geographical setting, but the exchange is that they are able to come into harmony with the features of the social and political environment in which they find themselves.[6]

A culture, take Turkish culture, for example, despite its color and richness, cannot express the same meaning to another group of people that it does for us. It cannot generate the same emotions in them. This is because culture is not made of the same stuff that material products are made of. They cannot be chosen, purchased, and taken home in the same form in which they were first encountered. It is a whole which is made up of elements of the very environment in which it developed. It is a combination of all of the different times and places and people, and belongs to this context. In fact, these two things, the culture and the context in which it exists, are inseparable. They are the same thing. In order to place it in a framework, unifying all the elements which make it up, it is necessary to think of it together with all the historical, social, and economic elements behind it. When we see it from this perspective, the first thing which becomes clear is that culture is a way of living and a set of behaviors for a given nation at a given time. The first thing that we notice is the mutual influence between the philosophy of life of a nation, reflecting its culture and its style of conduct. This is exactly what distinguishes nations from each other [these varied ways of thinking and behaving].[7]

However, Gülen believes that cultural differences are not capable of dividing the family of humanity into separate parts. According to him, despite all these differences there are common characteristics, which come naturally as a consequence of being human and are bestowed on humanity by the Creator as a gift. These common traits are what bring us together. Along with the satisfaction of having food to eat and a safe place to live, all humans desire justice, freedom, solidarity, spirituality, trust, protection, respect, and the opportunity to develop their personal talents. While they manifest themselves in different forms in different societies,

---

[6]   *Ibid.,* 72–74.
[7]   Gülen 1998a, 2.

in the abstract they represent the essence of civilization. Thus, cultures are like rivers running into an ocean called civilization. We can only in our own way, within in our own culture, retain our existence and, at the same time, become part of the civilized world. We can have contact with other cultures in the ocean of contemporary civilization and take from them contributions to enrich our own culture.

The area that this cultural exchange occurs the most is in the fields of technology and science. A society which closes its doors to the aforementioned interaction and mutual influence will have difficulty in both retaining its own existence and protecting its cultural individuality. In the end, it would be weakened because of it. In other words, we live in a world of our own, but also in a universe that we share with others. We do both of these concurrently. To the extent that we do it, we are both ourselves in our own cultural context and part of humanity at large; we are both local and global. When we deny this multi-dimensional aspect we confine ourselves within the castles of a limited identity, which is not in harmony with our character of being human. This sort of exchange also diminishes fundamentalism and brings us together with common human values. This is a very important point in Gülen's thinking. It is impossible to interact effectively with other cultures unless you are the bearer of a culture that will enrich the common civilization of humanity. Gülen believes that we are at a historical crossroads: We must revive our distinctive cultural identity—which at one time attracted great admiration from all over the world—to once again produce something which will contribute to the universal human civilization. Otherwise, we will never escape from the domination of other cultures. With these ideas, Gülen sees our age as the proper time for Turkey to become a world leader again, the writer of history and not the object of it. To this end, it is not surprising that he instructs the followers of his movement to contribute to this process with all of their talents and enthusiasm.

4. What changes took place regarding his world view and at what stages? Namely, what are the mental and philosophical stages in his thinking from the first days of his preaching until he became an opinion leader and held the influence that he holds today?

Gülen's answer to this question demonstrates that from early on, he took a holistic approach in his worldview, which evolved as time went by. It would be safe to attribute, at least partially, this perspective to his wide reading of the classics from the East, as well as the West, during the period of his childhood. For this reason, he believes that in all of the time that he has been preaching in mosques, there has not been a serious wavering in his thought. Of course, this does not mean that his thinking has not been enriched by the knowledge and the life experiences that he acquired later. Only, that he maintained a stable, solid course in his thought and general approach. As he explains it, there was "no change from black to white." He then adds:

> But, in my speeches and assessments, it is unavoidable to have small changes depending on time, place, and human factors. For instance, in my early preaching, when I considered the problems that arose from the behavior of the Jews, I used to consider them with an approach of generalization, and I used to interpret some verses and the sayings of the Prophet within that framework. But, in the atmosphere of dialog that began after the 90's, I distanced myself from that approach. I brought forth the idea that the counter arguments given in the Qur'an and the *hadiths* should be approached with a holistic view, rather than taken as specific accusations directed towards specific individuals. I did this because, it is more in line with the universal message of Islam, and I advise the people who are listening to me to take it that way as well.[8]
>
> A society which has been settled and stable for a long time and is open to reason will have a philosophy of life and a national manner of speech which is inherently unifying.[9]

Leaders who stress that differences among us are dangerous, rather than highlighting our common characteristics and our common needs, sow the seeds of doubts and enmity among their populations. At this point in time, peace should be based on common benefits and interests among communities.

According to Gülen, this unifying approach is the essence of democracy. The continuity of democracy depends on the interaction of the various segments in a society. Democracy maintains open channels of communications between the rulers and the ruled. Popular participation in decisions regarding community issues and common living must be unhindered by discrimination against members or groups within the

---

[8]   Doğu Ergil's interviews with Fethullah Gülen in January 2003 and February 2006.
[9]   Gülen 1998a, 3.

community. Agreements and peace in society can only be attained in this way. The primary function of government is therefore to facilitate this decision-making process and to organize the decisions into a set of laws.

Gülen's understanding of democracy, though, is not limited to a harmony between the ruling class and the ruled. He expresses a vision of a holistic democracy:

> From the teacher in a school to the preacher in the pulpit, from the writer for a magazine to the news commentator in front of the camera, from the literary artist to the painter, are natural carriers of democratic values and ideals, and the work that they do is inherently democratic.[10]

Gülen stresses that democracy does not happen by accident, nor is it exclusively available to certain cultures or societies. Extra effort is necessary to establish and maintain it, as well as an additional burden on the shoulders of the civic leaders and intellectuals:

> Leaders are people who think and produce, but they also encourage others to think and produce. By persistently broadcasting a message to the members of their community, they awaken it, they motivate it, and they prepare them for the difficulties that they are likely to face. They put them in circumstances in which their inherent gifts and talents can shine forth, and orient themselves and their communities towards every greater vision.[11]

Leaders continually expand the horizons of the people around them. They encourage others to transcend the material and spiritual limits into which they have been confined. Leaders would never encourage people to be passive and lazy, but to act on their ideas, and the leaders would guide them in their actions. According to Gülen, this is the way that you lay the foundations of a society that is dynamic and self-sufficient, rather than a society whose members are dependent on the authorities.

For Gülen, a mature society consists of citizens who ask questions and search for answers. It is a productive society which values sharing, takes care of its deprived and weak and, at the same time, critically assesses the orders and decisions coming from the authorities. A mature society rejects flawed decisions and constantly forces the rulers to improve their performance and to produce alternative solutions to exist-

---

[10]　*Ibid.*
[11]　*Ibid.*

ing problems. Thus, the government becomes the apparatus for the implementation of decisions made by the public. Demands and expectations that are diverse and potentially controversial are filtered through common interests and able to be reconciled. When such symbiosis is established between the ruler and the ruled, it is able to serve as a midwife for a new democratic political culture. In this process, the role of the social leader is important; but at the same time, every individual must work to conduct himself beyond the dictates of his own interests. Though a leader may guide, the future of the society is the responsibility of everyone involved.

Gülen attributes this phenomenon of responsibility to religion. According to him, a person can find in Islam the direction that they are searching for in life, as well as the source of the motivation necessary to reach their goals. But this does not mean that Islam is a closed circle and the only source of inspiration and knowledge:

> It is the duty of the members of an Islamic society to seek out the most beneficial ideas and thought structures, even if they lie at the end of the world, and put them to use. Yes, just as it always has, it takes the very best of physics, chemistry, astronomy, geometry, medicine, agriculture, industry and all other technologies, and uses them, develops them and leaves them as a legacy for future generations. There is no reason that an Islamic society would not continue this vigilant practice even today.[12]
>
> Mankind is the servant of God on Earth. This makes it part of his duty in such servanthood to cherish a deep love for the truth, a passion for knowledge, and research with dedication and commitment every field of human study. A believer should be as open as possible regarding matters other than those relating to the system of faith and thought. He should develop whatever he takes from the outside and develop and leave it to the future owners of it. This is the way that knowledge, science, and technology have traveled from nation to nation and from generation to generation, and has ultimately become the common heritage of all mankind. How can a Muslim deprive himself of this common heritage of intelligence and labor? It is out of the question to talk about the religion and nation of these matters, anyway. For this reason, societies that have self confidence are fearless against the modern world. If they can adopt the modern sciences as part of their culture, and if they have the right to express themselves freely, there is no limit on what they can accomplish.[13]

---

[12] Gülen 1999, 4.
[13] *Ibid.*

5. It is often noted that Gülen was influenced by Bediüzzaman Said Nursi and the Nur Movement. To what extent has Gülen accepted the teachings and social projects of Nursi? Can we talk about continuity or are there points where he differs from Nursi?

There have been people whom I recognize for their greatness and whom I admire deeply. For instance, I admired and tried to comprehend the intellectual and emotional dimensions and criteria of the great *tasawwuf* thinkers. Imam Rabbani, Mawlana Khalid, *Aktab-i Arbaa* [the Four Spiritual Poles], Abdulqadir Ghaylani, especially Syhayhul Harrani, Hasanul Harakani, Akil Menbici, and Muhammad Bahauddin are all great heroes of mine. Following in their footsteps seemed to me like walking behind the God's Messenger.[14]

He says, "I always mention with admiration the many numerous people from whose thoughts and interpretations I feel that I have bene-fited. I think of them as my teachers." However, the place of Bediüzzaman Said Nursi holds special significance. Gülen notes, "that he belongs to this age and reads this age well." He explains the influence of Nursi on himself as such:

The works Nursi produced are a good prescription for those who are searching for answers to their faith-related questions. There are letters which could be characterized as the summary of his correspondence with his students; He had offered there a model of a society without friction, without deviating toward radicalism or violence, without endangering the peace and tranquility of the society. A society based on justice, fairness, and respect for all people.[15]

Gülen says that through his upbringing he developed deep respect and love for the great personalities of *tasawwuf*. He points out that he always mentions their names in his prayers, and asks for their *himmet* (spiritual support). But, he also acknowledges that when he reads the works of *salaf-i salihin* (those belonging to the earliest age of Islam), which have benefited him very much, he has found passages that he believes contradict the Islamic understanding of love and respect. But this is not the case with Bediüzzaman Said Nursi. Nursi's work in chal-

---

14 Gündem 2005, 73.
15 *Ibid.*

lenging the age in which he lived had a great impact on Gülen. On this issue, he states:

> [Bediüzzaman] is like a *mihrab* [the semicircular niche in the wall of a mosque that indicates direction of Mecca] of the thinking system. If one faces something other than the *mihrab* in thought, he would be as if leaving the *kiblah* [direction to Mecca]. But alas! A lot of people in this country have turned their backs on this *kiblah,* which is just in their houses or very close to them, and directed their faces towards the West. With negligence, which is difficult to understand, they are deprived of him.[16]

The issue of Bediüzzaman Said Nursi which impressed Gülen the most was his criticism of the arbitrariness of the administrators. Nursi voiced his criticisms, not because the administration went against his own opinion, but, for the betterment of society. And he voiced his criticism in a time during which it was especially difficult to do so. In all of Nursi's ideas, one can see an underlying concern for raising the level of spiritual comfort in one's life. In letters that he wrote to his students, he attempted to convey the importance of building a moral society by starting from the individual. Gülen expresses the opinion that what Nursi wanted to do was not to generate a *tariqa* (Sufi order), but to save the "faith" or the totality of all the necessary beliefs and values that shape a good human being and a good society.

Gülen sees Nursi's collection of *Risale-i Nur* as the spiritual and mental mortar that holds together an aggregate social mass. According to Gülen, with his spiritual and social influence, Nursi is an important leader of a group of thinkers who speaks with a more or less unified voice. His complete works might not have the systematization and discipline of contemporary scholarly works, but the values that he emphasizes and the way he discusses topics and offers solutions have helped many people.

> These works do not only awaken the religious enthusiasm in the masses, they also strengthen the bonds of community among people. This bond protects them from the external distractions and internal confusion.[17]

In conclusion, Said Nursi and the *Risale-i Nur* collection had a great impact on Gülen and his movement. This impact, however, was in the

---

[16]   Gülen 2009a, 172.
[17]   Ergene 2005, 109.

spiritual and inspirational dimensions. The praxis of the Gülen Movement (the combination of theory and practice) is rather *sui generis* and is derived through the circumstances and conditions of our age. Therefore, the influence of the Nur Movement on the Gülen Movement is not direct or organic.

6. Is the Gülen Movement a continuation of any other previous movement?

Those who are within the Gülen Movement do not consider themselves the continuation or the extension of any other movement. At a certain time and under the perfect circumstances in Turkish History, the teachings of Gülen coincided with what a broad sector of Turkish society was searching for in their hearts. This is what allowed for the birth of such a movement.

The movement, in the words of Gülen himself, has produced a link between tradition and modernity. It has produced its own traditions, improved on the commonly held concept of Turkish society and moral life, and marked its own positions from which to view the world. Additionally, it has developed its own organizational model, and has shouldered a universal mission to disseminate its views throughout Turkey and the rest of the world.

Never before has such a social movement, which is able to spread the same message abroad that it teaches within its borders, arisen in Turkey. "There has been no heritage offered to us of this level, be it ideological, political, socio-cultural, or Islamic."[18]

Then, how does the movement produce the internal cohesion which is a source of dynamism and strength? Stated differently, how does the movement maintained and how does it generate the motivation necessary to maintain internal solidarity? The questions can be answered in two ways:

1. The values that Gülen represents and the interpretations are in harmony with the time in which he delivers them to a society that is searching for the exact message of solidarity and spirituality that he is delivering.

---

[18]   Ergene 2005, 108–109.

2. Gülen stands out as a strong and trusted leader. He, unlike others who quickly disappoint after the most brief encounter, does not contradict what he preaches with what he does; he is not after any material or political interest; he does not demand any position; his actions alone convince others of his integrity. He engenders loyalty among his followers, and he serves as both a civic leader and spiritual guide.

The movement is distinguished from the other Islamic movements. There are religious movements today involving many political and sociological researches in the East and the West, but they were born as a continuation of experiences in the past. They claim that they are the inheritors of a past socio-political movement. The fact that these movements anchor their future in the past throws them into an unrealistic thought-space: The tomorrow that they offer is a yesterday that they cannot bring back. Thus, they are attempting to construct an artificial "today." This often leads to fanaticism or violence, at times as far as justifying suicide bombings of innocents.

On the other hand, the Gülen Movement appears to have succeeded, in part, by correctly reading the change necessary in Turkey. The members of the movement are those who found meaning in the teachings of Gülen at a juncture when a traditional society was transforming itself into a modern one. Gülen encourages people to embrace the change and not to limit themselves to small worlds, but to become part of the larger one. They, in turn, have come to see the whole world, not only their own country, as the terrain of their mental and spiritual land. The fact that they go to every corner of the world as students, teachers, technicians, and businessmen is an indication that they have been united with this teaching and became citizens of the globe.

Above all else, Gülen is a religious leader and his followers are religious people. It is immensely satisfying to them that they have been carrying out the requirements of their religion through the inspiration that they draw from Gülen. They see their success as an indication that God is pleased with their work. While some certain men of religion interpret their religious texts and principles in a way which constrains abilities of the believers and limits their freedoms, Gülen interprets the same texts in a way that advocates individual initiative, self-improvement, and entrepreneurship. This provides the movement with a great dynamism and influence.

Another common characteristic of the followers of Gülen is that the majority has great upward mobility. They are among the modernizing population and they are seeking a foothold in this new space. For this reason, the Gülen Movement does not harbor any animosity towards other groups which may be slipping from their current position.

If there is any oppositional stance within the group, it is against those who do not sufficiently understand the movement, or against the practices that perpetuate moral degeneration. However, even in these instances, they prefer to express these disagreements with a cultural nomenclature (enlightenment and communication of the message), rather than with a political terminology.

The movement places great emphasis on both education and knowledge of world affairs in order to achieve this upward mobility. This motivates them to learn different languages and to live and work all around the globe. This sort of effort is a cure for both fundamentalism and obscurantism. This desire for cooperation and communication is further emphasized by the efforts for intercultural and interreligious dialog in the areas where they operate.

The movement takes extra care to share the common language of peace that it has developed with other religious and cultural groups. Followers view themselves as belonging to a social movement, a nation, a religion, and the great family of humanity. To neglect any one of these would make them lesser individuals. Because of this way of thinking, they do not see themselves as an isolated group. They have one foot in the circle of the nation and religion and the other in every corner of the world.

When the members of the Gülen Movement describe where they stand, it becomes easier to understand why they have no quarrel with the universal values of the West, as they have none with the values of their own country. This keeps them at a place away from political disputes and polarization. They simply do not have any time to worry about petty political matters. They are too busy working, teaching, talking, and learning under many different administrations within all sorts of cultures, all around the world.

Their concern is not with the behavior of political systems, but with people. How do they define this ideal that they are striving for? Is it simply religious, obedient, and otherworldly? After all, this is the classical definition of what it means to be a pious person. This is not the sole type of person that the members of the movement aspire to become. Through the inspiration and exhortation of Gülen, they seek to think, learn, work, produce and transcend themselves in order to be of the world and make sure to share with the needy the value produced in the process. Their lower limit is their families and the relatively modest situation from which they came, but they have no upper limit.

It can be observed that these views give the movement a great flexibility and compatibility. As followers become successful, their trust in Gülen's leadership and their loyalty increases. They no longer wait on the concrete directives of Gülen to act. Instead, they consult among themselves with the direction or inspiration they get from him. They make decisions on their own and move forward. Because the sense of solidarity and sacrifice among the members is so strong, the time between making the decision and executing it is minimal.

The Gülen Movement has been labeled "right wing" and has been criticized by the "radical right-wing." When asked about the reason for this criticism on both sides, the members of the movement emphasize that they are impartial: They are on neither side of the social and political polarization; they are not a party to any fight. They express themselves in the cultural field. What they desire is a society where differences are reconciled, ethical values are observed and good quality people lead. With their modest means and through solidarity with each other, they are trying to contribute to the production of people of ethical and sympathetic excellence. Many religious circles do not understand this social aspiration, and often criticize them as not being religious enough, as if being religious consists only of worship. All the principles, values, and advices are for the happiness of human beings, in this world and the next. Without the believer there can be no belief and the faith of the ignorant would not be in accordance with the will of God. For this reason they have no relations with any religious or political movement or organization.

7. What are the basic principles of the Gülen Movement?

The answer to this question cannot be separated from the fact that Gülen is a man of religion. Gülen has committed his life to understanding the principles of religion, commenting on it, and sharing his religious teachings with others. In order to understand what he says and does, it is necessary to keep this perspective. Misguided people try to seek out things in Gülen and his movement which are not present, from political ambitions to material gains. The person who tries the hardest to correct these misconceptions and who is the most offended by them is Gülen himself.

When his discourse and actions are observed over an extended time period, the obvious conclusion is that Gülen's aim is to reconcile tradition with modernity. According to him, a healthy modern society has three attributes: communal harmony, hard work, and productivity. The solidifying force to all three is the strength of the society's democracy. These concepts are realized in the form of investment and entrepreneurship and make the improvement of the market economy possible. Additionally, ethics and solidarity maintain societal stability. This last attribute implies that those who trust each other and resist social degeneration both increase their individual capacities for work and self development, and also elevate the quality of life of the society as a whole.

The basic characteristics of Gülen differentiate him from other theologians and opinion leaders. What is the source of this difference? First of all, Gülen was influenced greatly by Sufi teachings and tradition. This influence can be seen not only in his religious interpretations, but also in his general Sufi lifestyle.

His general conduct is modest. He does not consider himself superior to anybody else, and he holds tolerance in the highest regard. The way that these values reveal themselves in his personal conduct are that Gülen listens carefully to others before he begins to speak. He is also in general a very bashful person. His bashfulness is sometimes misinterpreted as secrecy. In his eyes, there is still so much to be learned and there is so much mystery in the world, and this posture of his reflects his respect as well as his astonishment.

Another attribute of Sufism is that the individual takes it upon himself as a responsibility to be a virtuous and perfect human being. An ideal person feels responsibility for society as much as he does for himself. He wants for others what he wants for himself. Gülen places this responsibility in the center of his conception of religion. According to him, a Muslim is a social being and to the extent that he has spiritual depth, he allows the wellbeing of others to factor into his decision-making. This sense of devotion to others is the foundation of his understanding of ethical conduct.

Gülen's teachings also have a constant national undercurrent. He exhorts his followers to strengthen their nation, to open up to other humans and to embrace the larger family of humanity. Gülen proposes three spiritual devices in this matter: modesty, tolerance, and the devotion of the self to humanity.

It is not an accident that the Ottomans spread across huge territory, embraced many groups from different religions and cultures, and were able to maintain their internal peace. The fact that there was no discrimination among the groups in its domain played a great role in this achievement. It is likely that the Gülen Movement with its numerous schools worldwide has derived lessons from the experience of the Ottomans. The followers of the Gülen Movement refer to this as the "line of Rumi and Yasawi," i.e. unconditional love, and view this perspective as a gift from the Turks to the world.

The ventures of the movement allow for relationships and dialogs to develop within the full spectrum of cultural circles. This dynamic of dialog between faiths and civilizations is critical. The Gülen Movement takes extra care not to lose this perspective. This is essential to Gülen's core beliefs, and his followers hold the same opinion.

According to Gülen, in the essence of all divine religions based on revelation lies the hope of reaching the absolute truth. In the Gülen Movement, this offer is more than an abstract promise. In all the actions and initiatives of the movement, there is the intention of turning this ideal into an active program. For that reason, as much as there is sacrifice and altruism in Gülen's faith and worldview, there is sacrifice and altruism in the movement. Empathy is one of the most important principles of the Gülen philosophy and expected from his followers. The ability to embrace others indiscriminately makes the individual closer to God, as well as making him closer to the human ideal. For this reason, this call is a duty that religion imposes on him. This is what Gülen refers to as "metaphysical tension," or "spiritual alertness." As the individual performs his action with this tension, he can approach the human ideal. Closeness to the ideal diminishes this tension and the individual reproduces himself as a perfect person in the process.

If empathy were not the fundamental principle of the movement, its members would not be willing or able to carry their message to the farthest corners of the world. They would not be able to communicate with people whose ethnicities, religions, and nationalities are so diverse and different from their own. Such sacrifices are found only in a strong belief. Gülen knows this very well and uses his religious interpretations to foster a mentality that produces a synergy between social work and spiritual development.

8. While today there are many Muslim thinkers and practitioners in the name of Islam, what is it in Gülen's teachings that seem to be so attractive to his followers?

There are three answers to this question.

    I.   The Gülen Movement is an open circle.

    II.   It is on good terms with the authorities.

    III. It does not hold a coercive moral approach. Morality and moral laws are not enforced by external forces.

Now, let us explore each point separately.

I. The Gülen Movement arose among pious men and women who wanted a modern interpretation of religion, cleansed of superstition. At the beginning, there were many among his followers who did not send their daughters to school. But through his inspiration began sending their daughters to school and even to the university. .

In the dynamics of the transformation of the movement, circumstance and the social milieu also played an important role. A rich, progressive city like İzmir, with a population of recent immigrants from smaller cities, played a primary role in helping the movement take on the character of a big city. The movement gradually began to employ those with a higher and higher social status. The movement became a spiritual refuge for those who searched for an interpretation where Islam was in harmony with modernity. Gülen understood this need well and satisfied it. For this reason, many began to understood the world better through his interpretation; they found answers to the basic issues of existence, duty, trust, sacrifice, tolerance, ethics, charity, goodness, happiness, peace and success.

This social body has become a community in harmony with the world. It is not fearful of the new era in which the world is heading and is in the process of being crystallized. It welcomes the changes that are occurring and is always looking to the horizon. Its followers have never been squeezed into the narrow confines of being merely a religious community. The Abant Platform, which began by the inspiration of Gülen, reached an important understanding at its first meeting in 1998: Revelation and reason do not contradict each other. When people put their social lives into order, they should use reason. The state should be impartial towards religion. State administration should not be based on religious principles. As a policy, secularism should not limit the legal activities in public life, just as it does not limit personal and private freedoms.[19] It is clear that the struggle of the Gülen Movement is not with others. Their struggle is with their own souls. They strive to become ever-improved and moral human beings; they strive to face their fellow human beings as they would like to face their Creator—with a clean slate.

There is another aspect of the Gülen Movement that allows it to transcend the bounds of a religious community. They have never approved the motto, "*Bir lokma, bir hırka,*" which translates as "one coat, one bite." It is a famous expression in Turkish Sufism and refers to the state of being a very poor person, and though he may have only one bite to eat and only one coat to wear, he is traveling on the path of the *dervish*. According to this philosophy, this state is desirable for the spirit. For Gülen, this is not enough to keep the body and soul together. God had given them reasoning and individual talents. To obey His commandments is to take these gifts to their highest level. This, in turn, means to work hard and to be productive. The harder they work, the more value is generated for the community. Is there a saturation point in this idea? Or worse, a breaking point? Worldly industry and blessings may serve to erode the very same values that inspired them. It can be said that the personality, character and the lifestyle of the leader in the movement does not allow for that. Gülen lives like a *dervish*—who is content with little, whose personal consumption is very limited, who never married, and whose personal integrity has never been compromised. He lives in this manner before the

---

[19]   "First Abant Platform Meeting Final Declaration,"
*http://abantplatform.org/main/component/option/frontpage/section/1/
category/135/content/40*

scrutinizing eyes of the public. Although he leads such a lifestyle, he advises his followers to work, to succeed, and to become wealthy. But he advises them further: Their wealth should be used to educate and to strengthen those deprived of it. In the West, this is called "human capital." Gülen believes that the richest and most influential societies are those with the greatest human capital. The result is a philosophy of life and ethics which puts one foot on the side of the lofty ideals of religion and the other on the side of the "human." It is the philosophy of those who do not lose perspective on the world in which they live. This outlook seems to be convincing and attractive to many people. As opposed to many other religious communities, its embrace of change makes the movement open to the world and does not imprison the members in the confines of one particular group by separating them from modernity. It is important to remember, however, that the Gülen Movement still sees itself as a community of believers first and foremost. But they see all the characteristics of being a modern person to befit them.

The followers of the Gülen Movement do not describe themselves as a political movement as some claim that they are. They absolutely refuse to be seen in that light. Gülen often talks about the debasing, corrupting, and polarizing influence of politics on people. The movement sees itself as the carrier of an offer for an ethical doctrine and a sense of solidarity. It is not afraid to rid society of its tendency to become divided and closed off from the world. It is these same tendencies which limit a nation's ability to compete internationally.

The movement has no revolutionary intentions or any political agenda of any kind. Gülen is defending the real revolution which takes place within each and every individual. He thinks that ethical, altruistic, industrious, and compassionate people can become the foundation of an ethical and productive society. Further, he believes that this is possible, only if we understand religion in its purest form, not imprisoned in a cultural context, and if we conceive and interpret religion in a way which allows humans to develop. He believes that the societies, which initiate change within themselves, can flow more easily in a world which is itself rapidly developing and changing.

II. The second answer to the question why Gülen's teachings are so attractive to his follower is because the movement is on good terms with the authorities. It is clear that this movement is a civil society project and not political. For this reason, it is not in a fight with political authorities nor other civil society groups.

III. The final point contributing to the attractiveness of Gülen's teachings is that it does not hold a coercive moral approach.

Morality and moral laws are not enforced by external forces. There are two types of ethics in Social Psychology: external and internal. The external ethics are the measures and types of behavior imposed on people from without. The individual obeys these rules and regulations only under the existence and observation of that authority. If somebody runs a red light when there are no police around, or if he thinks he can steal from the budget entrusted to him and get away with it, shows that a person has not internalized a sense of ethics. This reflects on the society as a whole, that this society views morality as a set of official rules whose subjects are under observation and monitoring. Morality is achieved through the threat of an authority with a stick in its hand. In societies such as this, to the extent that the authority is weakened or becomes incapable of oversight, the disregard for the rules and social degeneration only progresses further. Moreover, if the government fails to treat the population equally and does not monitor it in order to prevent unfair action, the sense of justice in the society weakens and ethical degeneration will lead to violence. There is a Turkish expression, "If meat is foul, you can salt it, but what if the salt is foul, too?"

For Gülen and his followers, ethics should be a tool for dialog with one's self and in interpersonal relationships. There is no need for an external authority. It is enough for people to guard themselves and internalize their own code of ethics. One who cannot be true to himself can never be true to others. If the individuals of a community cannot be compassionate and empathetic, then any dialog entered into would not come from a place of seeking common ground, but a place of self-interest. The resulting social landscape would not be based on solidarity and trust, but on egoism and materialism. The future of such a society is always ambiguous.

9. The ethical considerations of Gülen and his movement are made up of what components?

There are several components that make up Gülen's ethical considerations:

a. An appropriated and internalized ethics

Gülen accepts the concept of internalized ethics and morality. The Gülen Movement sees ethics as a social phenomenon based on the individual. In the basis of this conception of ethics lies appropriated and internalized ethics.

As a man of religion Gülen finds this conception in Islam but suggests that, in practice, religion is not the only source of ethics, as the decisions that people make also have some voice in the matter. For Gülen, the conscience is a bridge between faith and action. It has to be.

Ethical principles and good conduct are acquired through education; and therefore, he places great importance on education. For Gülen, being educated and pious are together, neither independently, the key to pious living. Part of piety includes self-control and the process of trimming and training one's carnal soul. In this training, a teacher can show the way, but it is the individual who must walk on this road. Whether he or she will be successful or not depends upon the will of the individual, and his or her efforts will finally be evaluated at the end of a lifelong struggle. Because of this, ethics, namely the vastness of conscience, is a bond which unites the individual with society, and makes the two parts of a single whole.

At this point, we are confronted with a seemingly perplexing concept in the Gülen philosophy: the notion of a modern Turkish Renaissance. As he developed his teachings, he stressed that an ethical, tolerant and just society would not waste its energy quarrelling or exhausting its resources through corruption. It would be a place where citizens could trust each other, where they would give no attention to their differences, and therefore progress and advance in their business and in their work.

The idea that a renaissance like the one which heralded the birth of Western civilization could be achieved in Turkey is very attractive to the movement's followers. Gülen's courage in submitting such a possibility is part of what distinguishes him from the other leaders and intellectuals of modern Turkish society.

What is the source of this great enthusiasm? For Gülen the matter is clear: the love of God and obeying his commandments. To the extent that one obeys God's commandments and purifies his heart, a kind of spiritual energy will come pouring out of him. This energy sooner or later will spread and a positive result will be obtained. The name of this spiritual energy is *tabligh* (communication of the message).

b. *Tabligh*

Tabligh first starts with enlightenment (*irshad*). Enlightenment starts within the individual and continues until the person feels the presence of God in this world in the entirety of his own soul–body–action. The human who can achieve this mental state is now both himself and all humanity. He is the person God created him to be. At this stage, the wholeness of the Creator–created has been achieved. The one who is enlightened can also enlighten others. To accomplish this, he has to find those who also are searching for the straight path. As much as this invitation is delivered to the larger masses, *tabligh* is spread. The individual quest for meaning is the struggle of the modern age. This struggle is not something which can be achieved by violence or weapons. Indeed, the call of the Gülen Movement in this regard is: Individuals should build a just, ethical and mutually supportive society without deceiving or exploiting each other; they should always help those in need, including with their education; and as a community, they should stand shoulder-to-shoulder with everyone else.

Just like the message of the movement, the method to achieve it is also peaceful and nonviolent. The method starts with an invitation and continues with *irshad*. The meaning of the invitation is this: If you want to be an upright and ethical person in the way of God, to be vast enough in conscience as to accommodate all of humanity, then "Come!" In statements such as this an echo of Rumi's call can be heard in our era through the voice of the Gülen Movement.

c. *Tabligh* and *tamsil* (representation)

For Gülen, the practices which represent the *tabligh* are just as important as the inspiration. Otherwise, even the most valuable ideals and the most beneficial thoughts could not go beyond abstract advices. Who can establish this bridge between thought and action? This question is about a phenomenon related to worldly talents and realities, as much as it is related to the organic wholeness between the one who offers his hands and the one who takes those hands (this refers to a famous Sufi practice in which the initiate holds the hands of the guide in order to initiate the process of a spiritual journey in Sufism). Every process of *tabligh* has an aspect related to *tamsil* (representation). The one who makes the *tabligh* should be able to represent in his own life the values and the knowledge he propagates at the same time. This means that the one who makes the *tabligh* should be able to practice it, to live according to the values he preaches, and to execute in his life the ethical rules he defends. The carrier, if he cannot represent the value and the measure he carries, cannot impart them to others. Gülen finds this relationship in the sincere, emotional, and trustworthy bonds of the Prophets, the Companions, and the Apostles. Otherwise, he believes, an ideal cannot turn into a movement, a movement into a cause, and a cause into an organizational activity. According to Gülen, *tabligh* and *tamsil* are the complementary parts of the same whole. He explains this relationship thus:

> Those who want to reform the world must first reform themselves. If they want to lead others to a better world, they must purify their inner worlds of hatred, rancor, and jealousy, and adorn their outer worlds with virtue. The words of those who cannot control and discipline themselves, and who have not refined their feelings, may seem attractive and insightful at first. However, even if they somehow manage to inspire others, which they sometimes do, the sentiments they arouse will soon wither.[20]

Gülen believes that the cause of all the chronic problems that we witness in the Islamic world is the lack of the representation aspects of the rulers and leaders. It soon becomes obvious that those who claim to be saviors cannot save anyone, other than themselves. Those who follow them are heartbroken and lose trust. According to Gülen,

> What is lacking in the Islamic world is not science, technology, or wealth. ... All of these have influences of their own; but the most important aspect of all is the image that we give out as a believer.
>
> The interpretation of Islam [by others] depends on our behavior and conduct. ...
>
> ... Further, just as we need the Qur'an, the Qur'an also needs us. It needs sincere people whose hearts have become the Qur'an in order to express it. For all of its awe-inspiring glory, if there is no one to represent it, it can do little more than sit on a shelf. The Qur'an has always served as a guide for people in the form of a concrete and unchanging soul, but there were times when its voice reverberated. It echoed across the four corners of the world.

---

[20]　Gülen 2005a, 105.

There were other times when it kept quiet, as if its lips were sealed, and it was locked in a drawer in the bedrooms, kept in velvet covers.[21]

Gülen expresses a social message through religious discourse. He is a man of religion and this is the language which comes naturally to him. He uses this discourse to communicate effectively the idea that those who receive the commandment of God and apply it in their lives can elevate our global community to a higher level. He states that the Qur'an is too often hidden in a remote place, like expensive jewelry, divorced from daily life by those who do not appreciate its importance. The aim of this correct and courageous ascertainment is to stress the fact that it is because of the ignorance of humans that this sacred text has not yet wielded the influence of directing life to a greater degree in society. The light is there, but it is the human who must accept the light or not. The human must be brought to maturity to choose the light; this is precisely the aim of enlightenment and *tabligh*. Gülen explains as follows:

> In brief, each one of us should work to provoke those who see us to say: "There could be no deceit behind this face." We must inspire those to whom we are speaking to say that "If the force that is motivating these esteemed people of great moral character is their religion, then their religion cannot be a lie."[22]

d. Social unity and the ideal of coming together as a community

When we examined the development of human social groups, we noted that we see groups forming by three different lines: the first by blood relations, the second by faith and the third, and historically the last one, by nationalism or faith in the existence of an "imagined group." The success of nationalism depends on two conditions. First, the state, before everything else, must meet the needs of justice, security, equality, and welfare. And second, social differences should be reconciled through equality, freedom, and participation, and the law should reflect this social reconciliation. These are no small achievements, and they determine the difference between the developed and underdeveloped, between democratic and

---

21   Gülen 2009a, 88–89.
22   *Ibid.*, 92.

authoritarian, nations. Gülen has never accepted arrested development or authoritarianism for his country and society.

Ultimately, the success of nationalism depends on the comprehensiveness and satisfying success of the nation state. Otherwise, nationalism, as it is seen in many examples, could become a source of compulsion and unrest. The turmoil and polarization (as a result of nationalism in this sense) could cause irreparable wounds in the soul of the society's spirit and its life, and these wounds could easily be transferred from generation to generation. Gülen had seen this danger. Instead of watching the events hopelessly, like the majority of society, he has taken the responsibility of action onto his own shoulders.

The period during which his teachings took shape and began to spread was during the dark years of the '70s and '80s. It was a period during which the integrity of the state diminished and when nationalism lost its unifying character. Gülen recognized the need for a call to bring people together. He saw the practical value in the unifying effect of religion during such a trying time.

This is a collective mission, one which does not exclude anyone and invites everyone to hear the call. Its success will be everyone's and no one will earn anything by exploiting others. There is no other call like it in Turkey. The implementation of it does not exist at all. The success of the movement to convert this call from potentiality into reality is there for anyone to see. It is not surprising for the movement to increase the number of its adherents and its effectiveness. What is surprising is that nationalism and the nationalists do not derive any lesson from this success.

Gülen finds the social mobilization that he calls for in religion, which he believes to be more comprehensive than any other ideology. For this reason, he has interpreted Islam anew to address the circumstances of our time. He seeks to find in Islam the most soul-stirring rhetoric in order to generate enthusiasm in virtue and ethics. It should be no secret why Gülen's teachings attract people who have lost hope and trust, as they believe that such a call would make them acceptable before God.

He expresses the importance of his call as such:

> The Exalted Creator and seeking His approval must have the first and foremost place in every activist's perspective. ... As for works undertaken to seek the Almighty's approval—a particle can have the worth of the sun, a drop the worth of the sea, a second the worth of eternity. ... If parents are

educating their children properly, if a place of worship is rousing its community with thoughts of eternity, if a school is awakening hope and faith in its pupils, we can say that they are serving their purpose and are therefore sacred. If this is not the case, they are no more than devilish traps that divert us from the truth.[23]

This philosophy provides a channel for those seeking meaning in their lives. It gives them direction that is both fulfilling and sincere.

e. Supporting each other

For Gülen, this principle is among the central values of his philosophy. It is so important to him that if a Turkish renaissance does begin, it will be with this virtue. This is the principle around which his movement has been formed, both in theory and in practice. This principle and its implementation make the Gülen Movement both more effective and more tightly connected inside the movement than other religious movements. The members of the group are can always rely on help from other members, in all facets of life, from their education to owning businesses.

f. Sacrifice

In order for these principles to be more than an expression of good will, Gülen attaches great importance to the virtue of self-sacrifice. According to him, there are many kinds of sacrifice, such as saving money and bringing expenses and consumption down to a minimum level so that children can receive a good education. Those who have lifejackets are still food for sharks. It is better to focus on keeping the ship floating than surviving in the water. This is accomplished by protecting the freedom, honor, security, and wellbeing of others, as much as we protect these for ourselves. The true salvation is that of the whole society. To achieve this, every individual must sacrifice. Sacrifice releases us from selfishness, greed, and jealousy. Indeed, what is the meaning of civilization, anyway? Shouldn't we desire for everyone what we desire for ourselves and to share our acquisition with other members of society? Our individual and communal knowledge, wealth, security, respect, good manners, and faith can all be augmented in this way.

---

[23] Gülen 2005a, 78–79.

The understanding of solidarity and sharing requires a *mefkure* (an ideal) in the words of Gülen, or a "utopia" in the language of the social sciences. Societies lacking this ideal are like a ship with a broken rudder. They lose their direction in the vast ocean of history and, in the end, become shipwrecked. The critical question here is whether it is possible to perceive and portray this sense of sacrifice as a humanist responsibility? According to Gülen, such a sacrifice can be made only by altruistic people who seek nothing other than the pleasure of God and who bring their worldly expectations and pleasures to a minimum level.[24]

The participants of the movement consider Gülen to embody this virtue. Their admiration for him not only stems from the fact that he satisfies them spiritually, but also because he encourages them to be act positively on society. To the extent that they are successful, individually or collectively, their commitment to him increases. They also express that these sentiments find a mutual response in expressions of Gülen:

> Today, we do not need just anybody. We need those who can say, "I am ready to be in the flames of Hellfire for the material and spiritual happiness of my people." They delight in setting aside personal interests and selfishness, in destroying their carnal souls in the path of God and the nation, by holding fire in their hands, lighting torches everywhere in order to struggle against ignorance and injustice, equipped only with their faith and their determination, to help those who have been left behind, by forgetting the desire for living, pushing forward with the pleasure of enabling others to live.[25]

He often stresses the role of the ideal in inspiring others to good work. Leaders must not only vocalize an ideal but also orient people to that ideal. He explains it like this:

> In my opinion, nowadays our society needs the heroes of ideals at this scale. The heroes of ideals who first extended the hands of mercy to our own nation, but then every time they open their hands to their Lord, praying for the goodness and well-being of others. Since others are incapable of meeting such a need, as a necessary consequence of where we are standing, expressing it, first starting form we are again left to us.[26]

---

[24]   *cf.* Gülen 2006a, 37.
[25]   Gülen 1985, 4.
[26]   Gülen 1998b, 389.

In order to deserve this trait, the leaders have to sacrifice and exhibit modesty. Again in his words: "The bearer of an ideal burns like a lone candle in the darkness and illuminates and enlightens the others around him."[27] And, "A true friend, even at the exit of Hell or at the entrance of Heaven, would know how to say, 'Please, after you!'"[28] Gülen calls the people who are equipped with these merits as the "architects of souls." If these people are not in majority or are not effective, there is no hope for salvation or societal revival.

g. The incredible resemblance of serving God and the people

A person takes refuge in God for personal salvation. He is a citizen of a country and a member of a society as much as a servant of God. He is a social creature. Social salvation is possible only with the help of other citizens. A global problem that endangers life on earth, such as global warming or the pollution of our natural resources, requires the cooperation of all humans and their sacrifices. The traditions of Rumi and Yunus Emre that exist in our culture point directly to this idea. The notion of loving the created for the sake of the Creator and that every service we provide to others is actually serving God has a central importance in the philosophy of Gülen. The one who is dedicated to God should prove this dedication by serving others. In Islam, the source of every kind of love is the Creator Almighty. For this reason, the spirit of devotion to God is the strongest motivation for the service to humanity. The spirit of devotion reminds us of respect, modesty, and embracing of all of God's creatures, without discrimination. In the eyes of Gülen, the one who is under the impact of this sentiment is:

> They are completely outside of the divisive, quarrelsome considerations like "us," "them," "ours" and do not have an implicit or explicit, overt or covert problems. Without these petty distractions, they could spend all their days thinking of ways to be helpful to the people around them. They would be extraordinarily careful not to generate any friction with the society in which they are living. When they encounter the problems in society, they act not as a warrior but as a guide. They act virtuously in order to call

---

[27] Gülen 2007a, 121.
[28] *Ibid.*, 136.

people back to their virtues. They stay away from the thoughts of politics or domination, or rule in any form or shape.

Knowledge, the persistent use of knowledge, a firm ethical foundation, and its employment in every sphere of life and a virtuous faith are their fundamental characteristics.[29]

In Gülen's teachings, individual salvation and communal salvation are two inseparable components of the same process. What is the motivational source of this "metaphysical tension" as he refers to it? Without any hesitation, Gülen says "the love of God."[30] But this love does not make one to face his mind and soul only on the hereafter. It calls the individual to engage the world through his intelligence, his willpower, and his internal compass. This is how, for Gülen, the love of God accommodates both the worldly and the other worldly. He does not give priority to one over the other. This approach conceives the human together with God and the individual together with society.

The reason that the "Gülen Thought" appears meaningful and realistic to his followers is that, to a great extent, his inspirations and encouragements guiding e their lives overlap with their life experiences. The idea that the individual can develop himself and become wealthy by using his intelligence and free will and at the same time please the Creator is very attractive to modern social segments.

These characteristics make the Gülen Movement distinctive from other faith-based movements, which are in conflict with modernity and some of which, even express their rejection of modernity through violence. What makes the Gülen movement effective is its link with the rising classes of Turkey and the importance it places on science and knowledge, which are among the most powerful agents of change in the world. Ironically, many movements directly oppose science for exactly this reason. For him, however, science is the external manifestation of the intelligence and creativity given to man by God. As long as it is respectful to the Divine Order, science is an expansion of Divine Knowledge.

Gülen's thoughts on the subject can be summarized as follows: God has given each of his servants a different face, voice, genetic structure, intelligence and set of talents. This is evidence that He intended for us to

---

[29]   Gülen 2006a, 38.
[30]   *Ibid.*, 37.

be different from each other. Thus, individual differences do not contradict Divine Order, as long as the individual is not selfish and arrogant. When an individual is selfish, harmony—which can be referred to in the seemingly contradictory phrase of "unity through diversity"—is threatened. The deeds of this type of individual turn into a futile, fruitless, and selfish materialism. This is also a part of his understanding of morality.

True sacrifice is not an ordinary sacrifice. It is the devotion of his entire being to the realization of the ideal that he has chosen. He also sees this as a yardstick of his piety. The efforts of the faithful and their generosity in sharing their acquisitions should not be without a defined purpose. It must be guided by intelligent aims. One end extends to the divine and the well-being of the soul and the other to the establishment of a better world and the well-being of all people. If an ideal is not shared by the community at large, it will never be realized. It must be spread. This is where *tabligh* comes into play.

> Sacrifice, too, is one of the most important traits of the men of *tabligh*. Those who do not accept and internalize "sacrifice" from the outset can never become the leader of a cause. The leader of a cause must be ready to abandon his property, his position, his fame ... at the drop of a hat. All of the things that most people are greatly attached to and accept as the purpose of their lives, he has no use for. With this degree of commitment, there is no doubt that the cause can be realized.[31]

When one sees the "Gülen schools and universities" that have been established in various countries or meets one of the hundreds of teachers and administrators who have dedicated their lives to the values of solidarity, knowledge, and respect of other people no matter what their color, religion, ethnicity or nationality, one cannot help but to be impressed. Why else would these people travel into the remote corners of Asia or the jungles of Africa? With what kind of devotion and faith do they go there and offer a service on behalf of humanity? The question then arises: Is there another civic organization that can carry the influence and culture of Turkey beyond its borders, as effectively and on such a large scale as this one? There is not. How does the Gülen Movement achieve this? By believing in their cause and knowing that they are fulfill-

---

[31]   Gülen 2008a, 226.

ing their obligation to worship their Creator and serve His creatures at the same time.

10. Does Gülen see himself as simply the representative of an Islamic teaching, or is he the carrier of a philosophy centered on the "human," which is a larger mission that also includes the former?

The answer to this question is implicit in the previous answer. But this time, partially because of Gülen's character and partially because of the things accomplished in the name of the service, he approaches the matter from a different angle. According to him, those who write the history of this movement are going to attribute its greatest aspects to different causes, ignoring that the main cause is the consent of God.[32]

Preconceived notions and biases repeatedly obstruct the philosophy before it has a chance to explain itself. For Gülen and the members of his community, this state of affairs has always been a source of pain and difficulty. For this reason, they are always careful to explain what they were doing and why they were doing it. Regarding this matter, he states:

> When our government gave permission for private schools to be established, a wave of people, rather than spinning away their days and wealth on summer and winter houses, chose to spend their energy in the service of their people. They did this not only for their country, but for all humanity and they did it with the enthusiasm that comes with an act of devotion. It would be impossible for me to know of all of the schools these volunteers have opened within Turkey and abroad. Not only do I not know most of the companies who have established these schools, as someone must advised me to record, I do not even know which schools are where. As far as I can tell from the media, it is common knowledge that these schools have opened in nearly every country where the opening of a school is permitted, excluding such places as Iran, Syria, and Saudi Arabia. From Azerbaijan to the Philippines, from Petersburg, the capital of the czarist Russia, from Moscow, the capital of Communist Russia, through the help of the Jewish businessman Üzeyir Garih, to the one opened in Yakutsk, they have proven to have the capacity to spring up.[33]
>
> Even if only one tenth of what I am saying was inaccurate, I would still fear for its accountability, because in the end I will answer to God. Only God knows the role that I have played in the hundreds of schools that have

---

[32] *cf.* Gülen 2006c, 186.
[33] Gülen 1997a.

been established. I did my part to encourage it for a short time, but the matter has grown with ten times the force of what I put into it. I have no contribution there. In fact, taking credit for even one tenth of the planning that was involved would be disrespect to that service. It would be disrespect to the labors of many people. Let someone else be unfair in this way, and overlook the good work that has been done. Let someone else say that there are a handful of people who carry all of the influence of this movement, rather than the movement itself which carries its industry and passion as a banner in a national struggle. No matter who says it, it will still be untrue.

... Something great is happening. Those who do not see it are welcome to go on not seeing. In my opinion, for the Turkish nation, a new era of prosperity has begun. God is accomplishing this through the hands of people whose names and faces we will never know. Though I may have advised that this might be a preferable direction, the matter has gone many times further than that. I am not convinced that I was significantly influential in this area, either. Maybe the nation is uniting around simply the reasonability of the idea. You propose an idea, it implies a certain kind of future, and then if it bears observable fruit and the people can see no drawback, why shouldn't the nation flock to it?[34]

Everything that Gülen has said so far is in alignment with his ideas about religion, morality, and community. However, after the other Turkic Republics freed themselves from the Soviet yoke and he advised them to seek out a place for themselves in the international system, can this also be explained in the same terms? He sees great benefits to be reaped from establishing cultural, economic, and spiritual relationships with the Turkic world. Since the late '80s, Gülen has been calling for businessmen, educators, and entrepreneurs who have the opportunity to establish a new life to settle in Central Asia. He more generally called on them to spread to the four corners of the world, establish families, and represent Turkish and Islamic culture in the societies they join. This call has multiplied Turkish influence on the world. After losing their Empire, the Turks were never again as influential as they are now. Hundreds of schools have been opened and thousands of businesses have been established. From these schools, tens of thousands of students have graduated and as they took their places in their respective countries, became voluntary ambassadors for Turkey. Businesses established by Turks abroad have opened places of

---

[34] "Bu Hareket Devlete Alternatif mi?" (Is this movement an alternative of the state?), *http://tr.fgulen.com/content/view/12134/9/*

work for other businessmen and technicians arriving from Turkey. Turkey has become the subject of discussion in the world as a country providing capital. Turkish language and culture are carried to these countries. This culture then mixes with local culture and a new synthesis is produced. These schools and social activities have added to Gülen's understanding of the ideal person and of morality.

In this big mission, there is also a personal side:

> Since my childhood, Central Asia was always in my prayers. The opportunity to embrace our fellow Muslims and Turks always seemed to me that it would be the cause for great celebration. There was a time when I advised from the pulpit that all businessmen, traders, industrialists and all of our friends go there.[35]

When asked why he has not visited these places and seen the work that his friends and followers had accomplished, Gülen responds:

> If we think in Sufi terms, one should not pursue mundane pleasures in this world. According to my philosophy, one should not even seek the spiritual pleasure which might be derived from the knowledge of God and the acts of worship. Even so, as a human, I had a desire to see with my own eyes the work of those who nobly work mostly without salaries, as laborers, scholars, diplomats, or whatever professional the task at hand calls for. For reasons known only to Him, God did not give me the opportunity to taste these pleasures.[36]

He also makes a personal point:

> In actual fact, to this movement which has become the property of the nation, my contribution is very little. Despite this truth, I am afraid that if I were to go to these places, there would be a misconception that I am somehow the author of all of those things done by these good people. I am concerned that people would assume that it was my thoughts and ideas that are the driving force behind these great works, rather than the devotion and enthusiasm of the people.
>
> Besides, people in general have a tendency to attribute the successes of others to the person who appears to be at the helm. I was also worried about what some might say. I was afraid to do anything that may provoke a reaction from certain portions of the population in those places. They might say, "Behind this is so and so," "They have a hidden agenda," or

---

[35] Gündem 2005, 62.
[36] *Ibid.*, 63.

other similar things even though they do not say it openly or explicitly. In this situation, I have buried my desires in my chest in order to keep an even keel and not to overshadow the services of our friends.

On a smaller point, if I packed up and went to the Turkic world as if I was the architect of what has been done there, people would look at me in the street and embrace me. These kinds of things do not seem natural to me.[37]

We can hear in his words the genuine desire to carry the spiritual values and the culture of his country to other communities of the world, no matter what their ethnicity or religion may be. Beneath that umbrella idea is the desire to have first an emotional, and then a concrete cultural and commercial connection with Central Asia. This is a significant need which he has felt since his childhood, as he feels this area of the world is where the roots of Turkish culture lay. For this reason, Gülen advised all who would listen that they first go to Asia and then open up to the rest of the world.

He believes that Islam has a universal message which can be transformed into a broad humanistic philosophy. He feels that this philosophy could be used to kindle the sense of solidarity which has been in decline and then spread it to the world.

11. Compared to the Arab interpretation of Islam, does Gülen offer a Turkish interpretation of Islam?

Gülen reminds us before answering this question that the foundation of his thought are the statements of the Prophet and his actions. He then draws attention to why and how the movement that he inspired was influenced by the way the Turks once lived and by the Turkish understanding of administration and its application historically.

For instance, he provides examples from the lives of the Prophet and his Companions:

> They used every opportunity that they could to reach people; they became close to people in the meetings that they held and the banquets they threw and then, they explained their message to them. They never waited for the people to come to them; they always went to the needy themselves. Just like they did in the following periods, during the Four Rightly Guided

---

[37]   *Ibid.*, 63–64.

Caliphs, they behaved in the same way. Even in conquest, the Muslims did not destroy churches or synagogues, they never touched the rights of the minorities, and they did not constrain freedom of thought. Salahuddin al-Ayyubi, Alparslan, Kılıçarslan and later, Fatih the Conqueror, Selim the Grim, and Süleyman the Magnificent all behaved in the same way. They protected everyone within their power without making distinguishing between religions, languages, or races.

... Our ancestors left us such a heritage that today we are proud of them. In Sarajevo, Macedonia, Greece, Bulgaria, or any other place where they ruled, they did not oppress any group and did not force anyone to change religion or language. The displayed democratic sensibilities well beyond what we have today. They accessed people's hearts and minds by using the vehicle of tolerance and understanding. Therefore, our basic texts as well as historical experience show that tolerance and dialog did not begin with our generation. It is the core of our past and the result of it. It is a duty and a task. It is no one's product as a result of his own compassion and mercy; it is the consequence of the mercy and compassion of Islam. The virtues which cause those who meet them to say, "You are different" stem from the essence of Islam, the Book [the Qur'an], the *Sunnah* [deeds and saying of the Prophet], and the aspect of religion which is open to interpretation.[38]

Tolerance, according to Gülen, is the ability to have unity in diversity and not to exclude any person or group because of religion or culture. It is not based on the Muslim ruler's personal abilities or goodness but on "firm, solid and durable sources," (Islamic sources) shaping his style of administration. One typical example often cited by Gülen is the "Constitution of Medina" (622 AD). This document is a social contract in which different religious groups participated as equal partners. It is a legal text whereby the rights of all groups were under record and through which they all came together around a common administration and a system of justice. By making reference to the Constitution of Medina, Gülen implies that Muslims today can live in peace and tolerance in a constitutional system which is based on legal equality. He views the establishment of such a system "as a duty for all Muslims." He also sees his followers, who act as volunteer ambassadors of culture in many different countries and who according to his teachings, as the people in the position to carry out that duty.[39]

---

[38]   Gülen 2005b, 231–232.
[39]   *Ibid.*, 237.

Up until this point, we see that Gülen finds the action of carrying a dialog of tolerance and the common values of humanity to other countries and peoples in the vessel of religion. Is there any significance to be attributed to the fact that those who carry out this duty are Turks? This question leads us to another question: Is there such a thing as "Turkish Islam"?

The concept of Turkish Islam might seem to contradict the notion of the universality of Islam. However, culture is an undeniable sociological reality. Yes, Islam is a universal religion, but the Turks (as did other peoples) accepted Islam, while still retaining their own customs and traditions. Turkey has a special place in the Islamic world, as do other Muslim societies.

The Turks accepted Islam early and they became a new rising civilization in the 9th century. Samarkand, Tashkent, and Bukhara produced eminent scholars such as Bukhari and the Tirmidhi. These scholars had important roles in the spread of Islam in the Turkish world and elsewhere. When Islam reached Anatolia, it mixed with Turkish culture and a new Turkish expression of Islam was born.

After accepting Islam, the Turks elevated their culture, which was already "civilized," to a higher level by employing, for example, Islam's universal message of tolerance for all humanity. Many thinkers and scholars among the Asian Turks emerged as a result of this cultural overlap. Bukhari, Molla Husrev, Molla Gurani, Merginani were all raised in Asia. With the contributions and help of these people, Islam came to Anatolia. The Turkish states of the Seljuks and the Ottomans practiced Islam demonstrated by with their exercise of power, justice and their pluralistic administrations; they also made elaborate records of their practices. To an extent, Turkish Islam owes its richness and peculiarity to Asia. This history explains the place of Asia in Gülen's thought, as well as why the Gülen Movement has given priority to Asia. A spiritual debt is being repaid. Yes, Islam was born in Mecca and Medina but,

> We owe a great deal to Central Asia, either in the field of *Tafsir* or *Fiqh*, or the renaissance which was carried out in the 4th and 5th centuries AH [11th and 12th centuries CE]. In the parts of religion open to interpretation, we have in our hands the Book, the *Sunnah*, the consensus of the *Ummah* [the global community of Muslim believers], and the analytical reasoning of the scholars. However, it cannot be denied that a society's ethical base, its psychological structure, and the state of the socio-economic situation all have

their impact on the field of *qiyas* [analytical reasoning]. Social structure in general has a strong influence as well. Turkish people interpreted the aspects which are open to the Book and the *Sunnah* in this way. They understood the "consensus" that way. For this reason, and also because it was ruled by the great empires, it has developed a style and practice of its own, different from those of other Muslim nations. In this sense, it is acceptable to talk about Turkish Islam.

Another aspect of this issue is that with us, Islam, in addition to the Book and the *Sunnah*, is more open to personal spiritual development. In addition to the handling of the spiritual aspect of Islam, we have a different approach to the natural sciences. All these develop together in partnership. We always retained the *takyas* [dervish lodges] and *zawiyas* [facility and retreat centers] along with the *fiqh* schools. This naturally brings about a distinction from other Islamic cultures.[40]

Gülen cannot find the same respect for science and spirituality in other regions of the Islamic world, as it is observable in Turkey. Indeed, he proposes that most Muslim nations or communities are closed off to this idea:

Fanaticism is widespread in even the simplest practices of Islam. I saw it in the USA, other parts of the Western hemisphere, Australia, and the Arab world. They hold to an understanding so rigid that it will continue to provoke backlashes from other nations for as long as it is continued. They fight constantly over details. ... If we are so inflexible even on matters of detail, how will we ever explain Islam to others? When I see reports of these sorts of events, I always think to myself, "I wish we could bring Islam as the Turks understand it to these places." Though they think they are serving Islam, such fanatical people do Islam a great disservice. What's worse is that this understanding is not what the Prophet commanded. He said: "Bring them good news. Do not scare them away." These people scare others away. "Facilitate, do not obstruct," the Messenger of God said. These people obstruct. They do not give good news, or facilitate. They make the way difficult and meaningless. This is another angle from which we can understand a Turkish Islamic identity from the perspective of the universality of Islam. When the expression "Turkish Islam" is used, then "Kurdish Islam," "Persian Islam," and "Arab Islam" also emerge. All of these together complicate the matter further.[41]

---

[40]   Can 1997, 34–35.

[41]   *Ibid.*, 35–36.

Gülen differentiates between religion as a system of faith and its practice as a result of historical, cultural, and sociological conditions. By doing this, he calls our attention to the importance of purifying religion from ethnic differences, but at the same time understanding that it is introduced into certain periods and certain places within the context of historical and sociological conditions.

Despite this need for purification, he is content with the expression of a Turkish Islam:

> This nation has represented this religion deservedly and correctly and left behind an important heritage. For this reason it could be assessed from a historical perspective, too. There are moments in history which we treat as a hump on humanity's back. We always try to get rid of it, to free ourselves of it. There are other moments which signify honor and we wear like a medallion carried around the neck. We take pride in them.[42]

Gülen is adamant that Turkey not become another Iran or Algeria. He also holds to a position of warning similar to that of former Prime Minister Bülent Ecevit: He also recognizes that there are "secularist fanatics" in Turkey:

> Every belief has fanatics, and secularism is no exception. All it takes for fanaticism to take place is for one to refuse to recognize any truth other than their own. Of course there are secular fanatics and just like any other fanatic, they are so confident that they will replace truth with brute force, and seek to enforce everything they believe simply through power.[43]

Continuing, Gülen assesses the relationship between rights, power, and justice in the following way:

> Right makes might. Might does not make right. But the tyranny of power is beyond that. It rebels even against common sense. It rebels against perfect logic. Those who are able to have power use brute force for things which could be solved with reasoning and dialog and a little patience. This is what we experienced in the 20th century. To me, this is the problem with Algeria. There is a serious conflict of values between the communities. The reference of one segment is its religion. But I wonder whether the timing is correct in some words and ideas. This will keep historians and sociologists busy in the future. But in some ways, the powerful feel that they are justi-

---

[42]   *Ibid.,* 36.
[43]   *Ibid.,* 37.

fied by their power. They erase their logic and reasoning and seek to beat their problems into submission. Then later, the other side will be portrayed as terrorists in order to legitimize the force that was used.[44]

Gülen refuses every kind of fanaticism and believes absolutely in pluralism. The paradigm, which is supposed to be democratic, is transformed into a sacred enigma, then is enforced by tyranny and finally morphs into dogmatism. The society in question becomes politicized and then extremely polarized. The dialog degenerates from a competition of ideas to a brawl of dogmas. Gülen attributes the polarization and tensions which are experienced in Turkey today to some extent to the war between these dogmas.

> A dogmatic front is fighting against another one. All of them are rigid. All are coercive and unfortunately, all of them have spread to the general population.
>
> In order for society to be freed from this polarization, the moderates who hold a majority must maintain their calm and stay out of the fight. Only they can soften the extremities and bring together the majority at the reasonable. This moderate conduct could bring Turkey back into a climate of tolerance, dialog, understanding each other, mutual respect, and accepting the differences. When this is done, Turkey could present to the world an important example of peace and democracy.[45]

Turks have been Muslims for ten centuries. As they expanded from Anatolia to Europe, they inherited the Greco-Roman civilization, which was the basis of the ancient world. They successfully ruled an empire through the synthesis of a culture brought from Asia, the spirituality and the law of Islam, and the universal values of Western civilization. The Ottoman Empire was a mosaic of races, faiths, and states. Its employment of pluralism allowed it to run this gigantic engine for centuries. What is the philosophical foundation of this practice? According to Gülen, it is the principles and values of Islam under the circumstances of time, along with developing a system of administration that met the needs of the society.

The Qur'an states that God created humans in different genders, colors, races, talents, and languages (An-Nisa 4:1; Al-Hujurat 49:13). God

---

[44] *Ibid.*, 37–38.
[45] *Ibid.*, 40.

has left to us the responsibility of the administration of these differences. For this, first we have to know and understand each other. It is only when people know and trust each other that cooperation can emerge. Unity and wholeness are born out of effort and understanding. Peace and civilization develop to the extent that these efforts to understand each other are successful. The Ottoman Empire understood this relationship very well and built an empire out of many races, religions, and states. Gülen places great importance on the example of the Ottomans and sees and presents it as a bright period for Turkish Islam and indeed, the world.

Gülen claims that it is only possible to administer such a heterogeneous state with a healthy and developing rule of law and scientific knowledge. Therefore, Turkish Islam does not shy away from science. Law is a discipline that must continually develop in order to accommodate changing circumstances. For this reason, numerous scholars in our history and teachings of *fiqh* have left us a rich heritage for today.

Starting from the perspective of Said Nursi, Ali Ünal (who researched Gülen's thoughts) adds the following comments to this assessment:

> Turkish Islamic jurisprudence [*fiqh*] and the form of its implementation consist of different approaches, depending on people, time, and circumstances. Here what matters is not absoluteness, but relativity. Making a relative truth into an absolute one and trying to apply it to every time, person, and condition will cause quarrel and conflict among Muslims.[46]
>
> Law is a critical element of Turkish Islam. The Ottomans, who wanted to implement Islam in every aspect of life established states in which different faiths, world-views, cultures, and races lived together peacefully. This resulted in their developing a vast and comprehensive legal system. Ottoman lawyers were helpful in developing Hanafi law as well as standard Ottoman law.
>
> Islamic jurisprudence had shown another important opening in the Ottomans and during the reign of Kanuni [Süleyman the Magnificent], in 1537. Sultan Süleyman had permitted Abu's Suud Efendi to utilize the interpretations of *mujtahids* [expounders of Islamic laws] with backgrounds in different creeds ... and this resulted in the composition of laws which earned Süleyman the title "Kanuni" [the lawgiver]. In the foundations of these laws and in the code of laws lies the idea that in the works of the state one does not absolutely have to be loyal to a sect, but to be able to

---

[46]   Ünal 2002, 149.

utilize the viewpoint of a particular *mujtahid*. In brief, Islamic law developed in the hands of the Turks in such a way that we do not witness in the history of other nations.[47]

Even if they belonged to the same religion, the character of every society, race, or tribe, the social, economic, political and physical conditions in which they operate, in the practice of that religion, it gave way to developing different molds and models.[48]

At this point, Ünal gives many different daily practices from the Kurdish and Bosnian groups to arrive at this judgment:

In the Turkish Islamic society it has to be recorded the existence of different traditions and lifestyles due to the geographical environment and historical courses, as much as racial factors.[49]

There are fields that Islam, without taking directly into its own field, but leaving to time, circumstances, dispositions, moods, and temperaments. For instance, Islam does not offer a form of state valid for all times; instead it establishes general principles of administration. It could be said there is not any rule for architecture; maybe it bans only wastefulness and luxury. In dressing, what parts of the body and how they have to be covered, and the main principle in this matter it lays. But it does not dwell on the form, color, design, and fabric. In the field of literature, it brings forth the abstract beauty; it admonishes loyalty to the fairness and the truth; while describing the universe, it sees it as a divine art and preaches the knowledge of the Creator.[50]

In short, every nation has its own culture and developed under its own circumstances. Just as it is possible to talk about being a Muslim of an Arab, Persian, or any other nation, Gülen is not disturbed by the expression, "being a Muslim of Turkey" or "Turkish Muslim." In Ünal's words,

This is so, because Islam was born in Mecca and Medina, spread swiftly and taking under its influence the cultures and civilizations it encountered everywhere, it brought into being totally new composition of a culture and a civilization. By virtue of this fact it did not have any difficulty at all to mold the native peoples of the conquered lands in their essential and original formations. While on the one hand, it chiseled its own essential elements into the geography and the lives of nations, on the other hand, it

---

[47] *Ibid.*

[48] *Ibid.*, 151.

[49] *Ibid.*

[50] *Ibid.*, 152.

never hesitated to borrow the elements from other cultures which are not in conflict with its own essentials. This way it spread faster and was accepted easily as well as it continually enriched its universal content, renewed it, and developed it.[51]

One of the most important successes of Turkish history is that when Turkish culture and the universality of Islam merged, the Ottoman Empire, through tolerance and inclusion, was able to unite culturally and racially distinct states and peoples, resulting in a thriving civilization that lasted for centuries.

12. What are the role and the function of Sufism in the teachings of Gülen? Since this approach opposes fanatical traditionalism, the label which religion is immediately imprisoned with under authoritarian regimes, does it carry the seeds of democracy?

Gülen is a thinker and a man of religion close to Sufism, but in his nomenclature, this concept becomes "lifestyle based on heart and soul." He often refers to the spiritual life of the Prophet in his writings and sermons. In these references, he draws our attention to the fact that some Muslim thinkers view Sufism as a source of inspiration for heretical currents. When he was asked to give a definition of Sufism, Gülen replied,

> Sufism is the spiritual life of Islam. In no period, those who represent Islam along the line of *Ahl al-Sunnah wa'l Jama'a* [Sunni way of belief] were outside that spirit and meaning. *Tariqa* is a set of disciplines within the thought of Sufism, by going to the core of religion, aims at earning the pleasure of God, therefore the bliss of this world as well as the next.
>
> Sufism was a lived experience in the Age of Happiness; and later it was systematized by those whom we might call *rijali tariqa* [important figures of *tariqa*] according to the character, spiritual disposition, and understanding of each. This is a normal act. At this moment, if I were able to read the hearts and minds of people, I would have given them this kind of duties according to their talents and capabilities within the criteria of the *Sunnah*. In reality what the *sheikhs* [Sufi masters] do is not different from that. According to the characters, their social standings, their general structure, by giving responsibilities in conformity with the spirit of religion, having everyone to progress spiritually according to their talents and capabilities, has aimed at to make real the necessary corollary of "the purpose

---

[51]   *Ibid.*, 152–153.

in the creation of mankind is to become *insan-ı kamil* [the perfect human]." Now this is what Sufism is all about.[52]

Gülen responds to those who call his system of thought and teachings "an unnamed Sufi movement" as follows:

> If by that, it is meant the people who are in the path of approaching God trying to get close to Him or who are after becoming *insan-ı kamil*, this would be correct, and in this sense, there is no believer who is not a Sufi or on the way to becoming one. But if by that it is meant either because of the differences of the addressees or those who represent it in terms of making it into a Sufi order and present it to the public as such, then these activities are neither Sufism nor a Sufi order.[53]

Moreover, Gülen says in the context of Sufi thought, the Turkish interpretation of Islam carries a special flavor. According to him,

> Sufism is a discipline appropriating as its subject matter the spiritual aspect of Islam. It is an interpretation the metaphysical aspect of which is very dominant. Sufi training exists in every sector of our society, to an extent. Everyone has had a share from it. The impact of Sufism on the Turkish society is more, compared to other places in the Islamic world. The understanding based on considering oneself inferior to everyone, and everyone superior, preferring everyone to oneself, were gifted to this society by the people of Sufism like Ahmad Yasawi, Yunus Emre, Mawlana Jalaluddin Rumi, and Haji Bektash Veli. ... That soft, embracing understanding and conduct has an important place in the sight of God and in the life of the society a unifying factor. Although he is not from the people of Sufism, the same understanding and morality was represented by Bediüzzaman, one of the eminent scholars of the last century. He says, "I have forgiven those who oppressed me, sending me from town to town, accusing me with many charges, trying to convict me, and preparing places for me in the dungeons."[54]

According to Gülen, this understanding exists with almost all of the members of Turkish society, at least potentially, and is ready to emerge at any moment. He sees this in a relation with the Turkish culture and stresses that every faith system develops an organic (give and take) relationship with the cultural setting in which it exists.

---

[52] Gülen 2009b, 125–126.
[53] *Ibid.*, 126.
[54] The interview given to Nicole Pope, *Le Monde*, 28 April 1998.

About the relationships between Sufism and Sufi orders, Gülen explains:

> Sufism is a name given later on to the act of studying and researching as a scientific matter the spiritual side of what should be considered as the essence of Islam. What is important is performing the good deeds which belong to heart like *zuhd* [asceticism], *taqwa* [piety; the conscious performance of good and avoidance of evil], *ihsan* [perfect goodness], and *marifat* [spiritual knowledge of God]. This is inseparable part of Islam.
>
> Religious orders on the other hand, as a little institutionalized form of this spiritual aspect of Islam, had emerged five centuries after our Prophet. I have respect for the Sufi orders in terms of their goals, and in general, the positive functions they performed in history. But today do the Sufi orders conform to the needs of the age, should they exist or not? These can be open to discussion. But no Muslim can stay aloof to the aspect of Islam which is its essence, sustaining the faith, as a road guiding one to perfection, its spiritual aspect, namely Sufism. Every human organizes his life according to the pleasure of God; tries to live in the direction He desires. He would and should take as the ultimate goal to worship Him as if seeing Him and in the end to become a morally perfect human being. In order to realize these, it is not even necessary to have Sufi orders.[55]

In the period following the founding of the Turkish republic in 1923, Sufi orders and dervish lodges were banned. Gülen was asked to comment about this:

> From the general decay in the declining period of the Ottoman Empire, the Sufi orders, dervish lodges, and the religious schools had their share, too. They became incapable of performing their real functions. The same thing was experienced in the army, as well. In the Ottoman period, against all the innovations and reforms the Janissaries, sometimes taking along with them the religious schools, had reacted negatively. The rebellion of Patrona Halil, and in some other rebellions, this is the case. As for the religious schools, for instance for a period Kadızadeliler, as it were, became the representatives of the backwardness, and acted that way. In short, from the general decline of the Ottomans, all the institutions had their share, the military, the academics namely the religious schools and the dervish lodges. The same thing can happen today. As the decay is experienced in the Sufi orders, and as we witness, it could be experienced in the schools for civil servants, and in some other vital institutions.

---

[55]   *Ibid.*

In the years the republic was founded, they had gone after the decay in the dervish lodges, the retreat centers, and the religious schools; for both to deal with this and also to deal with the rebellions here and there, the Courts of Independence were established. But in both these courts and in the conduct displayed against the decaying from time to time extremities and exaggerations took place. These should be evaluated within the context of that period and the reaction which occurred as a result of it. That day what the state was against was not Sufism, it couldn't be. Because Sufism is the vocation of living Islam the best way, practicing Islam at individual level, and becoming a perfect human being. It is the vocation of sincerity, honesty, and the piety. But if under this name, the science and new developments are opposed and state is prevented, then the state takes necessary measures to deal with it within the accepted boundaries. Otherwise it would not be right in its interference.[56]

This analysis of Gülen also extends to the debate "religionist vs. laicist," which occupies lately most of the discussions among the Turkish public and the media.

As there is obscurantism in religion there can be obscurantism in the reaction against religion. No one can say anything to those who accept secularism in the legal sense. For those who make secularism into an ideology, who makes it into an element of fight, they are giving the name "laicist" or "laicist obscurantist."

Therefore, although I dislike the term and do not use it personally, I find them inappropriate for my manner of style in my speeches; unfortunately these kinds of people exist. For that reason, ... we should be, as a state and as a society, soft, tolerant, open to dialog, respectful for the differences, but bring to the fore the things we can agree on, peaceful and never go outside the boundaries of law.[57]

13. Can the Gülen Movement be characterized as a Sufi order? Is it possible to call it a Sufi order considering the teachings regarding the spiritual realm and practices of daily life?

Although the basic dynamics of the Gülen Movement and the dynamics of the classical Sufi traditions appear similar, in terms of organization as a civil initiative and in terms of the form acculturation (the basic values and their applications), the movement differs from Sufi organizations. The

---

[56] *Ibid.*

[57] *Ibid.*

Gülen Movement can partially be analyzed through the concept of "worldly asceticism," a concept that Max Weber developed in his analyses of Protestantism and Asian religions, but in reality, it is a movement organized with civil initiatives. There are many concepts in the classical Sufism such as modesty, sacrifice, altruism, the spirit of commitment and devotion, to be with God while living among the people, to live for the goodness of others, giving service in return for nothing, and the depth of the heart, soul, and spiritual life, expecting no reward in intention or action. Many of these concepts take their place among the intellectual and practical dynamics of the movement. But unlike what it is in Sufi orders, this does not take its direction only towards the internal aspect of the person. As much as it is directed toward the internal, it is also directed towards the outside and the social. For this reason, the religious depth and the consciousness of being the servant of God are more comprehensive and carry social goals. Weber, in his conceptualization, considers this as "rationalization of the religious and social relations." In fact, even Weber's analysis is not comprehensive enough and does not cover the entirety of the Gülen Movement's rational and social dynamics.

Sufi orders deal with private and intimate aspects. It makes the person (initiate) aloof towards the worldly. It extracts the person from the social life and directs him or her towards the individual, private, and spiritual experiences and sufferings. Even if the order does not cut off the relationship of the individual from social life completely, the initiate is held in a rigid, more resistant discipline, as far as opening up to outsiders. The Gülen Movement carries a social content in the line of Rumi, Yunus and Yasawi, rather than an institutionalized Sufi order. In the Gülen Movement, the "religious sentiment" and the "social action" move together in great harmony. The internal purification, improvement, the effort for understanding, comprehension, and enlightenment are necessary to reach the Creator, but reaching to the "created" and extending helping hands to them are also necessary, necessary for being a good servant of God, necessary to be pious. The person who unites both of these in self becomes a perfect man. There is not a discontinuity between the person's religious and social world. To benefit from the worldly blessings at a minimum level or not to be extreme makes the person individually mature and improved, but it might also direct him or her to feel socially the same way with others and act in tandem. This, in turn, might result in the partnership in the ideal and action (participation in the social with similar sentiments and goals).

The Gülen Movement's approach—which does not distinguish categorically the human from the society, the religious and the social behavior and therefore, does not break the wholeness of the person—seems to invite those who want to be rational in daily life but are seeking the unification with the Creator in spiritual life. In this sense, it could be said that the movement receives its strength and dynamism from its philosophy that responds to the needs of the modern man.

It has been stressed that the critical concept in the Gülen Movement is *hizmet* (service). (In fact, the movement is widely known as *Hizmet*). Service as such resembles the principles enumerated by Max Weber in defining The Protestant Ethic and the spirit of Capitalism: not to go to extremes in pleasures, the responsibility to the society (to others), and turning values into investments to affect positively the lives of others, rather than consuming them. But here, "being content with little" or "modesty in lifestyle" does not exclude big goals. Therefore, Gülen's understanding of *hizmet* transcends the individual; it becomes a dynamic which is comprehensive and maintains continuity.

> Normal piety cannot carry the burden of such a sacrifice. It is because the limit of a normal religiosity is a certain limit: praying, fasting, giving prescribed purifying alms, making pilgrimage, etc. But Gülen's definition of *hizmet* is more comprehensive and continuous [lifelong effort]. Not only the religious basis, it holds onto the national, humane, ethical and the universal values and never leaves rationality. Those who took upon themselves the *hizmet*, in the sense Gülen defines, made the values of altruism, idealism, sense of devotion and rationality inseparable part of their personality.[58]

Turning back to the original question, "Is it a Sufi order?," Gülen advises sacrificing, devotion, and avoidance of extremes. He defends acting together and the virtue of sharing the same principles, as much as he stresses the necessity of producing the material and spiritual values which makes living meaningful and exalted. This call is both sincere and realistic. A typical social phenomenon came into being where the call became an action and the action became a movement. It must not be an

---

[58]   Ergene 2005, 56.

accident that such a movement had arisen in Turkey. When he says, "the interpretation of Islam under the circumstances of Turkey," it should be understood that Gülen must have meant this.

14. In today's world, fanaticism is becoming widespread and is overshadowing Islam. Is this an interreligious, intercultural matter or something originating from the Islamic world? If it is the latter, how can it be overcome?

To this question, Gülen replies that world fanaticism is both an interreligious matter and intercultural matter and continues:

> Outside the Islamic world as well, both in religions and in ideologies it has reached a level never observed before in history. Therefore when we look at it from this larger perspective, it is wrong to limit the matter to the Islamic world. It would be unfair to make the Islamic world a scapegoat or a whipping boy.[59]

Gülen attributes gradually increasing fanaticism to intolerance and the lack of love. In turn, he attributes this lack of love to the lack of empathy and a disinterest in each other's problems.

According to Gülen, fanaticism resembles the situation of a person who looks through the key hole from a dark room into the outside world and thinks the world is limited by what he sees and acts solely in respect to his own emotions. The one who acts with this narrow viewpoint sees everything in a distorted fashion and acts upon that distortion. This is the psychological state of a fanatic. For his cause, he does not care about the harm he might cause to himself, to his beloved ones, or the loved ones of others. Against the faith, objects, and the society that he hates, he declares a war and makes it into a sacred cause. This artificial sanctity causes the fanatic not to feel any moral responsibility when he kills innocent people or blows up buildings. In this sacred cause, everything, including himself, is not important and can be sacrificed.

One can arrive only at such an irrational and immoral belief by rejecting the fundamental principles of religions and the sacred books. Only people under extreme pressure, captivity, poverty, and helplessness (in other words, under siege) can find salvation in extreme doctrines. The setting in

---

[59]   Doğu Ergil's interview with Gülen.

which they live is conducive to these beliefs. If they also have access to teachers who tell them that these extreme teachings will provide them salvation, the combination results in a situation ready to explode. Fanaticism, under this assessment, can be defined as the psychological state in which the given circumstances are interpreted as helplessness or captivity, and salvation is found in extreme reactions (limitless violence) by sacrificing the individual and every kind of human value.

For this reason, Gülen calls our attention to the drawbacks of interpreting the fundamental principles of religion, according to certain times and places. In order to overcome fanaticism, Gülen advices us to hold onto the values that make one a good human being (for instance, thou shall not kill, thou shall not steal, thou shall not do to your neighbor what you do not want to be done to you, etc.) and to implement the teachings of the Prophet Muhammad. What has been said so far is related to the reading of the Islamic world from within. There also is an aspect concerning the outside.

According to Gülen, the Islamic world was held under direct occupation and colonization for centuries by the West. In many Islamic countries the administration allied themselves with the West or behaved like Westerners, but was unable to develop their countries or free them from imperialism. This generated a climate of resentment in the society. This resentment has grown over time, intensified, and has gone so far as to encourage rebellion against the unjust administrators, as well as the foreign yoke.

The salvation expected through socialism, was not realized in the Islamic world because the material conditions of socialism did not come about. The expectation of justice, freedom, solidarity, and ethical administration was looked for in a religious climate. When these expectations, which are the promise of the religion, could not be realized through politics, a political role was assigned to religion and through religious terminology and sentiments, justice and freedom were sought. This state of affairs led to politics and religion to be concentric, overlap, and interchangeable.

With a hope that every kind of negative thing would be eliminated, religion became the arena of the daily politics, became worldly, and the focus of every kind of fight. Through sacred concepts and a search for legitimacy the way to extremism and violence was opened. The sacred text, through the interpretations of some men of religion, gained a new meaning and presented as a document of hatred. The young people who felt they were under siege were taken under their influence, and the sentiments of helplessness were exploited, for the sake of a cause that they were made to believe divine, allowing them to accept killing and being killed as a form of worship.

The Westernizing elites ruled with iron hands the countries that they colonized. In this climate of helplessness, fanaticism was adopted as a way out, and this, of course, has been an extremely unfortunate development for the Islamic world. Breaking this vicious circle is only possible by the development of the countries where fanaticism was produced as a way of salvation, by the illumination of the darkened minds through contemporary education, and by the separation of religion and politics, and religion returning to its honorable and deserving place.

15. The early followers of Gülen sought a lifestyle that centered around community and religious values. Solidarity and mutual support were very important to them. How was the role of the individual determined in the structure of community?

"Society" and "community" are two foundational terms of sociology. Societies are the largest organizations of solidarity and division of labor. They contain different cultural and professional groups. Society is too broad of a term to represent the individual; the individual might find himself in the society uprooted, powerless, and anonymous. For this reason, in every society, traditional or modern, individuals seek groups that embrace them, that provide the means of solidarity, and that give meaning to their lives. This is true for every society.

This is especially the case for those who come from a rural environment (the relations, values and the basic principles of which are acquainted), who find themselves in limbo in an urban environment, where the laws, social rules, and codes of behavior are foreign to them. People in this position often search for others who have the same values and code of behaviors. This is only natural, and it is a phenomenon experienced in the process of development of every society. In Turkey, where development has come relatively late and where traditional features are still maintained in the country side, this process is ongoing. The Gülen Movement arose in the midst of this process, meeting a crucial need.

One of the most important concepts in Gülen's works—and a security valve preventing the loss of the individual in the society—is the phenomenon of consultation (*shura*). Consultation, which is based on injunctions in the Qur'an, is a mechanism through which the participants of the movement make a decision by consulting with each other in a sense of solidarity. According to Gülen, consultation is one of the most important features of a believing community, because it makes equality, participation, and solidarity possible.

Gülen finds consultation significant, both as a necessary corollary of faith and social solidarity:

> In Islam, consultation is an absolute essential, which both the rulers and the ruled must obey. The ruler is responsible for conducting consultation about state politics, governing, legislation and all affairs related to society; the ruled are responsible for expressing and conveying their views and thoughts to the ruler.[60]

According to Gülen, consultation is the first condition that must be taken for any decision in any issue to be correct.

> We have all seen how all decisions made without having been thought through thoroughly, without having taken into account the views and criticisms of others, whether related to individuals in particular or to society in general, have resulted in fiasco, loss, and great disappointment. Even if a person has a superior nature and outstanding intellect, if they are content with their own opinions and are not receptive and respectful to the opinions of others, then they are more prone to make mistakes and errors than the average person. The most intelligent person is the one who most appreciates and respects mutual consultation and deliberation [*mashwarat*], and who benefits most from the ideas of others. Those who are content with their own ideas in their plans and deeds, or who even insist or force others to accept their ideas, not only miss a very important dynamic, but also face disagreement, hostility, and hatred from the people with whom they are associated.[61]

Here, Gülen advices discussion and collective decision making, which is *sine qua non* of a democratic society. This view, being far beyond the

---

[60] Gülen 2007b, 43.
[61] *Ibid.*, 44.

classical frame of a Sufi order, is bringing to the fore a partnership which is open to novelty and human will.

Without consultation, one might venture into risky behaviors, such as the criticism of destiny and blaming of the environment.

Concerns such as "We are under the unending threat of foreign forces" and "They are going to divide and colonize us," result from the rulers, sound in mind but divorced from reality, those who make decisions without consulting the public's opinions.

According to Gülen,

> Consultation is one of the prime dynamics which keep the Islamic order standing as a system. To consultation belongs the most important mission and duty of resolving affairs concerning the individual and the community, the people and the state, science and knowledge, and economics and sociology, unless of course there is a *nass* [divine decree; a verse of the Qur'an or a command from the Prophet, decisive on any point in canon law] with a clear meaning on these matters.[62]

16. It is obvious that the concept of consultation prevents the melting or eradication of the individual within the society and contributes to the composition of collective decisions. What kind of a role does Gülen attribute to consultation in the framework of rulers and the ruled relationships?

Gülen stresses that for Muslims the decisive statements of the Qur'an and the clear *Sunnah* must be given priority. He then says:

> Even if the head of state or the leader is confirmed by God and nurtured by revelation and inspiration, he is under obligation to conduct affairs by consultation. There have been some who have neglected to do so, but generally the number of nations or communities which have retained this institution under different names and titles at different times is not negligible. In fact, any society which has ignored or disregarded it has never prospered, but rather has perished. So the Messenger of God saw the salvation and progress of his community in mutual consultation: "Those who consult do not lose."[63]

---

[62] *Ibid.*, 45.
[63] *Ibid.*

The importance that the Gülen Movement places on consultation explains why it continues to increase its members throughout the world and why it has become a movement that accommodates different sectors, unifying them around common sentiments and deeds. The evidences confirming the assessment made here are implicit in how Gülen interprets consultation and deliberation:

> Consulting with his Companions on every matter, the Messenger of God took their opinions and perspectives into account, and thus every venture he planned was presented to and adopted by the collective conscience; he made use of every feeling, emotion, and inclination that arose from the collective conscience as a foundation, and thus he supported and gave extra strength and endurance to the work he undertook. That is, by uniting everyone and involving everyone mentally and spiritually in the work to be done, he accomplished his projects on the strongest, soundest basis.[64]

Gülen reminds us here that in the life of a society the dualism of ruler and the ruled is not permanent and institutional; it is only functional and a division of labor directed to meet the needs of the society. This understanding, which is the foundation of modern democracy, refers to the principle that the religious does not interfere with the political and the political does not interfere with the religious, each acts in its own autonomous fields.

> Clearly consultation does not take priority over Divine Commands as a source of legislation. It is itself enabled by Divine Commands, and though it may be the basis for some laws and principles, consultation is restricted as it depends on true legislative sources. Those matters on which there is a clear divine decree remain outside the intervention of human beings, and people may only turn to consultation in order to ascertain its full meaning. Matters on which there is no such a decree are considered completely within the boundaries of consultation. On such matters, there is an obligation to abide by the results and decisions reached by consultation, and one cannot act contrary to the decisions taken and cannot continue to expound or defend other opposing views and opinions. If there is an error or mistake in the decision taken, even if it was taken by the majority, it must be amended or corrected by consultation again.
>
> Although the divine decrees about consultation are, in a sense, general, they are restricted by the decrees on particular issues and also by the acts and deeds of the Messenger of God. In fact the decrees in Islam, with a few

---

[64] *Ibid.*, 46

exceptions [those which express universal principles and general rules], do not dwell much upon or go into details of matters which can be deemed secondary. Issues on which there is no decree fall completely within the boundaries of consultation and are of the matters open to deliberation.[65]

Thus, in Islam there are a limited number of judgments in the field of political and social matters that came through revelation. In all other areas excluding these few concrete decisions, the decision is made or should be made through consultation. If a decision is made, but later or under different circumstances no longer serves the purpose, this situation should be reassessed and changed through consultation. In short, the society should be ruled, not by coercion or coercive people according to their whims and wishes, but by consultation with the members of the community, through their participation in a shared reasoning and decision-making process. Gülen finds this democratic principle in the essence of Islam. Secularism, which is respectful to religion, can be reconciled with Islam:

> The following are among the first principles at which Islam aims: to establish equality among people; to strive against ignorance and to spread knowledge; to interweave and interlace every issue and affair around the Islamic identity so that Muslims are not left to contradict their own essence; to direct the people of a country to protect their place and standing in the balance between states; to achieve the right balance of social justice between the individual and community; to develop and advance in every individual and the whole nation feelings of love, respect, altruism, striving for the sake of others, sacrificing their own material and spiritual benefits, and aspirations for the sake of others; to maintain and retain the balance between this world and the other; to order and organize domestic and international politics; to follow world affairs closely; and to prepare, as and when needed, all the resources to cope with the world as a whole...[66]

Gülen mentions here the main problems of human history, which, he argues can be met when both religion and worldly politics are functional.

Gülen continues with what consultation promises:

> Consultation, within its remit, promises some effects and also follows some rules which lead to positive outcomes. In this regard we may mention an increase in the level of thought and intervention in society;

---

[65] *Ibid.,* 49.

[66] *Ibid.,* 49–50.

reminding society of its own importance by taking its views on all new events; by reminding it in this way, leading it to produce alternative ideas... in every event, getting ... the majority of the highest, most able individuals ... to join in the administration to some extent; to ensure by public supervision of the administration that the people remain aware of the necessity for questioning and calling to account the administrators whenever the situation requires them to do so; and by preventing irresponsible behavior of rulers by limiting their executive power.[67]

What Gülen proposes is very close to the modern definition of democracy, namely, "participatory and deliberative democracy." His vision is more in conformity with a human-centered, political system that is based on the supremacy of law and which is seen in many developed countries. Furthermore, he calls upon the people to participate in the decision-making process, stressing that this is a right, as well as a responsibility. Individuals who do not fulfill this responsibility are, in fact, shirking the duty of citizenship. He holds responsible those citizens who do not let their opinions and demands known, as well as the administrators who do not resort to the preferences and demands of the citizens:

As a consequence of the verse, consult them in the affairs (Al-Imran 3:159), it is incumbent on the ruler or administrator to bring the matter on which consultation is required to the attention of those of sound judgment, otherwise he will be held responsible. The ruled are responsible for expressing their views when they are asked to. However, if the ruled do not express their views when asked to, then they are equally accountable. In fact, they are considered not to have fulfilled the duty of citizenship if they are not determined to be heard when their views are being taken, and still more if they neglect to voice their views and opinions.[68]

Gülen invites the individuals to become active citizens and participate in decisions that influence their destiny; he also considers it a weakness not to be decisive. He implies that such citizens cannot escape from the distress of rulers or demagogues who do not share the power in their hands and who do not let the decisions that they take be questioned. Another point he makes is that in the cases where unanimity cannot be obtained, the majority decision rules, with the proviso that the minority rights are safeguarded.

---

[67] *Ibid.*, 51.
[68] *Ibid.*, 52.

Under these given facts, in Gülen teachings it is impossible to find an understanding of a political system based entirely upon the principles derived from the Divine Decree, where there are unquestionable rules, immutable, or unchangeable. On the contrary, he brings forth a vast area of private enterprise and defends a rather developed system of a democracy in the worldly sphere, outside the divine one, in which only religious commandments are prevalent.

It is not possible to talk of a religion, if there were no principles related to worship. Moreover, any religion provides the fundamentals to develop into a good human being. For this reason, it is not reasonable and meaningful to say that there is a threat of *shariah* waiting behind the door, just because divine commandments are mentioned.

No matter how much Gülen believes in the importance of the individual's participation in the decision-making process on matters regarding their own lives and the merits of close supervision of rulers who implement those decisions, he is aware the need for the pioneering efforts of opinion leaders or wise men. He says:

> I am in favor of solving all issues in the collective conscience. I am of those who see three minds better than one and preferring the majority sentiments of my friends to my own sentiments. Then in that case, let us make the mechanism of mutual consultation operational. Let us grind the grave problems of the future in the wheels of it and never act individually.[69]
>
> People who know are numerous, but the numbers of people who represent in conduct what they know are very limited. The fact that knowledge transforming itself into virtue and its reflection on our behavior and conduct is our shortcoming. Both the one who knows [the wise man] and the one who has the merit of leadership, would shoulder the task of, in Bediüzzaman's words "division of duties, ordering the work, and facilitation of mutual help." In a society there are all kinds of works for everyone, from A to Z. For this reason, everyone should be given a task that he can undertake. Hence, the spirit of unity would not be damaged.[70]

When we are talking about the importance of opinion leaders, the topic of the relationship between Gülen and his followers inevitably arises. To what extent do Gülen's followers feel comfortable to offer their opinions in a consultation with Gülen? He replies:

---

[69]   Gülen 1997b, 69.
[70]   Gülen 2010a, 152.

Some of our friends, maybe as a result of their respect, do not want always to express themselves. But the moments that you would like to see are not few. Sometimes they are very talkative, they express their opinions. I am always advising these friends: Let us not say with a submissive spirit, so and so always says the truth. I am making a self-criticism, by questioning if what I am doing might be wrong. My interpretations are my personal interpretations; you might not agree with them. But there are certain things, if they are right and they are also confirmed by the Book and the *Sunnah*, then just for the sake of arguing you cannot quarrel by saying I am going to hold a brainstorm, it would be meaningless.[71]

When asked if his influence and his ties to the movement produce pressures on the followers by destroying individualism and freedoms, he replies:

It must have some pressure. Feeling respect and being crushed under that respect might occur, but it is not an oft experienced matter. We have to solve this, all of us, all together. Like a debate, namely keeping the courtesy, we can always discuss the matters. I think this would and can be realized over time. At this moment, here everyone is comfortable to bring the issues to be tabled. If it is right, it receives approval.[72]

After this assessment, Gülen returns back to the topic of the need for opinion leaders and what would happen to society if they did not exist:

In terms of their vision of thinking, if the individuals could not overcome their egos, those who did, could not vocalize them, and after vocalization, if they could not make the society of which they are members, appropriate with all its sectors, then it would be inescapable for such a society to decay, dissolve and swallowed up by others.[73]

17. What is the view of Gülen on secularism?

While in the second article of the 1982 constitution it is stated that secularism is one of the basic attributes of the Republic of Turkey, in the article 24, it is stated that everyone has the freedom of conscience, religious belief, and opinion; and the religion could not be misused. Although secularism is not defined in our constitution and in other legal texts, in the reason given for

---

[71] Akman 2004, 77.
[72] *Ibid.*, 78.
[73] Gülen 2010b, 45.

article 2, it is explained that secularism can never mean irreligiosity, and it is stated that it means for each individual to have any faith he/she wishes and not to be treated discriminatorily because of religious faith. The freedom of religion is defined as for the individuals to believe in the religion of their choice and without the fear of being disturbed to be able to practice the requirements of the religion they chose freely.[74]

Gülen, by looking at the current legal rules, proposes that secularism should be understood as follows: Religion should not interfere with the worldly life and the administration should not interfere in the religious life; everyone should be able to practice his faith freely in his social milieu. But in reality, this is not the case. Because it is not the case, many problems arise, including tensions among the society, the state, and the religious groups. According to Gülen, each individual in society should decide on their own whether to belong to a religion or not. No one should be forced to believe in a religion or to meet the requirements of a particular religion. He states with respect to Islam, his own faith:

> There is no coercion in the core of the religion because coercion is opposed to the spirit of the religion. Islam takes the will and the choice as real, and establishes all of its treatments on the basis of these traits. None of the actions and performances, whether they are of the kind of faith, worships or transactions, carried out by coercion can ever be taken as valid and acceptable. This situation would be in contradiction with the principle, "Actions are by intention."[75]

With these views, he stands diametrically opposed to radical interpretations or movements that relate Islam to brutal force or violence. Indeed, Gülen considers the politicization of Islam as the exploitation of religion and vehemently opposes it. He is aware that as a result of this abuse, it is unavoidable that the politics would meddle in religious affairs. If religion is a sacred phenomenon, it becomes necessary that it must not be used as a tool for anything else. He goes one step further and says:

> ... So much so that religion should not be used as a tool in the spiritual sentiments of *füyuzat* [effulgence, spiritual manifestations] in order to individually enter Paradise. Secondly, when we base our political opinions and

---

[74]   Dinçkol 1992, 67.
[75]   Gülen 2010c: 195.

our views of parties, in some ways, our shortcomings, faults, and defects reflect into the religion. The reaction which is felt about us is also directed to religion. In another approach, the religion also takes its share when hatred is felt towards us. The reality of religion should be represented in such a way that it should be above all political considerations. Whereas when religion is politicized, it is tantamount to say, "We are representing it." Then as it were we consider others outside it. Here I am not thinking of anyone or a political entity. I am directing attention to what kind of reaction could be generated by the politicization of religion. Even if that attitude is adopted in the name of defending religion, since we blacken it by our acts, the religion takes its share from the hatred felt against us. Those who politicize are doing a great disservice to religion.[76]

Religion is a matter between the human and God, the foundation of which is based on cordiality, sincerity, earning God's pleasure, ... the internal depth of heart. It is a matter of passing one's life on the emerald hills of the heart. It would be wrong by ignoring this side of religion, practicing it like a ceremony, and as if to make a show.[77]

He further states,

In Turkey which is a secular state, politicizing religion is treason to the spirit of Islam. Religion should not be a tool of politics.[78]

Despite his clear words to the contrary, Gülen has been subjected to persecution and many indictments for years that he is anti-secular and anti-Atatürk. An oligarchic network making these unfounded accusations desire to impose its own understanding of religion on the whole society. This power has made its creed dominant in the institution which has been entrusted with religious affairs. It has organized that institution as part of the state apparatus and by governing it; it has itself violated the principle of secularism.

Gülen explains the difference between secularism and secularization. Secularism is politics. There is a political authority behind it and this authority directs the institution of religion that it holds under its authority to put the society in a certain course. In this way, religion is a part of the political authority and is subject to it. When the political authority is weakened, the society interferes in the field of faith, which is already

---

[76] Özsoy 1998, 30.

[77] *Ibid.*

[78] The interview given to Hulusi Turgut, *Sabah*, 25 January 1997.

politicized, and tries to release religion from the claws of politics and the state. But this is a painful process. Because in order to pull religion from the hands of the political authority into the autonomous and respected field of faith, struggle in the field of politics might arise. In leftist and nationalist societies, this has generally been the result.

Whenever a society matures and develops, the educational and income levels and the standards of living increase. The religion moves from the political arena into the deserving cultural field, a politically neutral field where faith has the respect it deserves. Secularization is just that.

In summary, secularization is a process. It purifies religion from politics. When this happens, religious and worldly matters are not in opposition and confrontation; they are together and complement each other. In this sense, according to Gülen, Turkey is a country which has yet to complete its secularization.

18. Secularism is a policy; it is interpreted according to the political force behind it. There also is a process called secularization—as societies develop and the educational level of the members and cultural diversity increase, the religion leaves its position of being the only reference point for thought and conduct. The references influencing the thoughts and behaviors of members become numerous. Gülen's teachings and influence came exactly at this juncture in Turkey. For this reason, his inspiration, exhortations, and conduct seem to represent the secularization of Turkey from within and bottom up, rather than enforcing from top down, and they also provide the intellectual basis for it. Does Gülen share this interpretation?

Gülen replies,

> In Turkey democracy and secularism existed for years, even during the Ottomans they existed partially. The founders of the republic took from the Ottomans and developed secularism. In later years, it became a concept entering directly into the constitution. Nevertheless, not much said about the definition and the framework of it. The information was not provided. For this reason, the problem has stemmed from the ambiguity of the framework of the concept of secularism. It was not a matter of disturbance with the concepts of democracy or secularism.

For instance, when some said secularism, they thought not to recognize a place for religion. Of course, they could not say so to the Christians or the Jews in Turkey, because there was the USA behind them, there was Europe, there was the world. There was no one to defend the rights of the wretched Muslims.[79]

According to Gülen, the wretched Muslims, the majority in the country, should have been protected by the rulers, the dominant elite. They did not fulfill their duty of protecting the poor and deprived Muslims, which resulted in a widespread belief that if secularism and democracy do not bring us freedom, dignity, and welfare, they are not right for us. Believing people could not find the free environment that they were hoping for with respect to their individual, social, or family lives, nor in matters related to worship and worldly transactions. This caused a considerable portion of the society to stay aloof from these concepts.

After making this assessment Gülen, suggests that the people would not have any cause for concern relating to the concepts of democracy or secularism executed properly:

Our nation has a good mannered-culture that it had inherited from the past. For this reason, we never witness up until today, the uprising of those groups who are anti-democrats or anti-secularists. Therefore, the majority of the nation, we can say 80%, are not disturbed by either democracy or secularism. They said, "If they come with the Western standards we would say yes,"[80]

At this point, Gülen makes an interesting comment:

When they came to power, they said, "In reality we are more secular than anyone else, we are more democratic than everyone, we are more republican than everyone." And the public did not object to these statements. Those who were in favor of them did not give any reaction. That means this matter was not a great problem for the public. Even looking at their circumstances in terms of practicing their religion, they found Turkey more comfortable. Surely, there were some antidemocratic things, but Turkey was benefitting from democratic rights and freedoms, and utilizing them which could not even be contrasted with the prevailing situation in the Asian, African, and North African nations. The rest was not the concern of anyone. I think, later they made this matter problematic artificially. And

---

[79] The interview given to *Time*, 30 May 1997.
[80] *Ibid.*

some people, with political considerations, owned up this issue. Thus, they presented Islam as if it was opposed to democracy and secularism. Sovereignty and the issue of politics comprise only 3% of the teachings of the Qur'an. 97% concern the individual, his religion, his religious views, his relation with the divine, upbringing of his family members in good character, the rights and freedoms to educate his children, the rights and freedoms to earn his livelihood. None of the worldly preferences like these is in contradiction with Islam. Therefore, the nation never felt the contradiction with them.[81]

With regard to bending democracy or distortion of it by the groups seeking sovereignty and power, he states:

They say, "Can we channel the democratic thoughts into our service." It is not possible for us to channel democracy into any place. It runs its course in its natural setting. But till now others made it a tool for their different sensibilities, thoughts, and different understandings. ... While saying Marx, they said democracy. While saying Lenin, they said democracy. While saying Mao, they said democracy. Now adding some other attributes to it, they are still saying democracy. In fact, Marx, Lenin, Stalin, Mao are miles away from democracy. They are dictators at global scale; the advice they give to humanity, and the systems represented by those are the totalitarian systems. They have nothing to do with democracy. If a system has somehow a relationship with democracy to any extent, in my opinion Islam is very close to it. Islam and Muslims benefit from its many rules. There would be numerous things for a Muslim to perform in that democratic atmosphere.[82]

After expressing these thoughts, he makes a call to the Muslims to benefit from the blessings of democracy:

Instead of declaring a war against it, in the vast atmosphere it awards you with, you have to be making efforts to establish your institutions, efforts to serve your religion, your nation, and the ideals of your nation.[83]

Well then, is it possible in a future time to go beyond the familiar concept of democracy, to transcend it? Gülen answers yes:

It is theoretically possible to find a more humane, more perfect system. It is theoretically possible to establish a more progressive system, what-

---

[81]   *Ibid.*

[82]   Doğu Ergil's interview with Gülen.

[83]   *Ibid.*

ever humans expect from democracy with its reason and reasoning, its sensibilities, concept of freedom, philosophy of freedom, the structure of family, and system of governing. This does not have to remain at theoretical level. The new ... system might be represented by its architects and pioneers ... And there would be a new tendency along this line in the world. In history those paths had been tried, and this search of humanity would continue. Therefore, the current system ... could be changed by improvements.[84]

These views display the faith of Gülen in democracy and his belief that he does not see it as a frozen reality. He, by directing our attention to the fact that democracy could be improved along the lines of human needs and to the extent of human creativity, shows that he is looking at politics from a progressive perspective, rather than a conservative one. Ironically, Gülen, who has been labeled as an "obscurantist," appears more progressive than the ones accusing him!

This observation is strengthened further by the call to Muslims to reap the maximum benefits offered by democracy. After discussing the power of democracy and its ability to advance developing and maturing individuals and societies, he asks this question:

Why do not the people, who believe and love their country, think of utilizing such an atmosphere efficiently and benefit from it?[85]

The logical follow-up to Gülen's question, which carries a tone of complaint, is whether Islam and democracy can be reconciled. He responds,

Sultanate [the sovereignty belongs to the sultan and the political system he represented] was squared with Islam in the past. The messenger of God says "Caliphate," but later starts monarchy, they say "mighty monarch." And we applauded all these people. We applauded even the sultans. We accepted their administrations as the implementation of Islam. But in actual fact, none of these regimes could be considered as being in the footstep of the Prophet. Neither the status of Umayyads nor that of the Abbasids could be said to be in conformity of the Prophet's understanding of the administration. For this reason could it be said that the states of affairs in the Karakhanids, Ilkhanids, Seljukids or the Ottomans are com-

---

[84]   Can 1997, 130.
[85]   *Ibid.*

pletely in conformity with Islam? ... But all these things were owned up. Despite the administrative shortcomings, they were owned up.[86]

Gülen does not find a sultanate (or a similar governance under a different title) to be in congruence with the innate disposition of humans, their integrity, and the lofty ideals they carry in themselves. Of course, this is not tantamount to claiming that among those sultans or monarchs, there were no examples of extremely good, just, and capable rulers. What he disagrees with is their oppressive rules and returns to the discussion on democracy:

> If there is a good rule of democracy in our country that would see what harm in it? ... There remains the fact that democracy is an ongoing process. It is a process which has to continually progress. The West is not saying, "We have reached a point in democracy, we can go no further," either. If democracy is a process in reaching the perfect ... it could be said that we are progressing towards the perfect.[87]

Gülen is then asked if we have internalized democracy in Turkey. Is the relationship between religion and democracy problematic or is it just conceived to be?

> Democracy is a rule by the people. It is a profound form of "republic." It is its life; it is the more humane dimension of it. For this reason, in a sense ... it always existed in the past, although it was not named. We can even talk about a republic and existence of a democracy without a name during the Rightly Guided Caliphs. ... Maybe between the systems there is an overlapping. It is possible to reconcile them. For that reason, it could be thought that republic and democracy might make up a conveniently proper ground for Islam, Islamic thought, and the possibility of practicing Islam. Considering them as against Islam, in my opinion, is a wrong interpretation, a wrong approach. But I wish there could be a more developed democracy, the Westerners want that, we often want that, too. I mean I wish a democracy which could solve all our problems.[88]

Even if there is no inherent contradiction between democracy and "religion," for Gülen, faith as a political ideology presents dangers for social stability as well as for religion.

---

[86] *Ibid.,* 132.

[87] *Ibid.,* 133.

[88] The interview given to Yalçın Doğan, Kanal D, 16 April 1997.

They say religion is politicized. Accepting such a maxim means some circles are politicizing religion. But politicization of religion is dangerous for religion rather than what it is for the regime. In fact, it means blackening the soul of religion, because religion is everybody's religion, it is the name of something everyone respects, through which everyone finds worldly tranquility and happiness in his heart. It is the name of everyone's connection with God.[89]

When reminded that secularism in Turkey is in serious danger, he replies:

If the state would protect religion, but it would not interfere with it, others would not interfere in religion, if it is to be understood that the religious would not interfere in others' affairs while practicing his religion and if the state would maintain the matter in complete impartiality, then there is no problem at all. But, I think some people are creating artificial problems. Maybe sometimes, some are being harsh in the name of defending secularism. This agitates and provokes others. But I would not be able to say who starts first. Sometimes, some are also attacking secularism and democracy unjustly. They are also causing the other side to move and act.[90]

Her replies to those in some Islamic circles who claim that he is pacifying people in politics:

Islam is not democracy, and democracy is not Islam. Democracy is a system that the whole world has turned towards, but it is still being embellished, in order to find itself it is shedding its shell. It is not claimed that there is complete democracy in Turkey. That means democracy is going through a process in order to reach perfection. Democracy is an ongoing process; it is not possible to be aloof to it. The believing people should benefit from it as much as others do. Of the injunctions of religion those related to state [governing] are about 5%. If democracy is used and utilized well [possible frictions between religious interpretations and the laws and their applications by the modern state] can be eradicated to a great extent.[91]

When reminded of the accusation that he is anti-republican, Gülen is saddened: "I am a republican before them. I am even of those who accepted Islam in its early period as a republic."[92]

---

[89] *Ibid.*

[90] *Ibid.*

[91] Akman 1995.

[92] The interview given to Reha Muhtar, TRT 1, 3 July 1995.

Gülen's statements make clear that democracy can continue to develop to meet human needs. He has no problem with a secularism that does not oppress religion, thereby forcing it to become politicized. It is likely the "danger" that some in official circles artificially produced around the name of Gülen stems from their distrust about every citizen initiative and action of a civil society, which is not under the inspection and control of the state.

This doubt and fear delay the development of our democracy and distort and deviate secularism from its aim and the philosophical source. It has created an authoritarian and centralized administration, which holds the society under guardianship and subject to the state. Since Gülen does not like to quarrel, he prefers to point out these realities by way of understandable hints.

It is important to remember that Gülen is a man of religion and an opinion leader. He has earned the respect and interest of others, as his interpretation of the Islamic traditions meets the needs of an increasingly complex society, which is being forced to adjust to tremendous change. He stresses that democracy is insurance for everyone and the best governance to reconcile differences.

With regard to secularism, he believes it should have a "live and let live" philosophy, where it neither gives permission to politics (in a narrower sense, government) to interfere with religion, nor permission to religion to interfere with politics. He bases his thesis on Islam, as Islam does not contradict democracy or secularism. He believes that in a modern society, democracy and secularism do not have an inhibiting effect, but a developing and freeing one:

> The first article of the Turkish Constitution states that "Turkish state is a republic." Just after that in the second article, the attributes of this republic are enumerated, and it says, "Turkey is a democratic, secular, and social state governed by the rule of law." Again as you know, these two articles cannot be changed, and even a bill to change it cannot be introduced in the parliament. Yes, these two foundations are under guaranties, and you cannot touch them. But, maybe you can improve them, perfect them, and make additions to democracy. You can open and expand the definition of secularism; you can elevate it to the human horizon to contain more humane values. You can dwell on the "social state." You can dwell on the concept of "welfare state"; you can work on it and make it a little more humane and a little friendlier. But you can do all of these by remaining

objective and benefitting from the developments in the world, then you can improve on them towards perfection.[93]

What Gülen says regarding democracy is related to how to interpret the world and social life. Whether this interpretation is secular or religious brings the discussion to the source of sovereignty. This phenomenon implies that if the source of sovereignty is Divine, then the law and public administration have to be based entirely on religious rulings and judgments. In such a case, ruling the society and interpreting and applying the laws are for men of religion to perform. This situation is unacceptable for a secular vision of a society, as Gülen explains:

> Democracy means a system based on the sovereignty of the people. The matter expressed by "The sovereignty belongs to the people without any condition or reservation," [the famous phrase hanging on the wall of the Turkish National Assembly] is democracy. This word does not mean taking the sovereignty from God, and giving it to the people. On the contrary, it states that the sovereignty is taken away from the representatives of oppressive and crude force and given to the people [nation].
>
> Yes, democracy is a system of administration which entrusts the protection of basic rights and freedoms to the representatives of the public and is based on the principles where the views and opinions of the people become effective in the administration of the nation.[94]
>
> *Intihab* [election] comes from the word *nuhba*. *Nuhba* means "dish of sweetened clotted cream." Do not forget, whatever is in the essence of a thing, its *nuhba* would be the same. On the surface of milk would be milk cream; and on the surface of the stack would be the cream of stack. These words consist of a delightful interpretation of the *hadith*: "You are ruled as you deserve." Now, democracy is the administration of those who come from the people and represent their demands exactly.[95]

With this comment, Gülen points to the fact that the type of a democracy that a society has depends upon the extent of that society's level of development, the level of relationship it establishes with the world, the knowledge of its citizens, and whether its citizens are equipped with a conscience. In summary, societies where the religious rules are sovereign or the secular rules are prevalent are the preferences of the members who make up that society.

---

[93] Gülen 2010d, 190.

[94] *Ibid.*, 190–191.

[95] *Ibid.*, 191.

At this point, he carries the discussion to a different dimension: the contrast between secular state vs. theocratic state:

Laic, is a word borrowed from French; it means a system which is not clerical, religious thought or institution. After the famous revolution, the French disestablished theocratic order, purified the state from religious and clerical elements by separating the church from the state ... and called this a secular state. ... By the way ... it would be wrong to characterize and interpret theocratic order as a religious administration, epistemologically and terminologically. Theocratic order does not mean a kind of administration based on religion and religious texts. Namely, by the expression "theocratic state," it is not meant "a state administration based on the Torah, the Old Testament, or the New Testament." To express it as a kind of government based on the Qur'an or authentic *hadiths* is totally wrong. Mentioning theocracy together with Islam is either based on a grudge or malice against Islam and is aimed at oppressing and destroying the Muslims or an indication of not being in complete command of the terminology or ignorance. Theocratic state is a kind of administration based on the domination and control of the clerical class and the authority of the church. It means a state ruled according to the interpretations and decisions [of the clerical class].

In such a state, the words of the clerical class are the final judgments. Whatever they say, for sure they would mean the will of God in that matter and can never be questioned. Therefore, the concept of secularism was born in the West, within the context of religious, political, and social circumstances, out of a need to make a distinction between the church and the state, as a result of never ending civil wars which took place as a response to the oppression of the clerical class and their different opinions and interpretations. From this perspective, the problem of the Western societies is not with the religion but with the men of religion and the church organizations of the time for their use of religious commandments, for their own interests.

So much was the animosity that the matter, in a certain period had extended to the distinction between religion and science. Descartes who came out by a thesis saying "Metaphysics cannot be a science," by claiming that knowledge can only be obtained by investigating the measurable and divisible things, had confined the subject matter of science to material things; and later the Cartesian [the way of Descartes] philosophers had always spoken in the same vein. They had taken religion and science as if they were two different fields and insisted on not trespassing any one of the fields. This matter of not trespassing changed forms from one period to another and by the passage of time it became the basis of secularism defining the line of demarcation for religion and government, the separation of worldly and other worldly matters, and prohibition of mutual interference in each other's areas.

Nevertheless, secularism was not applied in every society in the same form; it was interpreted in different ways in different parts of the world. While *laïcité*, applied at a certain place, has provided the guaranties for everyone the freedom of conscience, religious beliefs and opinions, the right to participate in the religious ceremonies, the right to express and propagate individually or in groups their thoughts and opinions, in speech or text, or some other ways; in other places it was applied harshly, *laïcité* was taken entirely as secularism and ... almost all the religious life was banned, the right of people to explain and to propagate their religious thoughts and opinions were entirely infringed.

In this regard then, it is necessary for us to acknowledge that *laïcité* has to be developed. Like democracy, this matter is also going through a process on the way to becoming more humane. An important aspect of the Republic of Turkey defined by the constitution is its being a social one. By virtue of being a social state [or a welfare state] it has to recognize the basic rights and freedoms of individuals, and has to ensure the achievement of them. These rights and freedoms were determined by the constitution. For instance, everyone has the right to demand private life and the privacy of family to be respected; the secrecy of private and the family life could not be violated. A social state has the responsibility to protect that freedom, in addition to recognizing it. At the same time, everyone has the right to dwell any place one wishes and the freedom to travel. Within the framework of the social state this freedom has to be provided by any means; otherwise there can be no talk of a social state.

If some rights and freedoms are determined but individuals are not given the chance to benefit from them, for instance, believing in something ... is prevented and if the expression of different opinions are banned, again no mention of the existence of a social state can be made in that place. In order for a state to be considered as social, as it is necessary for everyone in that country to have the freedom of thought and opinion and to express and propagate his/her thoughts and opinions in different ways [by different means], it is also necessary for every individual to have the freedom to receive education in different fields of art and science, learn and teach, to do every kind of research, and the right to publicize them. However ... never your expression of your thoughts and opinions should result in disturbing others. As you have personal rights, so do others, they have also individual rights and freedoms.[96]

---

[96]   *Ibid.* 192–194.

19. In order to have an ethical society and an ethical human, do we have to resort to religion? Isn't it possible to have secular ethics?

As of the level humanity has reached now, one of the things considered important is to recognize the right to believe and to be able to practice what one believes. In a certain period, in order to consolidate the system, a different practice might have taken place; but today in Turkey, democracy has been accepted and internalized. Maybe, 10 years ago one might have said, "Democracy is an irrevocable process" [he is referring to his speech given at the opening of the Foundation of Journalists and Writers in 1994], he was criticized. But, now since everyone talks about democracy with its many forms, it means from now on, we are going to seek the remedies to the problems within democracy.[97]

He then states that the humans cannot meet at a common denominator if different sides insist on basing their positions on fear, personal interests, and prejudices, instead of looking at the essence of things. But, if one of the sides softens a little bit, the other side will soften its attitude, as well. As an illustration, he mentions the process of Turkey's joining to the EU. Somehow, there is a concern that membership in the EU will push the nation to a radical religious line; integration with Europe is viewed with doubt. Notably, those who feel this way are the ones who call themselves Western and modern.

The question arises, "Does religion really encompass every aspect of life?," to which Gülen unequivocally answers:

Religion is life. As it is lived, it would exist. There are priorities while living the religion. For instance, basic principles, called the *muhkamat* of religion [decisive and clear injunctions], have a priority, and no one has a right to compromise on them. Second, however a Muslim understands the individual and family matters in the Qur'an and the *Sunnah*, that Muslim should be given the chance to practice individual and family matters that way, by limiting the borders, the field of life should not be narrowed. On the other hand, those who want to live as a Muslim must take extra care not to confuse certain things.[98]

Here, he is suggesting that a religious person, while trying to live his life according to the injunctions of religion, should not force his faith on others, claiming that there are absolute rules to be obeyed, and he

---

[97]   Gündem 2005, 100.
[98]   *Ibid.*

should not carry these rules to politics for that end. For this reason, he is giving the warning that "sometimes the *furuat* (details) of religion is replaced with the *usul* (basic judgments)."[99]

After reiterating that religion can be reconciled with democracy, he draws our attention to the fact that today there are many views on democracy, such as those of Christian democrats, social democrats, and liberal democrats. The movements' approaches start from different points, but are directed toward the same end.

> Why should not there be a democracy which has a place for Islamic sensibilities? If a humane democracy is to exist, it should embrace me with all of my attributes and should be developed to meet my needs.
>
> In my opinion, in a developed democracy an opportunity should exist in order to live the secular as a secular person comfortably, and also to live the hereafter as a person of the hereafter. Anyone, who wishes, should be able to live like a Companion of the Prophet.
>
> Democracy is also going through a process of evolution. For instance, we live in a democracy for a long time now, but the Copenhagen criteria made us aware of the proportion of our shortcomings. This process will mature by development. As a matter of fact, the Europeans are also still going through democratization process. It is difficult to say that they have completed and captured the "perfect" yet. I believe that one day a milieu will come into existence where under the umbrella of democracy, we are going to meet all our needs, needs relating to heart, soul, thought, and sentiment. I am seeing that we are progressing toward that direction. I believe also, the harshness between the assertive secularist and the Islamist sides—I have to state that I do not like the terms—would be softened. In addition, the educated, intellectual people should understand this fact; they should stop acting on their illusions and release themselves of the imagined fears in life.[100]

After expressing his ultimate faith in democracy, Gülen discusses the necessity of readjusting the public sphere to accommodate different groups with different religious backgrounds or worldviews, so all can live together without frictions. As for the main actor in this matter, Gülen offers the name of the "state" as the representative of everyone.

> In order for the people to live their religion in peace, there is a need for the state to spread its wings of mercy and prepare the convenient environment

---

[99] *Ibid.*, 101.
[100] *Ibid.*, 102–103.

for it. The religion needs an undefeatable power in order to improve the individuals to perfection, to put the family and the society into an order, to open the hearts by dominating the conscience and through that means to prevent many vices which could otherwise not be prevented. With a good religious education, the state should take this power behind it. The humans are not made up only by material traits; they have aspects related to the hereafter, too.[101]

What can be said about the claim of some people that, as a result of so much emphasis on religion in either formal education or education given in the family, Gülen's beliefs will result in anti-secularism? According to Gülen, morality can be sustained from different sources, but the main source is religion. Our Creator brought to the fore ethical and moral behavior in interpersonal relationships in order to give order to the world and to the realm of humanity. Ethics and morality are implicit in the foundation of religions. The state or administrations can benefit from this.

Our statesmen should not ignore the effect of religion. ... Only the consciousness and fear of God can tie the hands of evil people. Furthermore, there are the sick, the handicapped, and the aged at the threshold of the grave. The death swings in front of their eyes. What is there other than the faith in the hereafter which can calm down the lamentation in their soul? Then in that case, our statesmen could turn individuals into people of spirituality by benefitting from these undefeatable principles of religion and thus make it easier for themselves to establish law and order. This does not mean that there would be no more need for the law, order, the law enforcers, guardians, and the courts. They will still be needed but their job would be a lot easier since it will help lower the number of people with problems.[102]

As much as ethics is a necessary condition of an improved humanity, it also is a social security. According to Gülen, the source of ethics is conscience and what directs the conscience, primarily is religion. Religion is where good manners and morality are acquired. In his words,

Religion is the collection of divine principles that guide people to what is good, not by force, but by appealing to their free will. All principles that secure our spiritual and material progress, and thereby our happiness in both worlds, are found in religion.

---

[101] *Ibid.*, 103.
[102] *Ibid.*, 105.

> Religion means recognizing God in His absolute and transcendental Oneness; acquiring spiritual purity by acting in His way; arranging relationships in His name and according to His commandments, and feeling a profound interest in and love for all creation on His account.[103]

He emphasizes the complementarities of religion and science. Similarly, he does not confuse religious judgments with laws that organize worldly life and envisions two different fields for them.

> Religion and science are two faces of a single truth. Religion guides us to the true path leading to happiness. Science, when understood and used properly, is like a torch that provides us with a light to follow the same path.[104]

20. What is the place of the "state" in Gülen thought? How does he interpret the never-ending debate about the concepts of "nation of law" and the "deep state"?

Gülen values the state, especially the state based on the rule of law, and sees it as the major component of life and peace in society:

> The state based on rule of law is a state which holds the field of activity within the border of individual rights and freedoms, loyal to the principle of universality of laws and leaves open the juridical door in order for the individuals be protected against others and the state.
>
> The most important attribute of the state based on rule of law, is to be bound by the general legal principles in all its activities, not bound only by the laws. Every ordinance of the state for sure is made by certain measures, and before its application everyone is informed. Everyone, including each administrator, is inspected and supervised by the institutions of courts of law. The bills introduced and adopted must be in line with the spirit of the constitution. If the spirit of the constitution recognizes to you this and that right as individuals, families or as a society, the laws to be adopted cannot be against it at all. Otherwise, there would be contradiction between the constitution and the laws. A total chaos would prevail in the society.[105]
>
> Everyone must seek his rights within the legal system of the state of which he is a member; otherwise, when individuals or groups of individu-

---

[103] Gülen 2005a, 8–9.
[104] *Ibid.*, 9.
[105] Gülen 2010d, 195.

als would like to take their rights on their own initiatives, there would be a total chaos and disorder in the country.[106]

At this stage of his analysis, Gülen discusses the events leading up to the 1980 coup:

In Turkey, in the rather long period before 1980, some people started seeking their rights in their own way. As for the rights, they approached the matter with a Lenin-like, Mao-like, Fidel Castro-like means and said: "The rights are not given but they are taken," and poured onto the streets. They said "freedom," "proletarian dictatorship," they screamed, destroyed, and tried to have their rights. Some others, as if it was their duty, stood in front of them, challenging them, in order to protect the country. In those days, people were tense and the tensions were very high and years passed in this atmosphere. The hearts had always beaten with a desire to shed blood. The youthful brains thought only about blood, they spoke blood, and every individual caught the collars of others as if they were bloody murderers. By shedding blood and killing the souls the process of taking the rights went on and on. Those who died could not understand why they died; those who murdered did not know why they murdered. Unfortunately we saw all these in different periods.

Those who try to handle some matter outside the law would push others to handle some other matters outside the law. Either the state or those who put themselves in the place of the state or seem to be on the side of the state, when they try to handle the matters by means other than what is allowed by law, would cause more serious problems and complications. Such an attitude triggers everywhere entities outside the law gushing forth everywhere. Underground world would come into being; the number of unsolved murders increases and everyone does something on top of their heads. Yes, as those who put themselves in the place of the state, cannot perform such illegalities, the state itself cannot either. Even if, in the matter of seeking justice everyone is at fault, the state should never take faulty steps; it must not come close to any illegal interference. If that is the case, then everything should be handled within the framework of the law. The solution to the problem should be sought in resorting to the institutions of legislative, judicial, and executive organs.[107]

This reasoning leads Gülen to the conclusion that those who claim they are going to solve the Kurdish problem are making matters worse:

---

[106] *Ibid.* ,196.
[107] *Ibid.*, 197.

The state can fight against the rebels; it can kill during the fighting those who fire at the security forces, since the war has a rule of its own. But if a person comes by his own accord and surrenders, the state can never carry out execution without trial. To kill a person surrendering would be against the spirit of a state based on rule of law. Furthermore that person would make acknowledgements; there would be things he would tell. There what is at issue is the interests of the state. With the clues to be extracted there, the further vices and mischief and corruption can be prevented. As the state of affairs is this, if someone feels regret and comes down from the mountain, and makes petitions somewhere to make confessions and says, "There are things I will tell you, I will give important, vital information relating to the center of the rebellion, the nest of the mischief," and if you reply, "We do not accept you, your place is the mountain," and if you refuse him, then certain convictions would enter my mind relating to the encouragement of the mountain, something that you are fabricating. Then I could not help but think: Maybe, I think, you are managing some tricks, something fishy there. I wonder if you are dealing drugs. Are you producing weapons or trading them? Do you have an interest in the continuation of fights going on for years? On what basis are you opposing something that is an open matter in a state of law? When people come and surrender, if needed, you can proceed with a trial. You could give them punishments, imprison them, evaluate their confessions, or reward them. You might arouse others' envy and by this way you can succeed in bringing many people to come down from the mountain. If you are opposed to the solution, it is beyond any doubt that you have some plans, opposing the basic principles of the state. Now, this could not be reconciled with the spirit of a state, based on the rule of law.[108]

Gülen draws our attention to the fact that when official personnel and some state institutions, under the pretext of national security, violate the law, the state's legitimacy is destroyed and disgraced and social instability prevails.

In a state of law, it is not possible to talk about state in state or deep state. But unfortunately, some people came out in our country and said: "I have murdered people. I am asked to murder for the purpose of establishing law and order to maintain public order and public security." There were those who said: "My state said to me 'Shoot,' and I shot." They could have been told: "If the state says 'Fornicate', will you fornicate! Are you going to steal, if it says 'Steal'?" Any state encouraging thievery, is a state which lost its honor; the state encouraging fornication, has lost the character as a state.

---

[108] *Ibid.*, 198.

Even if it stands as a virtual state, like a statue, in reality it is without a soul. Likewise, it is not possible to talk about honor and dignity of a state which says, "Kill the man." If that is the case, then leave that official job; be on your own, but do not murder. Even if the state orders you, you cannot carry out actions in opposition to the universal legal values and the system of law in Turkey.

There are many unsolved murders. Still it is not known who were behind these murders. Since it is not known, without any delay, new murders take place the same way, similar scenarios are played out. Yes, the state cannot murder even if it is for the state. State punishes, but it punishes after a due process of law. But it cannot execute without a trial at all. As the state cannot do it, likewise those who put themselves in the place of the state or those who claim they love their state cannot do it either.

In order to punish some rebels, the existence in the body of the state some secret services can never be accepted. As a matter of fact, was he or was he not, I cannot know, but sometime there was this Yeşil [the code name of a shady hit man] who claimed to work on behalf of the state. If the state is using such people, as it used Yeşil [Green] yesterday, if it uses a "Red" for the illegal things today, and if it is going to ask the "Purple" tomorrow to do some dark businesses, with such ugly things it is impossible to reconcile the honor of a state and being a state based on the rule of law.

Again one of the prominent figures had said sometime in the past: "What you call Hizbullah in fact consists of the people who give service to their government." He had said that the state was using them against the PKK [the Kurdish Workers Party, a terrorist organization]. This matter has become today a topic of conversations and discussions and still continuing to be a matter of speculations. If you use the rebel against a rebel, then you are going to have to find another rebel against the latter. In the end against any rebel, you will have to find another rebel and without being aware of it you would go into a vicious circle. The criminal who thinks he has stepped down on the ground, would break unilaterally the agreement and would no longer listen to you, he would not want to be your stooge. He would think, "Since I have my foot firm on the ground, I can do something on my own." Now this time you would have to find another group of rebels. Hizbullah is followed by "Mizbullah" and that is followed by "Tizbullah," this matter goes on and on. These are shameful things for a state based on rule of law. To give permission to these and to pioneer as an instigator is an historical disgrace. Those who generate these groups using them as puppets making them headaches for both themselves as well as for the state ... they will be tried in the court of history and will go into history as a black spot. And of course, before God, they will account for these crimes.[109]

In this analysis, Gülen points out that many retired generals have acknowledged that "We made a mistake," and that the politics of security, which has far exceeded the legal parameters, has produced an unstable, not secure society. He also emphasizes the age old mistake: "The enemy of my enemy is my friend." This mistake is costly to the country, as much as the legitimacy of those who practice it is over shadowed by it. When the states uses one armed group against another, it has entrusted its security to these illegal groups and swept the state itself into illegality, thereby damaging its legitimacy. The fact is that the enemy of my enemy is his enemy, but not my friend. Most likely, the enemy of my enemy will soon become my enemy too after a short lived partnership. This is because as long as illegal and blood-shedding methods are condoned, its tactics will continue, even if the aims are changed.

Gülen also calls our attention to the critical role that public opinion plays in the decision-making process. He advises us to avoid bringing frictions to the level of confrontation:

> For the sake of circulation and ratings, we should not be duped to blacken the future of Turkey. Under the pretext of struggle against terrorism, we should not cause the infringement of rights and freedoms, the cessation of the effort for democratization.[110]

As if he has seen today's events years ago, he warns against repeating the mistake of creating a Turkish-Kurdish (Turk-Kurd) opposition:

> It would not be right to make a judgment in general by saying, "Among so and so there are some rebels." Some time past now; weren't there some among those who said, "I am a Turk," but screamed everywhere "Mao, Mao"? Is it not the case that some of those who state that they are *Ulusalcılar* [literally, "those who are for the nation state" as opposed to "nationalists," a new term adopted by themselves to designate a particular ideological stand] were among those in the past to run after Lenin or Stalin? Just like from among us some people who are crooked emerge [outside the rules]; of course among others some spoilers might arise. The security forces should find them, surrender them to justice, and if

---

[109] *Ibid.*, 200.
[110] *Ibid.*, 204.

they have something deserving punishment, the law should punish them. But one has to absolutely stay away from using a language by bringing this or that interpretations to this matter, causing different fronts to come about to confront each other.[111]

Gülen expresses a stand expected from anyone with a common sense: We should not blame the whole community because some so-called "bad apples" cause animosities among larger groups or communities. If we do so, it will not be possible for us to solve our social problems and disagreements, and these problems will only increase to a point where our country becomes instable.

21. How does Gülen view the issue of multiculturalism?

According to Gülen, the idea of *Devlet-i Ebed Müddet* (the Eternal State—a phrase of hope for the continuation of the Ottoman Empire until the "end of days") during the rule of the Ottomans results from its view of plurality. He believes the Ottoman period illustrates how they embraced multiculturalism. For instance, the Ottoman Empire with its unique legal system was able to achieve the flexibility to administer the state for centuries. For this to be possible, the principles and judgments derived from the fundamental sources of the religion were utilized, and the other principles were reinforced by new interpretations and legislations. This brought together the social order and the philosophy of government.

For instance, in the conquered areas lands, the relationship of the government administration with its subjects was just and functional. Groups from different ethno-religious backgrounds were autonomous in practicing their daily lives and administering their cultural institutions.

> Another issue is that it was made possible for the people from different faiths, Christian, Jewish, and even atheists [under the roof of the same state]. Buddhists and Brahmans were treated very well. Even from the services of these people were benefitted. As of the earliest period, Ghazi Mihal takes his place next to Osman Ghazi, meaning they are acting with a Christian. It is not known whether he converted later or not. But one of those who fought in the front of Muslim armies was this man. Evrenos Pasha, Zagnos, Ghazi Mihal, etc...

---

[111] *Ibid.*

I think the fact that more than pure blood Turks from Anatolia among the subjects of the state, there are people from different races and tribes points to that phenomenon. No one had carried within himself the doubt and concern that by joining the Ottomans he would be deprived of some advantages. This matter is ... an application of the richness and facility of the core of the religion. What is beautiful about it is that the Ottomans did not do this facilitation only for the Muslims, but Christians, Jews and other faith members alike. The Ottoman administrators have implemented the principle of tolerance, and therefore they left the doors of the state always open. This must have meant a great meaning that the joining in the empire steadily increased. This feature of the state being pluralistic ... as providing the flexibility to the laws, it put the men of the state at ease. The universality was captured.[112]

At this point, Gülen enters into a much debated topic. He believes that during the reign of Fatih Sultan Mehmet, the principles of tolerance, pluralism, and the coexistence of different groups, prevailed. Whether these principles could once again be revived in the form of religious injunctions is the issue.

As long as you do not bring the logic to be able to interpret the principles of Islam together along, you can never bring about a universal function to this matter. When you are open to this matter like the Ottomans, the success could be obtained. But, in this matter, if rigidity takes place in the name of the religion, like the Kadizades did in the Ottomans, if the natural sciences are thrown out of the religious schools, saying these are evil sciences, and if the deliberations like why are there next to the higher Islamic knowledge, why do you have to recognize to the unbeliever the right to life, why should the Jew benefit from the rights we benefit, why should we allow others to earn in trade, what is the meaning of trading with the unbelievers, come to the fore, very important aspects of our universality would be trimmed. In reality, this would have been tantamount to trimming our own our arms and wings.[113]

These assessments explain why, under the pretext of creating a nation state and as a result of practices attempting to produce one type of human being, Turkey has lost a great majority of our non-Muslim population. Does it only explain the state of non-Muslims? Unfortunately, not. It also answers the question: "Why is our Muslim population, comprised

---

[112] Can 1997, 125–126.
[113] *Ibid.*, 127.

of diverse ethnic groups and sects, alienated and resentful?" Gülen suggests that the cause is the "loss of real Islamic logic" or loss of the logic of interpreting Islam within its own framework and its open nature to universality.

22. Does Gülen suggest that today's Muslim has a duty to address those distorting Islam from within or from without and, if so, what is that duty?

According to Gülen, those who commit vices against the nation or religion to which they belong are the ones who do the most damage. It is because they are from within. With a known enemy, by contrast, you are ready to face the challenge.

> The most unbearable test would be this one. To see treason and unkindness from the place you expect fidelity is painful as well as something to be considered seriously. From yesterday to today, from time to time, from the enemy but sometimes from the adversaries in the guise of a friend, the Muslims who encounter always disloyalty and ill treatment, during all history have seen the heaviest and the most painful tests. They were subjected to most dreadful treasons. Maybe ... in the future they will see some more tests. They will face hills made of fire, the oceans made of blood and pus; all of these will help them to renew themselves and acquire metaphysical tension. This is because, he will recognize his friends and foes through these, he will be sharpened, and he will learn the ways to stand up after falling down.[114]
>
> If there were no adversity and prejudices from his adversaries and no ignorance and disloyalty from his friends, today the entire humanity would have united around the divine table spread by Islam and shaken hands with each other. When the hearts do not lends ears to Islam, it cannot make its voice heard, either; if when conduct and representation do not deepen the words, its voice would be lowered and it would absolutely fail to generate attraction in the souls.[115]

What does Gülen mean here?

Evaluated with what has been said on other occasions, he is highlighting the fact that religion has been distorted by incorrect interpretations and practices and exploited for worldly benefits ,because of some

---

[114] Gülen 2008b, 39.
[115] Gülen 2010e, 16.

of the co-religionists' conservatism, lack of vision and disloyalty, and the enemy's hatred, vindictiveness, animosity, obscurantism, and fundamentalism.

In reality, religion becomes something other than itself (not a faith anymore) and turns into a vehicle for blind ambition, power, and politics.

> But in fact the religion was sent, to speak on its behalf, as itself, to enter into hearts as itself, and to say whatever it wants to say as itself. It had not appointed as its advocate and no one had the right on its behalf. But you can observe that many of us, without shame or embarrassment, we are able to speak comfortably about it.[116]

Gülen believes that the source of the problem is the personal preference made on behalf of the religion. It results from the specific conditions of a known time and place. Thus, the source of the problem is not the religion, but the adherents of that religion. A person's sincerity, intention, and humanity, and how he practices his religion and lets others practice theirs are the determining factors.

> ... The Muslims who make an effort to live in an atmosphere of tolerance, peace, and tranquility should know that Islam from yesterday to today is subject to attacks and after today some people might act with a sense of hatred and animosity.[117]
>
> Abu Bakr had struggled against Aswad al-Ansi on one side, and also the liars who claim to be Prophets like Musaylima al Kazzab, Sajah, Tulayha, and disloyalties arising from within the community. When entering the First World War, the Arab tribal chiefs [being caught by the influence of the foreign propaganda] committed treason against the Ottoman soldiers at the defense of Medina.[118]

According to Gülen, these sort of people have existed exist and will exist in the future. We have to live with them. It is one test on the way of becoming a perfect man or woman. Then, how should we conduct ourselves? First, we should not produce vehicles conducive to enmity:

> We are in favor of to chain the mistakes of the past in history books, and not to revive the sensibilities for animosity. In the past, certain events had caused other chain of events; animosities had given way to other animosi-

---

[116] *Ibid.*, 249.
[117] Gülen 2005b, 158.
[118] *Ibid.*, 158–159.

ties; the people were estranged and alienated from each other, and opposite fronts were built up. Today, by making mention of these, establishing them as reason for new fights, and creating new gaps are meaningless. Whatever they say, whatever they do, no matter what they say, we have to continue on the way of tolerance that we are walking on, despite the hatred, vindictiveness, and animosity. We have to reach some "islands of peace"; we have to establish the "islets of peace."[119]

These words are especially relevant at this time when the process of "democratic opening," better relations with non-Muslim minorities, and normalization of the relations with Armenia, is taking place. It is encouraging to witness a man of religion's sermons that were once considered mere abstract advices to turn into a reality. And, of course, for those who disagree with Gülen, it is a source of irritation and disturbance.

How then can peace be achieved? According to Gülen, peace is achievable through mutual respect, based on the acceptance of differences and dialog in order to get to know one another, thereby engendering warm relations.

> Let us say tolerance and go beyond it, let us think to "friendly share"; let our intention, our determination be in this direction, and let our planning and projects be made according to that intention and determination.[120]

There are, however, limits to what can be achieved.

Let us not forget that we do not have power to soften all the people in the world. We cannot force everyone to say "dialog," we cannot get them to say "tolerance and respect for every position." Not even in Turkey, you are able to carry everyone to the atmosphere of tolerance. Even sometimes, they are complaining to everywhere about you, by claiming, "They are Christianizing the people by saying tolerance and dialog."[121]

He also is asking people to be alert:

> Yes, as Muslims our problem is not only the animosity outside. Inconsistencies incongruousness among us, disloyalty, insincerity, not being able to endure, and infidelity are our greatest problems.[122]

---

[119] *Ibid.*, 159–160.
[120] *Ibid.*, 160.
[121] *Ibid.*
[122] *Ibid.*, 162.

As a man of religion, the solution is "to strengthen the Islamic thought and sensibilities, releasing the masses from the clutch of aimlessness and establish their bonds with higher ideals." And then he adds, "If you will, you can call these redirecting humans toward living with heart and soul."[123]

Gülen attaches significance to the rescuing of the soul and strengthening the faith. But while doing this, he is not overlooking the changes to be realized in the material life, social structure, economy, and law. He is only pointing out that these are not enough and that the process of change will be adversarial and shocking. Spirituality would be helpful at exactly this point in the process. Gülen believes that today the language used among the people and in societies is inappropriate in style and far from egalitarian in content. He worries that from this style will not emerge a desire to live in coexistence, willingly and peacefully.

> For years now in our society we are experiencing a slipping of our thoughts. And a distortion of manner of speech, increasingly spreading is, as it were, imprisoning all the senses and thoughts. Statements are rather indecent, the expressions are transgression as much as possible, the behaviors are lower than the ordinary, the tone is altogether torn up; the emotions and the logics which form the basis for these immoderations are as dark as the intentions of the scorpions. What are you going to listen to, who are going to trust, and what thoughts are you going to rely on? In the arena of these fighting spirits, locked into criticism and destruction, even the most innocent ideas, the most cohesive and consistent plans and projects, are eschewed in the tooth of the truths and put aside and the most sacred values are stepped on under the feet.
>
> I wonder what it could be to cause our people to lose altitude, in terms of humane values. What are the incentives making us wolves to our fellow men? If with this tone and manner of speech—of course if this could be called a manner—they are thinking to arrive at somewhere, they are mistaken; especially by way of this, if higher ideals are aimed at, that is altogether an illusion. But what a pity that for years we have been going through one illusion after another, we have been making unthinkable mistakes. Also, by boasting about what we have accomplished and trying to show off as if we had achieved something on the global scale, we have been making great mistakes. Some foolish talks, such as, "We are going to be an example for the rest of the world, to change the shape of the earth, or at least we are going to put our country in order," have become com-

---

[123] Gülen 2006a, 39.

monplace in this period. But here is this blessed country which is in the claws of the want of peace and tranquility and here is the victimized nation with a high-pitched screaming! In fact, with this deterioration beyond recovery, it would be possible neither to change the map of global thought, neither to transform our society's misfortune to prosperity nor to open up new horizons for our people. In my opinion, out of these circles of palpitation or feeling exasperation from their ideas each one of which could be considered as delirium, nonsense, convulsion, and agitation; if there is anything, disorder can result. But never a renewal can.[124]

Gülen's ideas can be summarized as follows:

1. Instead of starting from our history, from its social and cultural realities, we have interpreted them through an ideological prism; we have ruled the country with a vision of a nation, far from reality. Naturally, this state of affairs has produced tensions, conflicts and fights in the society.

2. In this foggy sphere, we became rude and crude. Our language has become vulgarized and carries a warlike tone. We have forgotten to respect and love one another. Therefore, we have lost the sense of commonality and the common values on which we could unite.

3. We have boasted about ourselves. We have deluded ourselves into thinking that we are successful. But according to all reliable international criteria, the fact is that we are an underdeveloped society with numerous shortcomings in the field of democracy, which are there for everyone to see. Additionally, while we are venturing into the role of ambassadors of peace in our region full of conflicts, we are overlooking the fact that we cannot bring to a positive conclusion our internal conflicts.

4. These weaknesses are nourished by two main sources: a) running away from reality and deceiving ourselves, namely making logical and rational mistakes; and b) ignoring our conscience and higher values such as justice, fairness, and love.

> For the humans who are defective with these weaknesses, it cannot be considered seriously at all, these people will develop the world to be a better, livable place, to contribute in any way to the happiness of human beings or to be beneficial for their nations, and furthermore to direct them to new horizons.

---

[124] Gülen 2010e, 168–169.

It is not possible because, they were never able to feel themselves in their innermost recesses, and could not conceive the reason of their existence, moreover they have forgotten to love, did not care about respect, considered the virtue as a fantasy, and always dreamed about what he is going to earn, how he will earn, whom he will con, and in what ways he will reach the zenith of welfare.[125]

People such as these "come back and seek the remedy in the doctrines like socialism, capitalism, liberalism,"[126] but could never save society from the vicious circle in which it is trapped. It is therefore necessary to identify the real center of the defect and the real causes of the deviations.

Where is the real center of the defect, according to Gülen? In this matter, Gülen is consistent and cohesive within his own system of thought:

> Although as a nation we had taken the initiatives to make so many reforms for couple of centuries now, we could not establish our own ethical and moral system, basing it on our own national culture; we could not develop our own metaphysical conceptions and made it into a system. We could not develop a coherent educational system and a conception of art which could reflect our own internal world life in terms of God, the universe and the realities of humans.
>
> But, in the world the core of ethical systems consist of a healthy and firm faith, an internalized sense of freedom and the conscience of responsibility that almost all of them are related subjects to metaphysics. In a society where the sense of religion is killed, the sense of responsibility is extracted from the hearts and thrown away; it is not possible to talk of metaphysics. In this milieu to talk about ethics and moralities is completely out of question. The societies which could not establish their own system of metaphysical thought, the individuals who could not determine their own internal identities according to such metaphysical considerations, over time would lose their faiths, but it would not be possible to maintain their family trees.[127]

There are two conclusions which can be derived from this analysis. First, if we lose our connection with our own history and cultural richness, we are plunged into meaninglessness. We have to decide who we want to be in terms of identity, philosophy, and faith. Second, our

---

[125] *Ibid.*, 169.

[126] *Ibid.*

[127] *Ibid.*, 171–172.

current understanding of history and society, which started with deny-ing the Ottomans, is based on the conceptualization of an artificial nation state, the characteristics of which are determined only by the administrators, as if it had come down from the heavens. This artificial nation state has no identity, soul, or organic unity, other than what the administrators have attributed to it. For this reason, we must search for a new identity and a spirit that begins with our nation's natural and historical accumulations. Only then can we become ourselves and dis-cover our cultural richness. A philosophy of life with an axis of God–universe–human, in accordance with the realities of our day, would allow us to find our identity and release the peace and tranquility inside us.

After pointing out what we need, it is reasonable to discuss the attri-butes of those who might lead the effort to meet this need. What kind of person could end our identity crisis and produce solutions for the indi-vidual and social discomforts and disturbances?

Gülen refers to them as "special humans"—"by triggering the dyna-mism of faith and action, those who would again start the period of faith, love, logic, and reasoning." He continues,

> They will be locked into an effort to correct the historical misperceptions, to establish a world based on better parts of the old and the new, to unite heavenly and worldly one more time. To the extent of the depths of their sincerity, they will be close to all considerations save the *Hizmet*, they will produce alternative thoughts against the faults, they will side with the right no matter from whom it comes, and they will take their place next to the building and repairing against the destruction and the destructive ... in the face of everyone—even if they do not share every point of view of them,—they are always respectful, elegant, and graceful people. They are a people of polite and courteous manner in language.
>
> They are not after a new sect, a new path, and a new system. But they are in the possession of the sensibility, the richness of thought, emotion, and reason, by making the old acquire new depths, to be able to produce from the old values new products. In our days when everyone seeks asy-lum into the material power and crude force, along with accepting the material within its own framework, they only trust the soul, spirit, spiritu-ality and divine help and support. They believe that their salvation as a nation depends on, rather than material victories and taking over other countries, but by embracing others, entering their hearts, and trying to open up the doors of their chests. They have believed so strongly that the doors of hearts which could not be opened so far with animosities would

be opened by love. For this reason, they would not exchange even an iota of love with the whole world.

As against everyone's display of harshness, hatred, and grudges, they act with tolerance and acceptance to the greatest extent, they would always search for the roads leading to universal peace ..., and they accept this as the purpose of their lives. So, instead of quarreling with this or that person, they would focus and direct, with all their strength, the power of struggle on their own carnal soul, and search for mistakes, weaknesses, inconsistencies, and shortcomings in themselves, and fight against them. They would ward off evil with goodness and kindness.[128]

What has been said so far represents an "ideal human" type. Gülen, beginning with his own yearnings and lifestyle, would like to see the number of this type of human being steadily increase and influence others by their example. This ideal human is so attractive that one can easily understand why participants in the movement try to live up to these expectations of becoming such a perfect man or woman. Our society desperately needs people who are equipped with these qualities and virtues.

There are two obvious goals in the philosophy of Gülen: the moral human being and a society of solidarity. And Gülen has produced a tremendous amount of material, regarding how to access both of them. Clearly, this material has been, at least, partially utilized in that a movement was born in his name, *Gülen Hareketi* (the Gülen Movement), even if that was not his intention or aim

Gülen sets forth the direction of the movement, which is a journey inward. It includes: training and trimming of the carnal soul to defeat blind ambition and appetite, controlling destructive drives, disciplining aggressiveness and temper, and once these are achieved, extending the hand to others. As such, it is a philosophy of ethics.

Many people try to categorize the journey Gülen is encouraging as a journey "toward the outside," namely, one that is politically motivated and a covert search for domination. Is that accurate today or, perhaps, in the future? It is unlikely, as long as Gülen is alive, as his beliefs would not permit that to happen.

---

[128] *Ibid.*, 89–90.

23. How does he view those who find compatibility between Islam and violence, and what is his thesis against the interpretations advocating violence?

Gülen refers to violence as a disease which is observed in every corner of the world, in every country:

> ... Everywhere, murders take place. And sometimes even mass murders occur. There is this much, when this kind of murders are carried out at a larger scale by some states, they are characterized as "operations," not "terror." Only when powerless, weak individuals commit them, these murders are called "terror" or "murder," and those who commit them are called "terrorists," "murderers" or "criminals." Assassinations and murders are sometimes directed toward individuals and they are committed by one or several individuals. Sometimes they are done by an organization, a secret association, or a government in the form of shooting down a plane, sabotage against a train or not leaving a stone over a stone in a city. In reality, in both cases whether the victim of a murder is one person or thousands of people, that event is a terror, a murder; whether those undertaking such a horrible act are one or two individuals, an organization or a government, should not make any difference, they are murderers and terrorists.[129]

> No matter who commits the murder against whom, it is a murder. And every kind of murder is accursed. No matter what the crime is, the individuals cannot apply punishments; the state does. The governments have the courts at their disposal. The punishment is their duty. Therefore, no believer can condone any murder. He can never stand soft against any murder. The person murdered must have said things against Islam; it is possible that at one time, he might have extended his tongue too long, attacked this and that person, might have done some mischief. None of these can legitimize the murder committed. There is a possibility and a probability to quite down and silence the voices of these kinds of individuals just through the system of the law. Therefore, let alone for a Muslim to venture into these kinds of assassinations, it is even unthinkable for him to be in favor of it in his heart. No one has the right to say, "So and so was the enemy of religion, of the faith, of Islam, of the Qur'an, he was killed and it is good that he was, he had deserved it anyway, how nice he was killed." A conduct like this in the face of a murder is not the conduct of a believer.[130]

Gülen believes that it is necessary to protect all the living creatures, not just human beings:

---

[129] Gülen 2005b, 203.
[130] *Ibid.*, 207.

In my lifetime, I have never, deliberately and knowingly, stepped over even an ant. I had ceased seeing and speaking to a friend of mine, who broke the backbone of a snake, for months. I have believed in the right of every living being, that all of them have a place in the eco system. I have stated that we have no right [authority] to bring ourselves to do injury to any living being. There remains the fact that the most honorable of the creatures, the most sacred is the human being. I repeatedly said that those who kill under the above-mentioned pretexts or considerations could not enter Paradise and they could not be considered as real Muslims. This is not my personal opinion. It is the voice, expression and breathes of our general considerations as Muslims; this belief has become part of our nature.

All of the acts of terror, no matter where and whom they come from, it is the gravest blow to the peace, and tranquility. No matter for what cause and to what ends they are directed, no act of terror could be condoned. Terror cannot be the form of the struggle for salvation.[131]

Under various pretexts and distorting religious texts, some murderers attempt to justify their criminal acts. But, as Gülen points out, this is in opposition to the core of Islam, as well as the values that Muslims should internalize. Before everyone else, the Muslims must oppose the violence that others attribute to Islam:

Muslims should stand up and say: There is no terror in real Islam. This is so because; Islam equates the killing of one person with unbelief. You can not kill a human. Even during a war, you cannot touch innocent people. Regarding this matter, no one can give a *fatwa* [religious verdict]. ... Islam has not approved wars; it has tied it primarily to the goal of defense, and then as a last resort. In addition, within the framework of the principle which is elucidated in the Qur'an itself, "... disorder [rooted in rebellion against God and recognizing no laws] is worse than killing" (Al-Baqarah 2:191) in order to prevent disorder, irregularities, oppression, and defeatism it has permitted wars reluctantly. Nevertheless, for the first time in the history of mankind, it has brought certain limitations to it, and in the earliest period, it had set forth the legal rules for it. The works on this theme were written 13 centuries ago by the Muslim scholars, experts of the field. Even at the heated moment of the war, do not take the fear of God from out of your hearts. Do not forget that without the divine guidance and assistance of God, you could accomplish nothing. Always remember that Islam is the religion of peace and love.

The courage, heroism and the *taqwa* of the Messenger of God should always be a model for you. "Do not step over the orchards and fields ready

---

[131] *Ibid.*, 207–208.

to be harvested. Be respectful toward the monks and hermits inhabiting the temples, and those who gave themselves to God; and do not injure them. Do not kill the civilians, do not treat the women improperly, and do not wound the feelings of the defeated. Do not accept gifts from the native inhabitants. Do not try to shelter your soldiers in the houses of the inhabitants. Do not ever miss your five time daily prayers at all. Fear God! And do not forget that at any time, death can find you, far from the battle fields. Therefore, be always ready to face death," and the commandments like those have gone into record in history as the advices of the heads of states, reminding the commanders when they were sent to the war- zones and they have been obeyed to the letter of laws, in minute details. It would be obvious that when required, only a state, within the framework of certain principles, can resort to, as the individuals or organizations on behalf of the Muslims cannot commit a terror, without any rules and directed against the values of humanity which needs to be protected...Terror cannot have any place in Islam.[132]

Why then is there this loud cry for *jihad* and what really does the concept of *jihad* in Islam mean? Many people are disturbed when they hear the word "*jihad*," worried that they might be swept up in a wave of imminent violence. According to Gülen, numerous Islamic concepts, including *jihad*, have been misunderstood, due to the loss of meanings that these concepts had historically, but also due to the misrepresentation of them by some Muslims and by some who want them misunderstood. With respect to *jihad*, he says,

> ...*jihad*, being a noun in Arabic, derived from the root *jahd* or *juhd*, means using all one's strength within the power of humans. Therefore, *jihad* means making an effort resisting every difficulty. *Jihad* as a term means the job of attaining one's essence. The internal struggle [the greater *jihad*] is the effort to attain one's essence by using all one's strength and power and resisting all the obstacles; the external struggle [the lesser *jihad*] is the process of enabling someone else to attain his or her essence.[133]
>
> In the words of the Messenger of God, the greater *jihad* is a struggle against carnal soul [*nafs*], purification of humanity, reaching purity, acquiring the merit in the sight of God, namely the purification of the mind from false assumptions, wrong thoughts and superstitious beliefs, with the acts like worship, repentance [seeking forgiveness], austerity [little food, little drinks, little sleep], the purification of the heart, learning the Qur'an and

---

[132] Sevindi 2002, 28–29.
[133] Ünal 2002, 192.

the wisdom with the purified heart and mind, and acts of acquiring some other forms of knowledge.

The lesser *jihad* is not restricted to battlefronts [by fighting], for this would narrow its horizon considerably. But, the spectrum of *jihad* is... a vast area. Sometimes a word or silence, a frown or a smile, leaving or entering an assembly, in short, everything done for God's sake and regulating love and anger according to His approval are all included in it. In every aspect of life, in every segment of society, in every effort maintained in order to improve [the life and society] are included in the meaning of *jihad*. In a sense, this *jihad* is material.

When both of these kinds of *jihad* are carried out successfully, the desired balance is established. If one is missing, the balance is destroyed. The lesser *jihad* is our active fulfillment of Islam's commands and duties and the performance of what is being expected of him. As for the greater *jihad*, it is the fulfillment of these commandments with sincerity and conscientiousness; it is proclaiming a total war on our ego's destructive and negative emotions and thoughts, it is a rather difficult and complicated task to perform.[134]

24. How does he view suicide bombings? Does he call the suicide bombers "martyrs" in religious terms?

Gülen's answer is short and clear:

No one can be a suicide bomber. No one can rush into crowds with bombs tied to his or her body. Regardless of the religion of these crowds, this is not religiously permissible. Even in the event of war, during which it is difficult to maintain balances, this is not permitted in Islam. Islam states "Do not touch children or people who worship in churches." ... This has not only been said once, but has been repeated over and over throughout history. What the Messenger of God said, what Abu Bakr said, and what Umar said is the same as what, at later dates, Salahuddin Ayyubi, Alparslan, and Kılıçarslan also said. Later on, Fatih Sultan Mehmet [the Conqueror] also said the same.

Thus the city of Constantinople, in which a disorderly hullabaloo reigned, became İstanbul. In this city, the Greeks did not harm the Armenians, nor did the Armenians harm the Greeks. Nor did the Muslims harm any other people. A short time after the conquest of Constantinople, the people of the city hung a huge portrait of the Conqueror on the wall in the place of that of the Patriarchate. It is amazing that such behavior was displayed at that time. Then history relates that the Sultan summoned the

---

[134] Gülen 1998c, 206.

Patriarch and gave him the key to the city. Even today, the Patriarchate remembers him with respect. But today, Islam as with every other subject is not understood properly. Islam has always respected different ideas and this must be understood for it to be appreciated properly.

I regret to say that in the countries Muslims live, some religious leaders and immature Muslims have no other weapon to hand than their fundamentalist interpretation of Islam. They use this to engage people in struggles that serve their own purposes. In fact, Islam is a true faith, and it should be lived truly. On the way to attaining faith one can never use untrue methods. ... In Islam, just as a goal must be legitimate, so must all the means employed to reach that goal. From this perspective, one cannot achieve Heaven by murdering another person. A Muslim cannot say, "I will kill a person and then go to Heaven." God's approval cannot be won by killing people. One of the most important goals for a Muslim is to win the approval of God, another being making the name of Almighty God known to the world.[135]

Gülen is saying that in the matter of those who resort to violence in the name of religion to legitimize their behavior they advance such reasoning:

War used to be fought in the past in the fronts. But now, everywhere is a battlefield. Therefore, they accept this also as a form of war, a kind of *jihad.* Moving from this point, they think that they are opening a door in Paradise. Whereas, the rules of Islam are clear. Individuals cannot declare war. A group or an organization cannot declare war. War is declared by the state. War cannot be declared without a president or an army first saying that there is a war. Otherwise it is an act of terror. In such a case war is entered into by gathering around oneself; forgive my language, a few bandits. Another person would gather some others around himself. If people are allowed to declare war individually then chaos would reign; because of such small differences a front would be formed even between sound-thinking people. ...They are weakening Islam. ...Unless state declares a war, the war could not be attended. Contrary behavior would be opposed to the spirit of Islam... The rules of peace and war in Islam are clearly set out.[136]

To the question, "If these behaviors are in opposition to the spirit of Islam, then why are such kinds of distortions and deviations taking place

---

[135] Akman 2004, 20.
[136] *Ibid.*

in the Islamic world?" The answer to this question has been sought for a long time. Gülen's response is rather striking:

> In my opinion, an "Islamic World" does not really exist. There are places where Muslims live. There are Muslims in some places and fewer in others. Islam has become a way of living: a culture; it is not being followed as a faith. There are Muslims who have restructured Islam in accordance with their thoughts. ... The prerequisite for Islam is that one should "really" believe, and live accordingly; Muslims must assume the responsibilities inherent in Islam. It cannot be said that any society with this concept and philosophy exists within Islamic geography. If we say that they exist, then we are slandering Islam. If we say that Islam does not exist, then we are slandering humans.[137]

According to Gülen, Muslims do not now have the accumulation of knowledge and skills to be able to start an "enlightenment":

> I do not think Muslims will be able to contribute much to balance of the world in the near future. I do not see our administrators having this vision. The Islamic world is pretty ignorant, despite a measured enlightenment that is coming into being nowadays. We can observe this phenomenon during the pilgrimage to Mecca. We can see this displayed during conferences and panels. You can see this in their parliaments through their television channels. There is serious lack of knowledge and know-how. At this moment, they cannot solve the problems of the world. It may be possible in the future.[138]

Moreover, Gülen tells us that there is no place that can be called "the Islamic world" that has a civilization of its own. For this reason, there is group of people in solidarity, who have common characteristics and share common interpretations and values. He states:

> No such world exists. There is an Islam of the individual. There are some Muslims in different places of the world. One by one, all have been separated from one another. I personally do not see anyone who is a perfect Muslim. If Muslims are not able to come into contact with one another and constitute a union, to work together to solve certain problems, to interpret the universe, to understand it well, to consider the universe carefully according to the Qur'an, to interpret the future very well, to generate projects for the future, to determine their place in the future. Since there is no

---

[137] *Ibid.*, 21.
[138] *Ibid.*

"Islamic world," everyone acts individually. It could even be said that there are some Muslims with their own personal truths. It cannot be claimed that there is an Islamic understanding which has been agreed upon, approved by qualified scholars, reliably based upon the Qur'an, and repeatedly tested. It could be said that a Muslim culture is dominant, rather than a sound Islamic understanding.

It has been so since the 5th century AH [12th century CE]. This started with the Abbasid Era and with the appearance of the Seljuks. It increased after the conquest of İstanbul. In the periods that followed, doors to new interpretations were closed. Horizons of thought became narrowed. The breath that was in the soul of Islam became narrowed. More unscrupulous people begun to be seen in the Islamic world; people who were touchy, who could not accept others, who could not open themselves to everyone. The narrowness was experienced in the dervish lodges, as well. It is said that it was even experienced in the schools of theology.[139]

Gülen mentions in this excerpt that even the Sufis (i.e., dervish lodges) have not escaped from the narrowness of thought that has distorted Islam. Specifically, they have deviated from their *raison d'être*, to convey the highest ideals of Islam to new generations and to lay the infrastructure of an Islamic Civilization in accordance with the changing times. As such, does he condone the disestablishment of dervish lodges and retreat centers? Unlike many other men of religion, he does not give an emotional reaction in favor of their continuation, by thinking that even though they lost their functions and became the focus point for resistance to change, they are still religious institutions.

He then discusses the subject of radical religious organizations, especially Al-Qaeda which has displayed many bloody acts in Turkey:

One of the people I hate most in the world is Osama bin Laden because; he has sullied the bright face of Islam. He has produced a contaminated image. Even if we were to try our best to fix the terrible image that has been done, it would take years to repair. We speak about this perversion everywhere on many different platforms. We write books about it. We say, "This is not Islam." Bin Laden replaced Islamic logic with his own feelings and desires. He is a monster, as are the people around him. If there are other people similar to them anywhere, then they too, are nothing more than monsters. We condemn this attitude of Bin Laden. However, the only way to prevent this kind of deeds is that Muslims living in the countries seeming to be Islamic, and I stated earlier that I do not perceive an Islamic

---

[139]   *Ibid.*, 21–22.

world, there are only countries in which Muslims live, will solve their problems. Should they think in a totally different way when electing their leaders? Or should they carry out reforms? For the growth of a well-developed younger generation, Muslims must work to solve their problems. Not only their problems in the issue of terror, an instrument that is certainly not approved of by God, but also those concerning drugs and the use of cigarettes, two more prohibitions made by God. Dissention, civil turmoil, never-ending poverty, the disgrace of being governed by others, and being insulted after having put up with government by foreign powers are all problems that could be added to the list. All of these are anathemas to God, and all of these have been placed primarily on our nation. Overcoming these, in my opinion, depends on being a just human being and a human being who is devoted to God.[140]

Gülen states that the road leading to terrorism is a complex one. He believes that salvation starts with the individual; and therefore, we should not forget the importance of being a good person. And the way to becoming a good person lies in the essence of religion and its undistorted values. He defines this as "servanthood to God."

But the question arises that because "being a good servant to God" is subjected to so many interpretations, how can we get out of this chaos?

It is our fault, the fault of the nation, fault of education. It is inconceivable for a true Muslim, for a Muslim who understands Islam inside out, to be a terrorist. It would be difficult to remain a Muslim for a person who is involved with terror. In order to reach the goal, Islam does not permit murders. But of course, what efforts did we make to raise these people as perfect humans? With what kind of elements did we bind them? What kind of responsibility did we take in their upbringing so that now we should expect them not to engage in terror? That is not the only issue. Both Turkey and other countries that have a large Muslim population suffer from drug abuse, gambling, and corruption. There is almost no one left in Turkey whose name has not been involved in some type of scandal. There are some implicated individuals that were supposed to be reached that have been reached. Yet there are many possible suspects that still cannot be reached. You cannot bring them for questioning. You cannot call the people in charge to account. They are protected, sheltered and thus they have been left alone.

---

[140] *Ibid.*, 25.

All these people are the people who grew up among us. All of them are our children. Why have some of them become bad guys? Why were some raised as bullies? Why have some of them rebelled against human values? Why do they come to their own country and blow themselves up as suicide bombers? All these people were raised among us. Therefore, there must have been something wrong with their education. That is, the system must have some deficiencies, some weak points that need to be examined. These weak points need to be removed. In short, the raising of human beings was not given priority. In the meantime, some generations have been lost, destroyed, and wasted. Dissatisfied youth has lost its spirituality. Some people take advantage of such people, giving them a couple of dollars, or turning them into robots. They have drugged them....They have been used as murderers on the pretext of some crazy ideals or goals and they have been made to kill people. Some evil-minded people have wanted to achieve certain goals by abusing these young people.[141]

Gülen diagnoses the problem in Turkey and in other Muslim societies—self interest, political competition, and authoritarian rules, which cannot be questioned, disorient people and divide societies, causing different sectors to fight against one another. He believes that these deviations are rooted, to a great extent, in detachment from morality and the relinquishment of responsibility. For example, if a fanatic activist gets his motivation from a man of religion he trusts, he will not feel guilty or responsible for his murders. No matter how wrong and sinful his action, he does it in the name of a high ideal or for the sake of Paradise promised to him; he is without a conscience and heartless.

Gülen uses as an example the suicide bombings of 2003 carried out by Al-Qaeda in İstanbul:

> The same thing could be said about İstanbul affair. Those who carry out the terroristic activities are not people who are sane, believing, coming out of the mosques and did that infamous thing. Their knowledge of religion is weak. He must have a leader, a teacher who said that person should be killed. Not few people were killed in Turkey. This group caused the death of that person and that group caused another killed. On 12 March 1971 people were holding bloody knives. The army came in and interfered. Again on 12 September 1980 people were killing each other. All of them were terrorists. That side was a terrorist and this side was a terrorist. But they were naming them. One says, I am doing this for Islam. The other says, I am doing it for my land and people. Yet another says, I am fighting against

---

[141] *Ibid.*, 26–27.

capitalism, against exploitation. All of them were just empty words. The Qur'an talks about such "labels" and calls them exactly "empty words." They were things of no value. But people just kept on killing. Everyone was killing in the name of an "ideal." Somebody at a higher echelon was saying: Let him be taken away, and then someone's body was being destroyed. So and so and so and so also should be taken away he was saying. All of these were terror. Not only the Muslim was doing it but everybody else was. Repeated by everyone, it became something ordinary and normal. They made everyone accustomed to it. They brought the society to the state of affairs we altogether know.[142]

Gülen points to a significant truth. Violence is atomizing the societies that it falls upon; it is destroying the sense of solidarity and trust. Once violence is made into a vehicle of influence, political calculations, and a source of power and becomes ordinary in a society, the legal system evaporates and becomes nonexistent. Violence tears apart the fabric of society and permeates every field of life and the collective consciousness.

Every chaos ends with a renewal. Societies in chaos start looking for a "savior." Some of them become victims of false saviors. These "saviors" offer them collective or totalitarian methods. They ask them to internalize, from morning until evening, from birth until death, "similar" and "one type" behavioral codes, without opposing them. They try to completely dominate their minds and hearts. These experiences result in failures and, most of the time, with disastrous consequences. Fascism and communism are this kind of totalitarian conceptions and understandings. Organizations such as Al-Qaeda try to do the same in the name of religion. They try to establish an order in the name of God, by placing themselves between the individual and God. The human (Muslim) here is not founder or organizer but organized, and even a victim—he is an insignificant accessory whose objection is met with an execution. Gülen offers a different road: Let us look at Islamic societies of the past when there was peace, prosperity, and social solidarity. However the religion was interpreted, what kind of higher ideals and values were prevalent and reflected in the daily life? Let us find out. Let us again accept and internalize them; let us reinterpret them under the current circumstances and make them part of our living.

---

[142] *Ibid.*, 27–28.

The cure for the problem is teaching the truth. It must be explained and exposed that a Muslim cannot become a terrorist. Why should it be explained? According to the dictum, "Whoever does an atom's weight of good will see it, and whoever does an atom's weight of evil will see it" (Az-Zalzalah 99:7–8), it should be understood and this should always be stressed that killing a person is as if killing the whole humanity is a principle of the Qur'an. People should be reminded of the words of Ibn Abbas: "A murderer will stay in Hell for eternity." If the foundational spirit of religion is this one, then it should be imparted through education. But they do not.[143]

As readily seen, Gülen believes that education, especially a sound religious education, leads people to the straight path. If so, why are Muslim societies incapable of doing this? Does this stem from the fact that self-criticism in Islam did not develop sufficiently? The answer is important because an individual or a society who does not engage in self-criticism and look at his thoughts or behaviors critically, automatically blames the "other." This, in turn, impedes his development and prevents him from understanding others and establishing meaningful relationship with them.

Gülen is not in favor of accepting in the absolute sense, the maxim, "There is no self-criticism in Islam." He explains:

> There is self-criticism in Islam. Anything which is not bound by a revelation is subject to criticism. The arguments, debates, and discussions of Islamic matters among the legal scholars and theologians are so widespread that they fill volumes. In Muslim communities everyone had criticized everyone else. If today no self-criticism is practiced in the Islamic world the cause should not be sought in Islam but in the attitude of those Muslims who do not read and understand Islam, or rather misunderstand it.[144]

25. How does Gülen explain the differences between those who interpret Islamic teachings to justify violence and those who use the same sources but derive peace, brotherhood, and tolerance from them? How does he transcend this dilemma?

This question has two parts. First, it is directed to the religious interpretations of fanatics such as Osama bin Laden, who formed and continue to form their teachings and acts with a feeling of hate, jealousy and destruc-

---

[143] *Ibid.*, 28.
[144] *Ibid.*, 29.

tion of the "other" (and this "other" can be a Muslim) and Gülen's interpretation, which is based on a philosophy of life aiming at peace, tolerance, mutual understanding and living together. Second, it seeks to find the answers to these questions: Whether in the soul of Islam does it condone violence and hatred, which from time to time, comes to the fore with proper interpretations? On the contrary, is an interpretation condoning violence and hatred a total deviation from the spirit of Islam? The answers to these questions and Muslims' criticism of their own faith are significant in that they offer an ontological proposition regarding humanity.

Gülen initially responds that fanatics who resort to violence are a minority in Islamic societies:

> It is possible to consider the emergence of such three or five bandits in the Islamic world of 1 or 1.5 billion as the secretion of the Islamic body ... Besides; terror makes numerous innocents as victims. The terror activities filling the last 50 years of the human history, even if at the beginning, seemingly harming the subjects of terror [victims], in the final analysis, have always been harmful to the terrorists themselves. Terror cannot be used at all, especially for an Islamic cause. A terrorist cannot be a Muslim; a Muslim cannot be a terrorist. A Muslim could only be a symbol of peace, prosperity, and reconciliation. Even if there are 9 criminals and 1 innocent in a ship, Islam does not allow the murder of those 9, for the sake of one single innocent. In Islam, a right is a right. There can be no greater or lesser of it. The right of an innocent individual cannot be sacrificed even for the sake of the entire society.[145]

Then he discusses suicide bombers:

> The people on the four corners of the world, for instance, the Palestinians ... though they go through much painful days, suicide bombings would not be proper. To venture into attacks in which the target and who would be killed are not known; just in order to kill tying the bombs around the waist, and pulling the trigger among the people and innocent children, unaware of what is happening, cannot be an Islamic act. Islam has set forth some rules and regulations, even for the heated moment of a war, regarding how to be killed, whom to kill, and how to struggle against the enemy. There is no such a thing as killing women, children, or the people who do not participate personally in the war. Although I understand the hopelessness of the Palestinians, the fault of being drawn into such a

---

[145] Sevindi 2002, 29.

struggle, and in the face of the conduct by some people, the condemnation of Islam and all Muslims I feel really sad.[146]

This assessment emphasizes that the use violence and suicide bombings as a vehicle of revenge, defense, or a political manifesto is not compatible with the religion of Islam. He stresses the peaceful aspects of Islam; its spiritual side, the human aspect, which opposes a radical stance loaded with violence.

> The fanatics like Osama bin Laden might say that they base their views on the Qur'an and the *Sunnah*. If the practices of God's Messenger and those of the Rightly Guided Caliphs are to be taken as a foundation, there you cannot talk of Bin Laden; what he does and the acts of God's Messenger cannot be considered along the same line at all.
>
> If we take the acts of the Prophet as a base, it would become obvious that Bin Laden is unable to look at the issue from a holistic perspective. He is not looking at the understandings, the viewpoints of the Book, the *Sunnah* and *Salaf-i Salihin* [the earlier generation properly practicing religion in the period of the Age of Happiness] with a birds' eye, he is taking certain parts only.
>
> There is an oft cited example: Without taking into consideration the context in which it occurs, people take the part from the verse, "Kill them wherever you may come upon them," (At-Taubah 9:5) and reach similar faulty conclusions.
>
> The meaning of this is that: "If there are people who accepted you, entering into your company, and later appropriating antagonistic behaviors, they betrayed the nation, then punish them." Against this kind of rebellion every nation would defend and protect itself, and would punish the perpetrators. Many events of this sort occurred in the Ottoman period as well as during the republican era.
>
> Continuing the subject, later comes back, prays, and fasts and if the old lines are, as it were extracted with tweezers, then considerations of Bin Laden and his likes take place.
>
> In summary, there is a problem of methodology. The matter is approached from one perspective only. When it is said, "There they are the unbelievers, you have take a stand against them or against those who rule the world by oppression," the matter changes form, loses its meaning, it becomes politicized. If we look at the acts of our Prophet, the acts of those Rightly Guided Caliphs ruling after him, the practices of the *Salaf-i Salihin*, as a recent example the practices of the Ottoman rulers, we will quickly find out they never acted in that way at all, on the contrary, they

---

[146] Gülen 2010a, 179.

opened their hearts to the Christians, the Jews. Besides, they left their doors wide open to those under oppression in other countries, those who were subjected to massacres, they protected them. While others were killing them, these rulers spread their wings of compassion. Since the general consideration was to open arms to humans with love and compassion, they would not have been able to act otherwise, anyway.

With our rude and harsh conducts, which are not based on the Qur'an and the *Sunnah*, we are doing harm to the religion. Whether today Bin Laden is alive or not is not known. I wish he would be dead, so that the Muslims could release themselves from such a distorted conception.[147]

Gülen knows that fanaticism neither started with Bin Laden, nor will it end now that he is dead. The solution, he believes, is in the root causes of fanaticism; he provides the example of those who commit "murders in the name of religion," declaring that they are doing so in an effort to release the Muslim nation from foreign occupation; they massacre thousands of their countrymen and fellow Muslims without any mercy:

Instead of fighting when necessary, you would kill there the innocent people in order to kick out the Americans, that cannot be. If the Muslims there are doing it, they must have been committing a serious murder. It is because of the dictum; "No soul, as bearer of burden, is made to bear the burden of another" (An-Najm 53:38) is one of the important principles of the Qur'an. Even if the whole members of a family commit a murder, save one, that innocent person cannot be touched, namely his blood, his honor, property are under protection, they cannot be sacrificed. It is not possible for them to reach an aim through this way. I do not see that it would be possible for one who believes in God, to perform these acts. He must be seeing red that he could do all these things.[148]

In Gülen's view, it is impossible to square Islam with terrorism. If violence cannot be justified with defense, what alternative road does Islam adopt? Gülen answers this critical question as follows:

On the other hand, there are many conflicting interests in the Islamic regions, as well as many competing and clashing groups. Problems such as antidemocratic practices and human rights violations have resulted in the foundation of various disaffected and disenfranchised groups. Being ignorant and inexperienced, many of these groups can easily be manipulated and used by some. Some, manipulating these groups, have worked to

---

[147]   Gündem 2005, 111–113.

[148]   *Ibid.*, 109.

reach their goals step by step. Moreover, there are multi-national covert or open organizations that have based all of their efforts on destruction and the creation of fear in society. To extend the borders of their activities, they agitate the unhappy segments of society by stirring up trouble and fomenting violence.[149]

So, in this case the first thing to be done is to expose this game and dissuade those local groups and organizations for their false causes.

He continues,

The role of the double standard in this terror game is also rather great. Although the big players of the world politics say, when it is convenient, "democracy, human rights, living in freedom," if their interests warrant, they easily oppose the values they have been defending all along, and when necessary resort to brute force. When it is a matter of bleeding wounds, their disinterest is a clear proof of that, like the issues of Kashmir and Palestine.[150]

It is seen from these passages that Gülen favors exposing this double standard and the two-faced ethics, as well as exposing their owners in the world public opinion.

Gülen also offers to explain, in every occasion, how wrong it is to produce a global paranoia out of Islamophobia, and how harmful it is to set nations against nations: "It is both ironic and grave to observe that some of the rulers in the Islamic world believe in this enormous lie."[151]

Gülen continues to explain his refusal to accept the use violence in his teachings and his acceptance of the philosophy of life around the axis of love, tolerance, and coexistence in peace:

It would be unthinkable for the religion sent by God, whether its name is Islam, Christianity, or Judaism, let alone ordering terror, to permit it to take place. Before everything else, in the eyes of God, life is very important. Because of that, through the religion he revealed, God considered it one of the five basic values to be protected. So much that since it considers every individual human as a species, compared to other creatures, Islam has accepted killing a sole human being as equal to killing the entire humanity; and saving the life of one human being as equal to saving the lives of all humanity.

---

[149] Sarıtoprak and Ünal 2005, 467.
[150] Akademi Araştırma Heyeti 2006, 182.
[151] *Ibid.*, 183.

In addition, in evaluating the issue of right, saying there would not be greater or lesser rights, it considered the right of the individual and the right of the society was equal, it did not sacrifice one for the other. Besides, Islam reminds us that in the movement and acts of individual Muslims, the goal has to be legitimate, that those who march on to the legitimate goals through illegitimate means would be punished with the opposite of their intention or aims. From this perspective we can say that terror can never be a vehicle in order to accomplish any of the Islam's aims.[152]

A Muslim cannot be a terrorist because Islam reserves the heaviest punishment in this world for those who have a design against the human life and the security of humans; and in the hereafter it is reserved, along with denying God and associating something else with Him, again for those murdering a human being, and has made the threat that those who deliberately aim at someone else's life would be in the Hellfire eternally. While there is such a punishment set for an act, a person, remaining as Muslim, can never commit it at all. Therefore, it is not possible according to the religious judgment for a terrorist to be real Muslim, and a real Muslim to be a terrorist.[153]

After making this assessment, he says that it is impossible to escape the reality which is happening before the eyes of everyone and must be confronted:

> Either in the Islamic world or in other places if there are terroristic acts and if they continue, first of all a healthy assessment and diagnosis of it has to be made, then according to this diagnosis a way has to be found to cure it.[154]

What could be the cure? As a man of religion, he has been reiterating constantly to those who consider or call themselves Muslims to explain, as a first priority, the basis or the principles of religion and its authentic rulings. But this undertaking is far beyond the capacity of a single person or even a single country. In the Islamic world, a common understanding must be reached using the main sources and then it must be spread. But even this is not enough. Administrations that undermine justice, that are far from honesty and productivity, should be transformed to meet the needs of their population and to respect their citizens' rights. If this is not achieved, opinion leaders and interpreters such as Gülen, who try to

---

[152] Interview with Fethullah Gülen, *Kenya Daily Nation*, 30 July 2004.
[153] Sevindi 2002, 29.
[154] *Ibid.*

make clear that Islam is peaceful and respectful of differences and try to engender a sense of solidarity, could lose to fanatical men of religion, who produce a language, loaded with anger and violence, and a logic that, in the end, would drag to extremes those who are full of anger and hopelessness. This is not a religion, but politics. Politics divide people, make them clash, and steer them away from faith.

Gülen believes that the high ideals of religion can contribute to the shaping of human relations on ethical and peaceful foundations, maintaining the social stability:

God has set forth the religious injunctions for the individual and social happiness of human beings. Believing in One God and worship to Him requires all believers to have a sincere relationship with all animate or inanimate objects. To the extent of the depth of the individual's faith in and submission to God, his interest in other creatures and responsibility he feels would be sincere.

The religion which is a contract between humans and God and the stipulations of which are always in favor of humans, is based on the principle of submission to the divine system to which everything other than humans bow. Namely, the entire universe, our planet included, obey the laws God had fixed, and in the end a unity, an order, and harmony takes place. Unlike other creatures which obey in this fashion, we, the human beings have something called "will." This will and the responsibility as a necessary corollary of it are given to us in order to bring our existence into harmony with all beings and thus to mature and progress.

God does not like the mischief and oppression at all. He desires us to live in peace and according to the standard of justice. Therefore what is expected of the worshipping believers in Him is to try to work towards realizing peace, brotherhood, and justice in the world. Religion brought primarily the following basic disciplines:

The power is in the right; on the contrary the right is not subject to power.

Justice and the rule of law are the essential principles.

The basic rights like the freedom of thought and belief, life, private property, reproduction through marriage, the mental and physical health can never be violated and infringed.

The privacy of individual life and inviolability are under protection.

No one can be accused of anything unless there is good evidence and cannot be punished for the crimes of others.

The individuals are in a state of cooperation in order to live together.

Religion declares, *"He who kills a soul unless it be (in legal punishment) for murder or for causing disorder and corruption on the earth will be as if he had killed all humankind; and he who saves a life will be as if he had saved the lives of all humankind,"* (Al-Ma'idah 5:32), for the reason that every individual represents the entire humanity and the individual rights are revered as much as the rights of all humans. Besides, killing one human being opens up the door to the idea that all people can be killed.

In the eyes of religion, the basis of social life is not power, but the right.[155]

In the words of Gülen, it is possible to envision a broader framework of a constitution that so far have never able to grasp: a civic constitution. It is a constitution in which the responsibilities are in balance with freedoms; the minorities are not oppressed by the majority; the administration obeys the dictates of the law themselves; (and social justice is realized It is indeed exiting to hear from a man of religion that religion can contribute, not as it is feared by to obscurantists and fanatics, but to ethical purification and social justice, along with the establishment of a system in which the freedoms are protected.

Who can object to the conception of a religion which does not in quarrel with the world and a modern lifestyle? Exactly for this reason, Gülen's interpretation of religion is rather significant. But, there is something that saddens him: those who apply violence in the name of Islam:

> They have become such a burden on the shoulders of everyone that, with the effort made in order to escape from them, it would have been possible by explaining the beauty of Islam, to enter the hearts of many people. But now, the Muslims everywhere, in the process of making exposition of Islam, have to start with trying to convince their audience that they are not terrorists, they do not behave in radical ways or they are not living bombs. More often than not, the turn does not come to explaining the beautiful aspects of our religion.[156]

26. Are the sources of inequality in life derived from social customs and traditions, and does Islam condone and strengthen this inequality?

This question was asked in order to obtain and understand Gülen's viewpoint regarding the widespread conviction in our society, as well as in the world, that Islam recognizes a lower status to women compared to men.

---

[155] Interview with Fethullah Gülen, *Kenya Daily Nation*, 30 July 2004.
[156] Doğu Ergil's interview with Gülen.

Here is a vision of a society which is based on peace, tolerance, solidarity and "understanding the other." Can it then also espouse gender inequality? If it does, is this contradictory attitude implicit in the foundational principles of the religion or does it stem from life practices, which reflect the culture and history of the Arabian Peninsula?

Equipped with the lofty inner drives, the woman is a monument of compassion; and her compassion is the end product of her creation and nature. If this pleasant nature is not defiled by faulty interferences, she always thinks compassion, says compassion, sits and stands up with compassion; for whole lifetime, she gazes those around her with compassion and makes everyone drink compassion, glass after glass. At the same moment she embraces everyone with compassion, and presents compassion to drink, as a corollary of her decency and refinement, she always chuckles with pain and suffering, and gulps in suppressing her emotions. When she sees the worry and sorrow in their mood, she fades like yellow leaves and she moans and groans with melancholy, grief, and sadness...

In terms of her spiritual horizon, the woman who found her counterpart and quenched her thirst through her children is not different from the Heavenly Maidens and her nest is not different from Paradise. We can surmise that the children raised under the shade of such a person of Paradise, always sipping compassion, would not be different from the spiritual beings. In this kind of a nest, even if the bodies appear separately, the soul which dominates everything and gives life to everybody is only one. This soul which always gushes out of the woman and envelops the nest, metaphorically speaking, like a magic, a spirit, makes itself felt always on everybody and, in a sense, it directs them toward somewhere. A blessed woman who did not darken horizon of her heart, whose road ahead is clear is just like a North Star in the family system. She stays still, she revolves around herself; the other members of the system always shape their existence around her and would march on to their goals, loyal to her. Yes, everyone's relations with the nest are temporary, limited, and relative. The woman on the other hand, whether she has a chore, a work to do or not, constantly stands upright in the middle of her kitchen where the mixture of mercy, compassion and love have been boiling and have been offering ... so much to our senses!

In our opinion, especially with the dimension of motherhood, the woman is a ball of emotions and thoughts, effervescent in her heart, as deep as the heavens and as many as the number of stars... Especially ... a fortunate, lucky woman has such a bright position as beyond imagination at a magical point, where we might call the mixture and unification of the material and the spiritual, concrete body and the souls meet, a point beyond which were any status or position we could assign to her, would look like dim candles, compared to her real value, shining like the sun.

In our world of ideas and the atlas of values, the woman is the most important color of the event of creation, the most blessed and magical pillar in the realm of humanity, a faultless, perfect projection of Paradise, in our homes the firmest security of our existence and continuity. Before she was created, Prophet Adam was alone, eco-system was soulless, the conceived human beings were subject to ending, the nest was a small cottage, not different from a cave in a tree and the humans were the inmates of their own cage. With her, a second pillar was formed and the pillars were bound together. The existence shouted with a different voice, and became joyful with a different appearance, the creation entered into the stage of completion, and the lonely human was transformed into species.[157]

We can summarize his thoughts as follows:

1. The woman is valuable. Her value is the phenomenon of her creation in complementing the man which transformed humanity into species. The formation of humanity was realized through Prophet Adam, but the birth of humanity was possible through the creation of woman.

2. Woman is compassionate, giving, and if she finds her place in marriage, there would be no limit to the love, interest, and positive contributions she can make to her children, her husband, and the other members of the family. Because of her, the firm families can be established and children are raised in an atmosphere of love and compassion. These kinds of people become a vehicle of goodness for others because they look at the world with love and compassion. In summary, as a good and happy spouse and a mother, the woman is important for the health and peace of the society. With this role, the woman presents a great service which is not always recognized and rewarded.

Gülen further states:

> The woman is not inferior to the man. If we are to think of the man and the woman like nitrogen and oxygen, both of them with their attributes and their special places are rather important and they are in need of each other to the same extent. To indulge in a comparing of man and woman in terms of superiority would be silly act and absurd. In terms of their mission in this world and their creation they are not different from each other and they are like parts of the same whole or different faces of the same coin.[158]

---

[157] Gülen 2000.
[158] *Ibid.*

After these statements, he reminds us that in many parts of the world the perception of a woman is negative, far from his own assessments; women are often characterized in a state, close to inequality and even exclusion. When an evaluation is made of several centuries, what one sees is inequality and even discrimination. For instance, Nietzsche was a representative of an age when he says: "When you are about to speak with a woman, do not forget to prepare your whip."

> Tolstoy, in his diary book regarding marriage, had jotted down, "I am happy that I am married, the happiness of the nest is enlightening my soul like the sun." These were proper and truthful words. But after a while he wrote a novel in which the hero of the novel was made to say: "Lo! Beware, do not marry, your spouse would prevent you from displaying a good work. She would suppress your interests and make you into a common, ordinary being. Since she is a lowly being, she would desire to make the spirit of her husband also lowly." Thus he had made an exposition of what he had thought of women clearly.[159]
>
> In the Arabian Peninsula where Islam first emerged, during the Period of Ignorance the state of the affairs was the same. It was a complete tragedy as far as the birth of women, growing up and their upbringings, and later their marriages, were concerned. On one hand the girls were considered as a burden on the family, on the other, even their existence was considered as a matter of dishonor and in some regions they were buried alive.[160]

Gülen, pointing out that this Dark Age had come to an end with the coming of Islam, notes that women's rights have been secured by decisive legal injunctions:

> The Qur'an stresses this fact unequivocally by the declaration, "*Women have rights similar to those against them (that men have)*" (Al-Baqarah 2:228) and elevates the woman to equal position intended in the plan of creation. In his farewell speech, it was stated: "I advise you to respect the rights of women and to fear God in this matter; the women are the trust of God to you." In that inauspicious period, when women were bought and sold like merchandise in the entire world, elevating them to a respectable position, is an event with an historical proportion in the world of women. The position and the rights of woman are emphasized in the Qur'an so much so that it would not be an exaggeration to say that she was emancipated from the slavery.[161]

---

[159] *Ibid.*

[160] *Ibid.*

[161] *Ibid.*

Yes, not for anything else, God created woman as a partner and a spouse for man. Adam could not be without Eve; and Eve could not be without Adam. This first couple was given the task of, in the name of God, as well as in the name of creatures, being a mirror and a speaker on his behalf. They were like two bodies and one soul, and they represented two different faces of the same truth. Over time rudeness in understanding and in conduct broke this unity. By the corruption of it, both the family as well as the social life was corrupted.[162]

According to Gülen, the right and the status of a woman do not depend on the man's decision (or "kindness and favor") and she is not at his disposal. Her right and equality come from birth. By uniting with man and establishing the family of "humanity," there can be no relationship of superior and inferior between man and woman.

Nevertheless, because of the woman's delicacy which originates from creation, the Prophet Muhammad had given the task of her protection to man. Man's transforming this task into oppression and domination is not something related to religion, but it is a historical and de facto matter.

He establishes the bridge between women's rights and the human rights as follows:

The human is the sole creature on the face of the earth, deserving the title *halifatullah* [the vice-regent of God on Earth]. In Islamic religion humans are made into a sultan, vice-regent of God. He was given the right to interfere with things. He was equipped with the rights like the right to defend himself, the right to protect his progeny, the freedom to live and work the freedom of enterprise.[163]

As for the rights of women, in Islam the man and the woman makes up a perfectly running system like teeth of a wheel. Therefore we should not understand different creation of the woman as her shortcoming. First of all, it should be accepted that these things were created in nature, to a certain extent, in different ways. In terms of the tasks that they can perform, and at the same time some responsibilities they are under, and even in terms of some other things they are subjected to, there are some differences. As a corollary or as a consequence of their nature, they will have their share in the division of labor, and the other side will have their own share.[164]

---

[162] *Ibid.*

[163] Gülen 2009b, 94.

[164] The interview given to the NMO (Dutch Muslims Broadcast), 19 October 1995.

Recognizing the possibility of being misinterpreted on the point that the natural differences he mentions could be used as a barrier for women's participation in social life and the work force, Gülen adds:

> Woman can work in normal regular jobs. Nothing can be demonstrated from Islam which prevents women from working. But in the issue of giving her a load of work which is beyond her capacity, the Messenger of God had opposed it. For instance, at one place he says: It would be unfair to give her weapons and send her to the front ... to let her undertake heavy work.[165]

Gülen's interpretation is inspired by the Prophet's interpretation: Both the man and the woman should not be forced to work in a field that is not consonant with their traits, which he refers to as "creation." For example, instead of caring for the child in pre-education, it is more appropriate for a man to work outside and in heavy work, where conditions are difficult.

The woman, on the other hand, in the home setting and where compassion is required, would be more productive and beneficial to nurture and guide her children. But, in the words of Gülen, "The woman would also help her husband to shed the stress he was afflicted outside the home, she would have mutual exchange of ideas with him."[166] Thus, although the woman has the right to work both in- and outside of the home, her load should not exceed her capacity. In other words, the woman should not be over exhausted, as a firm family structure can only be realized through the efforts of a woman who is not worn down and happy. He believes that healthy societies are the products of this sort of family.

This view might be found too traditional in some circles but Gülen believes that when a division of labor is established appropriate to the nature of the genders, it is beneficial for the family, as well as for the society.

He moves from here to several themes that have been offered as examples of discrimination in Islam against women. First is the issue that two women are required as witnesses in the place of one man in the courts. Gülen states:

> Some women are employed as officials of the state, some work in the fields. But most of women are at home and have taking to their shoulders the fam-

---

[165] *Ibid.*
[166] *Ibid.*

ily responsibility. This state of affairs was more realistic in the ancient times when the views and principles concerning the social roles of women were constituted.

For this reason, the women outside home might not be following closely what is happening outside home. Then if we say that the testimony of a woman who is not involved with legal matters, as much as a man does, is valid just like that of a man, I wonder if we would not have based legal rulings on the minority view. In terms of philosophy of law, I wonder if this would be acceptable.

God had equipped the women with different things. ... To be equipped with compassion ... maybe negative in the process of a trial. In testimony, the compassion might take priority... the woman might not be objective there. ... But what should be important there is fairness. Therefore, the compassion of women was assessed as a weakness there. For that reason, the Qur'an in that verse approached the matter from that perspective.[167]

Gülen continues:

Constantly taking the women from their homes ... bringing them constantly to the courthouses ... it is worth to dwell on this matter in my opinion, even in the name of women, and on behalf of feminism.[168]

Gülen believes that the relationship between men and women should be assessed within the framework of the institution of family. He again refers to the Qur'an and *hadiths* of the Prophet: "The Qur'an calls people to family life and points out many reasons and benefits of marriage." After this, he provides the following examples:

If you fear that you will not be able to observe their rights with exact fairness when you marry the orphan girls (in your custody), you can marry, from among other women (who are permitted to you in marriage and) who seem good to you, two, or three, or four. However, if you fear that (in your marital obligations) you will not be able to observe justice among them, then content yourselves with only one, or the captives that your right hands possess. Doing so, it is more likely that you will not act rebelliously. (An-Nisa 4:3);

According to customary good and religiously approvable practice, women have rights similar to those against them (that men have), but men (in respect of their heavier duty and responsibility) have a degree above them (which they must not abuse). And God is All-Glorious with irresistible might, All-Wise. (Al-Baqarah 2:228);

---

[167] *Ibid.*

[168] *Ibid.*

Mothers (whether married or divorced) are to suckle their children for two complete years if the fathers wish that the period be completed. It is incumbent upon him who fathered the child to provide the mothers (during this period) with sustenance and clothing according to customary good and religiously approvable practice. (Al-Baqarah 2:233);

Give to the women (whom you marry) their bridal-due (mahr) willingly and for good (i.e. without expecting a return); however, if of their own accord, they remit any part of it to you, then you are welcome to enjoy it gladly. (An-Nisa 4:4);

But if you still decide to dispense with a wife and marry another, and you have given the former (even so much as amounts to) a treasure, do not take back anything thereof. Would you take it back by slandering (for the purpose of contriving the kind of divorce that allows you to take it back), and so committing a flagrant sin? (An-Nisa 4:20);

O (most illustrious) Prophet! When you (Muslims) intend to divorce women, divorce them considering their waiting-period (as appointed in Law), and reckon the period (with due care), keeping from disobedience to God, your Lord, in reverence for Him and piety. (While the divorce is taking effect, during their waiting-period) do not drive them out from their houses (where they have lived with their husbands), nor shall they themselves leave, except in case they have committed an open indecency. (At-Talaq 65:1);

House them (the divorced women during their waiting-period in a part of the house) where you dwell and provide for them, according to your means; and do not harass them so as to straiten conditions for them (thus forcing them to leave). If they are pregnant, maintain them until they deliver their burden; and if (after the delivery and the waiting-period has ended,) they suckle (the baby) for you, give them their due payment. (At-Talaq: 65:6)

As a man of religion, Gülen expresses that in every injunction found in the Qur'an there is wisdom. It is evident that some of the examples that he mentions are taken from the Arab society and the social relationships in those times. Naturally, the question arises whether they are still valid for today's lifestyles and social relations. Gülen is aware of this issue as well and advises to take cognizance of the spirit of these precepts:

The Qur'an, as in many cases in this matter, in addition to reminding spouses about their duties towards one another, emphasizes the main principles of human morality, and invites individuals to be respectful to God and virtuous towards each other. Such an atmosphere of respect is necessary for the continuation of humane and legal relations. That is because institutions such as marriage with a unique aspect of privacy can hardly be controlled by outsiders. As a matter of fact, it is a considerable issue to refer to a judge or a referee in the case of disagreement between spouses. Yet, the fundamental issue is to prevent the problems from the very beginning, or to solve them at the very time of occurrence.[169]

In short, Gülen aims at protecting and preserving the family institution and believes that it is the foundation of healthy social relationships and a social structure. He states that Islam's principles and values are not behind the West, but even ahead of it on many issues:

> Until recently, it was not possible in the West to talk of women's rights. In our day, on the other hand, going into various extremities and deviations, as it were a reaction to the previous periods has been displayed. As a matter of fact, all of these remain in theoretical plane. How many female presidents are there in the whole world? In how many places are female officers are serving at the higher echelon of the armies? I wonder if women whose proportion is equal to that of men are represented in the parliaments proportionate to their numbers. How many women are there among the spiritual leaders of the world? We can add to that the justice departments, security organizations, secret services.
>
> Even today, there are ardent supporters in the West, of the position that it is supposed to be that way. We have never encountered in our realm such a thing. The French sociologist Gaston Bouthoul [1896–1980] talks about how women, because of their psychological aspects and with their particular logic and reasoning, could not undertake some heavy tasks and therefore in the days ahead the matters like the art of war will still be left to men.
>
> According to him, it would be wrong to consider women to be equal to men in political matters, as well. In summary, he makes some advices considering the physical structure of women that the numbers of those who share his views are not inconsiderable.
>
> Although it would not be an appropriate method to express the issues Islam has brought about by contrasting them to others, no doubt it would be more enlightening to explain some issues by comparisons.
>
> In the ancient Indian religions, the woman is a dirty, lowly creature with a weak character. In any case, at the beginning Buddha was not accepting the initiation of women into his religion. The law of the time did not recognize any right to women. In Hebrew tradition, the father, if need be, could sell his daughter, and if there was a male progeny, the female could not have any share from the inheritance. In the ancient Greece, the woman could be handed over to someone else. In China the women was not

---

[169] Sarıtoprak and Ünal 2005, 463.

considered a human being, she could not appropriate even a personal name. It must have been due to the alterations in both Christianity and Judaism, since Eve caused Adam to eat from the forbidden fruit by way of deception, the woman was considered the originator of this first sin. In a most civilized nation of the West, only in the 16th century, the woman was allowed to touch a copy of the Bible.

In Asia, too, the situation was not different from this. If he had the means, a man could marry as many as he wished; it used to be considered legitimate without any objection for the son to marry any step mother with the exception of the biological mother.

In the Arabian Peninsula, the situation was dismal. When the situation suited, she used to change hands like a merchant's good; as far as some tribes were concerned, due to the consideration of the difficulties of earning the livelihood, the female children used to cease from the beginning and they were buried alive. Even if she could manage to live, she used to be denigrated to the lowest of the low. The adultery was equal to that of our epoch. The immoral games played on women were, for those who still remained sane, who did not lose humanity, to an extent to drive them insane.

Islam marched on all these problems altogether. It took women as well as men as its addressee and at one thrust forward ... providing a new status; it has exalted her to a position of a blessed creature. Freeing her from being a door of profit honored her with giving the position of mother under whose feet lays Paradise. From now on, this exceptional being was not going to be forced into fornication, adultery, unchaste behaviors and never ever to be lowered to a position of a merchandise to be sold and bought. They would not be subject to unfriendly looks, no slander or degrading would be implied in words: *"Those who accuse chaste, honorable women (of illicit sexual relations) but do not produce four male witnesses (who will witness that they personally saw the act being committed): Flog them with eighty stripes, and do not accept from them any testimony ever after. They are indeed transgressors, except those of them who repent thereafter and mend their ways. For surely God is All-Forgiving, All-Compassionate. As for those who accuse their own wives of adultery but have no witnesses except themselves, such a person must testify four times swearing by God in each oath that he is indeed speaking the truth, and the fifth time, that God's curse be upon him if he is lying."* (An-Nur 24:4–7).

The daughters would not be taken lightly, and the murdering them would altogether be banned: *Come, let me recite what your Lord has made unlawful for you: that you associate nothing with Him; and (do not offend against but, rather) treat your parents in the best way possible; and that you do not kill your children for fear of poverty; it is We Who provide for you as well as for them; and that you do not draw near to any shameful thing (like adultery, fornication, and homosexuality), whether committed openly or secretly; and that you do not kill any soul, which God has made sacred and forbidden, except in just cause. All this He has enjoined upon you, that you may use your reason (and so believe, know right from wrong, and follow His way). (Al-An'am 6:151).*

What is narrated in the Qur'an is the creation of Adam first and then from his ferment or essence the creation of Eve. This picture is aimed at reminding that both of them are human beings, without making any discrimination. If we look at this matter from the perspective of the Qur'an's descriptions, it would be quickly understood that these two creatures are important phenomena complementing each other. Even if there is a difference between them, it is being a special design for many divine purposes; it is not an ontological difference at all. The verses in the Qur'an which gives the sense that man is superior over woman are the verses revealed... with the aim of expressing different talents and capabilities. "*(People differ from each other in capacity and means of livelihood, and it is not in your hands to be born male or female. Therefore) do not covet that in which God has made some of you excel others (thus envying others in such things as status or wealth, or physical charms, and so objecting to God's distribution). Men shall have a share according to what they have earned (in both material and spiritual terms), and women shall have a share according to what they have earned. (On the other hand, do not refuse effort and aspiration; instead of envying others,) ask God (to give you more) of His bounty (through lawful labor and through prayer). Assuredly, God has full knowledge of everything.*" (An-Nisa 4:32). In terms of the relationship between the servant and God, the worship to Him, there is absolutely no difference whatsoever between man and woman. Everyone's earning is to oneself. Everyone is the king or queen of his or her own knowledge and moral beat, and the considerations outside this have no value.

As in Islam it is out of the question to talk about a difference between man and woman in terms of being a human and being a servant to God in worship, in terms of basic rights and responsibilities, again there is no difference between these two genders. The women are not different from men in the fields of freedom of religion and thought, freedom of life, the rights of property and possession, to be treated with justice and equality before the law, the right to marriage and family, the right to privacy of individual life and inviolability. Just like those of men, her property, life, honor are under protection and for those who infringe on them there is a proper punishment. Yes, the woman is also free and independent person. Her being a woman is not a cause for restricting or destroying any of her qualifications.

Whenever any of the rights belonging to her is violated, just like man, she can address the grievances. If she has something rightfully belonging to her but in charge of someone else, she can recover it. In the religion of

Islam, some legal regulations were enacted, by taking into consideration some traits and attributes of men and women separately. For instance, the woman was considered as exempt from army duty, war, and the burden of taking care of close relatives, the responsibility to pay for the blood money in the face of a murder perpetrated by a relative. When it is added to these, the fact that the woman does not participate in different burdens of life due to her special private conditions, it would be evident that, compared to man, she would have less expenditures. For this reason, her taking half share of certain things in inheritance would offset the lesser debts she owes. When the antipathy which might arise in mother's home, due to the feeling that she is taking the property from the father's home, is added to that it would be obvious how this distribution is right and fair.[170]

Gülen explains the philosophy behind the legal system which was shaped in the Arab society where Islam first emerged and spread. Of course, he is aware that there is no corresponding environment today and stresses the necessity of retaining the spirit of it. According to Gülen, "The fundamental issue here is the realization of justice."[171]

When concluding this topic, Gülen discusses the following about the limitless and unprincipled sexuality which threatens the healthy life (which he refers to as the "moral" life) of the family and its protection:

> Islam has not prohibited one to fulfill the bodily and material desires at all. It considered having the pleasures within the legitimate boundaries as sufficient to enjoy life, and it discourages not to go into the illegitimate pleasures, in one drop of which there is a pain that could be measured in tons.[172]

27. Does Gülen defend the right of woman to enter every field of life as equal to man and to struggle to achieve this end?

This question was asked in order to learn Gülen's views regarding the widespread belief among Westerners, as well as Turkey's secular segment, that women in Islam recede to the background and are isolated from social life.

Gülen answers this question by calling our attention to the contradiction between the spirit and basic principles of the religion and their practices in social life:

---

[170] Akademi Araştırma Heyeti 2006, 174–178.
[171] Sarıtoprak and Ünal 2005, 465.
[172] *Ibid.*, 180.

Islam does not have a problem regarding women. If today there is seemingly one, it was produced in later times by those who had hardened Islam, narrowed the possibility of entrance, those who produced impossibility within the possibilities, allotting a narrow sphere for women. During the Age of Happiness, namely the times of the Prophet and the Rightly Guided Caliphs following him, the women were inside life; there was no problem whatsoever.[173]

Then he complained about the animosity and the prejudices of the West:

The Westerners see us as enemy and say there are no human rights in Islam. On the contrary religion does not confine women into home. Some economists are establishing a relationship between women's participation in the process of production and development. As long as physical aspect of women is taken into consideration and their special situation is protected, it is not prohibited in Islam for them to contribute in some fields of life. The women had contributed in every aspect of life according to their capacity all along, anyway. For instance, their participation in wars were permitted, their education was approved, preferred and encouraged.

So much so that during the period of Golden Age, Aisha, Hafsa and Ummu Salama were among the legal scholars and *mujtahids* [expounder of Islamic Laws]; even the women in the household of the Prophet in terms of learning religion, in a sense were the sources that the men used to recourse. Many people from *Tabiin* [the generation after the generation of the Companions of the Prophet] used to refer to the spouses of the Prophet regarding the things they wanted to learn. It was not limited to them and their period, in even later times, some competent women continued to serve as teachers for many.

That is to say, it is not a matter of consideration in Islam limiting the life and the field of activities of women. The points which seem to be negative as of today should be evaluated also from the point of view or considering the circumstances of the time and the practices of the contemporary governments. In addition, the fact that in some regions and societies, the customs and traditions continued after they became Muslims has to be taken into consideration. Islam should not be held responsible for any faults inherent in them.

What is important is thinking about the matter by taking into consideration the physical situation of women and their special states; for instance should the women work in heavy mining industry? Should they be con-

---

[173] The interview given to Nicole Pope, *Le Monde*, 28 April 1998.

scripted into the army as men are? Should they go through heavy military training?

If it is deemed there is a great necessity in doing these, then it is my conviction that nobody can say anything about it.[174]

At exactly this point, Gülen raises the issue concerning formal prayer and the requirement that women stand behind men, which indicates to some that women are seen as second class citizens in Islam. He recognizes the heated discussion on this matter in society. According to Gülen, it is not a matter of inequality, and he defends the practice, explaining that it is a formulation of convenience based on gender differences:

> I would kindly request that some of the realities should not be overlooked, especially during the daily prayers nothing other than God should be in the mind of the performer. I have to state that before Him one has to stand his arms tied one over the other as if ready to receive humbly the command coming from Him.
>
> Second, during the performance of the prayer, as well as the pasture of our body, the concentration and the orientation of our soul, in other words, without giving permission to our imagination to indulge in other fantasies, let's remind us that our hearts and souls are shut to all considerations other than God. Keeping in mind those two issues, let us ask ourselves: Why do we ignore some realities?
>
> I surmise that even if it is during the circumambulation of the Ka'ba, the men whose eyes capture a lady, slim and beautiful, cannot say, "We did not feel anything." If someone claims the contrary, I would say I beg your pardon, please, God is seeing you; at least here, let us not lie. Why are we exaggerating some matters and belittling and ignoring some others?
>
> In short, praying with a complete tranquility of the heart is indispensable for both the woman as well as the man. Now overlooking these, exaggerating the little things and approaching Islam with critical attitude, seems to be a decision made in haste.[175]

Gülen then states that women in our age should be able work in any place in the public sphere and occupy any position.

> The female could become a soldier, she could become a doctor. She can receive education in every field. What is important is be able to practice her religion. As there might be some who practice their religion while serving

---

[174] Gündem 2005, 174.
[175] *Ibid.*, 177–178.

in the public, there might be some others while staying home unable to practice their religion to the full.[176]

Moreover, he mentions the implementation of the Presidency of Religious Affairs regarding the employment of women in the local branches in order to facilitate the worship of women, thereby congratulating the administration.

The topic of conversation then turns to Catechism books written for the purpose of teaching basics of Islam. In the appropriate sections of these books relating to women, it is observed that women are treated as second class citizens. Does this have historicity? Are these interpretations bound by the circumstances of the epoch or do they directly stem from the precepts of the religious? This question comes up one more time regarding the status of women in Islam. The greatest criticism is leveled at the Muslim societies and it is claimed that this cultural background is not suitable either for human rights or social equality or the proper development of democratization. When asked his opinion on this matter, Gülen replies:

> Since the special conditions and physical state of women are taken into consideration, the responsibility and the arena of her movement had become a little different from those of men. For instance, the heavy jobs and the responsibilities outside the home are loaded on the shoulders of the man. The interpretation during the periods of legislation [period of the Prophet and the Four Rightly Guided Caliphs] and codification [of the books and the systematization], depending on the contemporary culture had come into existence in a particular direction. Perhaps it might be better to say that consideration of the special traits, attributes and characteristics separately for men and women played a role in particular formulations.
>
> No matter how you look at it, the woman is a woman, the man is a man. When they come together they make up the whole. We should not look at the matter from the perspective of equality or subject of a second class, because women in some matters are ahead of men. For instance, our Prophet placed women forward in some matters. He said: "Paradise lies under the feet of mothers," but no mention of fathers were made. Again he replied to a person who asked: "Whom do I have responsibilities to?" "To your mother." After repeating the same answer several times, he said, "After that to your father."

---

[176] *Ibid.*, 175.

In our day and age, the woman has positioned herself ahead of men in some places. In some other places she is told: "You should halt here. There is no need for you to guard the frontiers; you do not have to struggle with the enemy." Instead of interpreting this approach as a deprivation, and it is possible to approach it with a sense of appreciation, to treat it as an item to try to protect the right of the woman.

By freeing from the argument of first or second class, the differences in the duties and responsibilities, it would be more proper to assess it as a matter of division of labor that these kinds of things are also based on the historical experiences.

Here, commencing from a couplet from Mehmet Akif, I am going to say:

By taking the inspiration directly from the Golden Age,

We should make Islam speak to the needs of the contemporary century.

In some matters the woman comes to the fore, and in some other man does. We cannot see our Prophet making discrimination in this issue. In a society which had different conceptions and understandings, our Prophet held his granddaughters, as well as his grandsons Hasan and Husayn, and prayed with them on his shoulders and rectified the faulty conducts in that society.[177]

After making this assessment, Gülen notes that the precepts of the Qur'an were implemented in the best in the period of the Golden Age. If religious injunctions which came into existence due to special social conditions are to continue as they did in the past, progress is prevented as well as contemporary interpretation. Complaints would take place concerning the function of religious life (not necessarily of religion) and give way to conservatism and serve the status quo.

Gülen offers a solution: to consider the religious rules during the time of Prophet Muhammad; look at how they were implemented then and apply the Qur'an and its rules to the circumstances of our time.

In summary, it is understood that there are two main factors which make the issue of women in Islam complicated. First, the interpretation of religious precepts is done within the context of the past conditions, which entailed a lot of discrimination and inequalities, because they were dependent on the dominant patriarchal political systems of men. Many scholars insist on retaining these interpretations under the circumstances of our own age. This insistence pushes one to question the essence of religion, by taking the problem out of the social and political

---

[177]   *Ibid.,* 176–177.

culture. For this reason, Muslim societies should try to maintain the principles of equality, which they believe are contained within the essence of their religion, and should not be eroded in contemporary applications. But by setting out with the purpose of preventing the abuse of women, they should not end up with discrimination that results in their social isolation.

Second, the majority of the Muslim societies has not completed their development; and therefore, cannot yet incorporate modern equality and its praxis in every field of life (including the family). Against this, Gülen tells Muslims that, along with individual rights, the equality between human beings and between the genders are not prevented by their religion. While retaining the essence of religion and examining how that essence can be made compatible with current conditions, he is advising us not to fear innovations and go with the change.

To the accusation that Gülen's references are taken from the Qur'an and the *hadiths* and belong mostly to the early period of Islam, the response is: Gülen is a man of religion. He is neither a man of politics nor part of the judiciary nor a scientist. The role that he finds suitable for himself, and there is no concrete evidence to the contrary, is to contribute to Islamic research, to purify it of the superstitions and historical residues, to provide advice to raise mature and moral humans under the current circumstance, and to encourage the formation of stable societies based on solidarity.

28. How do Gülen and his followers view democracy? Do they see democracy as a vehicle or as goal? If it is a vehicle, then to what kind of social order or a regime do they aspire?

By and large, I had explained my views on the issue of democracy but I can add this much: Democracy is a system which gives people the possibility of living through their own feelings and thoughts. The tolerance is an important part of its depth. It could even be said where there is no tolerance, democracy cannot be talked about. But, unfortunately some wretched people who have no stomach for tolerance while saying democracy everywhere have desired to dry up the sources which are sustaining democracy. In a country where democracy prevails, it is necessary for everyone to be able to retain his or her life while benefitting from the rights and freedoms. If a segment of that society is to be disturbed by the existence of another segment, then this disturbed segment's claims, "We are democrats, we favor democracy," to say the least, would not be sincere and honest. Without the existence of tolerance it is impossible for democracy to take root. In actual fact, it is imperative for those who defend democracy to tolerate those who do not share their views and open their hearts to everyone.[178]

When Gülen remarks that ethnic and cultural characteristics of people and their differences should not be cause for their exclusion, he makes a preference in terms of faith:

> To accept people as they are and whoever they are does not mean to place the believers with the nonbelievers into the same camp. In our opinion, the status of the believer and the nonbeliever is according to their own value and worth.[179]

Would this difference (whether one is Muslim or not) determine the extent to which one is entitled to benefit democracy? Does Islam approach democracy with some reservations and conditions in the opinion of Gülen?

> Democracy is never opposed to the spirit of Islam. Furthermore, it is impossible to turn back the process of democratization. Democracy is of different kinds. There are social democrats, Christian democrats and liberal democrats in the world. I would like democracy to develop some day to such an extent that in that process of development, a setting is prepared in which all of the needs of individuals, material as well as spiritual, worldly and other worldly. One day democracy will develop so much that I think, let alone I, no one will oppose it. I never fell into hopelessness about this matter in my lifetime. In order to progress, it is necessary to leave hopelessness behind.[180]

To the question whether it is possible to find a more perfect system than democracy, Gülen replies that it is possible through two ways:

> It is possible that the creature called human being, with his logic, reasoning, senses, understanding of freedom conception, philosophy of freedom, the family structure, the structure of the state, could establish a higher system than what is expected from democracy. Second, this system could be shown

---

[178] "Hoşgörü-demokrasi birliği" (The unity of tolerance and democracy," *http://arsiv. zaman.com.tr/1998/10/07/yazarlar/6.html*

[179] Gülen 2006b, 144.

[180] The interview given to Taha Akyol and Cengiz Çandar, NTV, 27 February 1998.

and represented by those figures and architects to represent it. Namely there could be implementation of it and there could be a tendency toward it in this world. Of course these things we are talking about, in the end, are some assumptions.[181]

What can be said as of today?

The state of affairs at the moment is a human reality. When I said, "Democracy is a given today, it is impossible to go back from it," I had wished to mean these. As a matter of fact many anti-democrats, even anti-republicans always said "democracy" and "republic," but their deed belied their words and the values they defended. Despite this fact, democracy evolved and developed. Why would not believers think of taking advantage of such an atmosphere of freedom, and benefit from such a setting?[182]

Gülen reproaches both the faithful and those who try to narrow the boundaries of democracy in the name of democracy. This brings us to the question of tyranny and theocracy in Islam. According to him,

As some people might abuse anything, they may misuse Islam, and they may exploit religious in order to establish a regime of dictatorship. But this does not mean that there is a tyrannical side of Islam. Until today they criticized Islam with theocracy, but in actual fact, Islam has nothing to do with theocracy. Theocracy is a system of government which came into existence through the interpretations and implementations of the church fathers. In Islam there is neither the church nor the church fathers. In the sense the Westerners understand, the Presidency of Religious Affairs do not have the authority to make laws. The highest level in Islam is the level of servanthood to God. And the largest of the freedoms is this freedom. One finds the possibility of getting rid of all shackles by virtue of this freedom. Nowadays they have fabricated something called fundamentalism. This is also a concept originated in the West. Some referring to a movement in Iran and some others a movement in Saudi Arabia are reprimanding Islam.[183]

According to Gülen, the scholarly approach requires to treat the issues from the perspective of the contemporary conditions prevailing at the time. This is only natural, because democracy is a process and consonant with the development of the society it develops also. "Democracy is

---

[181] Can 1997, 130.
[182] *Ibid.*
[183] *Ibid.*, 131.

a process which has to steadily progress."[184] This state of affairs is valid for all the countries and for all humanity: "The West does not say 'We have reached the point we could,'"[185] i.e. Gülen implies: We should approach the matter in Turkey in the same way.

When asked how he sees the role of the state, Gülen remarks that a state, which is ruled with good principles and good laws, is in itself a value.

> Statelessness would mean chaos. Being without a state would be disorder. It would mean setting up different understandings against each other to clash. Statelessness would mean instability. It would mean all the enmities to get out of control and march on all the different thoughts. Think about the non-existence of a government temporarily in Turkey. Even if the administrators in this state are the socialists, think about non-existence of them for a moment, there would be such a fight, even among those who share nuances within that ideology; and the flood of blood would sweep aside everyone. Different Sufi orders would be at each other's throats. The differences between the sects would become a cause for war. People who use different languages would be up against each other. Just like the provincial principalities in ancient Anatolia, the mosque attendants in group of religious communities would become a mosque principality. A little powerful, a dynamic speaker would rise and take several people behind him, and start provoking others. For this reason, we are obligated to make a choice whether we would prefer to have a state or not. We still say the state which has an intrinsic value in itself. But if the talents or traits of the administrators of this state are very low, we do not have to make them a crown on our heads. It is out of the question.[186]

Gülen's views about democracy can be summarized as such: Democracy is for humans, without democrats, democracy cannot exist. Democracy is a good form of government. The guarantor of it is a just and egalitarian government.

Then, who is the guarantor of a just government? According to him, it is morally perfect and virtuous human.

> Authors of utopia like Farabi, talking about virtuous cities, brought to the fore the cities. But, what should always be given priority is the human. The city, civilization, the country, and the town should follow it behind. For

---

[184] *Ibid.*, 133.
[185] *Ibid.*
[186] Can 1997, 135.

democracy the existence of the meritorious, virtuous human beings is very important. In my opinion, Islam gives a very good education and training of democracy to the humans. Democracy can be reconciled perfectly with the virtuous people who have gone through Islamic moral training.[187]

If it is to be asked how many kinds of Islam exist, and then accordingly, how many democracies, Gülen replies it is a matter of their application.

The conception of democracy and its implementation in France is different from the conception of democracy and its implementation of it in England or those in Germany present differences. Islam has no problem with democracy. Even to a great measure, if you look at the codified non-canonical laws of the Ottomans, many people talk about the Ottoman period as one of secularism, as long as they are not in contradiction with the basic rules about the faith creed and worship, new innovations took place in making laws in legislation.[188]

In short, managing worldly affairs and solving extant problems require new rules and regulations. In order to meet them, the laws of common laws were enacted. If there is no principle in the Book, the *Sunnah* or the fundamental sources to be used as a guide, the current administration and ruler should govern. Additionally,

When this decision is made, if nothing could be found with a clear stipulation in the basic sources, then an effort is made not to contradict these sources. When viewed from this perspective, Islam has no problem with democracy and with secularism [as long as it is not repressive]. Although secularism basically involves legal discipline, if you say the system is completely a secular system and try to exclude religion, if you try to enforce a secularism, which is a philosophical one, which could be rendered as "irreligiosity," you would cause conflicts in the society. Then so many anti-secular and anti-democrat people would come into existence. It is incumbent upon us to point to the fault of the people who cause this disruption as much as those who do the disrupting.[189]

Considering Gülen's views that democracy is compatible with Islam, the question arises, "Why do so many Muslim countries not have a democracy?" To this critical question, his replies:

---

[187] The interview given to Nicole Pope, *Le Monde*, 28 April 1998.
[188] *Ibid.*
[189] *Ibid.*

On the issue of Islam and democracy, one should remember that the former is a divine and heavenly religion, while the latter is a form of government developed by humans. The main purposes of religion are faith [*iman*], servanthood to God [*ubudiyyah*], knowledge of God [*ma'rifah*], and beautiful actions [*ihsan*]. The Qur'an, in its hundreds of verses, invites people to the faith and worship of the True [Al-Haq]. It also asks people to deepen their servanthood to God in a way that they may gain the consciousness of *ihsan*. "To believe and do good deeds," is among the subjects that Qur'an emphatically stresses. It also frequently reminds people that they must develop a conscious relationship with God and act as if they see God, or as if they are seen by God.

Democracy itself is not a unified system of government; it is rarely presented without an affiliation. In many cases, another term, such as social, liberal, Christian, or radical, is added as a prefix. In some cases, even one of these forms of democracy may not consider the other as democracy.

However, in our days, democracy is frequently mentioned in its unaffiliated form, ignoring the plural nature of democracies. In contrast to this, many speak of religion as tantamount to politics, which is, in fact, only one of the many faculties of religion. Such a perception has resulted in a range of positions on the subject of the reconciliation of Islam and democracy. Even if these terms are not seen as being opposites, it is evident that they are different in important ways.

According to one of these conceptualizations, Islam is both a religion and a political system. It has expressed itself in all fields of life, including the individual, family, social, economical and political spheres. From this angle, to confine Islam to only faith and prayer is to narrow the field of its interaction and its interpenetration. Many ideas have been developed from this perspective and more recently these have often caused Islam to be perceived as an ideology. According to some critics, such an approach made Islam merely one of many political ideologies. This vision of Islam as a totalizing ideology is totally against the spirit of Islam, which promotes the rule of law and openly rejects oppression against any segment of society. This spirit also promotes actions for the betterment of society in accordance with the view of the majority.[190]

Both an understanding of religion as closed to democracy and a vision of a society that is isolated from religion are unacceptable to Gülen. Why shouldn't religion and democracy be reconciled? Why should they be incompatible? If religion, as an institution that meets the needs of humans, seems to be attractive and has followers, then it must have some

---

[190] Sarıtoprak and Ünal 2005, 451–452.

compatibility with politics and be able manage social life. What is important is how this is to be done, which is related to human intelligence and capabilities.

According to Gülen, religion is based on the sovereignty of God and democracy is based on the votes of the nation. On this point, Gülen does not compromise on the maxim that the sovereignty belongs to God: Sovereignty is "a matter left by God at the disposal of human beings." As such, who implements this sovereignty is crucial. He emphasizes that the sovereignty, namely the will, which is a determining factor for the management of the society should be taken away from a dictator or an oppressor or any other individual and handed over to the general public. And he likens this situation, in a sense, to the application during the period of the Four Rightly Guided Caliphs. He explains:

> Cosmologically speaking, there is no doubt that God is the sovereign of everything in the universe. Our thoughts and plans are always under the control of the power of such an Omnipotent. However, this does not mean that we have no will, inclination, or choice. Humans are free to make choices in their personal lives. They are also free to make choices with regard to their social and political actions. Some may hold different types of elections to choose lawmakers and executives. There is not only one way to hold an election; as we can see, this was true even for the Era of Bliss, the time of the Prophet of Islam, and during the time of the Four Caliphs, may God be pleased with them all. The election of the first Caliph, Abu Bakr, was different than that of the second Caliph, Umar. Uthman's election was different from that of Ali, the fourth Caliph. God only knows the right method of election.[191]

Lately, we are witnessing an intervention described as "exporting democracy" or "taking democracy" to some authoritarian nations. But according to Gülen,

> No nation has the right to establish pressures on another by saying, "You have to take this, you have to be civilized," or "You have to understand civilization in this way, you have to interpret democracy in that way," and to take what it wants by resorting to brute force or coercion. It is the business of no one to democratize another nation, according to their understanding to civilize another country. It is none of their business because this consideration is always open to mistakes, injustices; it can always be misused by utilizing it as a pretext to establish pressure and arbitrary

---

[191] *Ibid.*, 453.

enforcement. It can lead to playing with other nations' dignity, honor, and national unity [and national sovereignty].[192]

Such an intervention does not necessarily have to come from the outside; sometimes it comes from within the country. There are those who think that it is their right to interfere with the elected government by "arrogating authority and enforcing the rights on their own." For example, active duty or retired state officials and various civil society members (who act more like state officials rather than members of a civil society), have said as much. According to Gülen:

> To anyone, no matter what his or her previous position was, while looking into the eyes of the members of Turkish society, performing such shameful acts should not be allowed. We would like to believe we live in a free and democratic setting. We have difficulty in understanding such militant remarks in a democratic milieu. If it continues as it is, it would erode all the trust in democracy and the state.[193]

He states that the world order is shaped according to the preferences of the strong, powerful states:

> Almost everywhere, weak, powerless, and underdeveloped countries are ruled, to a great extent, by a brute force, and without any accountability to any authority. From one end to the other in the huge Islamic world, so far unparalleled oppressions and deprivations have been experienced in the most terrible manner. The representatives of crude force, who are in charge of the destinies of nations, who want to dominate, for a long time now, in order to legitimize the vices they have committed or to demonstrate the reasonableness of their deeds, have been saying foolish things like, "Official ideology is in danger," "Modernity is under threat," "There are enemies of democracy everywhere," "Secularism has is going away." They are creating fear and worry in the minds of innocent masses.[194]

After saying these, he is stating that resistance against oppression and injustices is a human right; however, individual acts to resist them are insufficient:

---

[192] Gülen 2005b, 150.
[193] Gülen 2010a, 199.
[194] Gülen 2004a.

It is another ill fortune for all of us that a heroic voice does not arise to say to all of these, "Enough is enough."[195]

He explains how the democratic rights and freedoms, like the right to life, the right of speech, the right to express oneself, could be gained through a collective resistance against the tyrants and the powerful.

29. What are Gülen's views on human rights? Does he, like many others, see these rights as "Western games" used to divide "our country and nation"?

Gülen replies, not within the framework of a legal discipline, but from the perspective of Islamic religion, on which his thoughts are based. According to him, all the rights and freedoms (including human rights) that contemporary citizens desire are provided by Islam, a balanced and universal religion:

> The Qur'an considers the murder of a human unjustly to be equal to the murder of the entire humanity. And whoever saves a life would be considered saving the entire humanity.[196]
>
> Our Prophet said in another occasion, "Whoever is killed while defending his property would be a martyr. Whoever is killed while defending his blood would be a martyr. Whoever is killed while defending his family is martyr, too." In all the legal systems of the world the values mentioned in the *hadiths* were taken under protection. These matters are dwelled on with great importance in our books of *Usul* [Methodology], which are the foundational books of Jurisprudence, under the rubric of *Dharuriyat* [Essentials]. From this perspective, religion, life, progeny, mind, and property are the essential elements for everyone to be responsible to protect. Islam thus approaches human rights issues from the perspective of these fundamental principles.
>
> The humans, not in any other system or religion, but only in Islam were honored with the title the "caliph of God" [this term "caliph" which is a theological term should not be confused with the term Caliph, in the phrase the "Caliph of the Messenger of God" which is a political term. The first is earlier, mentioned in the Qur'an, whereas the second is a construction, invented by the later scholars in political science], and it had stressed on the fact that he is the caliph on the face of the earth. Not only that, they were given the possibility to interfere with things in this world, and he

---

[195] Gülen 2003.
[196] Gülen 1997b, 92–93.

was exalted through the freedoms of work and enterprise. How would it be possible for a religion which values human beings so much to ignore the human rights?[197]

While citing examples from the implementations of Islamic injunctions in the past, which are in conformity with current practices, Gülen says that the violation of others' rights would be unethical and sinful. Furthermore, when he talks about "rights," he does not understand them as only human rights. He believes all the living beings have rights and gives many examples from the period of the Prophet Muhammad as to how the rights of animals were respected.

Gülen derives this philosophy from the "authentic *hadiths* of the Prophet" and bases human rights on five essentials, which Islam seeks to protect: life, mind, property, progeny, and religion. If one dies while trying to protect one of these, one becomes a martyr. Struggling in this path is considered a form of *jihad*. All legal systems in the world accept these five principles as foundations to be protected. He mentions that these principles exist in the books of Methodology (*Usul*). This analysis leads him to the following assessment:

> Let the contemporary world still crawl in some matters related to human rights, Islam, centuries ago set the standards of legality in the matters of crime and punishments; in the absence of a crime it proved conclusively no one could be considered guilty, the suspect has some rights just like others and could not be taken away from him at all, individuals could not be interrogated based on probabilities or conjectures. No one could be tortured; every right is to be respected, nothing relating to human rights could be belittled; the power must be at the disposal of the right and never a right could be sacrificed for the sake of might. It is reminding us of them seriously and is calling everyone to be respectful towards the rights; it shows it is always protector of the rights.[198]

Here, Gülen accepts Islam not only as the source of faith, but, as in the past and still today, also as the source of human rights and contemporary legal norms. As for the infringements of human rights and addressing those whose rights have been damaged, he notes:

---

[197] *Ibid.*, 94.
[198] Gülen 2010h, 176.

Today, it is known that many organizations came into existence and numerous foundations are established in order to serve human and humane values. Great majority of them have been giving services along the line of the aims of their establishments. In addition, there are worldwide organizations and institutions seem to be working in favor of humans. When we look at their constitution, bylaws, and their activities it would be demonstrated that their activities are not in conformity with their aims as stated at the inception.[199]

Gülen is implying that "justice" and "love for humanity" have permeated the Turkish society's soul:

They are full of pleasure to let live, rather than living themselves. They do not work with the philosophy of "If I do not see the fruits and results of my work, I would not invest, but they have been serving this country whose observed part, like the icebergs, is smaller than what is not seen below. And up until now, from these hearts no one rose to say, "So what, what took place" because of the tranquility and conviction in their hearts that whatever they did in terms of good deed had for sure reached its targeted place. Since they know the method and the system work in this way, they never bothered to dwell on the criticisms and slanders they received from others.[200]

Undoubtedly, Gülen refers to those who share his viewpoints and sentiments, not to society in general. He indicates this conclusion with the following statement: "I think this is the difference between 'a collective personality composed of those who dedicated themselves to the Ultimate Truth,' and a 'community.'"[201]

After explaining Islam's understanding of the "rights" and the justice of the Ottomans, he recognizes that the practice often does not reach the ideal and adds:

Until today the "might" has acted mostly as if it was the enemy of the "right" in the social, political, economic, and administrative life. The representative of the brute force always acted around the axis of self interest, interpreted life as an arena for struggle and fight; for that reason, to the extent that they have enough power and means, they did not care about the rights of others at all, even from time to time, violated many of the human rights and shouted "the power is with me!"

---

[199] Gülen 2007c, 201.

[200] *Ibid.*, 202–203.

[201] *Ibid.*, 203.

... When a time came for a breakdown in the important points of relationship like the faith, Islam, and perfect goodness, when the chinks began taking effect, the falsehood replaced the right; the "might" began imposing by force its obscurantism and obstinacy; the rights were violated; oppressing raised its head, everywhere was heard the moaning of brute force; as a result God rightly had taken away back the things He had given out of His grace, like the consciousness of brotherhood, the sense of trust, the sentiment of compassion, the reverence for respect for the right. Whether He would give them back one more time, I cannot tell, but He, up until now, had been always supplying them to those trustworthy, heroes of faith, Islam, patience, and defenders of rights. He had never left alone those who inclined towards Him with a sense of devotion and loyalty.[202]

In this analysis, two points stand out:

1. While the religion of Islam is the ideal, in practice (in terms of historical and social circumstances) Muslims have strayed far away from its essence.

2. He raises the question, "Whether it is possible to recover the innocence that has been lost?" Gülen's answer is conditional; if we return to the ideal values and if positive circumstances (relationships based on right and love) are established, a system based on human rights and justice can be resurrected. The analysis, which seems utopian in the face of life's cruel realities, is, in fact, inspirational, as he is "seeking the good" inherent in human beings.

Then, what is the relationship of Islam with humanism?

God Almighty has woven the universe with the threads of love. The strongest relationship between the individuals in the family, society and those making up a nation is the relationship of love. Love demonstrates itself when it originates from the parents toward the children in the form of compassion; originating from the children targeting the parents in the form of respect. The divine love displays itself as mutual help and solidarity between the particles of creation towards other particles.[203]

When justice and love are unified, human efforts not only serve self-interest, but also meet the needs of the "other." Only then can a comprehensive system based on "rights" begin to be established. But love is not sufficient—everyone must be respected and this respect is based on

---

[202] Gülen 2004b, 7.
[203] Gülen 2006b, 48.

mutual tolerance and cooperation. If this phenomenon can be established in communities, it also can be established in the larger society, and then it would be inescapable for the idealized societies of the past to come to life again.

30. Are the religious institutions to be considered as a social phenomenon and should be taken as independent from the political authority namely the state? Or is there a role for the state in this field?

According to Gülen, the status of a clergyman, which is seen as an intermediary between God and His servants, is opposed to the spirit of Islam. In Islam, there are no clergy. Everyone can be pious; and at this point, no one would be different from anyone else in terms of status. Only in terms of practicing religion some might be ahead of others and, of course, that is in the sight of God:

> Again in Islam, the duties and positions like *imam* and *müezzin* are not official positions. However, after the establishment of the Republic of Turkey, in a sense, as a continuation of how it was during the Ottoman State, the religious affairs were taken under the control of the state, and the duties were transformed into an institution. But in fact, such a thing does not exist in the essence of the religion; this is not an understanding derived from the foundational sources of Islam. It could only be considered as a convenient organization in order to manage some of the ceremonies of the pious Muslims. But no one would need an organization of religious affairs in order to practice religious life.
>
> A Muslim can perform all the acts of worship and ceremonies, including the burial of the dead, chanting of *mawlid* [a eulogy recited to celebrate the birth of the Messenger of God], and the recitation of the Qur'an. For these, one does not need an intermediary, a vehicle, or an organization.[204]

Regarding this matter, when he is asked whether he himself can be characterized as a "man of religion," he replies:

> In this sense, I have to say that I am not a "man of religion." However, since I had given sermons for a long time in the mosques, as a member of the Presidency of Religious Affairs, I could be considered as a "man of religion," as the title commonly used and understood in Turkey. But in terms of its real essence, this is officialdom [civil servant] in the state, rather than being a man of religion.

---

[204] The interview given to Nicole Pope, *Le Monde*, 28 April 1998.

Secondly, in Turkey, as is in all other countries of the world, not an insignificant number of people are seeking an organization, an association, or a leader, in terms of provision of religious services expected.[205]

I do not find reasonable the criticism that the Presidency of Religious Affairs is determining what kind of a Muslim we should be. On the part of the Presidency there might be coercion and pressure on us in different matters like our family life, economic life, and our transactions in the market. ... It could be stated that 90 percent of these are practiced freely. We are practicing our own religion. No one is telling me you have to live like this, or like that. ... Some people at the extremes who say that there should be no government are also saying that there should not be the Presidency of Religious Affairs. But they do not try to predict what would happen if this institution does not exist. As I had just mentioned, there would be different "provinces of mosques." There would be different provinces following different *müftis* [local administrators of religious affairs, again a government employee] Maybe, according to the ideas and judgments of people from different backgrounds, there would be different Sufi orders, but not for the purpose of reaching God. People would take to the streets in order to spread their methods and sects, and sectarian ideas. For this reason, although there may be some aspects of the Presidency deserving criticisms, I personally approve its existence. I am in favor of it. Some might consider the "position of approving the Presidency" to be in favor of an organization which is behind the official religion. This would not make any difference for me, because it is false.[206]

After this, he comments on the position of leadership attributed to him:

I say it sincerely, if I had given such an impression, through my conduct or behavior, if I had usurped leadership or respect that I do not deserve, then I would ask for forgiveness from God as well as the public. There are tens, even hundreds of people who represent Islam very well, who are aware of what should be done for the benefit of humanity. There are worthy scholars in the departments of theology. I am not fit to hold the candle to them. In spite of that fact ... in the activities of the people who are drawn to a common point under the circumstances and requirement of religion, those people who look for a leader or persuader behind these activities have instigated a curiosity among the public to find one. Those who have animosity toward these activities have done this partially deliberately, in

---

[205] *Ibid.*
[206] Can 1997, 136–137.

order to weaken the movement by discrediting a person. Otherwise there is neither a respectable leadership nor a man of religion in all these.[207]

31. How can the headscarf issue (banning of headscarves in the public sector in Turkey) be resolved?

As background, in Turkey the headscarf and its derivatives (e.g. turban) have become a problem with the regime. Secularism is one of the basic principles of the regime. But by deviating from its essence, secularism is reduced to a phenomenon of symbols and this has played some role in headscarf issue. The conditions of secularism are met when a spectrum of values larger than religion is resorted to make decisions related to daily life; the laws are based, not on the religious rulings, but on social will; and the political authority is taken out of cultural and religious spheres and stand at an equal distance from all cultures and religions. It is not important who wears what or what relationship a particular garment has to do with faith. But in Turkey, the headscarf has been used as a pretext to close down political parties. On this issue, the Gülen's views are along the following lines:

The following kind of understanding and argument has gained an official status: *Those who wear headscarves are traditional, religious, and conservative; those who do not are modern, contemporary and secular.* Traditionalism and conservatism, to some extent, could be met with toleration; in any case it is true that people with these traits are uneducated, local, or rural population. However, the following view is unfair and discriminatory: *The religious people have a secret agenda and this agenda or aim sooner or later will cause the erosion of secular values, and it will end up by the establishment of a state based on religion. Therefore, the headscarf and the people wearing them should be excluded from the public sphere and should be deprived of the public services so that they could not grow up.*

First of all, it is based on the dictum that "secularism should be established from top down and by force." This approach, which is devoid of every kind of historical and sociological notions, is ignorant about the four attributes of secularism.

---

[207] The interview given to Nicole Pope, *Le Monde*, 28 April 1998.

Secularism can be a policy, but secularization is a socio-cultural process and as a society develops, industrialized, urbanized, as its relationship intensifies with the world, as the level of its knowledge increases, its frame of reference gradually expands when making a choice and in its decision-making. It embraces a pluralist frame of reference, in addition to the established traditional source of references. In the traditional world, the most established source of reference is religion. In the modern world, however, some other sources of references have been added to religion. Secularization points to this change in the nature of references from being one to being many different ones.

Secularism is a phenomenon arranging the relationships among human beings; it is a phenomenon in which the cardinal ethical principles have as their sources not only religion, but human preferences and mutual human expectations. The "secular morality" produces a synthesis with the principles derived from religious sources in order to meet the needs of the modern age.

The laws are made, not by an authority which claims representing the divine power, but are made by a contract, namely through an agreement among humans. Thus, there would not be a problem of the laws promulgated by an authority to which is attributed sacredness, which cannot be criticized or amended. People who practice freely what they believe would rule the common lives and the relationships they establish with others, through the decisions they make, and the laws that are enacted by them through a common will. When these regulations become insufficient to meet the needs of newly arising circumstances, become obsolete, and lose their functions, again they make new regulations based on common decisions.

In a secular order, the sate or the political authority and the faith are separated from each other. In a process called secularization, the constant conflicts among the faith groups or a state representing one particular faith from among many and trying to enforce this faith on the others, to prefer one over the others led to many unwanted problems; many wars lasting for years had taken place. The history is full of its examples. Now secularization is a phenomenon to end all this turmoil. At the end of the process of secularization, the state or political authority stays at an equal distance from all religions and it tries to guarantee that all the religious groups, without force or interference, to practice what they believe, and to impart it to the next generation. In order to secure all these, it stays away at an equal distance from them. A secular state does not prefer a particular religion, but provides support to the devotees in order to meet their needs, and also provides legal and de facto security for them to be realized. Thus, by its impartiality between the religious groups, it makes sure that they would become tolerant, respectful, and peaceful in their dealings among themselves.

Under the light of these given, when the headscarf issue whether it is related to traditionalism or originates from conservatism in religion and should be considered part of the cultural stock, it is squeezed between the ideological and political preferences of the state and in the end it has acquired a political and ideological character. Furthermore the label attached to it is the "hostility towards the state and the regime."

With this label, the young girls with the headscarves are deprived of the right to education. The mothers, the aunts, and the grandmothers whose sons were conscripted into the army and were martyred, were not given permission to enter the *Ordu Evleri* (Army Guest Houses, where social gatherings take place) which are supported by the tax payer money and turned back. While all these take place, the most common pronouncements by the officials are, the "National unity and solidarity."

There is also a socio-economic dimension of the issue. Anyone who travels from the east to the west or from the north to the south through Anatolia cannot understand how such a country with an enormous agricultural potential, having human resources and power of labor can be so backward and poor. He would even rebel, and rightly so, because the reason for this backwardness and poverty is the bad administration.

Before us stands a state (the Republic of Turkey), which increasingly puts a distance between herself and the legal and political standards of those civilized societies which it had taken as a model to emulate, a state which wrote its history, not as it is, but as the ruling cadres wants it to be and instead of rather than accepting and managing the society with all its cultural, social, and religious diversity and richness, has been trying to squeeze it into a narrow format it drew and screw it under an ideological, cultural, and political press. The cadres dominant in the state, for tens of years now, in order to build a society at their whims (the most salient feature being obedient) and according to their wishes, have been implementing an authoritarian rule, had suppressed the political and cultural demands, instead of awakening the latent potential in individuals as well as in general society, opted to prefer to consolidate the state. So the society has not developed sufficient enough. What could it be more normal than underdeveloped segments of the society to be traditional?

As a result of intensive migration to the cities after the 1960s, the increasing visibility of those who come from the traditional cultural background from the hearts of Anatolia in the arena where always the domination of the secular state was felt firmly and the places where modernized segments were assumed to be living has produced an atmosphere of panic. The question, "Is secularism slipping from our hands?" became an oft-repeated question. Their visibility had an effect on them equal to that of encountering some creatures from space. But in actual fact, the traditional populace whose numbers were increasingly expanding in the cities were not some external, outside elements. They were the people coming from the large masses from the areas where the modernizing projects of the state could not penetrate and transform. But they were conceived as stranger and foreigner, non appealing, and even dangerous for their secular lifestyle and were treated as such, by the people who thought that in the identity tree of themselves the major branch was secularism.

To the question, "Is it obligatory for women to cover their hair?" Gülen responds:

> Women's covering their hair is not a matter of faith. These are not as significant as the obligation of worship and servanthood to God in general sense. They belong to the secondary level, the level of details. The matter of belief in God was revealed from the outset to the Prophet in Mecca. The five daily ritual prayers became an injunction for us. And later the alms giving became obligatory. But as for the *tasattur* [covering], it is little different. I think in 16th or 17th year of the Prophethood, the Muslim women head no cover on their heads.[208]

When he is reminded that the insistence on wearing the turban (a term assigned by dominant power to a special form of headscarf stating that only this would be allowed because it is reminiscent of the modern European dress, later only this form was banned) generated an anti-tur-

---

[208] The interview given to Ertuğrul Özkök, *Hürriyet*, 23 January 1995.

ban stance, which caused a break in social cohesion in Turkey, he replies: "When there are main issues to be discussed, I think it would be wrong dealing with the details."[209]

Gülen, who thinks that this matter should be left to free will—let those who want to cover do so and for those who do not, others should look at them with tolerance; they should not be forced to act hypocritically:

> It does not mean the following, either: When need be, let the people open their head and after a certain period they can cover. The matter of the place of covering in religion should be carefully deliberated and decided. Those who cover should be accepted as another segment within the mosaic of the society. In short, let us not be drowned in details. Let us not sacrifice big things for the sake of the small. That is to say, if the headscarf comes fourth or fifth in the order of ascendency in terms of its importance among the Islamic teachings, by making it as a cause for fight we are retarding to the background the matters related to faith. Namely, one might have a faith; he performs the pilgrimage and prays five times a day. But in this matter [covering the head] if he thinks differently [not covering the head] it could not be appropriate not to accept this person.[210]

Although Gülen has a flexible interpretation about the headscarf issue, there are still some who raise the concern that Gülen seeks the establishment of an Islamic state, after which he would force everyone in the society to cover. He responds:

> This stems from not knowing the principles and precepts of Islam. If such a mistake is committed, in my opinion, it would have been opposed to the Islamic teaching. This would have been done, without the knowledge about Islam. You have to leave humans alone with their own conscience and lifestyle. We have to know that suppression is not Islam. The matter of putting pressure on the nation and the public is not Islam.[211]

According to Gülen, coercion and suppression do not come from Islam but from the preferences of tyrants and political authorities. He implies that Islam could be exploited by political actors for the sake of power and political preferences.

---

[209] *Ibid.*
[210] *Ibid.*
[211] *Ibid.*

In order to take headscarf out of the political debate and to prevent the harm to youth by these quarrels, Gülen presents a practical and an effective solution in terms of consequences: If we approach the matter from the perspective of the fundamentals and the *füru* (in congruence with the fundamentals, but as compared to them, on a secondary or tertiary level) we are not faced with an issue as important as the five pillars of Islam: Then he is referring the matter of choice between wearing the headscarves and enrolling in a school to the conscience of the individuals. In order to expose the topic further, he continues:

> In Islamic religion the matters offered to the people in terms of faith and deeds are studied under two categories of *usul* and *füru*. Among them the fundamentals which have vital significance are the matters which come under the heading of *usul*. As for *füru*, it is always based on this *usul*. From this perspective, it could be said that in a place where there is no *usul*, it is not possible to talk about a systematic *füru*.
>
> According to this, starting with *La ilaha illallah, Muhammadur Rasululllah* [there is no deity but God, and Muhammad is His Messenger], the other articles of faith are considered proper subject of *usul* in the area of creed. The articles of faith could be summarized in four fundamentals: to believe in God, in the hereafter, the Prophets; worship God [servanthood] and justice.
>
> Five daily prayers, fasting, pilgrimage, prescribed purifying alms, or the other acts of worship are the deeds based on these *usul* and could be considered secondary kind of acts, compared to the *usul*. Nevertheless to say *füruat* [subdivisions] does not mean something as in Turkish usage "we could do without it." Any concept similar to it should not come to mind. They, being in the category of *füruat*, are a consequence of comparison and in relationship with the *asl* [primary] and absolutely due to the way we divided them up according to the abovementioned categorization. Otherwise, it is evident that a faith without acts of worship would not be perfect.
>
> When we examine the commandment of *tasattur* within the framework of these principles, first of all we see that it became obligatory in 7th or 8th year of the Hegira, that is to say 20 years after the inception of the religion of Islam. This would mean that in the first 20 years of Islam women maintained their attire from the Period of Ignorance.[212]
>
> In that case we also have to draw attention to this important point in *tabligh* and *irshad*. Considering the things as big that God considers them big, and considering the things as small that he considers small is from the *taqwa* of the heart. The issue of *tasattur* is obligatory but it should never have a priority over the faith and the truths of faith. And especially it could not be

---

[212] Gülen 2007c, 174.

claimed with an insistence on certain ways of dressing, of course in absolute sense the covering is reserved, because *tasattur* is something and wearing something like *çarşaf* [over garment covering the whole body with the exception of the face, usually black] are something else. It is for sure, *çarşaf* is one way of *tasattur*, and it is a kind of garment worn during the Ottoman Empire in certain regions. Its history goes back only several centuries. We even know that in those periods when it was in use in some regions, it was not used in Damascus and Baghdad. While this is the fact, to dwell on the issue of *tasattur* with an importance of a faith-related matter, and consider it as an essential would mean to put upside down the order of divine commandments. Though this is not a fundamental matter in religion, and it was only practiced after a while in history. Treating it as if it was part of a religious ritual would be in fact opposed to the measured spirit of Islam.

In addition, though it might not be accepted as an objective assessment, in the matter of interpretation of its usage with certain costumes, I would like to express my personal opinion: A Muslim's habits of eating, drinking, sitting or standing, at home, street, market, bazaar all should reflect his consideration of art, spiritual elegance, and kindness of his heart. From this perspective, a summary perusal of some dresses and garments even through the eyes of a plebian, it is difficult to say that there is an esthetic taste on them.

Then, we, the people who have the responsibility to apply the commandment of *tasattur* in our lives, can choose any style of dress with our own free will: It does not make any difference whether they are overcoat or *çarşaf*; red, blue, yellow or green. Going into standardization would kill the flexibility and therefore the universality to be found in the spirit of the religion. There remains the fact that, there is another beauty in diversity. For sometime in the past in China until Mao, everyone used to wear collarless shirts, and in this way they used to present an ugly image. At the same time, to standardize life like this and put it into certain format would mean to make life difficult for the public. And this is opposed to the spirit of Islam, which is the religion of ease and comfort.

On the other hand, some sectors under the influence of unfortunately a faulty understanding regarding some dresses and garments are provoked beyond words. Not provoking the people who do not know much about religion is a fundamental rule of our religion. Otherwise those who wield power in their hands, let alone the *füruat*, might not give the possibility to practice the *usul*. One can find our recent history with full of its examples.[213]

With respect to women who cannot enter universities if they wear a headscarf, thereby depriving them of education, he states:

---

[213] *Ibid.*, 175–176.

In the case of our young girls having difficulty, I would wish them to make their choices on the side of education. Of course, I am against the interference in the education of those who cover their hair for religious purposes. I am being saddened for them to be forced to make a choice between education and a matter related in religion which could be considered of details. But our society is going through a sensitive period. Everyone should take this into consideration. One side should not make this a cause for fight, and the other side, should not go to the fire with fuel saying the fight has already begun.[214]

According to Gülen, covering is not among the principles of religion related to the *usul*. A faithful and a pious person, after making an introspective accounting, might decide not to cover. This is neither a loss of faith nor a deviation from the religion. Furthermore, those who cover should not go to extremes in order not to provoke those who think they are posing a threat for them. They should make their preferences of style and color in conformity with the spirit of the modern age.

Finally, Gülen proposes not to take the phenomenon of covering in isolation, but to assess it within the broader set of rights and freedoms. He cites examples from other countries:

I would wish, just like in the Western countries, the women's rights should be treated together with the freedom of conscience and thought. I never forget, when we went to the Vatican, there was a female journalist with us. Because the Pope does not meet with women, she could not enter inside. Can you imagine about something like this taking place in Turkey, for instance the Presidency of Religious Affairs meeting only with men, refusing to see the women? You should be the judge, would this matter be a cause for headline in the next day's papers or not? But the Pope's meeting only with men is not deemed to be newsworthy.[215]

32. There are various sects within Islam. Is it a matter of freedom of religion and democracy for those adherents of sects to educate their children in their own ways, using their own methods? If it is not, what does Gülen propose?

On this issue Gülen is rather clear; he looks at the phenomenon from a larger perspective. He neither sees Islam as the only religion nor different Islamic interpretations as a threat for the religion. According to him:

---

[214] The interview given to Avni Özgürel, *Radikal*, 21 June 1998.
[215] Gündem 2005, 176.

The freedom of religion in Islam is one of the most important foundational blocks. Even God Almighty in the Qur'an says *"... whoever wills (to believe), let him believe; and whoever wills (to disbelieve), let him disbelieve"* (Al-Kahf 18:29), it would not be religiously permissible for us to develop a different discourse. It is imperative to have a free setting for religious preferences.[216]

In this environment of freedom and in the face of competition with other religions, he responds to the concern that Islam might regress:

We have no doubt in our religion. With its universal values, it is superior to the teachings of other religions in the fields of belief, rituals, and transactions. That would be the case as long as we expose them properly under the circumstances, and understanding of our age, and represent it properly.[217]

In short, Gülen is in favor of freedom through which religions are spread and taught without any obstacles. He also favors the adjustment and reinterpretation of religion to go along with the pace of change, meeting the requirement of daily life.

33. When was the Gülen teaching transformed into a social movement?

The Gülen Movement is a product of a structure inherited by the republic from the Ottomans, which was an aggregate of communities. The republic aimed at establishing a homogeneous nation state from this cosmopolitan and pluralist structure. And it tried to do this by modernizing the population of mostly peasant origin. This method worked in the urban areas, but not in the countryside where the dominant majority lived outside of this modernization process.

Two convictions of the elites of the last period of the Ottomans were shared by the architects of the republic who sought to modernize Turkey:

1. To educate the children in the countryside; and

2. To take Western science and knowledge and mold them with Turkey's own social values, customs, and traditions.

But that did not come about. Of course, education is *sine quo none* of modernization. But before everything else, there has to be a higher social

---

[216] Exclusive answer delivered to Doğu Ergil.
[217] *Ibid.*

setting for those educated people to participate in with their newly acquired knowledge and skills.

If you assign a young man who graduated from the department of agricultural engineering to a village where tilling is done with traditional plowing, and do not provide any devices and modern agricultural input and do not establish an economic system that produces a market, that engineer would start to plow behind an oxen as well. In short, it is necessary to transform the society in such a way to benefit from the newly emerging labor force, their skills, and their knowledge, and this has to coincide with the educational dash.

The Ottoman and the republican elite thought that importing the knowledge and the science from abroad that Turkey could not produce would be a sufficient factor to develop the country. But what is forgotten is that science and technology is a product of a certain social structure. In this structure, culture (social values, custom and habits) and economy come together, making an organic whole. If you break this wholesomeness, it would be like cutting off the lower part of someone else's body and then mounting it over your own, resulting in incompatibility. And this is what happened in Turkey. It could not be industrialized. Lacking sufficient capital and initiatives, the thrust for development was fruitless. The countryside, which was not be modernized, maintained the traditional structure of communities. Science and technology did not come to the country through domestic production but through imported consumer goods. They did not permeate the societal culture and therefore could not transform it. The gap between the city and the village was further widened.

The community structures prevalent in the rural areas were transferred to the cities with migrations beginning in 1960's. Of course, these structures were altered, according to newly arising needs in the new settings. The "familiar worlds" of those who were culturally similar became safe havens to their members, providing security and the possibility to cope with the problems in their new world. The ideology of the republic—which always stays away from individualism and emphasizes the nation or state (i.e., collectivities)—worked in favor of these communities and groups. Although they too were collectivities, the state stayed aloof to them or even took a stance against them, because they had different identities and cultural codes. The republic made many promises but could not fulfill them and, therefore, did not satisfy the expectations of these groups. These groups took it upon themselves to perform the tasks expected of the state, and with mutual help, increased the level of welfare for their communities and even supported some of their members to rise to important positions. In this kind of a setting in which individualism is not taken as significant nor valued at either the state or community level, people seek out communities or they help maintain those already in existence.

The Gülen Movement was born and developed in this social-cultural setting. In the words of Gülen, this movement is not designed as part of a master plan on the table.

> Now out there, there is a structure which came into being through the shaping effects of the events and the thoughts which came into existence through the exigencies of the needs and necessities. This dynamic structure has been renewing almost daily with the aforementioned needs and the necessities. But this does not mean that there is no kernel of thought independent of the events and circumstances. There is, but when the caravan was on its way, it was shaped and it is continually renewing itself today. For instance, when the schools were being opened in central Asia, there was no calculation of where they would be 15 years afterwards. And the planning was not made accordingly. For instance, the contests of Turkish Olympiads were entirely the result of the circumstances.[218]

34. What kind of individual and social needs is the movement responding to, such that in a short period of time it has spread to the entire nation and has even gone beyond the borders?

In Gülen's private conversations, writings and speeches, the emphasis is always on topics such as love, compassion, hope, tolerance, honesty, good morals and the wholeness of internal and external life, living for others, and letting others live.

With these aims, members do not expect in return anything worldly or other worldly. They simply want to contribute something positive to humanity, spreading the culture of tolerance and understanding, found in Islam. Gülen remarks:

> We have no eyes on anybody's land or country, or no desire of dominating anyone. But our eyes and hearts are fixed on every corner of the world in

---

[218] *Ibid.*

terms of taking what God has blessed us with, sharing them with others, to breathe into the soul of everyone, to pour the inspirations of our soul into the bosom of others. Our hearts beat for the whole world. No place will be outside this point of focus. This is also the thought of our Prophet. He says: "My message will reach everywhere the sun rises and sets." With the consideration of supporting life, we demand the whole world. I consider "demanding otherwise" as a flight from duty.[219]

Gülen seeks to spread the virtues of Islam. His understanding of Islam meets the needs of modern times and the newly arising necessities in the lives of the people, without deviating from Islam's basic principles. Gülen is talking about a *tabligh* which is ready to take all his thoughts, not only to Muslims, but to all of humanity. This approach assesses individuals, not according to their religions, but to the values that they carry as part of humanity. It is evident from whom Gülen derives his inspiration:

We move with the spirit our dear Prophet provided for us. ... Some people aim at establishing a state and the conquest of the whole world, we have none of that. No fruit of this world is expected, not even otherworldly rewards. Through the approach of the great thinker of this epoch [Said Nursi], I approach the matters: "I neither care for Paradise nor fear Hell. If I see my nation's belief secured, I will not even care about burning in Hell, for while my body is burning my heart will be as if in a rose garden."[220]

Despite his clear intentions, there are some in Turkey who worry that Gülen seeks to establish a political order. As against this, there is such a principle in Gülen's system of thought: The Qur'an makes mention of the "fly"; it has made the bee, the spider, the ant a proper title for its chapters, because their structures and lives demonstrate the existence of God Almighty. But it makes no mention of the state.[221]

Gülen, who appropriates the spread of Islamic principles and values to be disseminated as a directive of the Prophet Muhammad, has demonstrated that this *tabligh* could be carried out in every segment of the society and in every type of regime. The question then arises: If, as a result of all these efforts a common state structure and the institution of Caliphate-type rule are not the aim, then what is to be expected in the end?

---

[219] Can 1997, 65.

[220] *Ibid.*, 14–15.

[221] "İslam, siyasal İslam ve Fethullah Gülen" (Islam, political Islam and Fethullah Gülen), *Zaman*, 10 April 1998, *http://arsiv.zaman.com.tr/1998/04/10/kultur/12.html*

According to Gülen's writings and the speeches, it can be inferred that he believes that we are faced with a utopia or an effort to construct a transnational community, the members of which have common sensibilities and common values through which they establish communicative action, and they support each other, hoping to meet the challenge of global problems through perfect solidarity. This community, which transcends nations and states, is a moral and ethical community, not political. We are now observing the advent of a movement in which are people whose passion to consume and love for the wealth and power are tamed and disciplined and who set out to meet the need for a network, based on mutual support and solidarity and who derive their inspiration from Gülen. And we are witnessing all of these at a time when there is an erosion of values and diminished solidarity in the broader society.

35. What was the Gülen Movement at its inception and how can it be described today?

> This structure has never started as a movement, the grass root activities at the bottom started as small and moved into big projects, from the local to the global. In the reasonableness of these projects many people united, worked together and it became a movement. It did not have to be this way. For this reason, it would not be accurate sociologically to assess this set of activities as the "Gülen Movement."[222]

At the beginning, there was a group following Gülen as an *imam* and interested in his interpretations. Later in metropolitan areas such as İzmir and İstanbul, other individuals whose socio-economic situation was better, started searching for a spiritual leader, in order not to be trapped by immoral settings in their new lives and in the modern network of relationships of the cities.

Besides accepting Gülen as a man of religion, the more wealthy followers also began to consider him as an intellectual leader or a "life coach." Gülen's encouragement to transcend the local coincided with their national, or even international, aspirations. This role as an intellectual leader who could guide them enabled Gülen to transform his thoughts, recommendations, and exhortations from theory into reality.

---

[222] Doğu Ergil's interview with Gülen.

To the extent that the ventures and the projects he inspired became successful, Gülen's area of influence expanded.

Additionally, the Gülen Movement began "talent hunts" and "utilizing what was discovered," in order to perform the duty of educating the youth, especially those who were talented and hard working. They sought youth living in rural areas and the squatter quarters of the big cities, who wanted upward mobility and to receive an education. The movement provided them with support and established an infrastructure, including dormitories, scholarships, and peer groups.

Those young people who were enrolled in the countryside universities were encouraged to transfer to distinguished universities in the cities. But as time passed, even these efforts were found to be insufficient to spread the message of peace. Gülen advised that these talented boys and girls should attend prestigious universities throughout the world. So inspired, his followers helped to establish a network of support at global scale.

Now, with the encouragement of Gülen and through the support of his followers, students from Turkey study at universities around the world. Some of the students who graduate from these universities are encouraged to settle down in the respective countries where they completed their studies, get married, establish businesses, and support those who would follow after them; they also are encouraged to disseminate the humane Islamic values in the environment in which they live.

The so-called "Gülen communities," which exist in various countries, have established such good relations with the rulers and public that the administrators have sent their children to the Gülen schools, the standards of which are, in many cases, are superior to that of local schools.

Over time, the graduates of these schools have become fluent Turkish-speaking, volunteer members or sympathizers of the "Gülen community." Some of these graduates have come to power in their own countries and have been helpful to Turkish businessmen and investors arriving in these countries.

A Gülen community becomes a lobby establishment, a guide which solves the problems of and show the way to the Turkish businessmen. Some portion of the economic value produced in the process is returned back to the movement, thereby establishing a kind of "circulating capital." It augments the capital power of the community and provides the financial infrastructure to educational investments and humane projects.

Thus, the Gülen Movement has followed a line of activities from the local to the national, from the national to the global. It could be argued that this movement has become the most important and the largest export of Turkey.

36. Which social groups did the Gülen Movement appeal to at the beginning? Today which social groups does he see in the movement?

At the beginning, it was addressing totally the religious, pious groups, the mosque-goers. As for the place it has arrived now, it is addressing all people without distinction of race, language, and religion.[223]

This answer deserves reflection. How is it that a service which started by taking the basic teachings of Islam to the Muslims, and especially to the countryside or the more modest dwellers of the quarters of the cities, has acquired an international status? There are two answers. First, Muslims found in the teachings of Gülen the interpretations which would equip them to cope with new situations and newly arising problems, without losing their fidelity to their faith. Second, the Gülen Movement began to meet the need for peaceful coexistence.

It is possible to manage these differences through cooperation, which can be obtained through reconciliation, tolerance and coming to an agreement and understanding. In brief, it is cooperation obtained through common values. But if this difficult task cannot be achieved, societies and faith-culture groups will experience a constant doubt, exclusion, and a tension. The Gülen Movement, in order to minimize these tensions, offers a universal "partnership for living," which meets the common needs by deriving common values to reconcile differences.

As time passes and this message and these efforts become more prominent, people from different cultural and religious backgrounds will take their places in the proposed partnership.

Since no system of faith or religion can be reduced to another, the common precepts or principles, as well as common human values inherent in all cultures, can be synthesized to achieve common cultural human values.

This understanding is a composition counseled by Gülen. He begins with Islam, but at the same time he is a pluralist. This situation can be

---

[223] *Ibid.*

likened to rivers flowing into the same ocean. As all the rivers flowing into the same ocean, they feed that ocean, and in turn, the ocean unites all the rivers in its essence, producing a common pool. The general and the particular, the part and the whole, demonstrate unity.

It can be said that Gülen is defending a teaching which tries to reach the whole, the universal, by starting a journey from the local or the part. Otherwise, the acceptance and approval of the Gülen schools and universities in so many diverse countries, the attendance of the children of the elite in these schools, and their positive response to the call of the movement for a "universal shared living," would not have been possible.

37. What differentiates Gülen from other men of religion, enabling him to become the inspiration source of an increasingly widespread, modernizing movement?

Gülen does not accept, nor give himself the title, "a societal leader or social leader," which can be expressed in various forms. However, in sociological terminology, he fits the description of a "leader of a civic society." When asked why people gather around him, expecting guidance from him, Gülen replies that, perhaps, the reasonable projects embrace all of humanity and people consider religious rewards, and seek the pleasure of God. He categorically rejects the attribute of being a religious leader. He describes himself as:

> I am someone who tries as best as he could to practice his religion, not the one who is able to practice, but the one who is trying to practice. For that reason, namely since I am unable to perfectly represent the religion, I could not be considered a man of religion. Secondly, the status of the man of religion as an intermediary between the servant and the Creator is in contradiction with the Islamic precepts. In Islam there are no clergymen. Everyone can be pious, and from this perspective no one can be different from no one else in status. Only in terms of practicing the religion, and in the eyes of God at that, some people might be better than others. But, in fact people are, for sure, looking for a leader or an organization in the activities to be carried out or the services performed [in order to make them to be durable or reliable]. Whereas, just like in pilgrimage, millions of people are gathered by the commandment of religion, or these commandments bring together many people in a congregation during the Friday prayer or festival prayer. Today, some services which are falsely

attributed to me are in fact certain things consisting of the services according to the circumstances of the country, carried out by the people who comprehended the value of the service for humanity. Nevertheless, it might be the case that they might have been inspired by some of my sayings or encouragements. But for some unknown reasons, people are looking for a leader behind this, as they do in every other case.[224]

Gülen, who sees himself as only a message carrier, says:

There are many, valuable, prominent and worthy scholars in the divinity schools of theology. I am not fit to hold the candle to them. I am much inferior. Despite that fact, those who sought a definite leader in the activities and services of the people, the people who are pulled together by the religion and the circumstances without their deliberate attempts, have assigned a role for me. Otherwise there is neither a considerable clergyman nor leadership displayed.[225]

Gülen views his fame as such:

I consider fame like honey which is in fact poisonous, killing one's spirituality. If my Lord is going to cause me to serve, let me be at his service. But I do not desire to see that *Hizmet* to raise its head and be seen like a flower or a plant raising their heads from inside the soil for the fear of allotting a share for my own carnal soul as if I had something to do with it. This is the consequence of my special relationship with my Lord. This might not be understood by everyone. In order to understand it, one has to firmly believe in God.[226]

What does he understand from *hizmet*?

Since my childhood, I believed that the greatest service for humankind has to go through education. I believed it to be necessary to embrace all humanity. I believed in the necessity of tolerance, dialog, and acceptance of everyone as they are. I believed having tolerance and approving everyone as they are is the necessary ingredient for preventing the division in society and a strong barrier to the quarrels. Many number of people who shared the same belief set out to serve in this vein.[227]

---

[224] The interview given to Nicole Pope, *Le Monde*, 28 April 1998.
[225] *Ibid.*
[226] *Ibid.*
[227] *Ibid.*

As it is understood, Gülen thought that with this belief and aim he would be received with widespread approval regarding the things he was going to undertake, but again in his words:

> The things accomplished oriented some people to unthinkable, groundless fear and fancy. Since those who look at the world, the events and things through their own windows tend to see everyone in their own image, are caught baseless worries. The despots, those who had the intention of interfering with the administration began seeing them as a threat, those whose activities and intentions are never this worldly, never in favor of obtaining power, and even in tendency of running away from it and who only thinks of the pleasure of God, and therefore the only way to reach that aim has to go through "serving humanity." Even though they submit this as a threat for the state, in actual fact, they began seeing it as a threat lying before their plans. At least they should have thought of this that our use of power and theirs are not similar. One of us is in the path of justice, mercy, compassion, love and serving others; the other uses it on behalf of oppression, mischief, divisiveness, exploitation, and hatred. There remains the fact that we have nothing to do with power and force. We see the real power in faith, worship, ethics, living for others and in the servanthood to God. Those who see us in other ways are making life miserable for others, out of fear and worry. It is because they fear even the things which are not to be feared, they worry about the things which are not worth worrying. They are accepting things which did not occur as if they occurred and they are probable and they are making their own lives miserable.[228]

A new social leadership typology that is observed in the conception of leadership in the Gülen Movement can be understood as an effort to submit a new alternative to the society. As we often hear, "the world which lost its conscience," and the necessity to establish relationships with others that are not based on self-interest, as well as the need to submit a new alternative to the individual and to society, which has lost the capability to understand others.

38. What were the original goals of the circle gathering around Gülen at the beginning?

The main factor directing what members of the Gülen Movement do is, in their own words, earning the "pleasure of God."

---

[228] *Ibid.*

Gülen exhorts his followers to open dialog and develop cooperation and understanding, in order to support the education of the needy and to decrease the conflicts between different faith-groups. Members have never neglected to work in this direction. In the end, an international enterprise emerged. Those foreigners who took their place in this enterprise found it significant to act in harmony, seeking compatibility of the scientific with the moral, stressing common human values, speaking the Turkish language, mixing their culture with the Turkish culture, and reaching a world view that transcended the local. It cannot be denied that this enterprise carries an Islamic message that does not in conflict with the modern world.

The projects that members embark upon result in a synergy and spirit of togetherness, and the resources from the projects facilitate the expansion of the field of their activities.

According to Gülen, no matter how much one is equipped with material means,

> One always needs God Almighty. More than needing His blessings, one needs His support and guidance and His overseeing and protecting. The human beings who need things like air, water, and food, more than these material blessings, they need the nourishments along the lines of heart and spirit. Even if one is 60 or 70 years old and up until that time he led an impressive life to be envied, still he might make mistakes, he might be at fault. Then a believing heart should turn to God Almighty. He should say, "My Lord! Do not separate me even if for a moment from your guidance; do not leave me in error, in my words, conduct, speech, movements of my hands and feet, even with my mimics, no matter how small they may be.[229]

Gülen also tells us that one has to filter his thoughts and closely examine his reason and his conscience; he should try to see his mistakes and rectify any that he finds. Then, he should place his trust in God. In other words, one should first act according to one's reason and conscience. If he believes that he is acting properly, he should also believe that God is going to give him a reward. Success is measured by God's approval of the right act. No matter how much gain one has in the enterprise one undertakes, he should not be spoiled; he should not show off his successes; he should help others and work for goodness and kindness.

---

[229] Gülen 2009c, 160–161.

Gülen's teaching is reminiscent of the relationship between the Protestant ethic and the development of the market economy, proposed by the German social scientist Max Weber. According to Weber, the Catholic Church's tight control over the individual and its world view which constrains free will, did not allow the free market economy to develop. Furthermore, the church set a bad example in utilizing its resources by extravagant spending and showing off. On the other hand, Protestantism teaches its followers to be modest, hardworking, moderate, frugal, to use material resources productively, and to avoid conspicuous consumption—all very similar to Gülen's teachings and his thought. Both of these views see moral conduct, solidarity, work and rewarding them as a divine equation. Both try to achieve a balance by bringing together this world and the other world.

This teaching has created a shared bond among Gülen's circle of followers, from the beginning until now. What has made the strength of this tie possible is not the accomplishments that have been undertaken, but the soundness of the offer Gülen has made to the participants to be frugal, modest, altruistic and, especially, Gülen's exemplification of these traits in his personal life. His lifestyle forms an unshakable and trustworthy bond between the spiritual leader of the movement and its members.

Gülen expresses the character traits to be carried by the participants by the following words:

In this short life, to carry the goals, like to be known and famous, to be recognized as great and thus to receive respect or to be after some passions like benefiting from the blessings of the world is a shameful act against the Lord. While we have a duty of servanthood in terms of explaining Him and exaltation of our great religion, appropriating worldly aims would be infidelity to God.

I, for one, am considering, all worldly desires from having a passion for position or power to having a fame to be an esteemed person, as disloyalty to my Lord, my Prophet, and my religion. I do not want to have any passion or desire other than to renew ourselves as a nation over time, to display a brighter image, especially to know, to expose and present our cultural accumulation of the last one thousand years and explain our religion.

The sense of service to my religion and nation envelops my entire horizon, I am not thinking of anything else other than this. I even think that it is *haram* [religiously prohibited] for me to think of it or desire it. I am considering this world as a "place of service" and as long as I am alive I am performing the corollary requirement of this consideration."[230]

After making this choice for himself, he gives this advice to his followers:

> Today, according to the horizon of our knowledge, conscience and understanding, one more time we have to renew our faith. ... In the environment where we live, if renewals take place, the thinking changes, the logic and philosophy of science becomes something else, and despite that if we are still staying where we are, may God forbid, we would fall down. We have to constantly renew ourselves, and while doing this renewal, we have to walk together with our hearts. Our hearts should not be left even one step behind our minds; the heart has to maintain its vitality. We should not forget that if one, who has a progressive mind and has become a man of demagogy and dialectic, does not maintain a heart at the same level of development, then it means his dry logic and dialectic have swallowed up his heart. He has killed his life of heart and deprived himself of *latife-i Rabbaniye* [the spiritual faculty sensing God directly]. For that reason, you should paint one night of yours with the color of your daylight so that He would transform your night into daylight. You should make your worldly nights into days so that He would metamorphose your darkness in the hereafter into light.[231]

39. How can Gülen explain the fact that the Gülen Movement resonates in the large urban areas and with the recently urbanized and has become a social movement?

Some people in the cities could not adjust and became lonely; they found their identity eroding under the pressure of modernization and Westernization. These people, who were uprooted from their cultural roots, searched for a way to end the loneliness and ambiguity they found themselves plunged into. They wanted to rediscover or reconstruct their national and religious values in their new environment. This need was felt first in the cities, but today it is being felt in the villages as well. One of the main reasons for the rapid and far-reaching spread of the Gülen Movement is this phenomenon.

---

[230] *Ibid.*, 76–77.
[231] *Ibid.*, 136–137.

He adds, "Religion is a human need, and this movement is in the tendency of offering this need, avoiding the contradiction with the realities of life."[232] Thus, he remarks that his movement, developing a contemporary philosophy of life, inspired by the religion of Islam, aims at guiding the daily practices of living.

40. The Gülen Movement which is now international must coincide with global realities. When looked at from this perspective, what are the aims of the movement? How have the aims remained the same and how have they changed since the beginning of the movement?

Gülen, in his reply to this question, stresses the expectation of the "pleasure of God" and emphasizing the fact that there could be no change in this basic rule. But, in terms of worldly perspective, according to the developing and changing background and circumstances, taking on global projects that would support our country and religion and make them eternal is an important change we might have. He reminds us, however, that "these are efforts to reach the same pleasure of God from different roads."[233]

Later, he expresses the sadness that he feels from the severe criticism of this movement which set out with a sincere intention. He notes that until now Turkey tried and failed in expanding its impact through military and political means; what he is having difficulty in understanding is why to accomplish that through cultural means is regarded as strange:

> Some biased and prejudiced people with misconceptions, criticizing the Movement of Volunteers, are constantly reiterating the same claims. They say, "Organized activity." They slander by saying something like "They aspire to do this; they have that in their intentions." They are even able to filibuster the Supreme National Assembly of a nation with the same baseless claims, based only on grudges, hatred, and vindictiveness.
>
> I am unable to suit these expressions neither for myself or yourself; I am uncomfortable to make such statements in front of you. But in the face of these unfairness and injustices, not on my behalf, but if I do not speak up on behalf of the volunteers they are trying to slander, I would not be having fidelity to them, I believe. Think about it! They are against the educational facilities that they have never seen, never toured, never known; they write

---

[232] Doğu Ergil's interview with Gülen.
[233] *Ibid.*

against them, they try to plant doubts in the minds of others. How many times did we repeat it? The other day, we explained everything in detail through an interview. We said: "The schools do not belong to one particular person; these educational institutions belong to this nation."[234]

The activities and the schools of the Gülen Movement went through strict inspections, they were searched, investigated, but in his words:

> No crime was found, about none of them was started a trial. That state was the same state; the inspectors were the inspectors of the same state. Yes, what was happening was not an inspection but in a sense raiding. At the end of all of these, the institutions were cleared of any wrongdoing, proven to be clean, and are operating within the legal framework. Although these went into state records many, many times and these records are still in existence. If the gossips did not end there, there must be some grudge and hatred in this matter, and this is unfair; it is unconscionable.[235]

Fortunately, most of these doubts have been addressed and the pressures on the Gülen Movement have been relaxed for the last several years..

Gülen repeats his aim and the aim of the movement which carries his name:

> God knows our intention, for the last 30 years this nation knows it, too. We have no desire other than earning the pleasure of God and sharing with the world community our historical valuable acquisitions, to establish islands of peace in a bloody geography. As a nation, we believe that we have a lot of good things. We have an honorable and glorious history that we might call our Golden Age for the last thousand years, from another perspective, a history of 4000 years. In many matters we have become skilled. For instance, we have developed a serious understanding of aesthetic standards. It is both our right and duty to display this goodness and to display them in exhibitions. Now in our age, the places these exhibitions take place are our educational institutions, the schools, cultural centers, and even the business places established by those who went abroad for the purposes of trade. Because the things pouring out of their behaviors and conducts would be again our past, our *belle lettre*, our religious considerations, and ethical norms; and these values will be meaningful for the people of other civilizations.[236]

---

[234] Gülen 2010f, 220–221.

[235] *Ibid.*, 221–222.

[236] *Ibid.*, 222.

Gülen then turns to a frequently asked question about how the vast spectrum of the movement's activities is financed:

> If you would like to sincerely desire to learn from where the water comes to this huge mill, follow up the water from the original point. Follow them up in its canal and at where it turns the wheels. If you are not prejudiced, you are also going to see it. Whatever the strength and power which gave our nation its independence in some period in the past, it is the same power behind these educational activities. These are the services of our nation, displayed in some other ways, for instance the sacrifices displayed during the War of Independence and the source of it is their hearts. But, those who do not give without something in return, shall never understand this.[237]

Among Turkey's special contributions to the world are educational activities, which accommodate different cultural climates, and the tolerance maintained among many different faith based groups—a dialog which Gülen refers to as the "Movement of Volunteers, " evidently a special contribution of Turkey to the globalization.

Since the establishment of the republic the main political actor is not the social groups but the state. The state determines who and what citizens will become (identity): how they speak, dress, behave, and even think. Deviation has always been prevented and punished. For that reason, there is a "learned hopelessness and helplessness" in the society regarding doing different things and being different. Whoever entertains the thought of transcending the bounds of this narrowly defined "existential space," is marked as treacherous and treated accordingly. Although the Gülen Movement is not a political entity, it has committed the "crime" of a nongovernmental group's acting on its own, independent of the state, and like the similar groups of its kind, has been subjected to suppression.

According to the official ideology (and even Constitution), "the nation belongs to the state." Existence of another social will is "dangerous" for the state to exert absolute control over the society. It threatens its monopoly over power. The asymmetric relationship between the state and the people is at the expense of the civic society; all the initiatives of the civic society are considered "objectionable" and treated as such.

---

[237] *Ibid.*, 222–223.

The Gülen Movement, considering its beginning, development, activities, cadres and the material values it produces, is exactly and perfectly a civic initiative. It is based on the principle of volunteering and all of its initiatives are recognized as geared to increasing the human capacity, to make the individual efficient and sufficient for themselves, to do greater things in mutual solidarity and help others. The educational and human welfare projects, which are being operated with great zeal and meager means in faraway places, require an extraordinary ideal. Nothing less than a firm faith and confidence in the importance of the work carried out can make this ideal a reality. It seems that the core of that faith consists of "a particular kind of understanding Islam," and the foundation of the trust comes from "the respect and love felt for Hocaefendi."

Gülen refers to the movement that he has inspired as "the movement originating its own models." But as he always does, he calls everyone—the believer, as well as the detractor—to modesty and rationality:

> We do not consider appropriate and accurate to claim that because of this movement the face of the earth will change, all humanity will have smile on its face, and the face of the earth will become a worldly heaven or big claims like these...[238]

He defines the purpose of the movement as the sprinkling of water (through the contribution of the movement) over the plants (children) which have been left without water, have become yellowish, and are ready to fade:

> In a period when people are almost at the throats of each other, and in never ending disputes and quarrels, they are awakening to the truth through the contributions of the heroes of love. By finding the human values anew, they are functioning as the water breaker against the floods which would sweep away the world and humanity to disaster. We wish, under the auspices of their sincere efforts, everywhere islands of peace to come into existence; let the societies in distress run to their white islands. But, we can never approve of the exaggerated words like saying this movement is the sole effort to change the color of the world, by overlooking other beneficial activities, pointing only to them and saying they are marching to that or this point, they are going to accomplish this and that. We would consider a contradiction to proceed with such claims and statements with our understanding of servitude to God and our ideas of mod-

---

[238] Gülen 2010d, 174.

eration, ignoring the valuable services of others. Our duty is to serve religion and the nation within the framework of our own values, and while doing this, never desire to obtain the fruits of our efforts and be in any expectation.[239]

After stating the mission of the adherents of the movement, Gülen attributes the negative view of some to their prejudices and their passion for domination and power:

Some people are experiencing serious paranoiac feelings, thinking that the participants of the movement [Gülen calls them "heroes of love"], will change the world and are not going to recognize their right to life. They have their own system of thought, lifestyle, and economic, political, cultural, and administrative philosophies. According that philosophy they have established a world. In that world they feel comfortable and consider every voice rising outside their world as a death warrant for themselves. They conceive even the most innocent individuals as the monsters to blacken their world and dangerous people to spoil their comfort. These dark spirited people who see darkness as enlightenment and the light as darkness are worried even about the people who always speak love and breathe love. They are pronouncing this fear and worry through various slanders by calling the black as white and the white as black.

In actual fact, none of these people, who devoted their lives to tolerance, dialog, and education will in the future, let alone darkening the face of the earth, would make a shadow for even a sole individual. No, as we do not see ourselves with a special mission, we absolutely do not carry an intention outside the work in the service of mankind, in order only to gain the pleasure of God.[240]

No matter what others say, without being trapped by big claims, overlooking the slanders behind us, and in the face of the wickedness without being panicked, we have to perform our own tasks. Whatever the treatment we receive, we should not lose hope, we should not resent anyone injure and be injured by anyone. ... No matter under what circumstances we are, we have to make the best effort to meet our responsibilities. And even if we are left alone, we have to maintain this sensibility and act accordingly.[241]

Yes, our goal is the pleasure of God; we do not know anything greater than this *gaye-i hayal* ["purpose of one's life," one of the cardinal terms in the system of Gülen]. In order to reach this goal, we have chosen the road of

---

Ibid., 174–175.
[240] *Ibid.*, 175–176.
[241] *Ibid.*, 176.

[exalting the unity of God], and we do not recognize any task greater than that. While walking on this road, with God's permission, we are determined not to be boastful because of the greatness of the task or not to hesitate or worry in the face of the rebukes, reprimands, or curses of others.[242]

41. What kind of spiritual, human, and material devices, vehicles, or means did Gülen use in order to make a local Turkish reality an international one?

In Gülen thought, the religious element (namely faith) has always had a central place. Then is the concern to harmonize faith and worldly needs. This is the sphere of ethics, and it is proposed that a relationship could be established in which, starting from shared ethical principles, there could be more altruism, more understanding, and a sharing of grievances and difficulties. This is followed by the importance of solidarity. It is accepted that poverty and destitution can be transcended together, while welfare and productivity can be increased through cooperation. What kind of means is being utilized for that end? Gülen presents the following one by one:

- The pleasure of God and the hereafter, the belief in Paradise and Hell, the hope and fear of them.
- Historical heritage.
- Our standing as Turkish and Islamic world *vis-à-vis* the West.
- Every kind of material means that skill and technology has produced and left at the disposal of humanity.

Although Gülen mobilizes material and spiritual means in order for his movement to gain momentum, he foresees the possibility that the negative feelings and energy latent in his followers can be brought out. He proposes to use these energies for positive ends. According to him, under every envy, every inaccessibility, and every sense of failure lay a great energy to counterbalance this negativity. If this energy is activated in the right direction, opportunities lost can be recovered.

Tens of thousands of people from all over the world have known Turkey through this spirit of devotion become aware of the warmness of the Anatolian people and begun feeling sympathy towards Islam. Today thousands of people have been saying, "It is you who have introduced Islam to

---

[242] *Ibid.*, 178.

us and made us love it," and sustain a feeling of gratefulness towards them. So what that means is that, the people who are filled with a sense of gratefulness, got tired of hate and grudge, became thirsty for friendship, and were yearning for the atmosphere of peace, they were waiting the extension of a hand towards them. It means that they had never seen the smiling face of Islam, they had never heard of the message of Muhammad, peace and blessings be upon him, with its inherent beauty. When the laborers of thought stood a little closer by saying "dialog, tolerance and acceptance of one as one is" and presented our own values with a little smile on their faces, they responded, "Here it is, we have found it." They said if you had not come, we would have never known Islam and the Prophet Muhammad.

There are incredible people among these heroes who went to the remotest parts of the world in order to light up a torch. Yes, they set out in order to establish the thrones of love in hearts, in order to let humanity hear the tunes they had never heard of and to awaken sympathy for our own values. It was imperative to bring out the real face of Islam, the smiling face with all its beauties. They roamed among the people from town to town, in 72 nations [implying the diversity], in order to bring those who want to, to the constellation of faith with the principles of love, tolerance, dialog, and acceptance of everyone as they are.

... As a matter of fact, the path of tolerance and dialog was not opened for the first time through the representative of this movement. The Prophet Muhammad had used this style against the pagans in Mecca. At Hudaybiya Peace Treaty, he had dealt with the matter with practicality, he had consolidated this with the constitution of Medina. For the first time our Prophet announced to the world that no matter what religion, what race and what nationality one belongs to, the rights of belief, life, travel, proprietorship, and initiative could not be touched. He had advised to coexist and to establish the bridges of coexistence and dialog. He had repeated the same truths with a slightly different style and tone in the Farewell Speech.[243]

Gülen states that this tradition was continued later, with the exception of oppressive rulers and sovereigns who went to extremes and committed injustices; it continued also with the Rightly Guided Caliphs, Ayyubids, Seljukids, the Ottomans, and he stresses that the Gülen Movement is the continuation and extension of this same tradition.

Therefore both the basic foundational works and the historical experiences show that the path of dialog and tolerance has not started with us. It is the

---

[243] Gülen 2010f, 196–199.

essence and the consequence of our past. Yes, the things done by those people who are only expositors of our religious precepts and our civilization are not something invented by way of fabrication produced by their particular traits and as a corollary of their own nature. Saying tolerance, extending the hand of love, shaking the hands, being respectful to the special situation of others, never interfering with anyone's religion, all these do not derive from a specific, particular nature of anyone among them, or come into existence as a result of their moderate behavior or conduct, but rather they are rooted in firm and permanent sources. For that reason, this style is not temporary or transitory; it is something to continue in the future, a permanent and durable one, because the sources on which it is based are permanent and unchangeable.

When the matter is considered from this perspective, it would become evident that the people who say tolerance and dialog are in fact reiterating one more time what they heard in the Medina Constitution and therefore they are fulfilling their duty. Yes, entering into the hearts of others through such a path, to let them hear about God, to take the name of our Prophet to every corner of the world is an obligation on the shoulders of the Muslims. Therefore those people who act as voluntary cultural ambassadors in different parts of the world are also fulfilling this duty placed on their shoulders by the religion itself.[244]

It is possible to infer several conclusions, both spiritual and worldly, from what has just been mentioned:

1. Spreading all over the world, to imparting a modern and quality education and to teach dialog, tolerance, and the culture of living is a duty found in the essence of religion (Islam).

2. Fulfilling this duty is for the purpose of earning the pleasure of God on the part of a Muslim, by way of following in the footsteps of the Prophet; and therefore, it is considered an act of worship.

3. By carrying to various countries the Turkish culture and understanding of Islam, in order to disprove the characterization of violence attributed to them such as intolerance and antidemocratic stand.

4. After displaying that Turkey and the Turkish have a place and can contribute to the process of globalization, the desire to benefit from its blessings and letting others benefit also.

---

[244] *Ibid.*, 201–202.

5. To prepare the spiritual setting which will motivate and equip the members of the movement with the necessary skill and knowledge, in order to carry out the global mission.

42. In order for Turkey to have domestic peace and be regarded with esteem from abroad, what kind of actions does Gülen propose and what kind of a role does he assign to his followers in this regard?

Gülen gives different advice for domestic matters and international matters. Domestically, he emphasizes the importance of education and proposes to raise a generation, aware of world realities and understanding the meaning of change in the world. He believes that the republican elite (the founders) attached a great significance to education and thought that by educating the children of peasants, they could build a modern society. Looking at the result, it is obvious it was a futile expectation.

The educational efforts were not accompanied by developing a market economy and integrating into the world economy, which is observed in the model of development of Germany, Japan, and Singapore. For this reason, the well-educated youth had a great difficulty in making a progress beyond being employed by the state and could not contribute meaningfully to Turkey's development, which had a low growth rate. The people whose passion for consumerism increased, started consuming without producing, and the development was further delayed. For this reason, Gülen proposes with great passion a plan to encourage production and an educational policy in conformity with this plan.

However, starting from the assumption that everything would be possible by securing internal peace and security, the internal politics should not be carried out on the bases of ideologies and polarizations, but with cultural diversity and sociological realities kept in mind. Gülen notes that the problems that have so far eluded a solution cannot be resolved in a divisive, vicious setting, but by the segments of the society experiencing common problems and their political representatives agreeing on the common denominators.

With respect to his advice concerning international efforts, he again focuses on education. He believes that in the countries where the movement participates, Turkey's cultural, economic, and diplomatic influence will increase. But on this matter he is realistic. With the best estimate, he believes that the return for the human and material investment will bear results in couple of decades. Furthermore, that the real fruits will be reaped in the long run, and these activities will contribute to Turkey's global role, even if he does not live to see it. For this reason, he finds it important for the movement to establish bridges based on the sustainable global values through its activities abroad. He enumerates these values as, "justice, security, freedom, brotherhood, humanism." He wishes that a policy, which brings out empathy to the fore and based on these components, becomes the main strand of Turkish foreign policy. At this point, he touches upon the artificial debates which hinder democratization and opening up to outside world:

> In reality, there is neither Turkish-Kurdish fight, nor an Alawi-Sunni fight. No need for an Alawi-Sunni distinction; no need of a division between Kurdish and Turkish. There are only people who share the same fate. When they hurled themselves upon us, they crushed all of us; when they declared a war, all of us were united in one front and fought against them in unison. If there was a possibility to revive the martyrs of Gallipoli, you would see that they would use very different dialects and different languages from each other. But at one place, encountering the enemy, they gave a common fight altogether ... And we treat all of them with great respect and honor considering all of them as martyrs. We show our admiration, we applaud them saying that they have done their share. If your past was that, then today this is your fate, it is togetherness.[245]

Gülen's advice is to accept differences, but not by exaggerating them; common values should be stressed and people treated equally in getting their needs met. The importance of an economic infrastructure that would make it possible to have an honorable and free life for everyone is obvious. If Turkey can expedite its development which has been retarded, it can become an international "point of attraction, a center." Gülen points to the fact that for Turkey to become a center of energy and industrial production, what is required is only good planning and effort, which in possible through domestic peace:

> This is the first thing to do. Everyone in Turkey should work hard and thinking how Turkey could be made rich and wealthy, a great effort should

---

[245] "Bir Damla Ülke Kalmış Zaten, Yazık Etmeyelim" (There is only a small portion of the country left, do not ruin it), *http://www.herkul.org/kiriktesti/index.php?article_id=7105*

be made in this direction. How can the possibilities in our hand could be used and utilized in better ways? Some liberal activities are taking place in many parts of the world. If we go also into such a process, could we have the same advantages? Now we should look at this, and we should make Turkey a point of interest and a center of attraction. For this if you make use of your own potentialities. ... If you enrich your country, they would come to you.[246]

These sentiments also answer the oft-debated matter among the public: "Would the European Union accept us to join their association?" In this answer one finds self-confidence, a realistic proposal for planning based on utilizing the resources efficiently, hard work, and the expectation of social stability. In order to realize this social stability, he states that it is imperative to resolve the issue of the Southeastern Anatolia Region to be resolved:

> The Southeast has to be made a center of attraction. You cannot overlook the realities. Now there might be some people in Northern Iraq feeling differently from you one way or another. For some time, they were together with you; after an agreement with Sheikh Idris, for a period of four centuries they did not raise their voice and accepted you. They are always close to us; they are closer to us than the Europeans. Now if we make our region attractive, we would awaken the envious feelings in some other places, they would admire our country. ... No matter how much you stress on "Unitarian state" or "indivisibility," if you do not make your country attractive in terms of welfare and freedom, you would have difficulty in asking the loyalty of the citizens. The relatives of your people on the other side of the border would not take you as a model. But when you make your country attractive, the others would try to simulate you. Who knows maybe there, they would somehow go to the establishment of a confederation. Those in Iraq would say, "Let us have such an alliance with the Southeastern Anatolia.[247]

Gülen, who speaks in the same vein as Turgut Özal, former Prime Minister and President of Turkey, envisions a phenomenon of peace. Stability and welfare, spreading from Turkey, could develop into a network of regional alliances and cooperation centered in Turkey. For this reason, the problems prevailing in the Southeastern Anatolia Region have to end

---

[246] *Ibid.*

[247] *Ibid.*

and the residents of that region should not be against their country, but as a motivating force standing behind it:

> The peace of the Southeast would be the guarantee also for the peace in Turkey. The delay of the project of development and improvement regarding this region would be extremely objectionable. If you drag on these projects, and if the people living there become uncomfortable with this situation, that it would be an economic disturbance, then those who want to exploit it would exploit it, would lead the matter into another direction, they would provoke chauvinism and racism. These are acts of reaction. That is to say, if you say on your own, "I am this and that; I have come from the Altay Mountains." The others would stand up and say, "I for myself, I have come from Babel."[248]

If the administration leans on one ethnic element and bases the administration of the nation on that ethnic group, it could trigger negative sentiments among others. For that reason, Gülen agrees with the now circulating statement that "Kurdish chauvinism is the illegitimate child of Turkish chauvinism." He advises the civic society and the state to work together, shoulder to shoulder, to complement each other.

> Of course, we cannot do all of these; most of them are the business of the government; these are things that the state can handle with its parliament, respective ministries regarding different things, soldiers and civilians and its security forces. But as citizens we have to be present there, as well. What is left to us is the duty of advising tranquility and peace. If everyone takes the law into his own hands and starts applying punishments, then there would be chaos. In a state of law these do not exist and should not exist.[249]

In summary, Gülen proposes a unity and complementary role of state and society, which envisions a division of labor that stresses shared values and common needs and expectations, excluding no one. Gülen highlights the fact that the contributions of his movement have been met with approval, even in the problematic region of the southeast. He also emphasizes that these contributions are the inevitable consequence of the duty and responsibility of citizenship:

> The indigenous population of the region is open to tolerance and love. Even in the northern Iraq we are opening schools. People there are receiving

---

[248] *Ibid.*
[249] *Ibid.*

these educational activities with great appreciation. In different parts of the Southeastern Anatolia so many schools were opened. More or less since the 80's, the dormitories, youth hostels, university preparation courses were established. Neither in that university preparation neither courses nor in the schools nor in cultural centers so far nothing undesirable took place. Even one of the former prime ministers during his reign, had asked a survey to be carried out in that region. As a matter of fact this is the poll taken by the government. That poll showed that in the province of Van the number of those who went to the mountain to oppose the state through terrorism decreased after the establishment of the school there. The society seems, to a great extent, to be looking forward to the service given by the people of Anatolia. They seem to be saying come, do it!

Furthermore, many of your ministers are from the southeast. Turgut Özal, who served sometime as a Prime Minister and President, is a person from that region. İsmet İnönü was a man from that region. Again, Ferit Melen, who served as Prime Minister, was from the province of Van. I mean the nation has no problem. People do not have any problem with each other. The worst of it is that there might be some inside and outside the country who would take advantage of the chaos produced by some. In such a period, if they desire to make some laws to crush some people, they deem "undesirable," then societal peace could not be quite possible. Therefore, let us pity on the country and not harm it.[250]

Another source of grief for Gülen is for Turkey to remain a closed country. Unconcerned administrations, which closed the doors to the realities of the country and the developments in the world, have generated a society estranged to it and a stranger to universal standards. Now, Turkey would like to confront these domestic and international realities and meet the challenge, but the country is unable to find the keys to the door shut long ago. We are passing our days in vain, quarreling as to the place of the keys and losing time. As a remedy for this situation, Gülen submits the following:

I personally believe that a worldwide political vision must be in view. Until the moment we realize that, I carry the conviction that we are going to be in this closed cage. It is absolutely impossible for Turkey which has an important position, by cutting off the relationships with its neighbors, to retain its existence. Within the borders fixed by National Pact [which was made before the War of Independence], imprisoning herself in its shell. The first thing to be done for this country which is encircled by enemies is that,

---

[250] *Ibid.*

while preparing its citizens to face the challenge of this century, as much as the circumstances allow, to transform its environment as a halo of security. Yes, the citizens of the country have to be brought up along these lines.

... Especially lately, opening up to the world with the cultural and educational activities, I believe that this could be accomplished. These activities are admired nowadays anyway, by saying, "Turkey was inside a closed cage, these kinds of activities are very good for Turkey," and an image of a Turkish world from the Pacific Ocean to the Chinese wall. Besides, establishing strong lobbies by Turkey in various countries is very important in terms of securing the future. It cannot be said that there are lobbies in the world which support and defend Turkey, other than several artificial institutions working for a return of a price. If this country is in the defense of the ideal of *Devlet-i Ebed Müddet* [the Eternal State], it is absolutely necessary for different voluntary lobbies everywhere to be in existence.[251]

While making these practical propositions, Gülen stays away from imaginary and ideological fantasies as much as possible:

I do not believe in the imaginative things like "Islamic common market" to dwell on which are useless and futile. But when we become a centripetal force, I am of the opinion that this kind of unions or agreements could come into existence naturally. With this aim in mind, from education to economy from that to cultural activities through all efforts we should give priority to the development of these countries and let them feel that we are always behind them.[252]

43. This movement has spread around the world and has displayed great dynamism. Through what kind of process of exhortation or inspiration or education has this movement inculcated its mission in its followers?

In a *hadith*, it was stated: "The best of mankind are those who are beneficial for others. The meaning of expression 'good deed' is very vast. From the picking up and lifting a stone sitting on the path of people to the beneficial enterprises in economic life, to the establishment of educational institutions are all included in the meaning of that term. Those who enlighten the minds and hearts of people through disciplined knowledge; those who

---

[251] Gülen 1997b, 182–183.
[252] *Ibid.*, 183.

prepare for them different opportunities of employment, those who support the poor and the needy through almsgiving are the best of mankind.

When that was the situation, at every opportunity I got, as far as my tongue can manage, as far as my heart desired, I have explained to everyone the importance of education, the duties of every individual in economic development, to befriend others and remain to be friends, and the necessity of living open to tolerance and dialog.

These encouragements of mine found approval in the hearts of sacrificing people. For instance, Hacı Kemal of Aydın province was wealthy; he had olive orchard enough to sustain seven generations and a diamond mining business. After listening to my talks about education a few times, he sold his shops and even his house. He went into effort to provide scholarships to students. Whether I have done the right thing, I do not know, but one day, I told him: "Hacı Kemal! You and I must not have a house. Come; let us live in this world without owning even a small hut in this world. Let our state of affairs be the witness that we do not perform these good deeds for the worldly benefits, but only to earn the pleasure of God!" And this self-sacrificing and generous man, all his life lived in a rented house, in a modest room of a school, he did not leave anything worldly behind.[253]

Gülen likens this process of action–reaction, to the total mobilization of the sacrificial acts displayed by the entire public during the War of Independence. What is brought out are the "… services for the nation by the nation, the sources of these are again the hearts of this public, their faith. Perhaps in order to trigger those hearts, it is necessary to make a little encouragement and persuasion about the importance of what they do."[254] Gülen believes that by providing this encouragement and persuasion, he is fulfilling a divine, national, and humane duty. He attributes the interest he found to his call to the kindness and mutual help already found in the hearts of those philanthropic people, who live in all the villages, towns, and cities of Turkey. He just triggered this sentiment, after that all the rest is what the people who have the love of God and humanity in their hearts did.

He talks about "the sweat of the youthful teachers who had graduated from the most distinguished universities of our country, working for a salary just equal to a scholarship." He mentions how the teachers in one school abroad lived on potatoes for six months that the state had given them, how the cook preparing those potatoes brought his own food from

---

[253] Gülen 2009a, 92–94.
[254] Gülen 2010f, 222.

home, and how three families lived together in a single house because of poverty. In the words of Gülen, "... the water mill is running through sacrifice, sweat, tears, and the philanthropic sentiment of the self-sacrificing Anatolian merchants."[255] For that reason, he characterizes this "Movement of Volunteers" as a civic society movement, which is not dependent on any outside power.

44. The Gülen Movement provides educational opportunities to youth, who otherwise could not attend higher educational institutions. What inspires them to eventually volunteer as educators themselves throughout the world?

Since they were raised within the movement and since they were educated by the movement members extending their hands to them, many youth internalized Gülen's teachings regarding the human, society, and "right conduct" and shared his ideals. For the sake of their beliefs and nation, by pushing far beyond the borders of time and space, they have become volunteers, in order to share with others what they have learned. They have learned that, in order to do something for one's nation, country, or ideals, voluntarism does not require having great labels or positions. According to Gülen, those who are not seriously involved with faith and the hereafter cannot understand these motives, but they can be excused for not understanding.

> These people, without knowing anyone, went to strange countries. They have gone to Malaysia and Indonesia, they have gone to countries the names of which you are unaware of. They went to countries like that in Africa. They have said, "In our religion, migration is a very important factor. Our ancestors took advantage of this dynamic as well." They went with this thought. One went, another took him as a role model, learned a lesson, he/she also went. Another and another went. But wherever they went, they were able to find only one address or perhaps none at all. At different occasions, I had presented this. One of our friends, who went to Mexico, gave me a call. "I searched through the telephone book," he said, "I did not come across one Muslim name so that I could I ask him what I could do here." On the phone I cried sobbing, I could not speak a word, and I dropped the phone. And there are hundreds of people who went like that. I did not know the name Tuva. I did not know its place, either. If you say today, mark its

---

[255] Gülen 2009a, 95.

place on the map, I couldn't. We know the Mongolians a little, we know Mongolia too. We knew the place of the Orhun Monuments, too, but I could not mark its place either.

Those people, who left their homes and went, had gone in the name of the Turkish nation, in the name of Turkish state. They went like an exile. They went in order to reinforce the state they left behind. They went in order to establish lobbies in four corners of the world to favor, support and lift up the Turkish state. They went in order to raise people with your culture. Instead of some artificial lobbies that spend millions of dollars, they went to raise some people who would work voluntarily. They could not receive salaries. When I heard they could not receive it, my eyes were filled with tears, I cried here. They had homes and lives in Turkey. They had left; leaving everything behind, even their brides with their bridal gowns. They were so sacrificial that as you see they did not have any expectation in terms of worldly reward. If they had any expectations, they would have searched for an opportunity to jump into and sat at the sources of corruption. But they didn't. 80 percent of this nation today says "yes" to this undertaking. If they did not say yes, how could this amount of good deed have been being accomplished?[256]

It is understood from this explanation that the people who come together with the responsibility of citizenship derived lessons in terms of life, society, and humanity. As a result of these lessons, they took advantage of the opportunities that presented themselves to do service. They were convinced that what they do increases the quality of life of others, and they were not stingy in doing everything within their power to help. They convinced Christians, Jews, Buddhists, and others in far away countries that the reason of that they were there was only to develop a common culture of living and contribute to world peace. When they saw that others believed in them and accepted them as one of themselves, they worked with extra diligence and passion. Their passion and their actions have generated an international circle of volunteers involved in the movement. The children that they raised and the youth that they educated and helped expanded that circle and solidified and strengthened it. This resulted in the movement taking roots in many countries.

---

[256] "Bu Hareket Devlete Alternatif mi?" (Is this movement an alternative of the state?), *http://tr.fgulen.com/content/view/12134/9/*

45. There are some who would like to see the Gülen Movement as an alternative organization to the "state." Is this realistic?

When Gülen hears this skeptical assessment, he is dismayed, on behalf of the volunteers in this movement who work hard in four corners of the world as representatives of tolerance, that such slanders occur. But, of course, he adds that the real offended party is the volunteers themselves. Gülen believes that the source of the skepticism is this thought: "They are accomplishing something that the state cannot." In any event, he notes that this skepticism and doubt do not diminish the significance of the things done both for people in general or for Turkey. The habit of expecting everything from the government is neither providing the possibilities to the civil society to display its power and creativity, nor does it allow the hidden synergies of the individual to come into view. He says,

> As we think of the friends who carry out these and the chivalry of the people standing behind them supporting, sustaining, and financing the activities of these volunteers, we become stronger, and encouraged. The conscience of the society's owning up something, if you do certain things, is giving you courage in that matter. You are saying we are not on the wrong track, because it is not possible for a group which absolutely believes what it is doing is right. Even if a mistake takes place, it would be that of the oligarchic minority which desires to manage everything according to their whims and wishes. Those who are in the habit of calling the beauty an ugly one and considering everything which do not issue from themselves as ugly and dangerous, are now mistaken.[257]

He believes that those who do not perceive the change or see it as a threat for the regime, dangerous for their power, could do anything in order to protect the status quo which is gradually fading away. For that reason, the movement does not have to struggle only with the inertia of the system, but also with the protectors of the status quo. But he has hope:

> Beautiful things are taking place; let those who do not want to see close their eyes. In my opinion, a new prosperous period has started for the Turkish nation. For a long time all the things which were the signs of fortune in the past are again emerging one more time, our nation is going toward it. God Almighty is making it realized through the hands of people,

---

[257] *Ibid.*

people we do not even know their names. ... Even if I give advice, this matter went beyond my encouragements, ten folds more. There remains the fact that I do not believe I am effective in my advices. Maybe the nation and the people are coming together on the point of its reasonableness. Namely, you say something, let it be promising for the future, and let the people see its fruits, then this nation is flying to it. Therefore this movement has become an integral part of the nation.[258]

If this is the situation, how can the Gülen Movement be an alternative to the state? Gülen replies,

Some say, "You are acting as the honorary ambassadors, counselors, and attachés, are you the alternative to the state? My answer is as follows: If in the places where you cannot reach, some people are taking care of the business, you have to only admire and compliment them. That means there was a vacuum there. Regardless of whether they deserve it or not, if these people are filling that vacuum, we should appreciate it; we should stand behind them and support them.[259]

Participants of this movement also are taken seriously in many circles and accepted, raising the concern whether this unofficial group might eventually organize officially and become an alternative to the state; Gülen responds,

For a long time now, as those who are familiar with this poor man know, I reiterated over and over again my respect for the state to a degree of sanctifying it, always with a loud voice. I even received serious criticisms from some on this issue. They said, "Is it that important to make it sacred?" I have to say with all modesty, I know at least a little "what is to be taken as sacred and what is not." I cannot say I know it perfectly. I also know to whom belongs the sacredness. But I said: "The state is an important institution for the nation. It is an important factor, the worst government is better than having no government at all." I repeated these maybe 30 times: Not accepting the state is the source of anarchy. If you want to do something positive by any means, in the end you have to lean on a state. That is to say, I have said so many things regarding the state; in fact, it is not possible for anyone to say, "Are you going to be an alternative to the state? It is not reasonable. And no one must have the slightest thought, similar to it. If there was such an intention of the participants of this movement, they would have revealed it by now one way or another. For instance, they

---

[258] *Ibid.*
[259] *Ibid.*

would have desired politics. For instance, somewhere they would be after a position in the administration. For instance, they would have desired to be seen and to be known. For instance, they would have a passion for the world; prefer the blessings of this world. But none of these demands and desires took place so far.[260]

Furthermore, he proposes something radical, in order to eradicate these concerns:

Whatever we are doing, we are doing them for the nation, on behalf of the nation. All of it is for our state. If one day the state says to us, with soldiers and civilians, "Now, take your hands off of this business, we are overseeing this matter," we would say, "With all appreciation, your order has a place on our head," we would leave quietly. We would think in any case someone is doing it; there is no need for us. All our friends can declare this in a manly manner as loud as possible everywhere.

No civilian society, no team, no movement, no group should put itself in the place of the state; on the contrary, it should help and support the state, it should try to fill the vacuum somehow left and vacated by the state. While doing this, he should never distance himself from the thought that "I am an element of my state here. I am doing it on behalf of my state." He should always be behind the state, he should lean on the state, and he should be with the state. But some, unjustly and unfairly should not lower the morale of these people, serving on behalf of the state. They should not muddy them; they should not blacken them.[261]

As a spiritual leader of a civil society, Gülen approaches the state without any protective shield. But does he have to be a statist by virtue of that fact? I do not think so. He is so much pressed, pressured, and accused, he gives the impression that he has to exaggerate his assurance to make it abundantly clear that he is not competing with the state, nor does he have political ambition.

46. How is this global division of labor within the Gülen Movement managed?

Gülen describes the group attributed to his name as, "a movement of volunteers formed by those who come together with the purpose of exalting people materially and spiritually." He states:

---

[260] *Ibid.*
[261] *Ibid.*

I do not know 70 percent of the people who come to me. These people do not know each other, either. Some of them in Ankara, İstanbul, or İzmir, heard what was being said and explained, found them acceptable and started folding their sleeves and opened up schools. Later, saying "Let us carry this movement to abroad," they opened up to outside world. They did serious sacrifices, did not eat but let others eat, did not dress but let others have them. The teachers who went abroad were content with as little salary as they could meet their basic necessities. The fact that these sacrifices of those magnanimous heroes who spread to the four corners of the world being attributed to a sick and weak man like myself is a grave mistake and at the same time, it would be a transgression into the rights of these self-sacrificing men and women.[262]

In these explanations, we see the footprints of entry class whose influence is gradually increasing in Turkey, and not content with this national market, are opening to the world market. This class is different from the established urban capitalist class. The latter is a class that was enriched by the state for many long years and content with the import business aimed at the domestic market and with adopting Western habits, customs, and traditions. As for the people involved in the Gülen Movement or those who support it, they are different: Since they do not owe anything to the state, they have the ability to act with more freedom, and in order to make up for the support that they do not receive from the government, they require more solidarity and initiative.

It is difficult to say that there is a rigidly centralized (authoritarian) structure in this volunteer cooperation, which relies on the material support of entrepreneurs and where many people from all segments of society have taken upon themselves various tasks. But, on the other hand, it would be incorrect to say that there are no certain arrangements, orientations, and planning—that is to say, that there is no structure. A person you encounter in one part of the world as a teacher might be a hospital administrator at another time in another country. There is a division of labor, flexible and transferable, along with personal responsibility, requiring experience and skills.

Gülen says the following about the supports for the movement:

In fact, the volunteers of the movement, whatever was done in the fields of industry, trade, or cultural activities, from the smallest to the greatest, they

---

[262] Gülen 2009c, 95.

asked me about my feelings. I know some of them: The late Turgut Özal has written letters, maybe to 20 places that he was at the zenith of the state. As he did this while he was the Prime Minister, he did it again when he was the President. Even in his last travel abroad ... he said, "I am the guarantor and co-signer of this business" to a President of another nation. Süleyman Demirel, regarding this matter has written letters with authority to forty heads of states. This is a heroic stance. We have to applaud it. While serving as Prime Minister Süleyman Demirel did this, and he did it again when he was the President. Later another Prime Minister, Bülent Ecevit, did the same.[263]

But this support was, by and large, in the form of letters of trust and credit, for the purpose of and on behalf of the movement to easily maneuver abroad, mostly seeking permission to open up institutions. The funding and the efforts came from the movement.

47. The Gülen Movement, which originated in Turkey, has grown from a small religious group to a community, from a community to a movement, from a movement to a global organization. How did this happen? What are the characteristics of the participants behind this who transformed the spiritual inspiration "from virtual to actual"?

In reply to this question, Gülen begins with the following analysis regarding the state of affairs in Turkey:

> The economic situation of Turkey is not very good. A small minority maybe living well; they are milking the country; they are eating and drinking, but 80 percent is middle class, poor people. The small and medium sized enterprises, Anatolian Tigers, whatever you call them, are trying to open up to the world nowadays and this huge load and difficulty are on their shoulders. Sometimes I watch them with amazement, and my eyes are filled with tears; I say to myself: They cannot find anything to eat, but all businessmen, traders, industrialists, investors are going somewhere. Later, they send a courier asking; "Please, can you find and send several teachers to us?" Let us open up a school here. One looks at another, that one looks yet another so on and on. Maybe there will be a time in the future, no place will be left that they did not establish a school, a cultural center, a language course where they teach Turkish. They will search for ways and means to teach our language, culture, and national values that we inherited from our his-

---

[263] "Bu Hareket Devlete Alternatif mi?" (Is this movement an alternative of the state?), *http://tr.fgulen.com/content/view/12134/9/*

tory, in one sense, our richness and wealth reflecting 4000 years of history, in a sense acquired a different kind of its depth through Islam, and our religious values.

Therefore, they will no longer give in to the conduct of an oligarchic minority, who so far did not even like and approve its own people, who in the caste system they built, look down on their people, the masses, 80, 90 percent of them as if they were lowly creatures.[264]

Turkey has a problem with a small oligarchic minority, who do not approve of the majority of the people because of their different attributes and who constantly try to make them resemble themselves, sometimes transgressing the law, regulations, democracy, and the republic. According to Gülen, this oligarchic understanding of administration "... should not extinguish that passion, that excitement in the Anatolian people, should not deflate the hopes. This yoke, God willing should be carried to the target with the load as it was received at the outset."[265]

In the place of oligarchic and repressive mentality, which has proved to be quite detrimental for the will of the people, Gülen proposes a democratic system in which freedom and basic rights will predominate.

He expresses this desire with a metaphor of a dream, just as the American Civil rights leader Dr. Martin Luther King once did. He states that he is seeing a dream of a Turkey which is democratic, developed, having a high esteem throughout the world, and influential in world affairs.

According to Freud the dreams are the reflection of the unconscious in the outside world. If one does not even see the dream of a thing, if did not see one until today, it would mean he has no relationship to that thing.[266]

As for the question whether the movement shares this dream or not:

If you say, "Did you have any dream regarding the Turkish Nation's leap forward, followed by taking its deserved place in the balance of power among the nations of the world?" thousands of our friends would raise their hands. These friends of mine are sharing the same sentiment and the same thoughts with me.[267]

---

[264] *Ibid.*
[265] *Ibid.*
[266] *Ibid.*
[267] *Ibid.*

48. If it is possible to make a schema of the areas of activities of the Gülen Movement, what kinds of activities and groups of activities can be mentioned?

After stating that the movement consists of both societal and individual efforts, Gülen mentions six main activities of the Gülen Movement:

- Education
- Health
- Broadcasting and print media
- Finance
- Interfaith and intercultural dialog
- Business (investments, trade, services, and industry)

After enumerating the movement's activities, he calls our attention to what the state actors can do and what the civil society actors can do and the indispensability of each complementing the other.

> There are certain things that the state performs and we cannot. But there are certain other things that the state might not be able to do, like the establishment of schools and cultural centers. To an extent, those are some of the things, dependent upon international relationships. You might have very good relations for a while with a state. Your industrial, commercial, economic, and cultural relationships might be very good. But, there are constant changes taking place in the world. You see that France is standing next to you. Another moment, suddenly you see that she is against you. You observe that the Netherlands is with you, and after a while she is against you. Let us say the state is opening a university at one place, at another a high school, yet at another place a language course. When doing something like that depends on the international relationships, then at the moment that relation goes sour, they would close down all of them.
>
> In my opinion, an intelligent state would act with alternatives in this matter. It would activate the civil establishments. It would try to do certain things, at a national level, appropriate to the dignity of a state. But meanwhile it would have some other alternatives. It would say to the civil organizations, "You do also certain other things. By accident, if our relationship with this government breaks down, you would continue the same thing." And it indeed occurred as I have described. Because the relationship of a government in Central Asia with Turkey broke down, the educational activities there were prevented.
>
> In my opinion, a wise state would hold a lot of alternatives. It should not even say schools, language courses, and cultural centers, but it would and should establish also a theatre group, a movie group; when someone says,

"Get out!" and you leave, you would leave behind some others who would be permanent there. They would continue the same thought and the project, would continue the movement. We should hold many alternatives. Just like the different shoots of a plant from many channels, we should rise and go to four corners of the world.[268]

49. Is there a model of an ideal society for Gülen? If so, how do we create that society?

Gülen reiterates that he yearns for a society that is made up of virtuous individuals, who have self confidence and a sense of solidarity with the rest of the society; they seek to elevate the quality of life for everyone with the things that they do; they are not fearful of opening up to the rest of the world, and they aim high, always reaching for excellence. He again notes that the spiritual values necessary to achieve these goals are found in the religion of Islam and in the Turkish culture. He then points out the importance of human effort and the determining character of it: One is whatever one does. To the extent he performs goodness, he is good. If he does not do anything, having no vision for the future, he is nothing. He can only be the object of history and politics, having no role in them.

In order to arrive at this ideal point, a society and the individuals in that society must have peace and prosperity. This peace begins with knowing oneself, increases with the discovery of the universe, and matures through the bonds of love and solidarity established with others.

> Those who cannot comprehend the secrets of existence ... those who are the prisoners of their base desires are to be confined to darkness and irritation.
>
> For those who believe and are on the path of truth, absolute lack of tranquility is out of the question. They would receive good news of hope and security behind every discomfort and worry. The faith and hope are the first condition of peace. The peace first starts with the individuals, grows in the family, and finally reaches a point to dominate all sectors of society.
>
> For that reason, our entire tooth and nail efforts, as a nation, should be aimed at forming our people into a society of peace. A society of peace, devoid of any base desires, carrying only lofty ideals... A society of peace with its conscientious individual members, with its families providing security and happiness, with its nation promising peace and quiet...

---

[268] *Ibid.*

Then, if that is the case, while we are awaiting the arrival of hope and security, we should never forget the fact that we have to start with the individual. This is because it is the individual who would make up the family, and likewise it is the individual again who would be part of and a support for the society. A society, which is made up by sinful elements can have nothing to offer, in terms of goodness, hope, and happiness. All the goodness and happiness, security and peace are shaped around the individuals who have already reached a point to comprehend the secrets of self and the character, acquired spiritual and mental depth. At the same time the individual who has become such a healthy pillar would have been given the identity of a perfect citizen as well as a good part of the family.[269]

In this explanation, Gülen is talking about an organic society. A perfect individual reaches this maturity in the family circle. The society, in turn, is made up of families, which protect the individual.

A harmonious and a durable family is also the essential element of a future-promising nation. The nation comes into existence through the virtue and courtesy of this element and obtains depth. When it loses this trait, it loses all its vitality. A nation which does not exist in the family [or a nation which is made up by the individuals who do not have the sense of belonging to a nation] would lose also the identity and character of being a nation. All the love, respect, solidarity, and mutual help would reflect from the family into the dignity of a nation and such a nation would be exalted to the point where it becomes a witness and an observer of the balance of power among the nations; it would rule over the things and the events.

The cohesion [appropriateness] of the building blocks, belonging to this society, the unity in good-manners and upbringing and the altruism in the hearts tie together the parts firmly. In such a society, the citizens, carry the state and the public figures on their shoulders. The state and the public figures in turn act as honorary servants for the citizens.

... In such a society, the boss stands next to the laborer, in his eating and drinking, and in all his other legitimate desires. Just like a member of the family, he would make him eat from the food he eats; he would dress the same as he dresses, and would not burden him with the load he cannot carry. On the other hand, the laborer would be on the side of the work and the employer, far from being an enemy of property and wealth; he would be on his way of becoming a model representative of the labor and the effort. While he performs the work in the best possible manner, while struggling with sweat and blood on his body, he would do his work in total

---

[269] Gülen 2008c, 116–117.

peace of mind because he knows that he is applauded in the realm of the High and exalted and approved before Him.

In such a society, education with all its institutions develops the sense of virtue; opens the doors of love and goodness, teaches to have compassion towards the progeny and all humanity and how to be in harmony and reconciliation... And finally in such a society, the judiciary judges with a sense of fairness and a philosophy of justice, pursues the oppressor and the aggressor, becomes the protector of the innocent and the oppressed.[270]

Gülen finds disagreements and conflicts, both among individuals and within the society, as rather objectionable. He calls our attention to the necessity, which cannot be neglected, of bringing together around common values and purposes those who are estranged from each other, those who are so much opposed to each other that when one says black, the other says white. For that reason, he says that it is inevitable for social peace to achieve the unities of mind, conscience, and heart which make a human a real human. The mortar of the bridge between individuals is "tolerance." Tolerance is the essential element that must be adopted in individual and societal relationships. According to Gülen, tolerance can be taught and learned.

Gülen believes that cognitive dissonance, which is one of the major concepts of social psychology, is an important factor orienting and directing human and social behavior. Because of the sense of discomfort and dissonance, which is awakened by the state in which one finds oneself, one either wants to change that state or get out of it. In other words, people do not want to live under constant tension, discomfort, displeasure, and discontent. The inclination of both individuals and the society is in the direction of peace and stability.

According to Gülen, the chaos and turmoil has descended on earth because of the lack of morality. For this reason, high quality education is needed to lift the seed of discord spreading in societies and to make the climate of love dominant again. It is necessary to teach goodness, beauty, and truth, in addition to knowledge, and what is needed for this are "men of ideals" (*mefkure insanları*).

Gülen then names the people around him with this title and concludes:

---

[270] *Ibid.*, 118–119.

We have been searching for the ways of how to form this ideal society [awaited for centuries] and we have been resorting to every possible avenue to bring this waiting to an end. In order to realize it, we have been struggling desperately and have been scratching the surface of every possible means that we think might lead to that end. Let us see how long more, we will?[271]

50. Are there any groups targeted by the Gülen Movement?

Gülen expresses that his goal is not to target a specific group to diffuse his teachings. Sensitivity and attraction to his message emerges mostly at the individual level. Those who carry this sensitivity and attraction develop common projects or join projects already initiated in the Gülen.

Gülen believes that the most important factor to attract people to the movement is the importance that they attach to education and pioneering efforts in the establishment of the model schools. He discusses nurturing both "the light of mind and the ray of heart." He talks about the need for a type of human united with, on one hand, the comprehension of the mind and, on the other, the generosity and love of the heart.

He criticizes the groups which do not solve their own problems, but always wait for a "savior." These groups assess problems, not as part of a larger system, but as individual, isolated events, and they try to solve the problems accordingly, whereas according to Gülen:

> ... Social troubles, national problems, and natural disasters, the crises that besiege a society cannot be overcome or resolved by mundane measures. Solutions for such crises depend on the insight, knowledge, and wisdom, which become widespread in a society. It is of no use—indeed, it is a mere waste of time— to try to solve such crises with aimless, limited, unpromising policies that are like mundane political maneuvers.[272]

A man of ideals feels responsibility to the society in which he lives:

> To reach their targets, the first of which is, of course, the pleasure of their Creator, they sacrifice everything that God has bestowed on them, without giving the matter a second thought; they have no fear or concern for anything worldly, their heart is captivated by nothing other than God...[273]

---

[271] *Ibid.*, 119.

[272] Gülen 2007b, 123.

[273] *Ibid.*, 126.

... The future laborers of thought will be the builders of tomorrow and the guide for the generations to come. The world will be re-established with the thought, ideas, and ideals being synthesized in their hands. The future would be enlightened and illuminated with the messages they would give.[274]

51. In the beginning, the movement was sustained by private contributions. What are the financial resources of the movement today and how is the global network of activities now maintained?

Since this question is reminiscent of the polemics which has been going on for a long time, Gülen enters the conversation:

> They have tried to blacken with different various slanders and libels from USA's material support to being engaged with various intelligence services. These people who work with the philosophy of "Stain them with mud, if it does not stuck with them, at least there will be traces of it later," they never succeeded in their ideas [because they could never prove these]. Our head is high and our face is clean and clear. In no period of our life, we never entered into this sort of things at all which would embarrass us later. God willing from now on we are determined not to in the future.
>
> Yes, it is a truism that for these kinds of things to be accomplished, there is a need for material resources. We always tried to proceed on this matter the same way we saw in the *Sunnah* of our Prophet, by relying on the public support. We worked together and on many occasions, we resorted to the help of the people. They in turn provided the support needed. In this issue there is not a single penny worth matter we cannot account for, before God or before the public.[275]

No matter how categorical his answer is, some still argue that "A movement, increasingly growing and spreading to the face of the earth, would be taken to different directions, and it would be impossible not to meddle in politics or trapped by other organizations." What is the answer of Gülen about this issue?

> The greatest capital we have in the sight of God is our awareness of our weakness and poverty, our need of God, being aware of our insufficiency and with these considerations opening our hands and pray for His help and strengthen. It is not possible to explain away the services accomplished through miracles, with incredible intuitions or geniuses, it is

---

[274] Gülen 2008b, 66.
[275] Gülen 1997b, 75.

unshakable determination of our people to support. So, mostly without our knowledge or will, God is taking us to some point in order to give us a chance to serve our people. He is having us do good things, and we are filled with the sense of appreciation toward Him.

As for independence, again we have to express our thanks and gratefulness to God that the point on which the native and foreign academicians pay attention the most was the independence of the movement. It is very important for this movement to be independent. To make this movement to open its hands to others or to be directed in any way, for instance to get it meddle in politics would be a way to destroy it. This would be indeed very dangerous.

If this issue is one of faith, if it is an issue that only the volunteer heroes could carry out in terms of presenting the Turkish culture of several thousand years, ... if it is a matter of making the Turkish language a world language, the things like running after a worldly position or pursuing a future political intention would destroy it, would make that cause futile in the end.[276]

They say, "Why are the courses offered in English?" If you do not implement the curriculum of the country where you are, would they allow you what you want to do? Would they permit you to offer Turkish language in some places as an elective course and in some others as requisite?[277]

Gülen understands that in terms of sources of funding, there has to be transparency. Some people wonder, in particular, where the material support comes from for the schools to be established and operated, because it might determine what is the purpose and goals of these schools. This is a natural human reaction.

From his explanations, it is understood that the schools do not have central financing. Every school is financed by individuals in a city or town in Turkey or by wealthy businessmen. More accurately, those members of the community who take responsibility for the schools keep in touch with the directorate general of the schools in those foreign countries and send money that they collected from the wealthy merchants and members of the community.

As for the young teachers who offer the instruction generally in English, they are educated in Turkish universities, predominantly the Middle East Technical University, Marmara University, and the Bosporus Univer-

---

[276] Gündem 2005, 137–138.
[277] *Ibid.*, 139.

sity. Their salaries are low, between 400 and 600 US dollars a month, and it is nearly impossible for them to save. Almost all of the volunteers prepare themselves for this mission during their secondary and college level education.

This material support is provided with a sense of self-sacrifice and generosity, equal to that felt and performed during the War of Independence:

> Behind this project lie the support of the philanthropist people in all the villages, towns and cities of Turkey ... and sweat of youthful teachers who work for a salary, equal to the amount of a scholarship, the youth yet graduated from the most prominent universities of Turkey. ... Up until today, not even a single proof was shown indicating the receipt of any amount of money coming from other places, while hundreds of these schools are established and operated in front of the eyes of everyone, openly.
>
> The reason being that there is no funding resource other than the pure contributions of ... the sacrificing Anatolian men and women. ... This is a movement of volunteers, namely an enterprise of a civic society which does not depend on any foreign power.
>
> Those, who are unable to do anything without taking either several domestic establishments or a foreign nation behind them, might have difficulty to understand the movement of volunteers which does not rely on anything other than the public's attraction and approval and the grace of God. Those who do not know how to give without anything in return, might not be able to conceive the notion of sacrifice in order to serve firstly their own nation but also all humanity in general. But what is clear is that everyone knows, in actual fact, very well that these efforts, of which I am a part only in encouragement, is a public's enterprise and "water of this wheel" comes from the pure chest of Anatolia. But those who could not make the water of this Anatolian fountain flow in the direction of their choice, are trying to dry it through their jealousy, hatred, and envy.[278]

After this clear and absolute response, Gülen brings up another polemical subject: the movement's activities concerning the diffusion of a culture of dialog and tolerance. To the criticisms of, "Why are you so close to the foreigners, why are you accepting the strange ways of the foreigners?" he responds:

> If you do not take a step towards them, be respectful to them, if you do not conduct yourselves maturely enough to be able to share certain things

---

with them, they would not come close to you either. Approaching them would be the kind of a thing to facilitate for us to explain to them the values belonging to us. If not, even if the organization of the matters belong to you, if you retain the rigidity in your conducts, it would not be possible to explain anything to others. The reason for our inability to explain certain things after a period in our history is due to the artificial gap between them and us, anyway. We were unable to stand next to each other, how then one expects us to explain anything to them?[279]

Gülen understands the criticisms of those people who are not open to the world, those who do not even know their own society and its problems. But he does not attach much significance to the reaction of these people who cannot comprehend the enormity of the aim in this business. He says:

> Even though today some people find strange the things carried out, all these are being done for the sake of that lofty ideal, to express ourselves, and to contribute to the new formations in the world, and to prevent the likely future clash of civilizations that people like Huntington had pointed out, with every effort we can make within our means.[280]

The conversation then turns to another area of activity outside the cultural activities of the movement, namely, economic activities. At the center of these economic activities is the institution of Asya Finans. The questions arise: Why did the movement feel the need for such an institution? Who were the founders and where did they find the money to establish it?

Gülen states that for a long time (25–30 years) his friends felt the need for an institution where they could pool small savings together at a central place, believing that this would make up a considerable amount of a capital.

> I always used to say: Business activities in the future could not be carried out like corner store activities. In a little shrinking world, the small stores ... are leaving their places to the supermarkets. Play big, by bringing together their commitments. I had even asked some friends who would listen to me to open up several supermarkets in İzmir, when I was residing there. I said, "Establish supermarkets, you bring whatever you have, and you also bring some, and you can do it."

---

[279] Gündem 2005, 139.
[280] *Ibid.*

But my circle of influence and encouragement was narrow, then. It had consisted of three supermarkets. During the period of opening the schools in Asia ... again from the pulpit of the mosques, from the pulpit of Süleymaniye ... "Go to Asia and invest there ... If you cannot do it alone, by bringing together all the means you have, go there and invest; establish industrial plants, trade, do something there ... export from Turkey," I said. These words were only the encouragements for the necessary things to be carried out for the enrichment of the lives of the people of Turkey.

There are people that I know at the Asya Finans. I could only know ten of them, personally, bodily and by name. But I do not know their numbers. I think the share holders are above 200. ... It is not that I had them establish Asya Finance. Those who were influenced from the general encouragements, I think, took these encouragements seriously. There were finance organizations before that, like Al-Baraka, Faisal Finans, Kuwait Finans, Anadolu Finans, İhlas Finans. ... These had awakened a desire and enthusiasm among the public. When those desires and enthusiasms came together with the encouragements of this poor man from the pulpits of mosques ... they decided to establish this institution.

Relating me to this matter ... originated from that at the opening ceremony of Asya Finance, 5 to 10 people who knew me invited me to the opening but I think that day there were thousands of people there, and the former Prime Minister Tansu Çiller was there, too. But ... I became the subject of talk in the media, as if I had something to do with it; that became the perception.[281]

These answers show that Gülen, rather than he doing it, he encourages others to do; rather than owning, he encourages others to own; rather than saying "come and follow me" to those who are looking for a way to follow he manifest an example of leadership that guides people to the path he believes is the correct one. This is what leadership is all about. It is convincing others and moving them toward "a vision of a good future" and "good conduct," which he carries in his mind and heart. Gülen's special role is to present a vision which unifies the material and the spiritual, which consist of mind, conscience, and morality. He encourages people and helps them to understand the necessity of not deviating from spiritual values, while working in this world.

---

[281] The interview given to Yalçın Doğan, Kanal D, 16 April 1997.

52. Has the movement ever received any support from Muslim countries or Islamic organizations? Does it currently receive any such support?

Gülen's response to this question is short and clear:

> Absolutely such a support is out of the question. Earlier or later it was always closed to such offers. As it was not taken in the past, it is impossible to be taken from now onwards.[282]

Later, he makes a detailed and more philosophical explanation relating it to the perception or idea of "freedom":

> We understand freedom, from the perspective of Islam's spiritual aspect, as "not coming under the yoke of anyone or anything other than God, not bowing before anything."[283]
>
> Freedom is the title of being able to realize every wish and desire, not in opposition to the spirit of religion, without encountering any obstacle. Nevertheless it is not an unlimited liberty without any criteria; it is only the state of affairs in which there is no any suppression, domination or a yoke.[284]
>
> Another dimension of freedom consists of acting according to the principle that the power is in truth, never saying "I accept the defeat, I give in" in the face of oppressive powers and never being ready to accept the yoke of other powers.[285]
>
> Being in the place or position of "pay back" for a favor is a disgrace. When you lose your independence against some people, to the extent of the number of people you come under as their captive, you would have to pay the proportionate price, in order to stay alive.
>
> But the demands of each one of those who enslaved you would be different. One wants something, another something else. When you are under the obligation to meet each demand, you could not fulfill the obligations of even those to whom you really want to respond positively.
>
> ... In one sense, nowadays the situation of Turkey is exactly that. The European Union, the central Asia, The Middle East, and some powerful nations like the United States have all different demands, and sometimes these demands are in contradiction with each other.

---

[282] Doğu Ergil's interview with Gülen.

[283] Gülen 2010d, 88.

[284] *Ibid.*, 87.

[285] *Ibid.*, 89.

If you cannot stand on your own feet and you are forced to be part of some of the plans, if you are unable to have a say in some strategies from at the first degree and if you fail to raise your voice in the planning stage, it means you are not completely independent.

This situation is a proof that you are under some constraints and there is not even a partnership out there. When the state of affairs is like that, you can not satisfy any party, you cannot be adequate for any one therefore, and you cannot free yourself from the captivity.[286]

For this reason, it is very important for the dialog and educational activities, which is also called as the "Movement of Volunteers," to be independent...

... They, whom I call "heroes of love," said, "We will go to the bosom of the nation, but we will never be dependent on others and we will not have to pay a price as a *quid pro quo* to the foreigners," and set out...

The participants of this movement, first placing trust in God, and then taking the commitment of our nation on their side, without compromising on their freedom, marched on and never in their lifetime begged from strangers, never had indebtedness to anyone...

They did not owe anything to anyone, because the citizens of this distinguished nation by and large were approving the philosophy of dialog and the educational activities.[287]

When the participants join the movement and get to know each other, that issue which warms the heart of each one of them becomes a common denominator among them, receiving strength from each other, all are pitching in their personal commitment and together they are establishing that institution.[288]

Gülen believes that when people who made material contributions saw the result of their efforts, they experienced so much pleasure that their commitment increased. "Especially when they saw God gave them ten folds if they had given one, it increased the volunteers' generosity very much."[289] He believes that in these modern times there is only one thing which profoundly influences people, moves them, and gets them to act with a sense of renunciation, opening their hearts up to others: faith.

Gülen expresses that members of the movement take special care to make sure that the movement is independent, in order to continue the activities of dialog and education, which started as free civic-society initia-

---

[286] *Ibid.*, 90–91.
[287] *Ibid.*, 91.
[288] *Ibid.*, 92.
[289] *Ibid.*, 88.

tives, and to reach the goals set. Every effort is made and extreme caution is taken for the movement not to lose its trustworthiness and to stay away from all outside influences and political tendencies. According to him, this is a public movement (it belongs to the "people") and it has to remain so. At this point, he states that the activities of the movement can be in harmony with both the Islamic faith and institutional independence:

> While you say tolerance and dialog, and stay in a certain relationship with everyone, you would roam within the religiously legitimate boundaries, you would vocalize your servanthood to God, and you would taste a different aspect of freedom and be in an effort to have others taste the same independence.[290]

53. If no material contribution is accepted from outside of the movement, why are official circles so concerned with the Gülen Movement's outside connections, especially since between 1980 and 1985, Turkish men of religion who were supposed to be paid by the Turkish government, actually received their salaries from an organization headquartered in Saudi Arabia?

After stating that he is not the addressee of this question, Gülen remarks:

> I can say this much: Because they cannot comprehend the understanding of sacrifice of this nation, they do not see it possible, for this activity which is carried on in such a large area and which would require large amount of resources, to be accomplished just through the sacrifices, they find it mind boggling and are looking for a calf under an oxen [a Turkish idiom meaning to bark up the wrong tree]. Thus, they are trying to generate ambiguity and confusion in the public opinion. In no period of our lives, we have entered into such a thing which would blacken our face later. God willing, we shall not in the future.[291]

In 1980s when the Turkish economy was in crisis, Turkish *imams* working for the Presidency of Religious Affairs in Europe and especially in Germany, received their salaries from a Saudi organization. When the media reported this, the then current President Kenan Evren held a press conference with the leading journalists, defending the policy.

---

[290] Gülen 2010d, 96.
[291] Doğu Ergil's interview with Gülen.

In those days, most Turkish felt ashamed. The media and the educated sectors, which always claimed to be Atatürkist and secular but giving allegiance to the government, which did not care about Atatürk's principle of "absolute independence." They have always stated doubts and criticized the possible outside connection of the Gülen Movement, without any concrete shred of evidence. This contradiction has always dismayed Gülen and his followers. He states:

> Like every other believer, for the duration of my lifespan, I have searched the ways of becoming a beneficial human being, and as a consequence earn the pleasure of God. I have always lived with the ardent desire, love and passion, to be useful for others, share their grief, and search for remedies for their problems.
>
> I have made efforts to find the cures for the diseases of poverty, ignorance, and disunity which prevent our nation to improve. But I have never had material means to go to the help of the poor and the needy, the capital to construct the school buildings to be left at the disposal of the Ministry of Education.
>
> When that was the case, at every opportunity I got, as much as I could articulate, and my heart desired, I have explained the importance of education, the tasks which can be assigned to every individual in the economic development, to be friends and remain as friends, and indispensability of living open to tolerance and dialog.
>
> I have encouraged everyone in my speeches as well as in my writings to contribute to the educational activities. ... But unfortunately, the outside circles who are displeased to see this picture of friendships and their peons among us, have caused the individuals in society to lose trust in each other; they sow the seeds of worry and doubt in different segments of the society.
>
> Later, they produced and fabricated unthinkable slanders, about the representatives of education activities and tolerance, they turned upside down, even their most sincere conducts, and tried to connect them to some goals and aims, and they so to speak sabotaged all the beneficial activities. They raised doubts about the most positive deeds; they tried to find other intentions and goals in the dialog activities our friends offered to others. They displayed the most shameful illustrations of destruction.
>
> Now, these satanic efforts though might not be effective on the majority of the nation, nevertheless sufficient enough to confuse and make quarrelsome and noisy a marginal segment, since the time of its inception. They rebelled and almost declared a war against the concepts like "tolerance," "dialog," "love," "to accept everyone as he/she is," and "a world without fight."

They shook the hopes in hearts, destroyed the trust people had for each other, destroyed the major bonds tying together different segments with each other?[292]

They accused me of trying to take over Turkey. I have no desire for anything of this world. Even if they propose the sultanate of the world, I would not turn my eyes to that direction and look. They are accusing me of things I have never even dreamed of, the things which did not even enter into my imagination!

But in actual fact, behind these accusations lies the enmity for Islam, and also they do not want a Turkey which is purified of its corruptions, has handled its problems satisfactorily, and has taken its deserving place in the balance of powers of the world. For them it is more desirable and appropriate, to have a Turkey where it is now, in order to accomplish their own goals.[293]

54. Has the movement ever been convicted of a crime?

"No" is Gülen's short and categorical answer. Why then are he and the movement he inspired so much of a concern? They are worried because the civil society's growth in strength and declaration of its will would mean narrowing of the political arena where the state is the main factor. All the influence and privileges of those who participate in politics through the use of the state apparatus until now will come to an end. This worry does not generate a little resistance. In fact, the resistances we are talking about are displayed not only against the Gülen Movement. All the influential civil society organizations are subject to the attacks and pressures from the state or political organizations related to the state. TESEV (Türkiye Ekonomik ve Sosyal Etüdler Vakfı–Turkish Economic and Social Studies Foundation), a civil society organization, which was founded and managed by an elite class, is no exception. Because of its studies in the field of human and minority rights and its redefining the rights and duties of the armed forces within the framework of the constitution, the organization has received threats and was put in a blacklist. Other independent researchers and writers have been blacklisted as well.

Another feature of the Gülen Movement is its being religious. Turkish official identity is based on being Muslim, even Sunni Muslim. But Turks

---

[292] Gülen 2009a, 93–94.
[293] *Ibid.*, 96.

are not allowed to reveal this identity with a loud voice, especially in the public sphere; religion is not to be visible and influential. The religion, which is squeezed into the privacy of homes and on religious festival days, must be lived far from the eyes.

But over time the religious masses started standing tall in secular sectors in the big cities, in the schools that their children were attending, and even more, in the official positions of the state. When this happened, the alarm bells sounded.

The distinguished sons and daughters of the republic were frightened, as if they saw someone from space, when they saw the people with "funny and strange dresses" (although dressed the same way as their parents once dressed a generation earlier), frequently praying in public, and constantly making references to religion in their speeches. But they were their fellow citizens, living on the other side of their country, of which they had no knowledge outside the few cities, where they had been living. They were the traditional people of the regions that the incompetent administrations did not make any effort to develop. What is more, they were in majority.

The secular sector did not want to share their space with them. It wanted to prevent them from getting economically strong and from sharing power with them, through judicial decisions that were not quite within the framework of legality, through various administrative measures, and even through *coups d'état*. The mass media also shared in these antidemocratic activities. From this negative picture, the Gülen Movement got its share.

Although Gülen knows the answers, he asks:

> In my past, which of my acts, which word of mine, or which writing has aroused such a suspicion and concern? About a man who lived among the public for 45 years, and whose writings were published in tens of books, who has hundreds of articles, poems, well over 1000 sermons and again many lectures and conferences, but as against these, there is absolutely no finalized court decision or a sentence, with what kind of conscience, fairness, with what logic or reason, or which legal conception can it be explained or reconciled.[294]

---

[294] The interview given to *Aksiyon* magazine, 6 June 1998.

When reminded that he was arrested by the İzmir Martial Court in 1971, he explains:

> Martial law, as its name reveals, is an extraordinary state of emergency and its courts are not ordinary courts. The prosecutor of the İzmir Martial Court of the period had explained the reason for our arrest after the 1971 memorandum as, "We have arrested so many from the leftists and punished them. So what, if we have arrested a few from your side in order to balance it?"
>
> Later, the decision given about me at a lower court was overturned by the military appeals court, and the file for the retrial was closed due to the general amnesty declared still later. The case was dismissed. In this case, since the basic principle of legal systems is that "Until proven guilty, everyone is to be considered innocent," it would be obvious that there can be no talk of any crime of mine.[295]

Then, he makes an interesting comment:

> The 40 years of one's life passed almost under close surveillance, and during that time so many charges, accusations and slanders and inaccurate media reporting took place and yet there is no conviction about him. If there is a suspicion that he might do in the future just the opposite of what he represented all his life, then it means there is no one else in this country that might not be suspected. There remains the fact that those who are making these accusations have a lot of activities, anti-state and anti-regime and convictions in their past, and their present are dubious and stained.[296]

It is interesting that when Gülen made these comments, the Ergenekon case—the infamous case of a plot against the government—which might eventually include thousands from all walks of life, including generals, active duty and reserve, and hundreds of different crimes, including associations and involvement with the terrorist activities of the PKK)—had not yet been filed. Those who thought they were the owners of the motherland, the custodians of the state, and declared the majority of the citizens as enemy, and whose dirty linen had not been brought out for the public view.

---

[295] *Ibid.*
[296] *Ibid.*

Let us say that these so far are related to Gülen's person, but there also are criticisms about the institutions belonging to the movement, especially the charges and claims against the schools? Gülen responds:

> In every period, a certain sector had some weight with the current governments and against these institutions a bombardment of surveillance and inspections were experienced. ... They were subjected to midnight raids. They even raided the dormitories of the girls, and searched every inch of their rooms. They searched under their pillows, raised their beds. We did not know when they were going to inspect. But until now, they could not find anything contrary to the ordinances, rules, and regulations of the Ministry of National Education. Small or great, they did not witness any negative conduct of any student. We gave depositions. There were serious supervision, we were followed, there were listening, checking the books, entering the computers, everything was searched constantly, searched as in no other period things were searched; they could not find anything, one thousandth of a word worth, against regulations, democracy, republic or secularism. Then, what do you say? What do you say about those schools? Here is the state, checking everything, inspecting everything. They are state schools, under constant supervision of the Ministry of Education.[297]

55. Is the opposition of the East and the West or the so-called "clash of civilizations" a fantasy or a reality? If it is a reality, then how can we transform this clash into a tolerated togetherness and this togetherness into cooperation?

Some background is useful here about the often debated issue which is known in scholarly literature as the "Huntington Thesis," first articulated in 1993. According to many scholars and theoreticians, after the cold war a political order will appear consisting of human rights, liberal democracy, and a capitalist market economy. Francis Fukuyama, an American political scientist and author, said in 1992 ideological conflicts will come to an end, which would mean the "end of history," because history progresses through dialectical oppositions.

Another American political scientist Samuel Huntington arrived at a different conclusion regarding the global system which came into exis-

---

[297] "Bu Hareket Devlete Alternatif mi?" (Is this movement an alternative of the state?), *http://tr.fgulen.com/content/view/12134/9/*

tence after the cold war: Although the ideological period has ended, the end of conflicts did not arrive.

The world has returned to its normal situation determined by cultural clashes, and the axis of global clashes in the future will be cultural and religious. For this reason, the concept of "different civilizations" is the best vehicle to explain the phenomenon of clash as the most clear or the highest expression of cultural identity.

Huntington, in his article published by the *Foreign Affairs* (Summer 1993), stated:

> It is my hypothesis that the fundamental source of conflict in this new world will not be primarily ideological or primarily economic. The great divisions among humankind and the dominating source of conflict will be cultural. Nation states will remain the most powerful actors in world affairs, but the principal conflicts of global politics will occur between nations and groups of different civilizations. The clash of civilizations will dominate global politics. The fault lines between civilizations will be the battle lines of the future.

According to Huntington, the dissolution of Yugoslavia and the wars breaking out between Chechnya and Russia and between India and Pakistan have taken place at the fault lines existing between the civilizations of the world after the cold war.

Huntington also believes, contrary to many, that Western political values are not universal. Insistence on this naive belief, namely, the desire to export the democratic norms to non-Western countries, will generate reactions in other civilizations. The actors Huntington is especially calling our attention to are the "challenging civilizations," which he defines as Indo-Chinese and Islam. He claims that China will eventually become "a dominant regional power" by taking other nations under its influence. Since the Chinese culture is different from the West, which is based on values such as diversity and individualism, in the long run China will be a threat to the West.

Huntington furthermore argues that by the higher rate of population growth in Islamic civilizations, along with insufficient economic development, created enormous problems in these countries and at their borders. He points out that this instability causes an Islamic reaction and the fundamentalist movement. As an illustration, he mentions the Iranian revolution of 1979 and the first Gulf War. When Huntington advanced his thesis, there were no organizations such as Al-Qaeda and their acts of violence worldwide. After such violence occurred, the Huntington's thesis received more approval in the West.

The most controversial and debatable aspect of the Huntington thesis is the claim in that "Islam has bloody borders." He attributes this to several causes, one of which is an increase of population in the Islamic countries, with an especially large proportion of the youth. Additionally, Muslim countries are neighbors with civilizations of Indo-China, Orthodox, the West, and Africa. Huntington claims that potentially Islamic civilization is close to Chinese culture. In human rights and democracy, they contradict the West. Both civilizations emphasize armaments and they will conflict with other civilizations, especially with the West. Therefore, he claims, these two civilizations will establish alliance and alliance against the West.

According to Huntington, the major conflict is between the Muslims and the non-Muslims. The borders between these two civilizations are the "bloody fault lines," where the conflict is taking place. The conflicts start with Islam's entrance into Europe from two fronts. The Western front is the Muslim's conquest of the Iberian Peninsula and it continued for centuries until Muslims were forced to leave that area. The Eastern front is the occupation of Europe by the Ottoman Turks, which ended with the defeat in Vienna.

Huntington believes that there are three factors, sparking the conflict between Islam and Christianity, which is the foundation of the Western civilization:

1. Both are missionary religions, which aim to convert people from other faiths.
2. Both are universal religions, adopting the principle of "either all or none" and claiming that their faith is the "best."
3. Both are "teleological" religions, which claim that their own faith and values are the cause for this universe to come into existence; they claim that their religion contains the purpose of the existence of humanity and life.

This is the summary of Huntington thesis. Of course, as is the case with every other theory, there are those who criticize him. Amartya Sen from India is one of his critics. In his book *Identity and Violence: The illusion of Destiny*, Sen does not agree that civilizations will inevitably clash.

According to him, the clash can only occur when people recognize each other with only one identity, for instance Hindu or Muslim. But people have more than one identity and socio-cultural ties. For instance, a Hindu person can be a woman, an architect, parliamentarian, and someone's daughter. All these make up the sphere of one's identities and one continues a shared life with others in each one of these. In these what is regular is not a clash but one of reconciliation.

Paul Berman, in his book *Terror and Liberalism*, says that among religions and cultures, there are no longer rigid lines of demarcations and barriers; and therefore, an inevitable clash should not be expected. All cultures, to an extent, have permeated each other and the nations belonging to different religions share common human values and life interests. If that was not the case, how could the U.S. and Saudi Arabia be allies? Berman raises an interesting point: Many Islamic extremists spent a long time in the West, either to study or to live. Thus, the cause of the clash can be attributed to philosophical and political tendencies, rather than cultural and religious identities.

Many critics believe, contrary to Huntington, that social values can be disseminated and changed. For instance, Taiwan, Turkey, South Korea, and more recently, many of the Eastern European and Latin American countries, have acquired democratic administrations.

One of the most severe criticisms to Huntington thesis comes from Edward Said, a Palestinian-American literary theorist. In his article "The Clash of Ignorance," he argues that when Huntington sees civilizations as fixed and never changing universe of values, he is prevented from understanding the dynamic exchange and interdependence of cultures, which were always in existence. Huntington's views are based on clashes and conflicts between cultures, rather than harmony and reconciliation. Said states that the thesis that every culture is closed on itself is a viewpoint formed by looking solely at the map and depends on the notion that civilizational groups or races have their own special fates and psychologies. This refers to an imagined geography, legitimizing the establishment of certain policies (Western Imperialism). The thesis of "clash of civilizations," which contains an essential core of intervention and assault, is aimed at creating a psychology for the sense of urgency and a threat in the minds of the Americans, and the maintenance of the Cold War through other means. But, it also prevents the building of bridges among different cultures and the efforts to form a *Weltanschauung* or world view conducive to agreements, reconciliations, and co-existence.

Other critiques advance the argument that the civilizations Huntington defines do not constitute real unities at all; they even clash among themselves within each civilization. They point out that the Islamic world consists of Arabs, Iranians, Turks, Kurds, Berberians, Albanians, Bosnians, and Indonesians, and in these societies, important differences can be observed in both religious and cultural spheres. This strengthens the thesis that civilizations are not single value systems, placing all their members into the same formats.

In "Western civilization," two different cultural groups, Catholics and Protestants, have been living together harmoniously, although they had once fought against each other for centuries. One might mistakenly believe that there was never a conflict between them. When one looks at such kind of facts, Huntington's thesis is substantially weakened.

The more realistic thinkers opine that the most important cause of the conflicts in the Islamic world is "modernity," the conflicts arising from the traditional socio-economic structures and values and the desire to resist modernity; this is more important and severe than the conflicts arising from religion.

Another criticism is implicit in the words of the Pope John Paul II, who is an ardent defender of interfaith and intercultural dialog: If Islam or Christianity is envisioned wrongly under the impact of political and ideological aims, then conflicts will arise.

No matter what is said, pro or con, Huntington's thesis has stirred up a great deal of controversy. Serious initiatives took place in order to establish and protect world peace. These initiatives can be gathered under the heading "Intercivilizational Dialog." For example, the United Nations declared the year 2001 as the year of Intercivilizational Dialog. While many people attribute this idea to Iran's former President, Muhammad Khatemi, years earlier Gülen had visited Pope John Paul II, who pioneered this issue in the Western world, and at the time, Gülen proposed to the Pope to work in cooperation. The Gülen Movement was planned to be the Muslim representatives of the project. During the 59th general assembly meeting of the United Nations in 2005, under the co-chairmanship of Recep Tayyib Erdoğan, the Prime Minister of the Republic of Turkey, and Jose Luis Rodriguez Zapatero, the President of Spain, an initiative was begun: "The Alliance of Civilizations."

The aim of this initiative was for different societies to come together to cooperate, in order to prevent extremism and fundamentalism. It sought to prevent tension and polarization, stemming from differences in religious and cultural values, especially between the Western and Muslim countries. In the words of Giandomenico Picco, the former United Nations secretary general special representative to manage the activities of the year of Inter-civilizational Dialog, should always echo in our ears:

> History does not kill, ideology does not destroy, and institutions do not rape. The only entity on this planet who can do that is the human being, the individual.[298]

After this background, we can turn to Gülen's response to the question above concerning the clash of civilizations:

> As for the clash of civilizations, as advanced by Huntington: I am in the opinion that in this kind of claims, rather than realistic assessments regarding the future, the purpose followed is to condition others, the public opinion in determining new aims; and within the framework of those aims, and on behalf of the power, holding the domination of the world. Until the dissolution of the Soviet Union, the thoughts of humanity were divided along the clash between the West and the East or the NATO and the Warsaw Pact. This time, by fabricating an artificial enemy, a civilization clash is aimed based on the cultural and religious differences. Thus, what is intended is to generate a setting in which the dominant block can retain its hegemony in the world.
>
> As a matter of fact, until today the clash was something desired by some power centers. Namely, through the imagined existence of an enemy and presented as a threat, the masses were alarmed and in this way they were prepared to accept every sort of a war to come.
>
> In fact, from yesterday to today, whether represented by the Prophets Moses, Jesus and Muhammad, peace be upon them, no religion pleasing to God was ever grounded in the foundation of a clash. Let alone being grounded, these religions and especially Islam has declared a war against mischief, clash, conflict, and oppression. Islam means peace, security, and safety. Therefore, in a religion where prosperity, safety and the peace of the world is an essential part, wars and conflicts are just accidental, out of the

---

[298] "Dialogue among Civilizations," United Nations, New York, 5 September 2000, *http://www.unesco.org/dialogue/en/picco2.htm*

norm. Islam has taken the war as an incidental event caused by the human nature, and in order to offset the balance, it decreed some regulations and limited it. For instance, by commanding, "Your hatred for a group of people should not keep you away from justice and fairness," Islam established principles of justice and the peace of the world; it has built a principled front of defense by stipulating that the protection of religion, life, property, reproduction, and the mind is a legitimate right which is also accepted by the modern systems of law as basic rights.

As against this, while from the outset the Christianity was established purely as an abstract religion of love, in the matter of war which is a human reality, it did not set any determined rules. As it could not prevent the world wars, hundred-year wars, and many others, including the Nagasaki and Hiroshima, what is more, it in fact contributed to facilitate these wars manifesting themselves in their savagery, and catastrophic, bloody and violent. Yes, the Western history has been a history of wars, starting with the Muta and Yarmuk at the inception of Islam, continuing with the Crusaders and the wars in the following centuries against Islam and even the wars within itself. The perspectives of Huntington and the people like him are the product of the same mentality, and reflect the same psychological state.

We, with the grace and blessings of God, shall do everything within our means to continue the breeze of dialog and tolerance which started these days and promise a capability to spread to the rest of the world. God willing, we are going to disprove all the pundits in their predictions of the future. We believe that these winds of peace have enough power to overcome many deadly weapons, mechanized divisions and many other negative effects. This fresh message, the plan of which goes back well into the past, being exposed in every sector of the society and staged for everyone to see, is a divine complement for the heroes of love in our days. For this reason, we are saying that tolerance and dialog have to be represented in the best possible ways in our country and in this matter it should be an example, by any means possible. With the grace of God, if Asia is revived in this matter, it must not be an imaginary fantasy for the whole world to group around it. This would cause not the clash but the religions based on divine sources coming together around these foundations, and humanity, if God wills, is going to experience a new and a blessed spring, one more time.[299]

In this matter, the role that Gülen appropriates and assumes for himself is thus:

---

[299] Gülen 2008d, 231–232.

The thing which gives this poor man the love to orient himself to dialog at the world scale is benevolence and beauty which are inherent in the nature of man himself. My belief and my hope is complete that the humanity, whose ferment consists of goodness and kindness, one day will augment that ferment and will be forced by that ferment to come to the preordained line. I believe that at this moment, the humanity, who is tired of wars, conflicts, bloods shed, the oppressions committed, is ready for a universal dialog and peace, and the conjuncture is appropriate for such a dialog, and for such a blessed aim we are exactly at that proper point, if we do not take a wrong step.

It is obvious that nothing positive could be done by enmity, on a ground of fighting, and always taking a pasture against agenda of others, and acting in reaction. Because of that, in our days when the common civilizational values came to the fore, at least as a goal, one can resolve the issues by speaking to others. This means dialog. There is a truth, which was always prevalent among us but which the world had discovered only after the collapse of the iron curtain that in the next century religion shall have a dominant voice in the world affairs. This is a natural goal the humanity is marching toward. At this moment Islam and the Christianity are the two religions the adherents of which are the largest. Buddhism and Hinduism have also a lot of adherents. The Judaism, although appears small in terms of its numbers, is effective. Therefore, today it stands out as an apparent fact that the universal revival, peace, and prosperity of the world will have to go through a dialog, based on the common points between these religions.

We are not doubtful about our values, and as we are not asking anyone to join us, no one has it in their mind to offer us the same. From now on, the conquest of the hearts and minds, intermingling through mutual love and respect will follow. This is the real conquest, not gaining land. Now with this sentiment, our meeting with the Pope was only natural. ...

In no period of history, there was such an easy rapprochement; people of the world had a chance to coalesce with each other, to mutually accept each other. This shows that our hope is not unfounded. Political passions and historical animosities are taking place mostly in terms of quarreling on the worldly interests. We have never been in a fight to share the blessings of this world. We have no eyes set upon anything worldly, therefore we do not have to compete with anyone for anything, and we cannot oppose anyone. As for the rewards in the hereafter, they are like "light," they are spiritual, and therefore they cannot ever diminish by sharing. Six billion people benefit from the Sun, and one's benefit from it does not prevent someone else to do the same. The spiritual gains are similar. Therefore, those who act today with political passions, will realize that we do not have the slightest worldly expectations; and, God willing, the fact

that the political narrow passions do not benefit anyone will be comprehended; the real wealth will be discovered.[300]

56. Have Muslim societies succeed in coping with the challenges of globalization? If not, why?

According to Gülen, the answer to this question is very clear. The Muslim countries were caught unprepared with globalization and could not
respond to it effectively. One dimension of this weakness was structural
problems and not being developed sufficiently. The other dimension was
the ineffectiveness of the Muslim intellectuals in their duty of pioneering
and guidance.

To the question, "In the Islamic world, why haven't sufficient number
of intellectuals or the intellectual movements did not arise?" Gülen begins
with a definition of "intellectual":

> ... Intellectuals ... are aware and knowledgeable about their own existence
> and able to interpret and understand the creation correctly. ... [They] are
> aware of the time in which they live and ready to question it and able to
> voice with no hesitation what they know.[301]

Gülen accepts the fact that there are a few intellectuals in the Islamic
world who fit this definition; later, he elaborates more on his view:

> ... This standstill of development is not something unique to the Islamic
> world. There have been many nations throughout history whose yester-
> day was very bright, and whose today is dull. This is like the destiny of all
> nations; history repeats itself. Various civilizations and nations have such
> a destiny; similar to a flaming fire that is extinguished, or resembling
> equipment that becomes dusty and obsolete, or a human who is born,
> grows old and then dies. One can try to renew them in order to extend
> their life, however this can be very costly.[302]

Gülen suggests that Muslim countries are having difficulty in understanding the spirit of the age and in renewing themselves. He explains
why:

---

[300] The interview given to *Aksiyon* magazine, 14 February 1998.
[301] Sarıtoprak and Ünal 2005, 458.
[302] *Ibid.,* 459.

... There are three fundamentals of the Islamic spirit. The abandonment of any one of these fundamentals to a certain extent will paralyze the other dynamics. These fundamentals can be summarized as follows: Firstly, interpreting the religious sciences that draw from the Qur'an and the *Sunnah* in accordance with the understanding of the century, as was the case in the early period of Islam or the era of *Tadwin* [recording tradition]. Secondly, as we read the holy Qur'an, as derived from God's attribute of *Kalam* [speech], we should also read the book of the Universe and the divine laws found in nature, which come from God's attributes of *Qudrah* [power] and *Iradah* [will]. Thirdly, we ought to keep a balance between matter and the immaterial, body and spirit, this world and the hereafter, and the physical and metaphysical. One should be equally open to each of these.[303]

According to Gülen, these three basic fundamental principles were either neglected completely or partially, and Islamic countries lost the skill and capability to read the spirit of the age and the philosophical depth and, therefore, have fallen behind in the civilizational race. In this regard, he states,

> In a world where reason is abandoned, the heart has been ignored, and the love for truth and longing for knowledge has been extinguished, it is not possible to even speak of elite or intellectual humans.[304]

To the view that countries deprived of intellectual leadership fall behind, Gülen adds the blinding impact of wealth and power:

> ... Similar to the modern day West, the Islamic world experienced a great period of enlightenment. There were positives of the period, but when vital dynamics were neglected, there were no doubt negatives as well. In some cases, plentiful material possessions caused the laziness of people, industrial systems skewed people's sense of reality, victories and successes drove the people's passions for life, and extreme frivolity led to a decadent lifestyle. In a context where such an oppressive atmosphere is dominant, the intellectual cannot emerge.[305]

He adds that technology, which determines our age, came into existence outside the Islamic world:

---

303   *Ibid.*
304   *Ibid.*
305   *Ibid.*

... Today's positive sciences essentially and methodologically are not based merely on the search, experience, and analysis of Muslim scholars. Methodologically speaking, in our modern days, sciences are based on positivism, naturalism, and rationalism in the Western sense. In the world of sciences, all research and analysis are under the control of a certain understanding. This will continue until new geniuses emerge to reinterpret the world or the creation and to analyze and re-establish it within the filter of their own thoughts.[306]

Therefore, as long as the Muslim countries do not make their own contributions to modern science and technology, they will change and develop at a pace determined by the West and bound by its rules and regulations. As this separates them from their core essence, it deprives them of the capability to impact global processes.

57. In order to transcend the inertia or, in Gülen's words "freeze," that we are observing in the Islamic world, is Ijtihad appropriate?

The word *Ijtihad*, independent reasoning, literally means "to use all your power and effort in order to bring some hard and difficult works into existence." In Islamic terminology, the word means "to use all your power to deduct some hypothetical judicial decisions from the clear sources [*adilla-i tafsiliyyah*] of Islamic law." The one who makes this effort is called a *Mujtahid*. The issue in which these efforts are made is called *Mujtahadun fih*.

In principle, there are two conditions for *Ijtihad*. First, one must know the sources of Islamic law related to legal judgments [*ahkam*]. Second, the *Ijtihad* should be done by those who are able to penetrate into the spirit of the sources through their intelligence and the logic of religious law. Any *Ijtihad* that comes from an eligible person and is done within an appropriate case is valid.

Moreover, *Ijdihad* is not limited to analogy [*qiyas*]. It can be done through analogy as well as through the indications, clues, and the hints of the legal texts. It is also possible to deduce legal judgments from the linguistic aspects of the Qur'an and the *Sunnah*, including Arabic rhetoric dealing with metaphorical language and literary figures.[307]

According to Gülen, it is also necessary:

Islam, being the last and universal religion, is the epitome of solutions to the problems of humans for all time and for all locations. These solutions

---

[306] *Ibid.*
[307] *Ibid.*, 460.

are based on the limited texts of the Qur'an and the *Sunnah*, which address the unlimited problems of humans. This blessed activity started in the era of the Prophet and developed in the 3rd and 4th centuries under the names of *ijtihad*, *ra'y* [subjective legal opinion], *istidlal* [inference], *qiyas* [analogy], and *istinbat* [deduction]. It has remained alive within the practice of the dynamic systems of Islam and has been highly fruitful.[308]

Gülen believes that *ijtihad* is an essential vehicle through which religious regulations, rules, precepts, and the interpretations derived from the legitimate sources provide the flexibility for Muslim societies to adapt to change, maintain their dynamisms, and meet new needs. Indeed, after Muslim societies lost this dynamic vehicle of change and the flexibility it provided, the decline and the "freeze in time" began:

> This rich and original legal culture, unique to the Islamic world, has been fading for reasons such as exclusion of the active Islamic system of life from the public sphere, the absence of active minds similar to those of the early period of Islam, the lack of inspired spirits, and deficiency of superior intellects, knowledgeable of the Qur'an and the *Sunnah*. There are some who lack reasoning with insufficient intelligence, and are very behind in their knowledge of the Qur'an and *Sunnah*, and closed to inspiration. Since these types of people have risen to power in religious circles, the fertile institution of *ijtihad* has been replaced by unquestioning adoption [*taqlid*] memorization, and copying.[309]

Gülen points to other factors which led to the closing of the door of *ijtihad*:

> ... political oppression, inner struggles, the misuse of the institution of *ijtihad*, an extreme trust in the present legal system, the denial of reform, the blindness caused by the dominant monotonous present system of the time. All of these are among the reasons for this loss. Furthermore, the believers who were eligible to perform *ijtihad* based on their intelligence and abilities were at times included mistakenly among the groups of heretics who misused *ijtihad*.[310]

While he regrets the closure of the door of *ijtihad* for limiting change and renewal, he nevertheless notes that, even if unintended, it might be a blessing in disguise:

---

[308] *Ibid.*
[309] *Ibid.*, 460–461.
[310] *Ibid.*, 461.

The door, in fact, has never been closed by anyone. However, some *ulama* had the inclination to close the door of *ijtihad* against those who would like to promote their own desires and interpretations as guidance. The door was closed automatically in the face of those who were not eligible to make *ijtihad*. As long as society does not have quality scholars who can perform *ijtihad*, it is not possible to ignore the argument of those who are against *ijtihad*. ...

Despite all of this mentioned above, there has been a great revival of religion and religiosity in the Islamic world today. I hope—God willing— this development will result in the rise of those who are eligible to open the door of *ijtihad* in the near future.[311]

When asked directly, "Are you a *mujtahid*?" Gülen smiles and answers with a sense of humor: "No, I am not, but when I see one, I would recognize one from his eyes."

Gülen argues that the time has arrived for Muslim societies with their scholars, thinkers, and theologians to interpret the world and themselves outside the paradigms and categories of Western thought. He believes that *ijtihad*, made operational again, will generate new syntheses and movement of thoughts:

It is my conviction that when the proper season comes, such gushing spirit and ingenious intellect will compose groups comprised of specialists in their fields with an utmost sense of responsibility to undertake *ijtihad*. I hope that through such consultation, these groups will bridge the gap that has been generated since the loss of the spirit of *ijtihad*.[312]

58. Is the Islamic world unstable and backward because it forgot the humane, unifying essence of religion, and made religion subordinate to politics?

While answering this question, it was obvious that Gülen was unhappy to hear the negative state of affairs implied in the question. After mentioning that the first things that came to his mind were the "lack of faith" and the "narrowness of a vision," he added:

Islamic world, since its inception, in no period of history, has gone through as miserable time as it does now, and as far as I know, never was left behind its vision. Even worse, it is not even capable of assessing the size of

---

[311] *Ibid.*
[312] *Ibid.*

the gap between the miserable places where it stands now and where it should be. Despite that fact, it is as comfortable as it could be; it has neither an intellectual pain nor a constructive idea nor an intention nor an anxiousness which comes from the bottom of its heart. In terms of its tomorrow, with the exception of base desires it has neither a worry nor an ideal. Sometimes it serves the oppressors, sometimes a modern beggar, sometimes trembling in the hands of poverty and sometimes crawling with ignorance and fanaticism.

The religion of Islam commands its adherents to be virtuous to lead a life of honor, to be open to science, to read the existence correctly, to investigate the universe inside out and the things in it, to be creative in the worldly and religious arena and to interpret it in the ... most perfect manner. But who ... cares?

As we look at the power and richness of Islamic dynamics, one would like to see cities developed in every sense of the word, the settlement places as if they were projections of Paradise, villages, towns, happy and hopeful people, searching spirits burning for the love of truth, people coming and going between laboratories and the books. But how painful it is that what is being observed is just the opposite of what is to be seen! Nowadays, in this geography, it is not possible to see a dozen of intellectuals who would be the counterpart of those of sometime in the past who succeeded the development of the entire planet, nor a few apprentices who would repair broken parts of our ruin.

Whereas what was expected is that the adherents of this religion with its faith, decisiveness, determination and the projects for the future, to be in a mold to be able to guide the whole world, and to solve the problems of our day. We would expect that when justice, the superiority of law, the freedom of faith and thoughts, in everybody's imagination this world should appear. But is that the case now? No, Alas! Justice is like a commodity to have an eye on. The law is under the guidance of brute force and its power is a vehicle of oppression and molestation to oppress the weak; freedom, equality, brotherhood are the unknowns, we are yet fortunate enough to see. The respect for human and the humane values are the gilded topics of the conferences and panels which never have seen the light of day.[313]

Gülen attributes these negative things to the lack of political and social leaders at the top and the psychological state of defeat at the bottom. He attributes the lack of moving and embracing leadership to the lack of political and legal identity which should accommodate everyone. He relates the debates over the constitution and our inability to make a

---

[313] Gülen 2010b, 45–47.

new constitution, which all could accept, to the fact that we cannot agree on the common denominators in order to produce common values that would serve that purpose. He draws our attention to our inability to become a nation that represents all individuals and the society-in-general, but we live as parallel communities with its drawbacks:

> It is another reality that we are very behind in science and technology, in art and trade. Our esteem in the world is something like that. As against all these negatives, I wish we were at least in harmony inside. Alas! On top of that we are the ones who produce so much negativity: hate, grudge, to blacken others and establish all the plans on the basis of animosity. For so many years now, we always established fronts against each other in enmity, we invented artificial enmities and artificial threats; we seat the masses pitted against each other. And we made the blessed geography of the old into the valley land of ghosts.[314]

Gülen accuses the administration and political movements of having a narrow view; they do not see the Turkish people as a whole, but treat cultural differences as an excuse to discriminate and to establish privileges for themselves. They have divided the populace officially into two categories, "accepted" and "fearful" and treated them differently. In doing so, they injured justice. They did not attach significance to the superiority of law and opened the door of arbitrariness constantly; they generated the influence of authoritarian tendencies in politics. We observed with amazement how the seeds of hypocrisy were planted for the mere desire of not losing control of the central authority, and, hence, in order to prevent various societal segments from coming together to demand a more democratic regime.

The central authority did not only stay at an equal distance from the political and legal values which would unify the people, but also stayed at a distance from the faith-values, preventing democracy to develop. The belief in the threat, likely to come from religious and cultural demands, led to neither religion becoming in conformity with social change nor the establishment of a regime of plurality.

Today, the feeling of defeat in the society is sustained by the authority, which prevents the individual to develop. It also points to the determining and orienting impact of the West, which is ahead in terms of eco-

---

[314] *Ibid.,* 47.

nomical, technological, and legal developments on societal processes. The sense of siege and helplessness, as a result of this situation, often gives way to violent and extreme reactions:

> In the face of all these things taking place, who knows many, saying, "No longer any good can come out of this world, the future will be worse than this!" goes and sinks into the swamp of hopelessness; many are losing the hope to live for living. When everyone ventures to establish a world, according to one's own whims and whishes, they are in a position to demolish everything they see opposed to their criteria. That for the last one or two centuries, in this unfortunate geography, these things are working out in this way.[315]

Gülen refers to a line of Mehmet Akif Ersoy, the poet of the Turkish National Anthem, "The wretched fellow religionists who kill in the name of *ghaza* (war)."

Although he does not in any way condone the reactions loaded with violence seen everywhere in the world against this sense of siege, to prevent these reactions by viewing with doubt all the positive services in the name of ethics and morality and register those who undertake these activities in the black book is not the answer. Those who see everyone as a rebel, the tyrants and their so-called "yes" men, somehow never see the miserable, heart-bleeding situation of the world or they pretend not to see. He adds:

> Whereas, in this geography there is an inertia causing for concern; for centuries now, the minds are not producing anything, the power resources are idle; the sights capture everywhere the helplessness of the powerless and the jobless.[316]

From the picture he has drawn, Gülen believes that it would be impossible to derive unity, peace, and stability, and the only remedy to overcome this would be to agree on the common human values and make these values as the foundation of a new legal and ethical system. Later, he remarks that the leadership in the Islamic world is weak, and the opinion makers are lazy in recognizing the realities of the world. The faith, the thought, and the creative moves to direct and orient the societies, are prevented by the establishment and their dominant powers. As a

---

[315] *Ibid.*, 48.
[316] *Ibid.*

result, Islamic societies are deprived of the level of power and strength to contribute anything to modern civilization:

> How interesting it is! Although that exalted Prophet advices his *Ummah*, through hundreds of verses and *hadiths*, to seek knowledge and wisdom and insists on them constantly, for several centuries now, Muslims could not understand and comprehend them, they were always closed to the knowledge, skill, comprehension, and art; beyond being closed, they became so shallow in terms of thinking and research; became static and left everything go as it may, a time came when even coming under the tutelage of others did not wake them up, ... by waking up, they could not see what was happening around them.[317]

Where then is the salvation? How can this dark picture be illuminated? The *raison d'être* and the mission it arrogated to itself, is in the answer to this question:

> In this dark geography, we do not need anything else, but only to reawaken the love of truth, the love of knowledge and research, and letting the consciences hear one more time the religion in its original, purified form.
>
> Those who would save at this moment, this world from the terrible hole it is thrown into, are the minds who are raised with our own discipline and training, the souls devoted to God, sharing the same faith and the same goals; those heroes of will who run to the service of others without any hatred or rancor and determined to overcome every obstacle laying in front of them. They are the heroes of knowledge, skill, and determination, without expecting anything in return. Up until today, we have lived always with the hope of their arrival. We intend to do the same until eternity.[318]

In summary, Gülen dreams of a society in which the individuals consist of those whose souls are trained with Islamic ethics and morality—namely, those who do not steal, deceive, do not expand the gap of inequality through the habit of consumption, do not decay the administration through corruption, do not see the different as the enemy, and who are hard working, sharing, just, fair, and have not closed the door to innovations). Their minds are shaped with the discipline of science, researching and constantly searching after discoveries. With these attributes, they would contribute to the modern civilization and raise the development level of the society. His dream has led to a global organization. Seeing this,

---

[317] *Ibid.*, 50–51.
[318] *Ibid.*, 51.

while he is still alive is a sign that his preferences and the principles that he had adopted are in conformity with the expectations of people around the world. The Gülen Movement, which is the movement of volunteers, has come together, neither through legal enactments nor force nor as a political necessity.

Its expansion and development, despite all the pressure, can be attributed to the fact that people belonging to different sectors of society have found useful and beneficial things in what Gülen offers and advises, s which also result in positive developments in their own lives.

59. What is the reason which leaves the Israeli–Palestinian conflict at an impasse? What does Gülen think should be done?

Gülen proposes that this matter should not be handled by the super powers, as "big brothers." This method has not worked so far, since the countries involved are not sufficiently impartial. In his opinion, the United Nations should enter into the process and both sides should agree on the common denominators. For instance, they should abide by the rules delineated in Oslo and the like. More importantly, they should implement them without delay. In his opinion, the Israeli–Palestinian conflict is political and not a religious one; and therefore, the solutions lie in setting up canons acceptable to both sides and proceeding with negotiations based on these canons.

Additionally, he believes that another reason the conflict has remained without a solution is that it is no longer a bilateral matter between those two, but that of the whole region, and even that of the world. Another dimension of the issue is that the struggle is retained by taking it into the religious field; in the process, the essence of religion has been lost:

> Frankly, I view most of the activities carried out by some organizations in Palestine, and attributed to Islam, with doubt. Especially, it is a known fact how wavering activities the Palestine Liberation Organization is committing since the outset. Therefore, I am not sure the struggle along this line has gained or will gain anything for Palestine. Another thing: The matter should not be viewed as if it was a religious issue, because in this kind of a setting, the religion might be misunderstood and become an instrument of faulty causes. Second, religion should serve the peace in the region as well as in the world. We should not neglect the psychological dimension of the

matter. Namely, the land on which the struggle is going on is sacred for all the Muslims, Jews, and Christians.

In history, this region had been the area of *irshad* for many Prophets. Though majority of these Prophets were sent from among the children of Israel, it is the obligation of being a Muslim to believe in all Prophets, including them. Muslims as well as the Christians and the Jews accept these Prophets. Beyond this, the basic common points among Muslims, Christians, and Jews are not less than the points on which they argue. For this reason, when such togetherness, concentric and overlapping, requires living together, unfortunately some political factors give way to conflicts. Therefore, the Israeli–Palestinian conflict should be resolved in such a way that it should be handled through the framework of international law, and it should guarantee the basic human rights, freedoms, and security to satisfy all parties.[319]

60. How do you see the integration with European Union? What kind of meaning and importance, the idea of "Turkish identity of Islam," will gain in relation to European Union and Turkey becoming part of the world?

Gülen remarks that he finds it important for the European Union to be in negotiations for the first time with a Muslim country, in terms of Europe's identity and its vision:

> Regarding the EU, mostly the gains of Turkey has been talked about. I do not know if the European countries are aware of it, but what Turkey would bring to the EU is very important. If being aware of it, they are insisting on their course, it means their obstinacy is ahead of their sound thinking. In fact, for Europe, in this relationship there are a lot of gains, in terms of its future and its credit and esteem.
>
> Our intellectuals are after Europeanization for a long time now. We are in the process of Europeanization starting with Tanzimat which gained speed during the republican era. As is known, the first serious agreement was signed in 1963. Afterwards, there were conferences pro and con. Some very serious people that I listened to in 1966 and 1967 raised their objections to it. Their ideas are overlapping with what the people who are anti-Europe now are saying: "It is a Christian club, they are playing a game with us, and they would Christianize us."
>
> Today, some Muslims have written books and they have distributed them. They say: "If they come, they would have their impact on our youth,

---

[319] Interview with Fethullah Gülen, *Kenya Daily Nation*, 30 July 2004.

with their appearance, religious conceptions, understanding of God." Maybe, the Europeans had concerns about our poverty, and us being Muslims. Maybe, they did not have complete trust in the values of their religion, but they were not revealing them to outside. I would not know if they carry the same concerns, today. But it is obvious that up until now, they did not want to accept us.[320]

After this point, Gülen takes his analysis to a sociological dimension:

The Turkish community in Germany that they thought would be assimilated have maintained both its existence and also it came to itself after two or three generations. While it was a community under the impact of others then, now it has begun to be an influential community. We have seen at several occasions, we are listening to people, compared to other Muslim communities, both in Europe and in the USA; there is a warm interest in the Turkish community. They find the Turks softer, compared to other Muslims. Maybe from the perspective of democracy, republic, and secularism, it is easier for them to view it with a more positive attitude; these are the comforting aspect of our society for them. Turkish Islamic identity is pronounced more in the USA and Europe than it is in Turkey.[321]

Regarding the slow progress of joining the EU as a full member, Gülen comments:

Shall we join the EU or when shall we? Even though these are ambiguous at the moment, giving a date to review has had a psychological effect on the Turkish society. This appears as an achievement of the current government. Of course, there might be some aspects to be criticized, but thinking that they might be taken as a political deliberation on a political subject, I would rather avoid it. In reality, the Europeans should consider this as good news; they should have great interest in it, more than we consider we had received good news, in terms of membership in the EU.

It is because there are other powers which would like to have influence in the regions that the Europeans are interested. The Chinese entered into these areas long time ago, in virtue of their power of competition and the soft manner of their behavior. Neither the Europeans nor the Americans can compete with them. It is for certain that in the future there will be serious revolutions in the economic field.

Now, at exactly this point, Turkey can act as a bridge between Europe and the Far East. Europe needs a Turkey which has a deep and rich historical experience about the Middle East. They accepted Cyprus into the EU, but they

---

[320] Gündem 2005, 3–4.
[321] *Ibid.*, 4.

should have been able to understand Turkey was more important than Cyprus. Another aspect of the matter is that even if those at the head of the current administrations are unable to appreciate, when we come down to the level of the public, we would see that they have an enormous interest in and sympathy for Turkey, with its history, the psychological effect it has on the society, and the extraordinary credit it has. This is so in terms of our past and in terms of current times as we are ruled by a republic and under a democracy. In various countries where the educational activities are undertaken, we witness this clearly. Therefore, only if the EU wins over Turkey, it can become a power in the region.

The USA, too, would like to retain its domination in our region. Its administrators appear to support the membership of Turkey in the EU, as far as it is reflected in the mass media. The USA which wants to retain its domination in the region, would not want to lose an ally like Turkey or Turkey to take its place in another power network somewhere else.[322]

Gülen, when assessing the relationships between Turkey and the EU, does not want to see his country in this or that block, but wants to see it with many dimensions in the global system. He sees Turkey among the powers to have weight in the balance of power in the world or even as one of the powers to maintain that balance:

Turkey has a special history, national and religious values, as well as being a country bringing forth its own interpretations in the religious life. When considered from the perspective of the fundamentals of Islam, it is again seen, to a great extent, as a country which brings to the fore its own interpretations. Therefore, Turkey would have an inclination towards those who are closer to itself in interpretation of sentiments, thoughts, logic, philosophy, and life. Whoever has common values and interests with it, it would have some various great projects to accomplish with them. These are very important from the perspective of the international relations; but this truth does not constitute a barrier for it to enter the EU, and to develop certain projects with the Europeans.[323]

Gülen draws a vision greater than EU membership or even larger than any kind of membership of an alliance.

We should look at the horizon and we should see certain things more clearly. For instance, as we have to admire the things they produced in the fields of science, technique, art and civilization, and put them as a crown on

---

[322]   *Ibid.*, 5–6.
[323]   *Ibid.*, 74.

our heads, we have to see also that Europe has aged, and even the USA has grown a little old. Even if they seem today like a shining Sun, this Sun is very close to setting. Turkey, on the other hand is a country where the signs of dawn appears on its horizon, is a country experiencing a revival, a young and a dynamic country. We should not look at the dazzling brightness of them now, but at the things likely to shine in the future.

Turkey is more promising for the future. I am not saying these things on the top of my head. There is a Turkish reality, and it would not be possible to race with us in the future. We fell so many times, but we recovered each time. These days, the passion for searching is awakened and we are going through brainstorms now. Therefore, our state of affairs at the present time necessitates new searches, not a blindness by the system. If it can make good use of the dynamics at its disposal, Turkey would certainly take its place in the international balance of power that it deserves. However, the fact that it needs time, it cannot be done on the spur of the moment, should not be overlooked. Some day this nation would, for sure, display its own character. As the poet says, "Closed my eyes, I am gazing at such a Turkey.[324]

Gülen notes that a country which does not change in response to a changing world would be out of development and the balance of power:

It is a very important issue to determine the national course. Our relations with the national sentiment, thought, tradition, convention, the Book, the *Sunnah* and the religion are reserved. But it is also a reality that our national sentiments and thoughts are not in harmony with the needs of the age and are incapable of producing sufficient motivation where everything is changing. Of course, it is vital to keep our essence, our color, and identity, but would it be necessary also to develop different policies with various nations in the world; which is being globalized? We have to be open to the change experienced in the fields of science and technology. But unfortunately up until today, a period of interregnum was experienced in this area. Things like common heritage of humanity and the globalization were not thought out sufficiently.

Our dynamics should be reviewed one more time again and should be appropriated by the society. By adding the things promised by this new age, the richness and the inputs of the age to this business, as it is often stated in many parts of Anatolia, there is a need for the revival of the notion, "If everyone brings and pitch in from the things cooked at home, a rich table can be prepared." Of course, some time is needed for this, because acceptance is important. Just like the religions, this kind of an idea takes a long time to be

---

[324] *Ibid.*

accepted. ... The issues should be reviewed again, from the point of view of the modern conditions, and should explain well.[325]

Gülen believes, only through this integration, we can agree on the common denominators with people inside the country, as well as with the rest of humanity. In this respect, he believes that the differences are not barriers for a shared living, "Yes, despite all these differences, I carry the conviction that there will be no conflicts."

He believes that humanity and the nations have an obligation to share their accumulated knowledge and wealth with others—and from here a new type of relationship will arise, based on solidarity and justice. But, he says that this process will take time. Gülen is optimistic; he looks forward to the future positively. But at the same time, he is cautionary and patient:

> Because in some sense, we are face to face with the age to settle the accounts with it, embrace it, and then accept it. It would be more proper to leave certain things to the commentary of time, as long as this process we are in is accepted with its own peculiar features. Let there be no hurry and let there be a lot of efforts with regard to determining the course, and its nature.[326]

Gülen is offering, not to sit back and wait passively, but to understand the age and to meet the future under the best circumstances. Therefore, he is not afraid of the future and the change. On the contrary, he is advising people that with their personal talents and skills, as well as the flexible laws and institutions of societies, they should be ready to meet the challenge of the future. Unlike many opinion makers, he is not hesitant and closed to the outside world, in the face of change. For instance, while the politicians, and some other sectors influenced by them, remain at a distance with respect to joining the EU, he states:

> There is no reason for objection to unification with the Westerners and the Western thought, on certain necessary points. This is inevitable, anyway. So, that means in the nature of humans there is an inclination towards always seeking the good and the beautiful. If we have found our true self, the things we would be taking from them can only be good and

---

[325] "İslam ve Dogmatizm" (Islam and Dogmatism), *http://tr.fgulen.com/content/view/7860/15/*

[326] *Ibid.*

beautiful things. And there are many good things to be taken from the West. Mehmet Akif had expressed it succinctly: "Take the science of the West." Bediüzzaman has similar approaches. In this sense, I do not see any objection to be raised to becoming "Western."[327]

Gülen does not see the widespread animosity observed in the Islamic world towards the West as reasonable or beneficial:

I think, in the absolute sense [restricted and unconditional] the animosity toward the West would push us to a point to lose touch with the age. And you would be eliminated over time'. There remains the fact that, they did not hesitate to borrow from us what they thought they needed. Those who read little history of science would submit that before the renaissance occurred in the West, in a real sense, a Renaissance took place in Asia in the 5th century AH Al-Birunis, Al-Khawarizmis, Ibn Sinas [Avicennas] ... in Andalusia, in Asia to the extent that their voices were heard all around, they had become the breath of a great civilization. And again, according to many historians of science, the foundations of the Renaissance in Europe were laid in Asia. Some conservatives of the Westerners had adopted the names [of the sources] by distorting them. For instance, Al-Jabir was called El Gabir. The conscientious Western authors have acknowledged this. In my opinion, there can be no objection to take back from the Westerners what they borrowed earlier from us. We can take these matters and further advance them.[328]

When asked what role Turkey can play, he answers:

We are a new force. ... If we deliberate it with the methods of the sociologists and the social historians, out of 20 civilizations, people like ourselves, who came from behind, had established seventeen of them. In a sense ... without plunging into dogmatism, without being entangled with or being bound by the restrictions others set. We can form very original, different compositions. It seems that the dynamics for this is being prepared. Asia for a while was segmented completely; Uzbekistan, Kazakhstan, Georgia, and Eastern Turkistan ... All of them opened up to other civilizations under the influence of various cultures. In my opinion, the depths of thoughts dug by the rivers of these thoughts ... would take us to great visions. A rich culture, an unshakable civilization, these dynamics at the present is all promising such a result.[329]

---

[327] *Ibid.*

[328] *Ibid.*

[329] *Ibid.*

Gülen, who places a great deal of emphasis on the relationship with the East, does not ignore the West:

> It is inescapable for the Turkish people to integrate with the West in this age we are living in. I am convinced that if Turkey enters into this business, by reviewing one more time on this way with its own reasoning, logic, its own dynamics, and its own values, we are not going to lose anything. ... I have no concern about it at all. ... Let us leave it to Europe and the USA to be concerned about it. In some areas, like in sentiments, thoughts and understanding, we are at a point to export them. I see the West like an old woman who offered already whatever she could. Neither it can give birth to anything nor can it be implanted with anything new.
>
> If we reverse the situation, Turkish people, in terms of recent history of four centuries, is like a single person who never married, remaining virgin with its men and women, heart and mind, being capable of both giving birth or susceptible to implantation. The other side is also able to inoculate. Everything inoculated will be healthy and many kinds of thoughts will be born out of it. I believe that everything we would say and every thought we would display is still virgin. There are things that they in the West cannot find the counterparts for our terminology. It may seem to be simple, but when they go through the books belonging to us, and when we peruse them, a lot is to be found without the counterparts, they cannot render them.
>
> From out of our creativeness and productivity, a lot of things will be spilled over around. You may take it as a joke, but I have the conviction that it is true. Leave those alone, who do not believe, let them think that this is a dream or fantasy. I know that with the dynamics at hand, God will help us to make this dream come true. For this reason, I have no concern about the West. But there remains the fact that we have to review "living" with all its components. We have to revive the vital institutions that we can properly call ours so that this process, represented by our people ... can travel at a safe pace and strong steps, and jump to a higher stage.[330]

Although not explicitly stated, Gülen here is talking about the systematization of a thought which makes up the mortar of a formation, known as the "Gülen Movement." He is giving the good news that our society is distilled from its history and culture; it has a new philosophy which can fill the vacuum, vacated by the concepts of morality and humanism of the Western civilization, which can no longer comprehend the human in all its wholeness. He is so confident of it that he says:

---

[330] *Ibid.*

In the years ahead, we are going to run the long way in the international marathon, we are going to reach the finish line first in the Olympiads from science to art, from sports to culture. There may be some who might find what I am saying as empty talk. The sociologists, psychologists, the philosophers and the history writers might criticize them.[331]

61. Will the political differences between the U.S. and Europe lead to fracture between these two powers? Does Gülen believe they can reconcile their differences?

Gülen responds:

At this moment, they seem to be reconciled. As long as they are reconciled, it seems that the relationships between them will go on without any problem, but if their interests clash with each other, it is not that they are not giving from to time, the signs that they might go separate ways. In the future, only the circumstances would determine the matter.[332]

With respect to the USA's place and dominant status, he states,

The USA, with the power and status it has right now, could command the whole world. All the things to be done in the world could be directed from here. If the Americans do not wish, they would not allow anywhere in the world anything to be done. The USA is still the name of the nation which sits at the steering wheel of the world. Just like every individual, there is a lifespan for each nation; there is a hole into which it would fall down. The USA cannot be exempt from it, it cannot avoid it. But it has a democratic system, from the time it begins to decline; it would collapse in 25 to 30, or 40 years. Because the collapse of democracies is very slow like a feather falling down onto the ground due to gravitation. In despotic administrations like Russia, it is like the explosion of a propane tank, it takes place at any given moment. It is the consequence of the system. Because of that, the USA will play its role in the destiny of the world for a long time to come. This reality has to be accepted. No one should venture into any work here or there by ignoring the USA. Russia might support something, but if you do not get along with the USA well, they would spoil it. The USA would want its own affairs to go on in harmony; it would wish its own order not to be broken. It would want the harmony to continue and be permanent. And this would not be a

---

[331] *Ibid.*

[332] Doğu Ergil's interview with Gülen.

surprise for me. If the Ottoman Empire were in the place of the USA, it would have done the same thing. We should not view it as strange.[333]

62. Is the anti-Americanism prevalent in Turkey and throughout the world directed against the American public or the government?

Concerning hostility against the USA, which has increased lately, especially the intensive anti-Americanism observed in Turkey, Gülen advises moderation: "Hostility against nations, against people is not something which brings much benefit." But he interprets the reaction displayed against the USA as a sentiment felt against the foreign policy of that country and the administration. He adds: "I do not believe in the existence of any problem between the peoples of the respective countries."[334]

When the events of the past few years are recollected, Gülen's statements become even more meaningful. When the USA applied a weapons embargo against Turkey in 1974, as a reaction to the Turkish government landing at Cyprus, with the rising leftist thoughts in Turkey, the public's anti-imperialist reaction increased. The Islamic movements also were taking hold in the country. This psychology in the society was further sharpened through the belief that the United States protected Israel and the grave injustices committed against the Palestinians. But the real break off point came by the "Hammer Force" operations in 1990s, first by limiting the influence of Saddam Hussein's government in the Iraqi-Kurdish area and then preparing a setting for an autonomous Kurdish administration by occupying Iraq. Turkey was struggling against terrorism, as it was unable to solve the problem of ethnic Kurdish separatism. Now was added another problem from abroad: dealing with the problem of Northern Iraq which really constituted the nucleus of a future "Greater Kurdistan."

Turkey had a great difficulty in accepting this reality first, and it acquired a concern that these developments would lead to fragmentation. In this milieu, the anti-Americanism in Turkey increased more than what it was in many Arab countries. After Barrack Obama became President, the sense of anti-Americanism has diminished somewhat, but it is

---

[333] Sevindi 2002, 100.
[334] *Ibid.*

still too high. All of these are directly related to the foreign policy of the United States and the way in which the Turks perceive this policy.

63. What is Gülen's view on the "Greater Middle East Project?" Is this project feasible to implement or have the developments in Iraq forced the project to be shelved for now?

Greater Middle East Project was an issue which kept the world busy in recent past, and one of the issues the most talked about. But, the history of the project goes back to 70s. In the past, similar projects were developed and implemented. For instance, in some period in recent history in order to get rid of, and erase from the face of the region, the Sublime State [the Ottoman Empire], to change the balance in the region, in order to replace a state with it, the tribes were provoked, the Arabs were instigated to rebel against the Ottomans, they were asked to revolt against the Sublime State. With racist winds and the fantasies of establishing national states, they had sawn the seeds of hatred and anger among the neighboring countries and still in the hearts and tongues of the administrators at the head of those countries are buried hatred and anger towards the others. Furthermore, even among those who play the game of Arabism, there are those in whose hearts, the dominant feeling is hatred and anger against each other. All these are the consequences of some of the projects put into implementation at the beginning of 1900s.

As early as in 70s in a magazine, there was a talk of a plan to divide the Middle East and the near environs, of 20 countries. Later, when I saw that some of the plans were being implemented, I was not surprised. These were planned even earlier and maybe they were watching out for an opportunity to arise for 30 years. These divisions were, for sure, to be realized by someone. Among the places to be divided were Syria, Jordan, Egypt, Iran and Iraq. Considering our observation that they were tackling the issue of the Southeast in Turkey, if we think about it, it would be immediately evident that this region was also included in the perspective.

There is this much, what were said yesterday were different things. Nowadays, in the ideas they are pronouncing now, they have been saying that they are aiming at making the region as an island of stability. But, they were not speaking in those terms yesterday. It is probable that the implicit and explicit reactions they received from the region or outside the region, forced the owners of this project to change course. By way of claims that they are trying to establish peace and security, they are trying to soften their rhetoric and presenting a different style so that the countries in the region will see no harm in this project anymore.

Yes, while some talking about these kinds of projects; they are basing themselves on a pretext of democratization of the region. Before everything else, what has to be clear is whether they are sincere in these expressions or not. Are they really sincere in this assertion? In 1911, the man at the head of the force to occupy Benghazi was saying, "We have come here to democratize you." These days there is an oft-repeated claim: "Democratization of the region." No one can say anything to democracy and the word of Democracy is really such a soft expression to excuse the things which might come afterwards. The excuse however here is that for democracy to take root, one really has to sacrifice certain things; this is exactly a satanic thinking.

Second, some people, taking along some others also with them ... after setting various ethnic and religious groups pitted against one another, make the innocent looking claim: "The region by itself is unable to establish peace and stability, when there is a source of irritation in one place somehow that threat is reflected in other regions of the world, hence, to prevent such a problem is our human duty, it is an obligation on us and the like." Can these be a pretext to enter the region, and consolidate their position of being a referee? The thinking of the West can be this, and the aim and goal of another and another, too. ...

In spite of that, in my opinion, whether in the earlier or the later form, to the projects like "Greater Middle East" or "Northern Southern Africa project," or if there was any, the Far East projects, it would not be right to oppose them just as projects. The reason being is that what is important here is knowing by whom these projects are being planned and presented for implementation and what kind of ultimate plans behind and in front of these projects. If the owners of these projects are not the Middle Eastern countries but some super powers like the USA, Europe, Russia, even China and India with a view of dominating the region, then without knowing what is being stipulated at the beginning, at the end, and since we are not in it from the beginning of the project, supporting that project would not be right. At any stage of the project, entering into it and owning up the project might seem in our favor. But, since we are not in it from the beginning, and we have no say in shaping the rules of the game, it might generate very negative consequences which would hold us responsible in history.

I wish Turkey, in terms of its subconscious heritage, having a great credit, had prepared this project in cooperation with various strategy centers, with the participation of idle Eastern nations and then offer it to the super powers. I wish Turkey said to the Europeans, "I have such a plan, and you say that you fear terror, you are concerned about the people of the Middle East. Do not be afraid, here we are a source of security and guarantee. As long as we are here, no one would touch you." As a matter of fact, since some of the region's nations detect this intention and influence of

Turkey, they say we wish we can have the support of Turkey and try to maintain good relations with it. It will be strengthened with this togetherness. After all, Turkey has a Muslim past. At the moment, it has a regime which looks with tolerance at Islam and an understanding of democracy. It has a common past with the countries of the Middle East. It lived for a thousand years with this world. Therefore, we have a very important credit with them subconsciously. Yes, we have several thousand years of history and an honorable past. We are a nation dominated almost half of Europe. Even if we are poor today, economic situation is not good, and we have stayed behind some Western nations; still we are a credible nation in the region. In a sense, those who work with us can dominate that world through us. Despite the shortcomings we have, in the eyes of the regional nations, we have a superior position. We have to use this credit.[335]

Some might say we have a strategic partnership with other states, and it is the necessary consequence of that partnership to support this project. Well in reality, the strategic partnership does not mean to participate in the implementation of a plan of which we are not part! Why we were not consulted in the preparation of that project? Why aren't we consulted, "What do you think about this issue?" Why aren't we asked, "Should we proceed to do this, do you approve of it?" For this reason, I wish from the inception the plan and the vision belonged to us, we had prepared those arguments. I wish we had fixed the rules of the game. Then we would not have lost. Since the plan was ours, it would have been possible to revise and correct where we made a mistake.

On the other hand, saying in haste "no" to the project might be a mistake, too. Who knows, by not trying to prevent great loss, by not venturing to stop a wrong, we might be mistaken. By merely saying "no" to the matter and stepping aside would not be something right, either. That matter has to be analyzed seriously. In short, I do not know if those, managing the Turkish political life, those who are at the higher echelon of the state, with its government and opposition, with its soldiers and civilians, have properly deliberated on this matter. I do not know if they approach it positively. But, personally, I am not carrying the conviction that it will be in our favor, because the project was not over sighted by us from the beginning and we do not know exactly what the content of the project is. We cannot think of the existence of our interest in a project which is not placed there by us, by not thinking about the interests of Turkey and the people of the region, in a project in which we have no contribution or a project which is not initiated by us.[336]

---

[335] Gülen 2005b, 209–212.
[336] *Ibid.*, 213–214.

This analysis not only is viable from a strategic point of view, but it also had been vindicated over time. The destruction and the human drama, experienced as a result of the occupation of Iraq by the Bush administration with false pretexts, opened up the door for political instability that will last for a long duration.

From another perspective, if one goal of the Greater Middle East project is to establish stability, another one was to establish democracy. But it soon became evident that democracy does not come on the tip of bayonets. The bayonets are shedding blood, but the blood does not sustain democracy. On the contrary, it is suffocating it. Nowadays, Turkey is developing its own democracy and is preparing itself as the model that other societies can follow to challenge their own state apparatuses. And Gülen had foreseen this development three years before it occurred..

64. What is the view of the Gülen Movement about the concept of an "Islamic state"? Could there be such a state?

This question can be asked in three different forms: What is the concept of state in Islam? What is the place of state in the Qur'an? Can a state be established based on *Shariah*?

By negating all these three questions, Gülen says in summary:

> Those who study and put forward opinions concerning the Islamic perspective of state and politics usually confuse Islam, established by the Qur'an and the *Sunnah* of the Prophet, with the Islam as constructed through the historical experiences of Muslims and of course based on *Shari'ah* [legal] principles, and also the superficially observed Islam of the modern times. They come up with various shapes and forms in the name of Islam; sometimes using Qur'anic citations, a few selected sayings of the Prophet, or sometimes ideas and suggestions of one of our contemporary thinkers and they vow to make their interpretation reign if they have the opportunity.
>
> ... Islam does not allow any person to put his or her own thoughts or ideas, or nowadays' possibly fantasies or desires, at the level of guidance for people, and does not allow them to say "This is the religion," but rather considers such attempts as misguided.
>
> First of all, the thoughts that are proposed in the name of religion, if not originating from the Qur'an and the Sunnah of the Prophet, will result in as many projects and proposals as there are opinions, and this will result in a crisis of legitimacy. Any proposal that does not take its reference from the historical experience of Muslims upon which there is a consensus of the

majority of Muslims absolutely cannot be enduring. The needs of today's people, if not responded to through a reference to the main sources of religion, which are accepted and revered by the majority, will not be realistic and will not satisfy people.

In Islam, rule and sovereignty belong to God. The Qur'an emphasizes this point in several verses and declares that ruling and command belong to God: "Female and male believers, when God and His Messenger made a decision, they have no other choice anymore" (33:36). Through this, the Qur'an declares that rule does not belong to holy and infallible spiritual leaders, as in theocracies, nor to any religious institutions under their supervision, nor to any other religious institution organized in any other way. Islam says, "the noblest of you in the sight of God is the one who is the most righteous." By this, it does not allow any privilege based on family, class, race, color, wealth, or power. Instead, Islam established righteousness and merit and honesty and the sentiment of justice as a principle. In Islam, which is based on the Qur'an and the sayings of the Prophet, there is neither absolute monarchy nor classical democracy as known in the West; neither dictatorship, nor totalitarianism. In Islam, ruling means a mutual contract between the ruler and the subject and it takes its legitimacy from the rule of law, and from the principle of the superiority of the law. Accordingly, the law is above the ruler and the subject. It belongs to God. It cannot be changed and cannot be usurped. The law is to be applied according to the Creator's command, and the way in which the Prophet expressed and applied it. For Islam, an administration based on tyranny is illegitimate. Islam does not approve any kind of dictatorship. In an Islamic administration, those who are at the top have to obey the law like ordinary people: They cannot violate these principles and cannot act in their practice against these principles.[337]

More questions immediately arise: "In this system, where is human will?" Who is going to promulgate the laws? Who will decide whether these are in conformity with the rulings in the Qur'an and the *Sunnah*? Who will decide that the laws are divinely inspired or not? Is this process itself this-worldly? Where are we going to locate the human factor in this process? Gülen responds,

> In Islam, the legislative and executive institutions have always been allowed to make laws. These are based on the needs and betterment of society and within the frame of general norms of law. On domestic issues in the Islamic community and its relationship with other nations, including economic, political, and cultural relations, Muslims have always devel-

---

[337] Sarıtoprak and Ünal 2005, 449–450.

oped laws. The community members are required to obey the laws that one can identify as "higher principles" as well as laws made by humans. Islam has no objection to undertaking *ijtihad* [independent reasoning], *istinbat* [deductive reasoning], and *istikhraj* [derivation] in the interpretation of *Shari'ah* principles.

In fact, in a democratic society the source of law is colorblind and free from ethnic prejudice. It promotes the creation of an environment for the development of human rights, political participation, protection of minority rights, and the participation of individuals and society in decision-making institutions which are supposed to be the characteristics of our modern world. Everybody should be allowed to express themselves with the condition that no pressure should be made on others through variety of means. Also, members of minority communities should be allowed to live according to their beliefs. If these sorts of legislations are made within the norms of international law and international agreements, Islam will have no objection to any of these. No one can ignore the universal values that the Qur'an and the *Sunnah* have presented with regard to the rights mentioned above. Therefore, it is impossible to prove in any way that Islam opposes democracy. If a state, within the framework mentioned above, gives the opportunity to its citizens to practice their religion and supports them in their thinking, learning, and practice, this system is not considered to be against the teaching of the Qur'an. In the presence of such a state there is no need to seek an alternative state. The system should be reviewed by the lawmakers and executive institutions if human rights and freedoms are not protected enough, as in the case of many developing democracies around the world. In order to make such ideal laws, lawmakers should reform, renew, and organize the system according to the universal norms of law. Even if such a renewal is not considered *tashri'* [based on *Shari'ah*], it is not conceived of as being against it. Significantly, there are some who think that *Shari'ah* rule would necessitate a state system based on religious rules. Without looking at the meaning and implication of the word *Shari'ah*, they display an attitude opposing it. Whereas the word *Shari'ah* is, in a certain way, a synonym of religion [*din*], it indicates a religious life supported by God's commands, the Prophet's sayings and practices, and the consensus of the Muslim community. In such a religious life, the principles that are related to the state administration are only 5%. The remaining 95% is related to the articles of faith, the pillars of Islam, and the moral principles of religion.[338]

What is understood from this answer is the following: The religion of Islam does not regulate politics nor does it require a specific form of gov-

---

[338] *Ibid.*, 450–451.

ernance. These decisions are left to the believers themselves, to be arranged according to the circumstances of a particular given time. But the Qur'an and the *Sunnah* fixed the basic rules and framed a general moral picture.

If people live their lives according to these principles and this spiritual framework articulated by Gülen, they also would meet their religious obligations by trying to practice their faith. Furthermore, these principles and spiritual framework do not contradict the modern understanding of law and freedom. Resistance to the change comes from the conservatism of the societies and the rigidity of the prevailing political system and the administrators.

Until recently, in the preamble of Turkey's constitution, the "state" was characterized as "sacred." But, can the state be sacred?

> In various periods in history, the state was sanctified, it was accepted as sacred. For instance, the "Sacred Roman Empire." This empire was established by the clerical class and became a prototype for the theocratic systems proper. That is to say, the administrative system of the sacred Roman Empire was not a divine system based on the sacred texts and divine sources. It was rather a system based on the principles developed and interpreted by the church authorities depending on the conditions, and the set of laws derived through *ijtihad*, at the convenience of the conjuncture of given periods. In other words, it was not a divine administration; but one, under the church fathers. In this system, the state is related to the political domination of the clerical class and is based on the superiority of the church authorities. For that, these characteristics are reminiscent of a "theocratic regime." It is true that in the ensuing periods, the state was still sanctified. Even in various localities and in the countries where Muslims make up the majority, as a reaction to the attacks on the state, the state was almost considered as sacred by some circles.
>
> ... Since it does not allow "monkery" [priesthood], Islam advices a form of state supported and strengthened by the direct participation of the public at the highest level, a state in which, there is no pressure of the conservatism of spiritual assemblies. The state is not a goal. it is a helpful vehicle and its task is to prepare a setting in which people can have a life in order to obtain the peace and bliss in this world as well as the next. Without falling into the error of sanctifying it, being respectful to the state is a duty of citizenship.
>
> The state might not be able to perform what is required of it or it might be at fault in its work ... but we have to look at the matter from the perspective of general principles and holistically.

Islam has a general viewpoint about the matters like sin and fault. One, although faithful, might commit sins, might be at fault. In the matters regarding the state, the same view should be retained. Namely, even if the state does not abide by the commandments of God, and loyal to the principles and advices of Islam completely, it still deserves the respect and support which is due to it. Because the people who make it up are us, the individuals. Then why should we be in opposition to it? When we are opposed to the state, this would be tantamount to being against ourselves. We have established it. You might say we have not established this state in this form; we never wanted it to turn out this way. Somehow it is thrown at us! But, I would beg your pardon, where have you been until it has come to this point which is annoying to you? Until it has become what it is, aren't there any negligence on our part?[339]

65. Is there currently a political agenda of the movement? Has there ever been?

Gülen insists that neither he nor the movement that he has inspired has any ideological aim. Therefore, the formation of the movement is not shaped according to any ideology. According to him, neither a political ideology nor an ideology based on religion is relevant. This has been the case since its inception. He especially dislikes the movement to be called by the lately fashionable term, "Islamist ideology."

He considers stamping every Islamic movement or all social and cultural "renewal" movements (which he sees as a renaissance) sustained by Islam, with the label of "obscurantism" as a mental residue, left over from Western colonialism. He considers labeling all the cultures outside the Western culture and civilization basin as "retarded, barbarian, exotic and from the third world" as an effort to make them the "other" and defines this as sickness of Orientalism. He says,

> For exactly 200 years, the West leaned on this ideology in its international and intercontinental relations. Orientalism was an ideology invented to make possible the cultural change to facilitate the political, military and economic expansion of the West and it served this purpose for two centuries.[340]

Gülen views Islamic movements from this perspective:

---

[339] Gülen 2005b, 51–53.
[340] Ergene 2005, 53.

Now, classical Islamic ideology in the Islamic world was born as an oppositional political identity against this colonialism. Today of course, the conjuncture compared to the conjuncture in which the Islamic ideology was
born has become different, to a great extent. It is torn apart from the foundations Orientalism was hanging on, it oriented gradually to more humane,
ethical, and universal values. This conjuncture development, to a certain
extent, changed and transformed the movements in the Islamic world. For
sure, in the Islamic world, still there are marginal groups acting with
political and ideological concerns of classical Islamism. But, in terms of
both, the material and mass [collective] power and ideological organization, they are movements, weak and with narrow visions. Therefore, it
would be wrong to perceive all the formations in the Islamic world as
movements acting with concerns of classical Islamism and as a threat oriented toward international relations.[341]

He defines the movement that he inspired as "independent as possible from political and ideological formation, which is a religious, social,
and cultural dynamic."[342] It also is clear that when talking to participants
of the movement the general impression is that they have not adopted
Islam as a political ideology, as advised by Gülen and oppose that it is presented as such. They note that this situation would make themselves and
the movement a party to conflict, and a movement that is a party to conflict cannot carry out its duty of *tabligh*. Gülen, both in his public speeches and in his books, frequently emphasizes this point.

Additionally, the movement does not see itself as just a religious
community. It has a social and cultural identity and a mission. Many
Western commentators present religious movements as being a hostile,
anti-modernity reaction of traditional societies or social sectors. They
consider the rise of these kinds of movements as the crises of traditional
societies. But the Gülen Movement is not a reactionary formation. It does
not have an anti-modern position. The individuals who shouldered the
main dynamics of the movement come from important segments of the
society—urban and well educated either in Turkey or abroad; they have
adopted modern values and have shown to be self-sacrificing supporters.
As they are not after an ideological state, they are not against the official
state ideology, or trying to develop an opposition. They are not acting
with a sense of deprivation, as is often seen in radical and reactionary

---

[341] *Ibid.*
[342] *Ibid.*

movements. On the contrary, all of their relationships are conciliatory and based on dialog and tolerance. In their conduct regarding the individual and social relationships, they value the positive. They express that they are trying to develop relationships, based on a healthier and productive foundation, not by using power or force, but by developing alternatives, without breaking the order of the society. They are bringing to the fore, in all their relationships, the ideal to serve the individual, society, and humanity.

> The state, the government, the politics, those whose purposes are these, and who tie their lives to the interests that they will derive from these activities have a tendency of assessing in the same vein those who do the things in the name of faith, the pains felt in the service of the Qur'an.
>
> We have never had any business with terror, anarchy, or anything illegal. They accused me of trying to take over Turkey. I am after no worldly thing; even if they propose the sultanate of this world, I would not turn my face and look in that direction. In the face of this kind of accusations, I say "O my Lord! I wonder if I made a mistake in my act of worship, in my servanthood to you. Was I at fault in sincerity? They are accusing me with the things I never thought of, the things which did not enter into my imagination or dreams![343]

Gülen appears to understand the meaning of "politics" differently than its current usage:

> In reality, politics is thinking today with tomorrow, and tomorrow with the next day, and an art of administration with a larger perspective of considering the pleasure of God together with earning the pleasure of humans; but today, politics is understood as consisting only of the party, propaganda, elections, and power struggle.
>
> The domination which is obtained through wealth, fame, power, or force is transitory; what is durable is the domination of the right and justice. For this reason, the greatest politics should be sought in the partisanship of the right and the just. Alas! When we look at many countries of the world, we cannot help but think: Where is the politics integrated with the thought of right and justice, and where is the street charlatanism consisting mostly of the lie and deceit?
>
> Unfortunately, in our day, most of the people consider as politics the daily political games, the deception of the masses, the struggle for power and interests, and all the activities in order to realize all these things, legal

---

[343] Gülen 2009a, 96.

or illegal. Because of this wrong interpretation and thinking, for the sake of my life related to heart, the straightforwardness of my thinking, and my relationship with my Lord, I have stayed away from every kind of political action, and I consider it absolutely necessary to remain the same for the rest of my life.[344]

66. Does Gülen prefer a particular political movement or political party? What is the relationship of the movement with politics?

Rather than party politics or cliquishness, our country needs disciples of knowledge, morality, and virtue who are well equipped with faith and hope, full of enthusiasm, and who have divested themselves of any wish, desire, and distress, be it material or immaterial, pertaining to this world or the other. Until we can find them and put ourselves in their hands, this intertwined exile and slavery, though relative, seems set to continue.[345]

Here I should also point out that, unlike some other religions or religion-like systems, Islam does not restrict itself to metaphysical considerations only, such as spiritual perfection of the individual, religious rituals, prayer, devotions, and contemplation. In addition to the emphasis on metaphysical considerations, Islam also sets out rules that order human individual, social, political, economical, moral, and legal life; and it promises safety from lawlessness and eternal rewards in return for the observation of these rules. Restricting the divine religion to only belief and individual religious rituals means compartmentalizing it and shaping it contrary to God's will and approval. At the same time, this will force individuals to hesitate about what they need to practice and live by and how and when to practice it. It would not be difficult to claim that such compartmentalization can even cause some sort of mental confusion. If individuals cannot live by the principles of their religion freely because of certain obstacles put before them, this means that they have been denied the freedom of belief and conscience.

According to the religion of Islam, the Messenger has been sent to provide principles for life in this world and the afterlife, with the promise of eternal bliss for its followers. In the message of the Prophet, this world and the world of eternity complement each other. Personal and social responsibilities are interrelated. Prayer, supplication, and remembrance of God, the life of heart and spirit, and social and governmental issues are all facets of one unit. Besides all of this, every Muslim should be very sensitive and conscious about his or her own rights as well as respectful

---

[344] *Ibid.*, 105–106.
[345] Gülen 2007b, 122.

about the rights and freedoms of others. Moreover, as they defend their own rights at the same level, they are very willing to defend the rights of others.[346]

... I do not think that the institutions constituting the state are against so and so, against you and us. In some institutions, some whose voices are louder and who dwarfs others with their voices, whose noises are ahead of their activities, might appear to you as the state. That is to say, those who are against you are not the state, but a marginal group. Therefore, it is a grave mistake, to consider a vital institution for the life of the nation, as if it was in opposition to you. To reprimand her for such a mistake, to denigrate, to constantly criticize her, that is a second mistake, and doubly so, especially to damage the trust of the nation in her therefore to weaken it, this is a many fold mistake. For that reason, we should not be caught in the flood of those faults and mistakes.[347]

When he is reminded that before going to the US, he occasionally met with politicians, he replies:

I am a regular citizen and as a citizen, I think I have the right to meet with anyone. In my meetings with the politicians, they might have some political concerns, but up until now, I had no political interests. The proposals for meetings always came from them anyway, and I had accepted them as an opportunity to explain the issues of the nations to them. I had told all the persons I met, "I wish all the parties from the left to the right, could agree on the national issues, and not go to opposition with each other." I am thinking that this kind of a conversation is just very normal.

There were times that I might have advised to take some measures in favor of the nation in matters related to the likelihood of our nation might be wounded. In those meetings, staying away from politics, I always tried to speak about the general and durable issues. For instance, I remember that once I said these things: It is important for a nation to say, "This is my government" rather than for a government to say, "This is my nation," and in my opinion this is always what is sought after. On the contrary, if the nation considers the government as a chain of caterpillar to fall upon itself, that would mean that for a long time now, that body and that head were separated from each other.[348]

Although there have been those who mentioned my name with some parties, all of these, if they do not come from a deliberate intention, surely it would be a mistaken assessment and inaccurate information. It is a com-

---

[346] Sarıtoprak and Ünal 2005, 448–449.
[347] Gülen 2005b, 58.
[348] Gülen 2009a, 106–107.

mon knowledge that as a consequence of my philosophy of service, I am opposed to every kind of internal division and anarchy, to the monopolization in the fields of religion, civilization, and democracy to using and utilizing them negatively inside the country and using them as a vehicle to divide the people. But there are those who imagine for a time or those who see some benefit in inventing such fantasies that I supported the Justice Party, later Motherland Party, yet still later, True Path Party and then the Democratic Left Party.

Up until now ... there was no one and never a meeting of a political nature, a bargain in which even the use and mention of one word can be irritating to anyone; and it would not be possible and it shall not be possible in the future. I am not after such and such chairs in the national assembly, but am after the pleasure of God, which is declared in the Qur'an as more valuable and greater than everything, including Paradise. Up until now, as I did not lend support to any party directly or indirectly, written or verbally, vocally, in this matter and during the election of any member of any party, I did not give any hint to even the closest people around me, to support or not to support.

The late Turgut Özal was someone I respected and admired, but the claim that I advised people to vote for him is inaccurate. The secret of the matter lies in the farsightedness and fidelity of the nation. Turgut Bey, all his life, had run after lofty ideals, he was always with a vision. He was a great thinker and statesman. He was a constant supporter of the philanthropic activities, carried out in the educational field. Our people who know him in this character were supporter of him with a sense of fidelity.

In the matter of voting for Mr. Ecevit, in no uncertain terms, I would like to state that I did not give advices or encouragements. In any case, Mr. Ecevit did not demand such a thing and he did not have an expectation in that direction. In his relationships, he did not have a goal of obtaining votes.

Mr. Ecevit became a symbol of honesty. He did not say something yesterday and something else today. He reshaped the left under the new realities of Turkey. He tried to renovate the left and to form a left-culture, reconciled to and in peace with its religion and national values. It was for this reason that he did not see every pious person as an obscurantist. He demonstrated that the left can be in peace with the sincere Muslims. The farsighted Turkish nation as a compensation for his honest and consistent conduct rewarded him with its votes.[349]

We are at an equal closeness to all parties. As I expressed earlier, I am not saying "at an equal distance," because the followers and sympathizers of each and every party there are our own people. The parties and the political view points of people are is not obstacles for us to befriend them.

---

[349] *Ibid.*, 108–109.

Those who embrace everyone, who fold their sleeves for heroism of love, would not exclude anyone for the sake of temporary political interests; would not imprison anyone in his/her political party or viewpoints. No matter who says what, no matter what imagination one has or vocalize his own expectation or suspicion, their line of thinking is well known: They neither support one party and set aside another nor are they conditioned and establish a front of hostility with a preconception against any party.[350]

What is understood here is that Gülen takes extra care to keep the movement outside politics, but not necessarily the participants as individuals. For individual preferences, he is neither guiding them, nor preventing them. He is aware that the partial and divisive spirit of politics would impact negatively on a movement that tries to embrace everyone, based on solidarity with everyone else. He knows that it would only sow the seeds of hypocrisy. His exhortations are in this direction.

67. Can religion and politics have common goals, work together and overlap?

Acceptance of religion's expression of its sacredness, another aspect of approaching it in this manner would be not to use religion for any worldly purposes. It would be not to exploit it for worldly or spiritual gains. Religion should not be used as a vehicle for the pleasures in heart for personal considerations, either. Politicization of religion, religion being the foundation for some political ideas and acts, looking at matters through the prism of religion, garbing our personal political administrative understanding within religion, would mean making our personal opinions sacred, therefore, it would be an insult to the religion. Second, when we base our political thoughts, considerations, party politics on religion, in some ways our shortcomings and faults and deficiencies are reflected in religion, reaction to us brings a reaction to it. In other words, those who hate us feel hatred toward the religion, also. The truth of religion should be represented in such a way that, it should be above all political considerations. Whereas when religion is politicized, when we say we represent it, in a sense, we would be seeing others outside of it. Even if it seems to care about religion, since we make a shadow over religion through our conduct and behavior, since we blacken it, and since the religion receives its share from the hatred directed toward us, in my opinion, those who politicize it would be doing a grave harm to religion.

---

[350] *Ibid.*, 110.

Religion is a matter between God and the servant, the foundation of which is sincerity, honesty, gaining the pleasure of God, it is a matter related to heart, to go deeper as much as possible into the inner recession, as well as it is about dealing with the external. It is one's passing his life on the emerald hills of heart. By ignoring or neglecting this aspect of religion altogether, understanding and practicing it as a ceremonial matter and trying to display it as if making a show off to others would be wrong.[351]

In Gülen's approach to Islam, there is no place for a political organization. He strongly advises against giving the impression that religion is being exploited for political purposes. Gülen advocates understanding Islam as a religion, with its basic precepts within the immutable framework.

68. Should religion enter every field of societal life?

Gülen's answer to this question is short: Religion encompasses every aspect of life.

The foundation and the beginning of Islam are *iman* [faith] and *iz'an* [realization] the end of it is *ihsan* [acting and praying as if seeing God] and *ihlas* [honesty and sincerity from heart]. To believe in the truth of *Uluhiya* [Divinity] in such a way that not to recognize even the possibility of the opposite, and bond the heart with God; to undertake the responsibilities, to fulfill the obligations with a sensitivity as if seeing Him, or being in the presence of Him; and everything to be done around the axis of gaining His pleasure and nothing else. This is the concise expression of the truth of Islam.[352]

Islam, the foundations of which are rooted in the messages of God and represented and practiced by the Prophet, is a divine religion from heavens. And those who make it as the life of his life are the believers and Muslims. The believers had defined this religion as the set of divine laws which orient people with their own free will and choice to goodness and kindness.[353]

Islam is the last and the most perfect religion that God had chosen for humanity and honored with it. Because it is the last and the most perfect, it is, as it were, the elaboration and detailed explanation of the previous religions according to the needs of the modern age. But, the fact is that nowadays, this perfect system is going through an unfortunate time, for being represented by those representatives who are not qualified and by

---

[351] The interview given to Yalçın Doğan, Kanal D, 16 April 1997.
[352] Gülen 2010g, 175.
[353] Gülen 2010h, 171.

those who have no sense of fidelity to the original memory. Hence, despite its vastness, today it is imprisoned within the confines of narrowness and it is unable to express itself with its own language. This also means, at the same time, that all of the divine religions lack their proper true representatives to give proper expression these religions desire. First and foremost, Islam, by accepting all the messages of the previous Prophets, has come down by taking along their messages and with a view in mind that it would represent them according to the understanding of the contemporary age, in a sense it consists of the summary of them, it is the voice of all of them.[354]

Islam may contain the meanings: the servant's surrender to God, to obey his commandments, to march towards security by entering into a path of security, to promise safety to everything and everyone; being a person, no one feels unsafe or uncomfortable from his hands or tongue. For this reason, those who see it as consisting only of faith, as well as those who could not accept and internalize it through the ego would be counted among the mistaken. It is evident that both of the categories would be deprived of the spiritual or material, this worldly or otherwise of the rewards God promised. Nevertheless, it would be wrong to consider the "practice" as part of "faith" relying on these considerations. Those, who believe that the practice is religiously obligatory but fail to practice as demanded by the tenets, would be sinful, but still considered as believers. According to the Qur'an, the element *sine qua non* is "faith." Islam is the sole path for it to become a depth of his nature, to become a second nature to human being. The practice without a faith is hypocrisy; despite the faith, not practicing it is a *fisq* [deviation from the truth] or hypocrisy. Since it is a secret, implicit unbelief, vices and immoral acts through the repentance, asking for forgiveness and again returning to God is always open to the possibility of forgiveness. Therefore, even if one does not do good deeds or practice the rituals, as long as one does not belittle them, or does not see them as insignificant, we should always think positively about him, and the judgment should not be passed as to his unbelief. At this point this should be pointed out, too, that the place where faith is born and develop is the heart and conscience, another important foundational component which God looks for in a faithful is: along with such a conscientious acceptance, doing good deeds and morality. Because of that, in either theoretical matters or the issues regarding the practice, as long as there is no coercion, the believer should stand by these matters that he or she has already accepted.

When that is the case, trying to present religion as if it was a matter of conscience only, is opposed to its spirit. The interpretation of *iman* and

---

[354] Gülen 2010g, 184.

Islam according to the whims and wishes of the individuals would make it as a non-divine; it would make it mundane, a human affair. In actual fact, Islam is a divine *tabligh,* freeing humans from their whims and wishes, binding them to God and to the guidance of God. It takes as its addressee the ones who have reason and conscience; it would orient them to this worldly and other worldly good, with their own free will and choice, and promises eternal bliss to those who respond positively. Religion is a divine complement from the will of the divine to the partial human will.[355]

According to Gülen, there is a total Will which creates and rules the universe. This Will had given the human servant the ability to make choices and the possibility of freedom, of orienting his life towards knowledge and wisdom. To the extent that the human utilizes this possibility of choice closer to reason and morality, he meets with religion, the divine vision, and happiness.

69. What is Gülen's view of the market economy? Where would he place the state and private enterprise in the economy?

Gülen, who notes that the answer to this question should be left to the specialists in the field, expresses that he has always attached great importance to private enterprise, and he explains how religion looks at this issue:

Islam is a religion which guarantees the bliss in both worlds to its adherents. With the condition of intention that every individual who has given heart to Islam, can make worth the reward of an act of worship every moment of personal, social, family lives. If the business life is arranged in the course of service, one can also make his entire life worth the reward of a life span.

Everywhere in the world and all the time the Muslims have to be wealthy and dominant force. This is necessary because today it is not possible for the Muslim to face the challenge in the world without having superiority, economically and scientifically.

God Almighty states in the Qur'an (An-Nisa, 4:141) that "... *and never will God allow the unbelievers to find a way (to triumph) over the (true) believers.*" He reminds the Muslims that He is not to appreciate to see the domination of the Muslims by the unbelievers, and with a sacred manner of style at that. Concluding from this, it could be said that whether indi-

---

[355] *Ibid.,* 175–178.

vidually or collectively, it is their responsibility not to be subject to the predomination of the unbelievers.[356]

Here we have to open a parenthesis. Gülen views all the religions as divine phenomena and encourages his followers to approach all of them with respect and tolerance. Then, what does the word "unbeliever" (*kafir*) mean in this verse? By this word, does he mean the definition commonly used among the public, which can be rendered as "non-Muslim"? Since the word *kafir* means those who do not accept the existence of God, His unity, and the createdness of the universe, this could not be meant. Christianity and Judaism, like Islam, accept these fundamental principles. Then, in Gülen's understanding, *kafir* must mean the one without any faith or who denies God or all of these religions. In that case, how are the religions outside of these three viewed? This problem seems yet to be explained in the Gülen Systematization.

Returning to the subject of economy, Gülen has a strong reaction to laziness, inertia, and backwardness, because he sees them as the reason for being subjugated:

> If always others determine the economic life in the world and we sit still where we are, and if there is no effort to escape from this poverty and disgrace, it means we are constantly committing a sin. The state in which the believers get under the domination of the unbelievers and live a life of captivity is a truth the Qur'an informs us about. For this reason, in every field a faithful has to utilize the dynamics to be able to carry him to superiority, and he has to jump to highest levels. In this world everything is subject to knowledge and science. Sometime in the past, the futurist Toffler had said it. So, any society which could not get hold of the dynamics of knowledge against the ignorance, would be knocked out by the age in which it lives and the technical developments. Likewise a society which cannot take peace and alliances on its side to fight against divisiveness would be defeated by its contemporaries.[357]

Gülen also calls our attention to multinational associations such as the European Union, the economic unions that Asian states have established among themselves or the association between North and South America. No nation can stay aloof to these formations and retain its influence:

---

[356] Gülen 2007c, 43.
[357] *Ibid.*, 44.

Looking at it from another angle, a nation which does not search for means and ways to become wealthier against poverty is bound to be under the domination of another, sooner or later. A Muslim nation which came under such domination, for being under the domination of a non-believing nation would be responsible before God, also. Starting from this fundamental thinking, every believer to be sure remaining within the legitimate boundaries has to find a way to become rich by any means possible. If need be, the capitals should be put together domestically or abroad, the investments must be made in a feasible manner and in the fields open to competition.

Through the help of people, raised with positive sciences and disciplines of religious studies, in order to embrace the future centuries and to turn the tide of time in our favor, we should not forget the impact of economy in this area. For that purpose in mind, the economic power should be snatched away from those who hold it in their hands at the moment. God almighty states in the Qur'an: "*We (recorded in the Supreme Preserved Tablet and then) wrote down in the Psalms after the Torah that My righteous servants will inherit the earth.*" (Al-Anbiya 21:105). Therefore, for their ignorance and not knowing how to work coordinated activities, the believers lost their place in the balance of power in the world. Now, they have to take it back. For this reason, the believers have to search for the ways inside the country as well as outside, to discover the ways to get richer, and become wealthy. These people who are locked into *hizmet* for human beings, with everything they got, have to earn money and save and protect it, because this might be a means to earn rewards also from God. Sometimes blessings come under disguise, some seemingly non beneficial things might be a blessing and beneficial.

In that case, every activity with the intention of contributing to the development of this country, economically and educationally, to maintain the unity among us and the Muslim countries to take their places in the balance of power among the nations, every technological and economical enterprise is tantamount to an act of worship.[358]

In Turkey, there was a need for a doctrine to state that economic development and capital and investment transactions are not mechanical phenomena. These activities raise the level of individuals and societies, engendering respect and the admiration of other nations and, therefore, good and beneficial. After Gülen vocalized this need to his fellow believers, the message travelled a long way and today the movement has

---

[358] *Ibid.*, 44–45.

a portfolio expressed in billions. This, in turn, increased the power and credit of Turkey and its citizens.

> Here, another issue to be reminded of is that the professional establishments have solidarity through good and serious organization. Yes, every member of a profession should unite among themselves, should work in an organized fashion and with the permission of God should become a force not to be transcended, overwhelmed. However, of course we have no intention to rival anyone or compete with anyone. But it is extremely important for the people who love each other and each one of them to desire for the other to earn as much as he does, who share the same thoughts and ideals to come together in unity. As in Japan, in our country the young, mature, and old people can get together, can organize camps, and seminars, and discuss profoundly the matters relating to their businesses. As a result of all these discussions, they can be a support for each other in the economic enterprises they are going to undertake inside country and outside, instead of individual ventures they can erect a collective consciousness, and under its guidance, they can march to the zenith of their professions.[359]

70. What is his view on projects such as "Islamic Common Market" or "Union of Muslim Countries"?

From what Gülen has expressed previously, it might be expected that he would view such associations favorably. But, his position is different:

> In a globalized world, establishing associations based on the common denominators like race or religion in today's world are looked at with repugnance or should be looked at with repugnance. Partnerships should be established which do not differentiate on the basis of religion or ethnicity and do not lead to the formation of divisive fronts. Front formations like Islam and Christianity or Islamic world vs. the West should never be allowed, at all.
>
> In a globalized world the way to have a say in the power balance, goes through establishment of alliances first of all, with the neighboring countries, and later with the nations having more common points, but without having an exclusionary attitude to others. Establishment of natural alliances, and instead of enemies, being encircled by the friends should be made the aim of every, and this should be realized by any means.[360]

---

[359] *Ibid.*, 44–46.

[360] Interview with Fethullah Gülen, *Kenya Daily Nation*, 30 July 2004.

Ideas turning into concrete politics do not only stem from the fact that those who advance them are bright, but also from their ability to foresee that the time is right for particular ideas to be actualized. It is a matter of wisdom and farsightedness. And while it is normal for alliances to be established to the advantage of those establishing them, it is imperative that these alliances do not harm other countries and extra precautions must be taken to avoid causing tensions. In this regard, Gülen states:

> For alliances and peace, it is not absolutely necessary to have various organizations; extreme caution should be applied not to give way to the establishment of opposition camps; all humanity needs it.[361]

While Gülen agrees the joining the European Union, he stresses the need to also develop and improve relationships with the Turkic Republics of the former Soviet Union in Central Asia:

> Our integration with Europe is very significant, but our opening up to Asia would be a bridge for the Turkish businessmen and investors, it would facilitate the competition with the rest of the world. Maybe, some joint ventures will be undertaken and in terms of our relationships, these things will give us strength. Of course, the same things might be true for the Pacific world. We are not bound to anyone with a rope; we can use the Pacific, or Asia as well as Europe. The existence of different alternatives would have given us the lee-way for bargaining. Our politicians ... our diplomats ... could not foresee this. Asia is an important security for the future ... For this reason, in order not to miss the chances in the long run, with the friends who think like I do, have established the institutions of science and wisdom to gather our enlightened ones under the same roof. We are trying to recover the chances we had missed. With the hope that maybe we can be able to catch them after 25 years or if the circumstances warrant it, we can realize it in 15 years.[362]

During the administration of Refahyol (coalition of Welfare and the True Path parties, this being the acronym of both parties) government in 1996 and 1997, it was desired to establish a Muslim economic and military pact (it was named "The Developing 8"). When asked his view on this, he responded,

---

[361] *Ibid.*
[362] Sevindi 2002, 93–94.

I personally see D-8 as a cheap message to some circles. It is a matter with a lot of risks. I do not know if they really believed that D-8 would bring something. First of all, the conjuncture was not conducive to it. As Muslim countries each one of them is in the hand of a Western power. Saudi Arabia is like that, Iran is like that. Without the permission of the countries at the steering wheel, no one would allow you to move to make such a pact. Also, there is the matter of how the Islamic world views you. Islamic world saying "the source of religion is with us" had always looked down on us. Even when we were trying to open schools in Asia, we had petitioned to them with the same aim. Saying "let us think about it later," they had dragged the matter and acted toward us with disrespect.[363]

71. How does Gülen see the "individual"? To what extent should the individual have freedom vis-à-vis the state and religion?

It is useful here to make two points:

First and foremost, Gülen's idea of "human" is a person who does not have a blind obedience to any authority outside of his will. This authority does not necessarily have to be political or administrative. It could be social, that is to say, it might be rooted in a group one belongs to. Both might oppress the individual. However, for the individual to be able to resist repressive authorities, he or she must have something to lean on, some kind of spiritual place of refuge. For Gülen, this place of refuge is religion.

The individual, who has sought refuge in religion (i.e., Islam, according to Gülen) and has resisted every kind of tyranny and oppression through the support he has received from his faith, also can protect his freedom. But, what about the binding regulations of the religion? Does religion have its own kind of repression? According to Gülen, religion is a holistic system; it is the sum total of a set of values adopted and accepted. It is not a matter of accepting or compliance by force. On the contrary, belonging to a religion is by personal choice, with a free will.

The unity of the believers frees the individual from loneliness and powerlessness. Their combined actions create a synergy that they cannot acquire individually and protect them against political oppression. Another benefit of religion is that it gives direction to one who is lost, hope to the one who is hopeless, morality to one who is seeking morality,

---

[363] *Ibid.*, 93.

and a norm to one who is seeking a norm in dealing with others. In the words of Gülen:

> The modern world and contemporary systems of thought claim that for the first time in history individuals have become the true, active subjects of their lives and their actions. According to these modern systems of thought, individuals have depended on the traditions that have come down from the past to the present day, imprisoning themselves within the limits of these traditions. Since the group attitude has become the norm, and as it is not possible to change the established standards of communal life, it has been the destiny of individuals to remain only passive, obedient members of the community. In the modern age, they have finally started to free themselves from this imprisonment, acquiring their individual personalities. Until the modern age, individuals were not free and were not independent. Although these thoughts on individualism are true for some cultures and some regions of the world, they are not true for every religion, for every thought, and for every community. From the perspective of *Tawhid*, which is the main principle of the unity of God in Islam, it is impossible to have unrestricted individualism. This is because humans are either both free with no acceptance of any moral values and rebellious with no moral criteria, or they are servants who are dependent on God and seriously obedient to His commands. Through being obedient servants of God, the individuals will not bow before any power and will not sacrifice an ounce of their freedom.

> A servant of God cannot be enslaved by anything but God—neither by worldly belongings nor by the corrupted traditions that cause individual misery and paralyze the spirit; nor by communal relations that lay siege to human reason; nor by considerations of selfish interests; nor by greed for more and more material earnings, a desire which dynamites morality; nor by oppressive tendencies that give priority to power over logic and reason; nor by immorality, such as jealousy, hatred, and slavery to carnal impulses. A Muslim repeats at least 30 to 40 times a day, "O Lord, You alone do we worship and from You alone do we seek help" (Al-Fatiha, 1:4). By saying this, individuals break the chains that bind their freedom and individuality and so take refuge in the infinite Power of God, which is sufficient. An individual who has not achieved this reliance on God and taken refuge in Him cannot be considered having fulfilled the task of being an ideal human.

> Thus, Islam, while asking individuals to be free and independent from anything except for God, also accepts as a principle individuals as members of a family, society, nation, and indeed, of all humanity, based on their needs. A human being is a social, civilized being that needs to live together

with other humans. In this sense, a society is like an organism; the parts are interrelated to and in need of one another.

It is very important to see such togetherness as a "greenhouse" that protects individuals against oppressive forces and helps them to meet their needs and assists in personal and social development, which is not easily achieved individually. This is the point where we differ from those who claim absolute freedom for the individual. Those supporters of absolute freedom leave the individual alone by themselves in the "desert" of existence, without any support against the forces that wait in ambush to capture them, under the pretext of freeing the individual from certain traditional ties. Such an individual, being under the tyranny of dictators or even social oppression, has paid for this individualism in a very painful way, by losing both freedom and honor in the name of individuality.

Here I should also point out that, unlike some other religions or religion-like systems, Islam does not restrict itself to metaphysical considerations only, such as spiritual perfection of the individual, religious rituals, prayer, devotions, and contemplation. In addition to the emphasis on metaphysical considerations, Islam also sets out rules that order human individual, social, political, economical, moral, and legal life; and it promises safety from lawlessness and eternal rewards in return for the observation of these rules. Restricting the divine religion to only belief and individual religious rituals means compartmentalizing it and shaping it contrary to God's will and approval. At the same time, this will force individuals to hesitate about what they need to practice and live by and how and when to practice it. It would not be difficult to claim that such compartmentalization can even cause some sort of mental confusion. If individuals cannot live by the principles of their religion freely because of certain obstacles put before them, this means that they have been denied the freedom of belief and conscience.[364]

72. What is his perspective on the environment and natural living?

When asking this question, the author was under the impact of what we can call a "natural Paradise," far from the noise of the city, in a rural setting in the upper Pennsylvania region, where Gülen resides. When there were several small lodges, unrepaired for years, at the beginning, this natural place, decorated now by the rich forest-like trees and bushes, is completely renovated. A major building was constructed where both Gülen can reside and meet the followers and he can hold the lessons with his students. Later were added some more single houses where they can

---

[364] Sarıtoprak and Ünal 2005, 447–448.

receive the guests. The landscape of the premise is done properly and some paths were opened, leading to the ravine at the lower part of the property. While the field resembles a campus of a school, without touching the natural appearance, it was made more beautiful. In short, before even receiving the question regarding ecology, Gülen and his team together have demonstrated their sensitivity about it. But the question was asked, anyway and answered by Gülen as followed:

Gülen sees protecting nature as a religious duty:

In Europe an environmentalist group arose who call themselves the "Greens." In addition to establishing political parties under various names and titles, they have organized themselves and began works in this field. They even, through these works, have connected with the dominant powers of the world, and integrated.

As for our situation, it is rather difficult to awaken the Muslims to this issue. It cannot be said that we have made a serious progress in this field despite the efforts of last 5–6 years. This was not taken as seriously as the schools and the dorms. It cannot be said that the state takes it seriously, either anyway. Although, for so many times we had applied to revive the forests which were burned down, in many of these cases we could not receive positive answers.

Yes, to patronize the environment, to protect the eco balance is among the major duties of a Muslim. If God wills, starting with our friends, everyone would be awakened and later it would be possible, to accept it as a religious and national patriotic duty, they in turn, explaining the matter to others, can achieve the establishment of a green and balanced world.[365]

He bases his views on the following:

Mankind, in terms of origin, was created in Paradise. Later as a result of disobedience to the divine commandments [it can be said to the harmony there] was put out of Paradise and sent to this new land. For this reason, as long as he lives in the world he has desired Paradise and he will desire it in the future. Yes, this place which is described with its one thousand and one beauties has always entered into the dreams of people, decorated their fantasies, has become a theme for legends, and is always pictured as a goal to be reached. So much so that in order to call attention to the beauty of a place beyond imagination, by using the expression "like Paradise," we try to stress on this passion of ours.

---

[365] Gülen 1997b, 239.

As a matter of fact, the place on which the mankind originated and opened its eyes to life is such a place, "like Paradise." Who knows, maybe it is the projection of it. But it is unfortunate and painful that deliberately or not, after the unlucky period, the mankind has destroyed this paradise with its own hands, has made it non-livable and nowadays has set out to search for one, by making descriptions of the "lost Paradise."

In this slice of history, Turkey has experienced this unlucky period that we have been talking about. Today, not only Turkey, but all the countries of the East and the West, sharing similar fate are in the same bitterness of heart and in the same search.[366]

He continues,

The place on which our dear Prophet had honored our world was a place of desert. In order to convert this place, encircled with deserts, into a worldly paradise, in addition to the Qur'anic allusive remarks in many verses, he has insisted on this issue through many of his sayings, acts, and deeds. If we make an exposition of his words about Medina, "I am declaring Medina as the Haram region" in modern parlance, we can render it: This vast area was declared as a "national park." The Messenger of God, in his statements, commenting, and making an exposition of it, said: "The flowers or plants cannot be plucked, the trees cannot be cut down, and the animals cannot be killed."

During wars when it was inevitable to bombard the interior of the castles through catapults, our dear Prophet went into doubt and expectation for guidance through revelation in the matter of cutting the trees and throwing them as logs to serve as canons. He showed the same concern about the burning of the crops. But, today when it becomes a matter of victory or defeat, it is resorted without any hesitation to both burning of the crops and cutting of the trees.

Furthermore, for the people, who go into state of *ihram* for the purpose of *Hajj* [the Pilgrimage] or *Umrah* [the minor Pilgrimage], it becomes absolutely prohibited to kill animals, to pluck the weed or grass or plants, to cut down the trees in the region of the Haram. This statement belongs to him: "Whoever has a plant in his hand, if he is able let him plant it into soil, even if it is the doomsday!"

In summary, the idea of protecting the nature and retaining it has to be appropriated by the masses. And who knows, maybe then, the mankind can reach the "lost Paradise" again.[367]

---

[366] *Ibid.*, 196.
[367] *Ibid.*, 196–198.

Based on various Islamic sources (e.g., Bukhari, Muslim, and the implementations of Umar), Gülen also concludes that, "The species of animals should not be extinct because, the balance in the nature would be tipped." He notes that Umar took many measures not to damage nature. In the matter of protecting the ecological balance, he interprets the principle that the Prophet and his early Caliphs had adopted: "If you are going to plant the three in your hand, while the end of the world is at hand, it means you have not lost the hope yet in this world."

Gülen attaches great importance to measures taken not to pollute the environment and to maintain the ecological balance. However, he also points to the double standards with respect to this issue, as well. For example, the West polluted nature and spoiled the ecological balance. He believes that this did not originate only in its passion for conspicuous consumption, but also it did not realize that so much industrialization would be so harmful. Now, that the West is trying to correct these mistakes, it should provide the developing nations with guidance.

While displaying his sensitivity about the environment, he makes an interesting comment. He states that the creature that needs to be protected the most is the human, because the human is the most beautiful.

> And human beings themselves seem to be the most beautiful among all this beauty. With our outward looks, our inner world of senses, thoughts, and faith, we are like a sample, a replica of the universe. It is therefore apparent that humans have been created as a key to solve the riddle of creation.[368]

Since the human is such a miracle and contains in his self the mystery of the worlds, he is a combination of all creatures through the Creator. In this situation, he is both the carrier and the implementer of the unity of creatures. The human accomplishes the acts related to this unity through art. In his own words,

> The nature in its entirety is an exhibition of wonderful things, but we prefer to call it a "book." It is because we hear it like a book, we read it like a book, just as if we were watching the gilded lines and decorations of a book in all colors, and we watch it in great admiration. Every morning we

---

[368] Gülen 2010i, 24–25.

see it painted anew, decorated in front of us with its dazzling height and gaze at it loosing ourselves in amazement and wonder.[369]

For Gülen, nature is the primary source of what is aesthetic. The human takes the talisman of beautiful things and utilizes them in shaping his own work. For this reason, every beautiful work of art is, at the same time, a wonder of nature. Gülen explains this relationship as such:

> As the architecture of a mansion or a waterfront house, the elegance and aesthetic in its architecture whispers to us something beyond the mansion and the house, a wonder of a nature likewise ... carries meanings beyond the existence. It whispers also the one who makes it and brings it to the place of display, the one who hints his existence through every work he produces, but somehow cannot be comprehended due to his awe the genuine, real source of all the order and beauty which is beyond the capacity of humans to understand and comprehend.[370]
>
> Unfortunately, we did harm to ourselves by turning this beautiful place, resembling Paradise, into a hell. If the mankind does not revive and bring back to its former glory and beauty, this world that they broke the order of and defiled and made ugly, it would be inescapable for us to receive a flood like the one of Noah, and through that calamity this beautiful world will be showered on us like the ruins of a collapsed building.[371]

After stressing the necessity of protecting nature and humans as part of it, along with its aesthetic values, Gülen complains about our establishment of ugly settlement units in natural spaces:

> Our urbanization is measured by the sand and the barns, our architecture is devoid of any aesthetic, to the extent that it can make even the beavers laugh at, and they are hastily put up. Our villages, our towns, our cities are as lowly as to be an illustration for the contest to destroy the nature, along with growing and expanding. Our plains and oasis are completely dry and in the pang of becoming deserts. Our streets are narrow tunnels between the buildings that mutually closed in on each other. Indeed, to call these houses as houses, to consider these piles of concrete as a dwelling place is disrespect to the words and concepts.[372]

---

[369] Gülen 2002a, 110.

[370] *Ibid.*, 111.

[371] *Ibid.*, 113.

[372] Gülen 2008e, 23.

Whereas, in the past, the elegance and beauty and art in these houses and buildings were so deep and in congruence with the book of nature.[373]

73. Does Gülen value art?

Gülen sees art as part of culture. For that reason, every society should develop its own culture, producing new forms and new expressions, in addition to those already in existence, that adapt to new developments in the country or in the world, as cultural stretch. He does not consider art separate from the societal changes. In other words, he is of the opinion that a developing country would have a developing culture. In his words,

> Cultural values have the same meaning and worth for a people as blossoms and fruits have for a tree. A community that has failed to produce a distinctive culture, or has lost or forsaken it, may be likened to a barren tree or to one whose fruit has dropped off. Today or tomorrow, that tree will be cut down and used as wood.[374]

According to Gülen, art is the soul of development; it is a phenomenon developing one's senses and his capacity to discover. Through art, one does not only develop the inherent talents and the capacity to understand, but, at the same time, he arranges anew life and the world. With the power of imagination, he could establish new worlds. He can transcend time and space, becoming eternal through his works. He believes that one can become a fountain of beauty, through the unification of faith (religion) and art, generating energy, which in turn creates enthusiasm and excitement in his imagination and creative faculties:

> It was by means of art combined with faith that, with its most magnificent places of worship, slender minarets pointing to the realms beyond, sacred designs and intricate patterns carved in marble each of which served as a distinct message, diverse kinds of calligraphy, brilliant gildings, and embroideries as beautiful and fine as butterfly wings, this once magnificent world of Islam became a gallery of invaluable beauty.[375]

Gülen notes that art does not reach perfection only through emotions, but also through the accompaniment of science, which is more durable and through it, mature works will come into existence.

---

[373] *Ibid.*, 26.
[374] Gülen 2005a, 55.
[375] Gülen 2005a, 66.

Gülen does not attribute the beauty of the human to its material existence. He views the matter like a work of an artist:

Man's height, form the cohesiveness and compatibility and geometry between the members, are as beautiful and perfect as to generate admiration in everyone watching. This is comprehended by the artistic genius of the Romans but since they could not orient themselves to the unity of God, they confined these sense to the narrowing geometry of the concrete.

I have been expressing my admiration for the human all along with the statements like: "If there was the permission to worship anything other than God, the human must have been worshipped." This expression seems to be supported by the angels being asked, in a sense with the order to prostrate Adam.[376]

The artist takes the sentiments of our inner world in its relation with the existence under close surveillance, and interprets effervescent emotion, excitement and vocalizes them. After vocalizing them, he would present them to us in different combinations in which he pictures for us to see that everything leaps forward to return to its origin. In other words, in the face of any elements from the existence and any color from the universe, the artist by tying together and mixing up the inspirations running into his senses and enveloping his soul, he would bring together the phenomenon and noumenon. He is a hero of metaphysics in presenting everything together in a holistic form.[377]

But even the artist should have his own share from science.

Because if he starts from the parts, if there is no real scientific references, he would be devoid of inspiring in others real vision of an art. In terms of our recent history, our inconsistencies, and murmurings in artistic thoughts, somehow never being ourselves, being monotone, therefore our dissatisfaction and non-contentedness must have been based on such a narrowness of a perspective.

... For those reason, we can state that the nations who do not have a horizon of a spirit, and hence could not establish their own metaphysical system of thought can never escape from fixed molds, they could not be themselves and can never feel their sense of belongingness.[378]

---

[376] Gülen 2010j, 164–165.
[377] Gülen 2010e, 82.
[378] *Ibid.*, 82–83.

74. Does he encourage his followers to take an interest in art? Is he interested in any forms of art?

When asked about encouraging people to art, Gülen replies, "Some circles are not ready yet to set out such a journey within our criteria."[379] He then discusses a parallel topic: He claims that when societies do not appropriate a holistic approach in either science, art, or metaphysical matters, it results in undesirable consequences. As a matter fact, it actually stems from the fact that they do not have a "civilizational project." According to Gülen, for humans to understand themselves and the universe, they have to have a holistic approach to existence and the realm of creatures. This would contain a civilizational project. In the words of Dr. Faruk Beşer, an expert of Islamic jurisprudence,

> ... No civilization can be a civilization without meeting all needs of its members within the framework of its own world views. If somehow there are in the nature of mankind music ... literature and other *belles-lettres*, the members of a civilization should be able to find these in a cohesive and appropriate manner for their civilization, in one way or another. Otherwise, if the artistic products of other civilizations are envied, admired and imitated, this would be tantamount to an opening up a gap in the body of own civilization, and that civilization resembles a ship receiving water from an opening.[380]

Gülen provides music as an illustration:

> When voice, instrument, and word [theme] which are the basic elements of music come together and present themselves in unity, they would be more effective. But when the wholeness of theme, voice, and instrument are not achieved, one cannot escape from emptiness of sentiments. In some cases of works, sometimes word rebels against harmony, the content against rhythm. Music is also a way, an art and a need. If that is the case, then this phenomenon that we call the "need" and is in existence in the society any way, should be handled along the line of our thoughts so that it can be ours. I firmly believe that in the near future in this country, our people, young and old, no doubt are going to be united with our understanding of music; our taste of music will acquire wholeness with our music ... but with our systematic efforts. Probably, then our country will be freed from the occupation in this area and again they will embrace the geniuses of music like

---

[379] Gülen 2007b, 42.
[380] Beşer 2006, 19–20.

Itri, Dede Efendi, Hacı Arif Bey, Saadettin Kaynak, Münir Nurettin Selçuk. Let us not forget, music is a need.[381]

The question arises whether Gülen listens to the music and, if so, whose music does he admire most?

> During my childhood, in Erzurum, I had connection with some Sufi people. Sufi music ... classical music was born in dervish lodges, in retreat centers. By that aspect, the things like *ilahis* [hymes] and *ghazals* [odes] attracted me to classical music. For instance, I liked Itri and Dede Efendi and listened to them. I liked Hacı Arif Bey and respected him. While coming towards our day, I liked Ahmet Özhan, and listened to him. I like very much our own music. My stance against the others is maybe because I do not understand them. I listened to mostly Sufi music. I liked it. For instance, we have a close relationship and familiarity with Reşit Muhtar. I have friendships with the old composers. I have some close friends among the artists, and they condescended and composed something from me. ... It is not possible to go through the list. As a matter of fact, I have interest in and love towards many branches of art.[382]

Among the musicians that Gülen likes are Cem Karaca (a Turkish rock musician) and Burhan Çaçan (a Turkish folk musician). He says, "We have become very close with them and embraced each other." Gülen also enjoys Hüseyin Efendi, with his touching works and implementation; he says he knows Bekir Sıdkı Sezgin (Hüseyin Efendi and Sezgin are Turkish classical music performers and composers) and Gülen expresses the importance he attaches to music as:

> A mind, which is close to music, would be close in inclination to anything in the world, because music requires elegance, flexibility, sensitivity and a perfect structure of sense. Therefore, it is not something that everyone can do. I can even say that it has priority over anything like sculpture and painting. So it would be impossible for anyone who does not have a talent for art to adjust one to music, to be able to make music.[383]

Gülen also believes that a woman's sensitivity gives her an advantage in the field of music:

---

[381] Gülen 1997b, 175–176.
[382] The interview given to Ertuğrul Özkök, *Hürriyet*, 23 January 1995.
[383] Gülen 1997b, 180.

A woman's inborn sensitiveness is an advantage for the field of music. Maybe for this reason, the proportion of the women who have talent for music is higher compared to men.[384]

The widespread desire among the youth for pop music and the constant support to it by the media, echoing of the stadiums with the noises of the pop music, ... along with very intensive and organized activities on their behalf, it is obvious how difficult it would be to inculcate the love of our own music. But facing all the challenges of these difficulties, by any means possible, we have to make extraordinary efforts in this cause.[385]

But, Gülen cautions that during the process of this search, we should not go to extremes:

In reserving a place for the kinds of music, which are favorites of the general public today on TV and radio, we have to think and assess objectively about the entirety of the society. You can isolate neither TVs nor the radios from this business. If you act to the contrary, you would isolate yourselves from the society, and left alone with several individuals who think like you do. For this reason, from among the kinds of music the society accepts, you have to execute the less harmful or harmless ones, you would meet the needs of them and thus you would give your message, too. Let us not forget, if the trustworthy hands do not provide what is needed in the society, it would degenerate in the hands of less worthy ones.

You cannot expect all the sectors of the society or all the members of it to be like yourselves. As there are some to be contented by listening to the Qur'an, by listening to the religious chants and hymns, there are those who share other sentiments. Then, we have to go to the help of those who are after satisfying their desires through "heavy metal" music and "rock music," with our own genuine music.[386]

He does not hide that he prefers classical Turkish music over others:

It is among the commonly accepted fact that classical Turkish music provides a certain level of refinement to many. The one who could go into depth in the music being executed, could comprehend the elegance in it, and after sometime could reach certain elegance and could get away from primitiveness in him. ... Namely, the musical elegance, finery and even aesthetic, these matters too require music. To deal with music and to spend time with the music lovers depend on orienting toward the meaning, rather than words and instruments. It can always be said that the classical

---

[384] *Ibid.*

[385] *Ibid.*, 178.

[386] *Ibid.*, 179.

Turkish music gains one this spirit. However, this should not be forgotten either that the source of this business was dervish lodges and retreat centers. When these institutions dissociated themselves from their real, genuine missions, and became the place of idle people, the classical music had lost one of the most important fountains. After that, people returned to primitiveness and adopted the taste again for *davul* and *zurna* [drum and double reed instrument] of the folk music. In other words, the people who experience the psychological spirit, represented by the drum and the flute, filled every place. By *davul* and *zurna* I mean the noisy atmosphere of the rude sentiments. Nowadays, the same thing is prevalent but I am personally not altogether hopeless.[387]

Gülen calls our attention to the fact that after social change, the society's taste also changes. As the social division of labor develops, new social strata emerged. They then carry cultural habits, originating from their own lifestyles and tastes, into the public sphere. In the last century, after the intensive migration from the rural areas into the cities, the sectors coming from the rural areas and small towns, lifted up by education, politics, and capital, have gained influence in the society. Their understanding of art and music was different from other sectors of the city, which had contact with the world earlier. It could be said that these sectors are living in the same space, but not in the same time period; they are carrying the tastes of different times and social realities. Therefore, their visions of the world and their understanding of art, in congruence with those visions, are different.

Gülen, who is aware of this difference, believes that this state of affairs is only temporary:

I believe that for sure; this quality crisis in music will come to an end. Because it is a sociological and historical fact that especially at the beginning of Islam and later the Ottomans, all of the nations who were dominant in the destiny of others had come into existence following such a crisis, just like the last curtain of darkness paving the way to illumination. ...

At this moment in the Anatolian land, which served as a cradle for many civilizations, we could be considered to be going through a revival, in the sense of returning to the true, genuine essence. This revival is marching on in every unit of the society. It is evident that the music will have its share from it. As a matter of fact, the works being done in the field of classical music is an evidence of that. If God wills, the days will come for us to be at an ele-

---

[387] *Ibid.*, 180–181.

vated stage, and with the kind of music which belongs to us, the union of mind, heart and spirit would be developed. Elevated individuals, who gained profundity, internally and externally, would be raised.[388]

Gülen then discuss other branches of art and says something interesting: "If in our day I am to bring to the fore someone modern ... I would be interested in Picasso."[389]

From there, he turns his attention to literature:

If there was no literature, neither the wisdom would have taken its magnificent place, nor the philosophy could have been extant today, nor could the Rhetoric have accomplished what was expected of it. Having said that, in a mutual effectiveness and service wisdom, philosophy and Rhetoric have not left, at the disposal of literature, whatever they produced in their respective fields as a limitless, inexhaustible capital, and made it immortal.[390]

Later, he comes to the genres of novel, story, theatre, and cinema:

The novel, the story, theatre, and cinema are lagging behind here compared to the West. Even if the posture of Islam played a role in this, the role of the negligence belonging to us has been enormous. Here I am deliberately using the expression the "posture of Islam." Because, regarding these matters, there is no prohibition by Islam for certain. It is only possible to detect an anti-stand from the implicit and explicit expressions. In my opinion, at one stroke to get rid of the genres of story, theatre, and cinema and to attach a label of "banned" on them must not be considered as accurate and authentic. ... What we have to deliberate is to understand what kinds of themes they may or may not contain. Praising and encouraging the matters that Islam says absolutely prohibited is out of the question. Any kind of description, representation, explanation, drawing, painting which might be considered as praising and encouraging ... has to be rejected absolutely. Otherwise, in general principle, as a rule of thumb, it would not be right to go against neither the novel nor story nor others like them.[391]

When asked, "What can be done in order to produce our own genuine literature?" Gülen replies,

---

[388]   *Ibid.*, 181.
[389]   The interview given to Ertuğrul Özkök, *Hürriyet*, 23 January 1995.
[390]   Gülen 2007a, 51–52.
[391]   Gülen 1996, 330–331.

"For this, first and foremost both literatures of the East and the West should be known very well. Second, there should be colorfulness and richness in narration."[392].

Gülen's emphasis on literature coincides with his view of religion. According to him, the first creation was a sudden event by throwing two letters into the chest of nothingness: *kaf* and *nun*, which compose the word *Kun* (Be!). This awesome moment started with a word and started a process of going from one to many, from oneness to multiplicity, to infinity. Everything owes its existence to the "word."

> If there was no word, we would not be able to hear anything belonging to beginning of time, and we would not be able to grasp the meaning of the mystery filling our hearts. By virtue of the word, the universe has become an exhibition and the books coming from God have become a declaration ... the meaning of existence was unfolded.[393]

The poetry also has a special place in the Gülen's perception of art. He sees poetry as music, made of words. For him poetry

> ... is the expression of the beauty and mutual proportion hidden in the soul of the universe, the expression of the smile and heartwarming sentiment on the face of existence.[394]

Gülen remarks that in Islam's understanding of art, lies picturing creatures in an abstract form, not as they are in actual fact. He considers this preference to be due to the influencing of thought by the faith.

> Islamic art, while stressing on the unity of God, opposes clearly resemblance and anthropomorphism, and it clearly expresses its posture. Leaving always the door open to interpretation, it tries to show the ocean in the drop and pictures the Sun in the particle, and it tries to express books in one word.[395]

Gülen attributes the fact that the art did not develop very much in the Muslim countries, other than in certain bright periods, to science becoming fruitless. When religious schools fell behind the developments, scientific endeavors deteriorated and retarded. According to him, "In order for

---

[392] Gülen 2006c, 153–154.
[393] Gülen 2002b, 29.
[394] Gülen 2010k, 499.
[395] Gülen 2010g, 64.

the great ideas to shoot out and develop, for the work of arts to come into existence," the vase has to permit it. As it can be expected, Gülen talks about these matters from the perspective of Sunni Islam and develops his interpretations from this angle.

> It is unthinkable for Sunni Islam to be against aesthetic, art, beauty, and the expression of beauty. If there was such a thing, the civilizations in Asia would not have come into existence. The period is the one in which the best efforts were made for [the compilation of] the works of *Tafsir*, *Hadith* and *Fiqh*. If there was a system of thought which would shackle the free thinking and art that could only be through the way of *Fiqh*. But if you make a little research, you would find that the period in which *Fiqh* is highly developed, is the same period the Islamic society is most forward in terms of art and esthetic thought and free thinking. Andalusia in this matter is the land of wonders. These days, the authors of the Islamic history of science, cannot help but reveal their admiration and adoration and even perplexities of that period.
>
> From Seyyed Hossein Nasr to Garaudy these admirations are expressed maybe more than 50 times. A civilization was established; a civilization in the chest of which was molded the aesthetic, free thinking and faith together, and where the peace, tolerance and love were represented.[396]

Gülen emphasizes here the decadence in the Islamic world does not stem from religion, but a particular interpretation of it by the society and the way religion was managed. According to him, Islam is open to every kind of freedom and the form of expression provided that they are compatible with the basic principles. The ones who blacken its horizon are the authoritarian and fundamentalist understandings; they are the governments that make Islam into a kind of regime and the rulers who preside over those regimes.

75. What is his concept of culture? What are the sources of Turkish cultural heritage?

Gülen sees culture as,

> ... the whole of social and ethical disciplines of conduct which a nation produces in history, and over time makes it into a dimension of national existence or subconscious heritage.[397]

---

[396] Can 1997, 103–104.
[397] Gülen 2010g, 85.

According to this understanding, although it appears as universal in terms of some of its fundamental features, it is obvious that in every society or geography a different culture is predominant. Of course, this difference is an influential factor, to a great extent, on systems of thought. For this reason, we can consider an individual's thought, bound by a culture, as his expression of himself within a certain framework of reference.

It is possible to define a culture as ... a given nation's displaying, in its entirety or partially, its own ethical values, considerations of doctrines, its thoughts about existence, universe, and humanity, its postures *vis-à-vis* the social and political behavior, the disciplines of behaviors, within the framework of national thinking and national sentiments, all the things which occur within its history like ideas, arts, tradition, conventions and customs.

In our cultural system, the relationships of human–God–Universe ... is the most fundamental principle and all mental, ideational, and concrete action take place according to this relationship. The modern European logic, that it is altogether a Greek heritage, relates all its thoughts to human, things, and events; therefore either it does not take into consideration the reality of the divine at all or considers it as a secondary matter to the former ... It dwells on only the results of events or facts in practice and relates everything the events and things.[398]

With this in mind, Gülen must be aware that Islamic societies, in general, and Turkey, in particular, did not go through a process of bottom up (soft) secularization, by going through the Reformation and the Renaissance. If such a historical process did not take place, the approach Gülen refers to would have been carried through Christian thought from the Middle Ages into the modern times. If the reverse had taken place, what he says about the Christian world would have taken place in our society. And this is only the natural result of mutual influences of the systems of faith and social life on each other. Gülen must have shared this evaluation assessment when he says:

We have to interpret and assess our culture carefully not only in order to open up to our region but also in terms of opening up in our life of thought and establishing a durably and firm bridge between us and the civilized world. In other words, on behalf of our nation, in order to construct a firmer, more cohesive and coherent, and more durable understanding of a culture, we have to take the ethical and moral values belonging to yester-

---

[398] *Ibid.,* 85–86.

day, today, and tomorrow, without sacrificing one at the expense of another, and make a synthesis of all of them as a dynamic whole.[399]

According to Gülen, while aiming at development, this synthesis has to secure the continuity within change and development. He also makes an interesting expression, "... cultural times, being different from what we know as time, it would be more appropriate to call it *above time*."[400] With this he is offering a conceptualization which always changes but carries the continuity in it, while always benefitting from different reference points. And this makes his approach autonomous from others and original. Because of this, Gülen's system is able to include different concepts, paths of thought, viewpoints, understanding of art, and ethical values, and produce a new synthesis from them.

Were we able to accomplish as a society what he is trying to achieve? The judgment of Gülen is categorical and impartial:

We are a nation, which along with so much adventures in innovations, could not establish our own ethical system based on our own national culture; could not develop and systematize our own metaphysical thoughts; could not display an artistic vision which would reflect our internal world in terms of God, universe and human realities, and develop an educational system according to our own spiritual roots.

Unfortunately, we have dried up those blessed resources of life with our own hands that had sustained us as a nation in all history, and we oriented ourselves to importation. So much so that, we have confused the minds altogether with the strange understanding of a nationhood which we tried to enforce on the people the things we brought from all corners of the world, that strange philosophy of life and a strange understanding of art. We have extinguished our own cultural torches which had been burning for several millennia, and submitted to the darkness like the bats?[401]

Gülen's observations, along with his assessment that we cannot hold on and we are swept by the currents, make it easy to grasp the secrets of Turkey's backwardness.

Nevertheless, Gülen offers hope and the remedy:

Right now what we need is not this or that person; this or that philosophy, but a magical prescription which would take us to the acquirement of our

---

[399] *Ibid.*, 88.
[400] *Ibid.*
[401] Gülen 2010e, 171–172.

soul that we had lost, which would save us from the depths of the anaphor of confusion and bring back the love for a new truth within the framework of our own understanding, our own customs, a new conception of science and depth of thought. This prescription consists of our own meta-under-standings which would be filtered through the prism of our national life of hundreds of years ... related to our philosophy of life and the reality of human–God–universe, our own voice and breath. And I think that until we find the values that we lost, it will not be possible to find our manner of speech, and free ourselves from the deviation of thoughts.[402]

How can we accomplish the great leap forward for which he yearns? How can we construct the civilizational project? Gülen offers a national renaissance where the language is Turkish. According to him,

> It will have been accomplished through the integration of Turkey with the Turkic world and the Western world, through the generations to be raised in the USA and Australia ... by making the Turkish language as a language of the world.[403]

Since language is another dimension of the culture, Turkish, which is spoken in many parts of the world anyway, should become a universal language. According to Gülen, the future will be an age of science and communication or oration in concrete form—the signs of it are already apparent. For that reason, language is as important as science for nations in the future, in their development and in finding a place in the rapidly globalizing world. In order for Turkish to accomplish such a mission, pri-marily the men of literature and thinkers have serious responsibilities.

76. Does he have any interest in sports? For instance, does he watch any games on TV? Does he encourage his followers to participate in sports? Have any well known athletes arisen in the movement?

Gülen first explains what the word "sports" means to him. He sees sport as a vehicle for communication and sharing between groups and indi-viduals.

> With the expansion of the network of communications in the world, the concepts of democracy, peace, dialog, and understanding are being expanded. Without doubt one of the vehicles of communication to be able

---

[402]   *Ibid.*, 172.
[403]   Gülen 2007c, 170.

to influence the social is sports. Everything regarding the sport in a moment goes from one end of the world to the other. In terms of the durability and its tomorrow, dialog and tolerance which we believe are necessary along with other vehicles should be disseminated through this channel, too.[404]

Why are sports a good vehicle for communication and mutual influence? For instance, 90 minutes on a soccer field provides an opportunity for people to share pleasurable moments and excitement, coming closer together. The gentlemanly contest displayed during the game, without seeing the rival as an enemy, encourages competing according to the rules. The notion that, "Winning does not depend on crude force but professionalism, doing its task well, and being well-prepared," spreads. Sports contests are not to destroy the rival, but to compare talents, to test, to see who is better in the field. A contestant, while testing his own skills and by getting the audience to participate in the game, is able to produce a great partnership and a group of emotional fellowship. At that moment, the masses, who feel the same excitement and concerns, understand that they share a commonality in the rules of the game and in human sentimentality. In other words, they discover their humanity one more time in the contests.

Gülen explains:

In a contest, in general, there would be winners and losers. To the extent that at the end of the contest, the rivals embracing each other in a gentlemanly manner and show that they have the same goals and aims, this friendship and sportsmanship can envelope the audience and even the entire society. This would be an important lesson for those who from time to time put the chairs on fire, curse each other, fight with each other in a bloody manner, and those who want to see or want us to see the sports as a vocation devoid of sentiments and thoughts. Yes, even if it is considered as insignificant today for the supporters, instead of fighting, shaking hands in a friendly manner and leaving the stadium with love and affection, this hatred and discord would be prevented, at least to an extent, and the world at this moment needs it very much.

Furthermore, every profession should be exercised appropriately; we should act according to the requirements of that profession. An *imam* uses his voice in the mosque; but an artist in a cinema or theatre cannot act in that way. He would bring it to the fore the body language, and acting skills.

---

[404] Gülen 2006d, 161.

If he is an author he would bring it to the fore his pen. He says whatever he wants to say with the tongue of the art, the literature. There is a benefit for it to be done in this way. Otherwise the impressiveness and impact of those messages would be broken and no benefits can accrue from them. The same applies to the sports. For instance, at the end of a goal scored, the statements such as, "I have done this with my faith, it happened with the permission of God" may lead some people to delirium and rebellion. Instead, the sportsman, an athlete should express himself through his achievements, gentlemanlike character, and his life.[405]

At this point, Gülen asking people to go after what they desire and to realize them in the way he wants, rather than just praying with words.

Unfortunately in our day, the importance of some of the concepts is not comprehended. Everyone has a need for religion, and the peace and security religion promises, more than bread and water. I am in the opinion that all of these will have positive reception if they are presented properly. Since almost all the people in the world, who want to do something in the name of Islam, are approaching this important matter with ill manners, and wrong methods, they are causing them to be hated rather than liked. And they are forming gaps unbridgeable between people. But what is expected from Islam is to be a bridge between the humans, a road, and an element closing the gaps among the people. In summary, we can say that an element like sports has to be taken advantage by any means to realize dialog and tolerance in the society.[406]

It is clear that Gülen attributes a great social role to sports and through his inspiration, sports is encouraged in schools. Gülen had implied that he prefers wrestling and soccer among the branches of sports, but he leaves the following question unanswered, "Do you watch matches?"

Gülen also was asked, "Has ever a known sportsman arisen from the schools and the movement?" After remarking that from the school in Georgia, Zaza Pachulia has been playing in the National Basketball Association in the United States, Gülen states that many sportsmen attended schools established by the movement in the fields of soccer and wrestling. He adds, "But determining them name by name is the subject of another study."

---

[405] *Ibid.*, 161–162.
[406] *Ibid.*, 162.

77. Why does the Gülen Movement attach so much significance to education? Why does it run an educational mobilization?

Behind the educational mobilization of the movement, which was inspired by Gülen to spread around the world, lies the notion that, it is possible by a society to become strong only with the help of humans who are self-sufficient and beneficial for others. Let us elaborate on this point.

If the individual is not learned, he would neither understand himself nor the society in which he lives. He could not discover his innate talents and trigger them to move. In this case, he would not be self-sufficient. A person, who is not equipped with necessary skills, would be a hireling to somebody else. He would be a subject to the chief of his tribe, his boss, his party leader, and authorities; he could not be independent. From a herd would emerge a nation, neither powerful, nor respected.

To be self-sufficient and to contribute to a shared life is only possible through knowledge. Knowledge is realized through education. Therefore, education is as important as the act of worship, because the self-sufficiency of the created, doing goodness and kindness, results in gaining the pleasure of God.

The Gülen Movement, which takes this philosophy as its foundation, ventured into educational activities by first establishing university preparation courses in Turkey. Later, it diffused to the rest of the world, and now it is educating over 100,000 Turkish and foreign students in more than 100 countries.

The movement, which started educational activities at the end of 1970s, spread to five continents in a 30-year-period. In addition to schools and universities in various countries, Gülen's followers opened up many cultural centers and language courses.

In these schools, which try to give a better quality education compared to their counterparts in the countries in which they are operating, the quality of the teacher is very high. The majority of the teachers are graduates of universities in Turkey, such as Middle East Technical University, Boğaziçi University, and Marmara University, where the language of instruction is English.

The curriculum and the course programs are approved by the ministries of education of the country of operation and English language is dominant. Of course, the language of those countries is taught. In addition, the Turkish language is taught to the extent that a student upon graduation becomes fluent writing and speaking Turkish.

The second focus in the course programs are positive sciences such as Math, Physics, and Chemistry. The students in these courses have achieved international success. For example, one of the students in Zamboanga, one of the remotest cities in the Philippines, won third place in the International Mathematical Olympiad held in South Asia. Students from South Africa school participated in a math competition with 30,000 other students and placed three students in the top 100. In Kenya, in the fields of Physics and Biology, the task of forming the team to participate as a national team was given to the Gülen school there.

Due to these successes in the countries where the Gülen schools operate, many parents from among the wealthy families prefer to send their children to these schools. The children of governmental officials in Central Asia countries prefer the Turkish schools as well. Most of the children of ministers or deputy ministers attend Gülen schools. Many of the graduates are achieving high government positions in their countries. Most of the schools charge tuition fees, but they have no difficulty recruiting students. Bright and talented children, who cannot pay tuition, are provided scholarships.

These schools establish not only cultural, but also educational and commercial bridges. Teachers and administrators of Turkish schools, by penetrating the societal fabric of the countries in which they are working, established friendships. If the students' parents are employed by the government, the administrators of the schools encourage Turkish businessmen to invest in these countries. By the help of these schools, the exportation of culture and capital are achieved simultaneously. Turkey's influence is spreading through civil actors. When this unofficial diplomacy and these economic relationships come together with official channels, Turkey is expanding the area of its influence as never before in its history.

Turks are seeking to be influential in many areas. For instance, Turkish businessmen are receiving contracts worth millions of dollars. Indeed, there are those who attribute the increase in Russian tourists to Turkey to the positive influence of Gülen schools in Russia.

How did the adventure of first opening up schools and its subsequent spread to the world begin? The mobilization of schools began in the mosque. The acceptance of this idea began in the 1970s through Gülen's sermons in the mosques. What Gülen did was to encourage. Those who believed in the importance and the merit of education started an educational mobilization, spreading to five continents, through their service, effort, or material support. Of course, the dissemination of Turkish values also was highly significant to them. These educators believe that they are accomplishing a contemporary mission, appropriate for their faith. Like Prophet Muhammad migrating from Mecca to Medina and spreading the Islamic faith, they adopted the same method by migrating to other countries, in order to carry their culture and made this a goal of their lives. The majority of the teachers are former students of these schools and, therefore, very close to this cultural endeavor.

Today, the Gülen schools are operating in a vast geography extending from Central Asia to Japan, from the Far East to the United States of America. Looking back, only 35 years have passed since the beginning of Gülen and his followers' interest in the field of education.

As a result of perseverance, selecting the right individuals, a quality curriculum, adapting to the political structure and the local culture, and maintaining an educational level desired by the students' parents has resulted in amazing achievement and success.

Why were these schools established? A series of conclusions can be drawn from Gülen's writings and conversations:

1. The people who had labored in the establishment and the operation of the schools believe that they have undertaken a religious and human task. These sacrifices require a devoted spirit that can come only through a firm fidelity to one's religion. In Gülen's words,

> In this world, this is the sole thing which could be done for Islam. And this can be accomplished by the altruistic people who forsake their own pleasure for living for giving the pleasure of living to others.[407]

2. The ideal of a "Grand" Turkey is a second source of enthusiasm. This greatness does not depend on the vastness of land. What is desired is for Turkey to reestablish its cultural influence.

> The Turkish nation, had never experienced this much weakness and incompetence, during history, especially in its geography and later in the

---

[407] Gülen 2010a, 59.

world in the face of the events taking place. It had never before in its history, it was excluded from the process, from the circle of power. This disgrace and dishonorable situation has to be overcome. ... The time to repossess the honorable position we had in history has arrived.[408]

Starting from this aim, Gülen says:

We are in love with Turkey. We feel an obligation on our shoulders to strengthen it again and return the honor it deserves, to make its weight felt at the world scale. If I will not be able to serve my motherland, nation, religion, and culture, I would consider living anymore absurd. If I am living for these aims, then there is a meaning of my life.[409]

3. [Through these schools,] ... today in the four corners of the world we have many friends and brothers. At a critical juncture of decision making, there are innumerable people who would use their preferences in the direction of friendship and cooperation with Turkey. In the future world, these are very important bases, namely basic building blocks for Turkey.[410]

At this point, Gülen states:

Do not forget it is no longer possible for a Turkey, isolated from the world to promise a future nor even to retain its existence. Now these educational activities in this sense have been securing the future of Turkey. Who knows so many friends meanwhile gained in the process, will form very strong lobbies in the future. There will be friends who will work as honorary workers, Catholics, Orthodox, Buddhist, Hindu, men or women, black or white, intellectual or common, at every level.[411]

4. Gülen seems to take the position that there are far more similarities between all religions of the world than differences. If politics and material interests do not pit societies against each other on insignificant matters, a new philosophy of faith will emerge based on these common values. This new philosophy will not be unfamiliar to the monotheistic religions. Gradually, the mutual agreement that we are all the servants of the same Divine Being will develop and mature. This, in turn, will form the basis of solidarity among societies and world peace.

---

[408] *Ibid.*, 60.

[409] *Ibid.*

[410] *Ibid.*, 61.

[411] *Ibid.*

Gülen firmly believes that the notion of the unity of God is nothing other than this:

> Winning with the civilized people has to be through conviction. Through power and force you cannot direct people toward anything. With your superpower, you can go occupy a place, destroy, burn, and kill; but you would attract the dire hatred of people. On the other hand, if you go in with reason, logic, and universal values, you would become a sultan in the hearts.[412]

These four conclusions inspired Gülen to start an educational mobilization. But only one flower in the hand of a person does not bring spring. Some followers—who understand him and who comprehend that his encouragement and inspiration will open many opportunities—believe that, through their support, they are accomplishing a spiritual task. It is common saying, "There is nothing stronger than the idea whose time has come." Let us add to this the proposition, "There is nothing stronger than a person who has conviction and the rising class who is searching for a new world for itself." Through them, an enormous power comes into existence. Moreover, this is a civic power and it produces its own means; it makes its own decisions through its own free will.

78. What was the inspiration behind establishing schools and educating a new generation? How did he convince his followers that this was a good idea?

Gülen responded as follows:

> Since my days of youth, I always thought about the state of psychology we found ourselves in, as if we were inside a cage, by saying like "No person of merit can arise among us, no discoverer, no inventor, no genius can arise from among ourselves." I used to say I wish we could break this cage, these chains, throw them away, and show ourselves to the world. ... As of lately ... in a sense we have broken this cage. Since the time past, I always attached great importance to education. I wanted to make up for the deficiency. ... In my personal life ... a period came in Turkey when private schools were allowed. This had occurred also before the 70s. But at that time ... I was an insignificant preacher. I knew I could not have an impact on people, but even then, I used to say education! Absolutely education!

---

[412] *Ibid.*, 62.

Open up schools, I used to say. Produce men of thought, produce the laborers of thought, produce the architects of thought, I used to say. I used to say, we have to bring out the talents of our people. Then, we did not have this opportunity. Neither I was so influential, nor there were people within the circle of my encouragement.[413]

Upon receiving this answer, several other questions arise which many in the public has asked. Where does the water of this wheel come from? People go to the other end of the world to provide education to children, why are they bearing so much of the sacrifices?

Before everything else, Gülen points out that the success of the movement does not belong to one person alone, namely himself. He is only an opinion maker, who defines this great mission and inspires the desire of those who would like to participate in the movement. The rest is the concern of those who make up the movement. It is as if Gülen is composing the song and his followers are playing the music. He plays his role by giving inspiration and mobilizing the collective reasoning and activities. The rest takes its natural course.

In the area of education, it is well known that Gülen was influenced by Said Nursi. But he adjusts the thoughts of Nursi to the new age and provides interpretations that are appropriate to the age. Said Nursi also had dwelled on the three vices which present a threat for the nation: ignorance, poverty, and disunity. He stressed that all of these had to be resolved through nonviolent means and reconciliation.

Gülen encourages capital formation by getting together small savings, investment, and trade, and he places great significance on education and defends insistently the expansion of a climate of tolerance. As a motivation behind these goals lies the same desire: to fight against the three diseases mentioned above which keep the country unfruitful. But it should not be forgotten that the society was trying to find a way to free itself from these disasters as well. A need was felt for an opinion maker, a trustworthy guide to orient the individuals. Gülen filled this vacuum. In short, Gülen's call, "Let us spread the education so that the ignorance can come to an end; do trade so that the country can get rich; let us show tolerance to everyone so that oppositions and divisiveness can be lifted" and "Be without hands in the face of beating, be without tongue in the face of

---

[413] The interview given to Yalçın Doğan, Kanal D, 16 April 1997.

cursing" are propositions that were made at the right time, at the right place, and to the right persons; and, as such, they have found reciprocity. This movement is the initiative by the civic society, and maintained by it; it is the most comprehensive project with the largest participants, and its impact has been to the same extent.

When asked why he encourages so many schools to be established and foreign students to be educated, Gülen gives two separate answers. One is an answer perfectly suiting a man of religion, and the other is the answer of a contemporary civic leader:

> In the final analysis, everything depends on the knowledge. Without knowledge nothing can be accomplished. It is important so much that today the source of all the emptiness in Turkey and in the world, even at every place, all the time, of all the problems, is the neglect of an education to be located on a realistic, firm, and sound foundation. While the West was experiencing the Renaissance, we were sleeping. While they were accomplishing the scientific and technological revolution we were again sleeping. These are some of the matters we have to consider seriously. I am sure it has been done from time to time, but the level is important.[414]

He also draws our attention to the fact that in order to integrate into the world, it is imperative to understand it, comprehend the change, and adapt to the new circumstances.

> The age in which we live has to be heard perfectly, has to be comprehended, and all the circumstances have to be understood. Then education is very important in integration with the world. Today, no country can be in isolation. The way to the integration with the world has to go through a modern education.
>
> If we are thinking an integration with these friends of us, these institutions of education can be very important platforms. I believe that by virtue of these institutions of education we can better know each other, and establish good, durable, and sounder relationships with the West. For this reason, as long as the state does not prohibit the encouragements and advices I have made so far, I shall continue to do what I am doing. I would not want to be in opposition with my own government. I always think to be with my government in tandem. If our government says, "What you have done is enough now," then as I am thinking a lot these days, I would

---

[414] The interview given to Nicole Pope, *Le Monde*, 28 April 1998.

go to a corner and pass the rest of my life in retreat, far away from people, in a remote corner.[415]

The existence and the goal of the schools also are related to the role Gülen assigns to Turkey:

A nation must have an important place in the balance of power in the world. But at this moment with a sense and thought of a nation which missed the boat, I am hoping that just like a worm becoming a butterfly through metamorphosis, this nation is going to break its shell, again it will branch out to the four corners of the world, it is going to make itself felt with magnificence. Let our nation open up with its dervishes to the four corners of the world, let it take that spirit and meaning. Let it express itself at different platforms and let us regain our status in the balance of power among the nations. Another aim of the schools that we were able to establish in almost every nation of Euro-Asia is exactly this.[416]

In addition to the aforementioned aim, spreading of a peaceful and humane religious understanding holds great significance, in order to prevent gradually increasing radicalism and to prevent some people from achieving legitimacy by exploiting religion and recruiting prospective members. Gülen's philosophy and terminology demonstrates exact opposition to radicalism.

We have to be a light for humanity; even if it is as strong as a candle, we have to seek ways to enlighten our environment with the light of faith. Enlightening the darkness could only be possible through good Muslim attributes.[417]

At this point, another important feature of education is revealed: All of this effort is made to become a good Muslim and to share the highest values of Islam with people from other faiths and nationalities. He explains:

What we mean by education ... is to explain the beauty of Islam to humanity. We will try to stay away from political fights and goals, we are going to learn our religion solely for the purpose of gaining the pleasure of God and then without expecting anything in return, if need be, we will do any work, simple or hard, and earn our livelihood through our own sweat, but in any

---

[415] *Ibid.*

[416] The interview given to Taha Akyol and Cengiz Çandar, NTV, 27 February 1998.

[417] Gülen 2009c, 93.

case and by any means possible we are going to carry the name of Muhammad, peace and blessings be upon him, into the desirous and needy hearts! The purpose of our existence is to know God and to enable others know Him and love Him. This is the reason of our existence. If we do not do this, then there is no sense of being in this world, no sense of breathing anymore.[418]

79. Where, when, and how were the schools first established?

The first fruits of Gülen's encouragements and inspirations were obtained in 1979, by opening in İzmir a university preparation course, under the administration of the Akyazılı Foundation for Secondary and Higher Education. It was followed by the opening of student dorms in İzmir. During a period of ten years, the courses and the dorms spread to other countries. Before the establishment of the İzmir Yamanlar Koleji High School, it served as a university dorm, without any charge to the students, between 1975 and 1978. In 1978, the building became a university preparation course. The Yamanlar High School, which started academic studies on 15 November, 1982, is the pioneering institution of the Gülen schools.

Over time, the scope of the movement's activities expanded further. A series of schools were opened like Fatih, Yamanlar, Aziziye, and Samanyolu. All of these schools, which charge tuition fees, became centers of attraction.

In 1991, when the Soviet Union collapsed, the Gülen Movement had ten years of experience in the field of education. Furthermore, even before the collapse of the Soviet Union, some names close to Gülen had begun to search for ways and feasibility of establishing some schools in Central Asia. Indeed, Gülen had already begun talking about Central Asia in his sermons, in various mosques of İzmir and İstanbul.

Gülen always credits Atatürk for the ideas of carrying the educational activities to Central Asia. With a quotation from journalist Nazlı Ilıcak,

> Many years ago, Atatürk had told us what we are supposed to do today: "Today Soviet Union is our friend, our neighbor, our ally. We need this friendship. But no one can predict today what will happen tomorrow. It can break up just like the Ottomans, just like the Austria–Hungary. The nations that it holds inside its hands firmly now, can slip away. The world can come

---

[418] *Ibid.*, 96–97.

to a new equilibrium. Turkey has known what to do then. Under the rule of this friend of us are our brothers, whose faith and religion and essence are the same. We have to be ready to help them. Being ready does not mean quietly waiting for that day. We have to be prepared. How do the nations get prepared for this? They do by keeping the spiritual bridges firm and sound. Language is a bridge. Faith is a bridge. History is a bridge. We have to descend to our roots and we have to unite in history which was divided by incidents, we cannot wait for them [outside Turks] to come close to us. We have to approach them."[419]

In summary, Gülen saw the dissolution of the Soviet Union as an opportunity and directed and guided his fellow workers.

In his sermons, after retelling the story of Hijra (the Muslims move from Mecca to Medina), Gülen talks about going to the aid of fellow Turks in Central Asia, in order to emulate that event and encourage businessmen and teachers to go there. He made his greatest proposal regarding Central Asia in 1989, in his sermon that he gave in Süleymaniye Mosque of İstanbul, where he explained the process of the new world order to a vast audience.

Gülen's encouragement gave its first fruits in January 1990. A group of 11 businessmen visited Batumi province of Georgia. In May of the same year, a second group of 37 persons went to Batumi first and then to Azerbaijan. This group was both travelling and, at the same time, was studying the legal regulations to transfer students from Azerbaijan to Turkey. After this trip, in every part of Turkey, corporations were established for the schools to be founded. The grand "mobilization" had begun. In many countries of Central Asia schools were opened. They were followed by universities.

By the things it achieved, the movement was carrying Turkey to the world, while it was carrying the world to Turkey. Turkey was now becoming a central power, which could not be torn apart from the world. Gülen explains this phenomenon as follows:

> Turkey cannot be torn and separated from the world, when it is separated, it cannot be left alive, just like a branch which is separated from a tree. It would dry out. Turkey has to be in integration with the world. In such integration, at the head of the countries to have a sincere relation with us are

---

[419] Ilıcak 1998.

the Central Asian countries. Namely, there is a sort of Asian unity. In a sense, we are different branches of the same tree.

For this reason, I have oriented my friends to Asia. Maybe, this was a fantasy. But I thought there should not have been any vacuum for others to come there and establish schools. Even the Europeans should not have found vacuum there. The Turkish people with a sense of fidelity supported, and the schools in Asia were opened. Some of them are now able to stand on their own feet. If there were no support for them until now, it would not have been possible to retain this business there. We had an opportunity; we wanted to make use of it, by believing in it firmly, with a sense of responsibility.[420]

One of the individuals who took a personal interest in Turkish schools was the President of Turkey, Turgut Özal (from 1989 to 1993). President Özal did not hesitate to have personal contacts with the Kazak and Uzbek leaders on behalf of the Gülen schools. Gülen notes that during the February 28 process (the military memorandum that has been labeled as a "postmodern coup") which started in 1997, no pressure was sensed in the schools aboard. And as a matter of fact, then President of Turkey, Süleyman Demirel, wrote a letter to Eduard Shevardnadze, the President of Georgia, expressing his personal support for these schools.

With the experience in Central Asia, the Gülen Movement became a global player in the field of education. The most successful in the educational mobilization is Kazakhstan, as 29 schools were established there in two years by the people who came to this country in 1992. Four years later, Süleyman Demirel University was opened. After Turgut Özal wrote a letter of recommendation to the President of Kazakhstan, Nursultan Nazarbayev, Gülen's followers found better opportunities to operate in this country.

The schools are now operating in Africa, as well. Turkey, for the first time since the Ottomans, returned to Africa through something outside of the state, the Gülen schools. At this moment, the schools have encompassed the continent of Africa from one end to the other. The most talented and the brightest children of the local population find places in these schools. The children are accepted, sometimes through tests and sometimes through mere selection, are only 1 out of 20 of those who apply and, in some places, 1 out of 40. While these schools have been charging

---

[420] Turgut 1998.

tuition fees, the rate is adjusted according to the conditions of respective countries.

80. What are the goals of the schools? What were they at the beginning and what are they now?

Although these questions are constantly asked, Gülen does not show any impatience and explains:

> Raising generations who take as their life principles love, peace, tolerance and intercultural dialog, who are respectful for their own national and spiritual values, who could read the world correctly, establishing bridges between these countries and Turkey as well as among themselves, and thus through these contribute to the world peace. ... The aim of opening these schools is to lessen the load on the shoulders of the state, at the same time to raise the generations who give priority to national and spiritual values, owning up to the universal values. This aim was the same at the inception of the schools and it is continuing in the same way now.[421]

There are two points worthy of consideration here. First, there is the desire to encourage the students in the schools to have an attachment to their cultures and their national values; second, there is the goal to develop manifold ties between Turkey and various countries, in order to place Turkey in the center of the alliances to be formed in the future. If both of these aims can be reconciled in a global vision, the movement's followers believe that there are no serious obstacles to seeing the 21st century as the "Turkish Century."

In the course of this aim, the quality of the people to open the way and the correctness of the methods chosen are important. Gülen stresses that it is absolutely necessary for those people who would accomplish the ideal advanced here by the movement to be faithful and not to avoid any sacrifice. For this reason, Gülen places significance on those persons having a strong faith.

He also believes that the most influential of the educational vehicles is language. Since there are various religions in the countries where the participants are present, he defends that the main bridge to carry the universal elements of Turkish culture should be language, namely Turkish. Therefore, all Gülen schools attribute a special significance to Turkish

---

[421] Doğu Ergil's interview with Gülen.

language education. Indeed, in the Turkish Olympiads held annually, the Turkish language is spoken by youth whose races, colors, religions, and nationalities are extremely diverse. Notably, their Turkish is at a higher level compared to the Turkish spoken in the less developed rural areas of Turkey.

Gülen summarizes the matter as follows:

> The business of introducing the 1000 years of culture could only be accomplished by the volunteer heroes ... by making the Turkish language a world language ... If things like desiring politics or administration in the future enters into this business of education, if it is mixed with it, that would defile the matter, it would cause decadence.[422]

With this warning, he sets a limit or barrier in front of his followers in the movement—not to deviate from the course or goals set for them today.

According to Gülen,

> Everything depends on knowledge. Nothing can be done without knowledge. So much so that in the world and in Turkey, the main cause of the problems observed all the time is the neglect of an education with a sound and realistic base.[423]

For this reason, the Gülen schools take extra care to make sure that the education they provide is of the highest quality. Of course, it is indispensable that the program executed must be in accordance with the local and national ordinances. Gülen explains,

> If you do not implement whatever the curriculum of the countries where you go, would they permit you to do the things you are planning to do? Would they allow you to include Turkish in some places as an elective course and in some others as a required one? We are saying dialog and tolerance, even that is also questioned in some places, if you do not take a step towards them, you do not respect others' laws and status, if you do not conduct yourselves as mature as to be able to share certain things with them, and then they would not come closer to you.
>
> These are the things to be considered as facilitating our job of explaining ourselves. Otherwise, even if the organizational aspect of the matters is yours, if you retain rigidity in your behaviors, it would not be possible to

---

[422] Gündem 2005, 138.

[423] The interview given to Nicole Pope, *Le Monde*, 28 April 1998.

explain anything to others. Expressing ourselves, contributing into the new formations in the world, is being done in order to prevent chaos that people like Huntington are predicting, through every effort within our means.[424]

Furthermore, he states,

"...education, besides being the best way of serving our country, is the way to serve the entire humanity and the most important means for a dialog in the age when our world shrunk like a small village. After all, education is a humane service for others. All humans were sent to this world in order to be perfected, to be improved through education."[425]

Here, Gülen is referring to Rumi, because Rumi once said, "One of my feet is on the center and the other, like a leg of a compass, in the realm of 72 nations." Rumi was able to open the door of a dialog to anyone receptive to it.

81. What is the quality of education?

Before everything else, these schools impart every good and quality education. This matter has been proven by all the students graduating from these schools to have a good chance of entering one of the universities. It is also confirmed by their successes in the Scientific Olympiads held in the region or internationally, by winning the highest levels and therefore bringing the medals home. In the Scientific Olympiads, these schools have become competitors with their counterparts in Turkey and they are contesting among themselves now.[426]

The schools under consideration are very successful in the respective countries. For that reason, the foreign mission representatives in the respective countries, in general, prefer these schools to enroll their children. For example, the mission chiefs in Romania, who represent Czechoslovakia, Indonesia, Congo, South Africa, India and Iran, as well as other diplomats and businessmen, have enrolled their children in these institutions.

The curriculum in the schools does not prioritize Turkey or Islam. Indeed, this would not possible according to domestic laws. A secular

---

[424] Gündem 2005, 139.
[425] Gülen 2006d, 243.
[426] Doğu Ergil's interview with Gülen.

education is provided, and there is no religious education, only the history of religions. Therefore, it is not possible to disseminate the *jamaat* values, as some claim. The educational model adopted seeks to reconcile the divisive approaches between secular education and faith, reason, modernity, and tradition.

Despite the fact that the main language of instruction is in English, through the inspiration and encouragement of Gülen, the goal is to make the Turkish language also an international language of communication. In all Gülen schools and universities, an intensive education of Turkish is maintained. Gülen sees the language as a cultural bridge and wants it to be built firmly. Diligent teachers between 22 and 35 years old, originating from Turkey, perform this task and believe what they are doing is part of their worship to God. All of them, men and women, are well educated and fluent in English. They are young; mostly coming from a rural background and from families with meager means, but they had the opportunity to be educated in high quality universities in Turkey. For most, the Gülen Movement gave them this chance. They believe that they are doing a service to humanity by being in the movement. They also believe that they are repaying the movement for the opportunities provided to them, by showing fidelity to it, when needed. They reserve most of their time to their students. Their salaries vary between 400 and 600 US dollars.

Another thing that circulates about the Gülen schools is that these schools not only impart an education at the highest level of quality, but also that they provide a good education in the fields of social relations and human values. For example, when foreign students who are being educated in these schools are interviewed, some remark that they did not get along with their parents prior to the admittance into these schools, but now they have good relationships with them. Some report that they quit bad habits such as drinking alcohol and smoking. In general, students say that they gave up thinking about themselves only and now feel more sensitive and responsible towards others. Gülen attributes these changes to the fact that these students are being raised with the customary and traditional manners of the Turkish nation.

In this educational endeavor, the aim is not to give religious knowledge or to inculcate the consciousness to establish a religious regime, but to make the students gain an ethical and moral worldview which sits on universal human values. Of course, the teachers and administrators are sensitive in making sure that these values do not violate the basic Islamic values. But these values are imparted as a cultural element, not as an infrastructure for a political project.

One of the areas where extra care is taken is that the education provided is to form a setting of peace where the operation is in progress for reconciliation, societal peace, and tolerance. When the students diffuse the values in society that they have acquired in school, everyone is proud of their achievements and the youth raised in these schools become role models for others. This state of affairs makes it possible for others, who did not have the chance to enter these institutions, to be won over, who otherwise would be left on the street, prone to any radical extreme ideology. For example, since the majority of the Gülen schools in the South-eastern Turkey are boarding schools, parents know where their children are and feel secure and safe; they know what their children are doing and live in peace, feel at ease.

What is understood is that Turkish schools, which have spread to many parts of the world, have indirect effects, in addition to imparting the values of becoming fine individuals and good human beings. For instance, after the collapse of the Soviet system, a period of ambiguity took place in Central Asia. In this milieu, in Central Asia and Azerbaijan, the impact of fundamentalism was felt strongly. By the interference of the movement, through its schools and foundations, religious extremities were to a great extent prevented.

There is a Turkish school in Zamboanga, Philippines, where one half of the students are Muslims and the other half, Christians. Its name is Philippine Turkish Tolerance High School. The city is located in a region where the anti-government forces are effective in their fight and struggle against government forces; the region is unstable and going through a civil war. The school in this region selected its students from among both Muslims and Christians. Along with providing education to over one thousand students, the school is teaching tolerance and living peacefully together. Thus, the school has become a source of stability in a place of instability; it shows that peace and the culture of shared living are possible. The society has embraced this peacemaking school and supports it.

In the schools, Gülen's philosophy is reflected in the culture of shared living that it tries to impart; the dominant thought among the participants is to leave behind the ethical notions that is derived from militant secularism and materialist and the modernist ideology which alienates human beings and separates them from spiritual foundations, and instead, to erect a contemporary ethical understanding derived from Islam. Then later, the effort is to establish a marriage between this and the daily or contemporary technology and scientific thinking which has been lost in the classical religious institutions. If this cannot be achieved, Gülen fears that our national unity will be destroyed.

The movement's educational projects are neither backward nor reactionary, as some claim. Gülen believes that there was "a golden age" in the past, and it was the time of Prophet Muhammad and his Four Rightly Guided Caliphs. He takes as his reference point the period in which the society ruled itself; the notions of justice and morality and individual virtues were derived from the shared common interpretation of the religion, and these were not defiled by politics. Nevertheless, his referencing of this time is limited to the dominant ethical norms and the notion of justice, that is all. He does not seek to go back or to establish a political system that resembles the one at that time. In fact, Gülen severely criticizes fundamentalists who hold these views.

He remarks that the expression he often uses like "spirituality" and "spiritual values" do not signify an aspiration to make the religion dominant in the secular societies, as some believe. Spirituality for him comprises virtues such as morality, logic, spiritual balance, empathy, and an open heart.

Therefore, in his definition of spirituality, justice and peace-loving are included. He defines a genuine Muslim as one from the hands and tongue of whom no one is disturbed, no one is harmed. The function of education is determined accordingly—both equipping the student with knowledge and skills, necessary in later life, and, at the same time, making these virtues a second nature for that student.

What he expects from the teachers is to have the students gain a good personality, beyond their courses to enable that student to see the world in a holistic manner. What he offers in character building is to enable the students to become useful individuals, to have empathy, to think of others, to be tolerant, supportive, and not going to extremes in passions.

Gülen sees teachers, who teach only, in return for a salary, without taking any interest in formation of their students' character, as "shepherding the blind by the blind."

In short, the schools, established by following the inspiration and exhortations of Gülen and according to his philosophy, are trying to repair the broken relationships between secular institutions and faith. In this sense, he represents a modern and national illustration of the Turkish Islamic identity.

82. In which countries are there schools? How many schools have been established? How many are universities?

After a moment of hesitation, Gülen replies:

> In fact, it is difficult to say the number of schools definitely. It is because, though there is a serious bond of heart between them, the Turkish firms in many countries have been acting independently of each other and without fail almost in every month, a new school is being established in one or two places. Up until now, no list or tally regarding the number of schools has been prepared; no study about the sum total has been made. Nevertheless, some newspapers have published estimates of numbers. It would not be a lie, if I say that no one knows the current numbers.[427]

Nevertheless, information about the schools abroad can be obtained from the participants of the Gülen Movement. At the time of this writing the following schools were identified:

North America
Canada: language course
Mexico: 1 school and a cultural center
USA: 5 private schools, above 50 cultural centers

South America
Argentine: cultural center
Brazil: cultural center
Chile: cultural center
Colombia: cultural center

Africa
Algeria: language course
Burkina Faso: 1 school

---

[427] Doğu Ergil's interview with Gülen.

Cameroon: 1 school

Central African Republic: 1 school

Chad: 1 school

Congo: 1 school

Egypt: language course and student youth hostels

Ethiopia: 1 school

Gambia: 1 school

Ghana: 1 school

Guinea: 1 school

Guinea-Bissau: 1 school

Kenya: 4 schools

Madagascar: 1 school, 1 cultural center

Malawi: 1 school

Mali: 1 school

Mauritania: 1 school

Morocco: 4 schools

Mozambique: 1 school

Niger: 1 school

Nigeria: 4 schools, 1 cultural center

Senegal: 1 school

South African Republic: 4 schools

Sudan: 2 schools

Tanzania: educational complex (dispensary, complex with sports fields comprising primary and high school)

Togo: 1 school

Uganda: 1 school

Oceana

Australia: 7 schools

Indonesia: 4 schools

Philippines: 4 schools

Asia

Afghanistan: 4 schools

Bangladesh: 4 schools

Burma: 2 schools
Cambodia: 2 schools
India: 3 schools, 1 language course
Iraq: 4 schools
Israel: 1 cultural center
Japan: 1 school, 5 language courses, cultural centers
Kazakhstan: 29 schools
Kirgizstan: 12 schools
Malaysia: 1 school
Mongolia: 4 schools
Nepal: 1 school
Pakistan: 6 schools, and 1 cultural center
South Korea: 1 cultural center
Tajikistan: 13 schools
Thailand: 3 schools
Turkmenistan: 20 schools
Uzbekistan: 1 school
Vietnam: 1 school
Yemen: 1 school

Europe
Albania: 4 schools
Austria: 1 language course
Azerbaijan: 12 schools
Belgium: 1 school, student dormitory, language course, and cultural center
Bosnia Herzegovina: 2 schools
Bulgaria: 3 schools
Czech Republic: 1 cultural center
Denmark: language course, and cultural center
England: student dormitory, language course, and cultural center
Estonia: 1 cultural center
Finland: 1 school, language course, and cultural center
France: cultural center, and language course
Georgia: 3 schools
Germany: 3 school, language courses, and cultural centers

Hungary: 1 language course, 1 cultural center

Italy: 1 cultural center

Latvia: 1 cultural center

Lithuania: 1 cultural center

Macedonia: 4 schools

Moldova: 2 schools

Netherlands: student dormitory, and cultural center

Norway: language course, and cultural center

Poland: 1 cultural center

Portugal: 1 cultural center

Romania: 4 schools

Russian Federation: 6 schools

Slovakia: 1 cultural center

Spain: cultural center, and language course

Sweden: cultural center, and language course

Switzerland: student dormitory, and cultural center

Ukraine: 2 schools

Universities

Azerbaijan, Georgia, Kazakhstan, Kirgizstan, and Turkmenistan

83. Do the schools provide religious education, as well as secular education?

Gülen gave his answer without hesitation:

> In the schools religious education has not been provided. The courses of "Religious Culture" and "Ethical Knowledge" which are part of the curriculum used in the primary and secondary institutions has been studied. The number of hours in these schools and in the public schools is the same. Of course, these schools have adopted secular educational system and in the main they are following the same line as the basic principles of the Ministry of National Education. These schools, with their programs, superior technical capabilities and laboratories, have been established after the model of the familiar Anadolu Lisesi [public first class high schools]. These schools are operating in conformity with the legal regulations and educational philosophy of each respective country.[428]

---

[428] Exclusive answer delivered to Doğu Ergil.

Those who visit the Gülen schools in Turkey report that they have not seen female students with headscarves. On the other hand, Gülen states that if the local customs and traditions require the girls to wear a headscarf, namely if the student is wearing the headscarf outside the school, then they are not interfered with in the school, either.

Religion in the Gülen schools is not seen as a vehicle consisting of certain symbols, in order to develop a consciousness for a regime based on the *Shari'a*, but as a source for a culture of solidarity and ethics inspired by the religion of Islam. This culture of solidarity, on an individual level, consists of the principles of respect, love, mutual help, and training for a common effort; at the social level, it consists of not going to extremes and extravagancy, not resorting to violence, tolerance for differences, becoming frugal by escaping the attractiveness of consumerism, and producing surplus value by investments.

Gülen states that these values are inherent in the Islamic and Turkish national traditions as an essential part of Anatolia. Therefore they are easily accepted by society and by working on them, a "civil society initiative" can be achieved easily. This approach is very different from the political function that is given as a task by the state. According to him, this is "a civil mobilization"; it has neither a political feature nor a political aim. Gülen sees religion as a system of values orienting humanity. He opposes that the religion be used as a source for a political agenda to rule a society. For this reason, he believes the relationship between religion and state should operate in parallel spheres, within the framework of the principle of "live and let live." This notion is the source of modern philosophers' and political scientists' formulation, "secular society and religion respected by the state." Therefore, the aim of opening these schools is not to establish another alternative system, opposed to the one in existence.

Gülen remarks,

> ... Rather than one perspective, formal education, based on certain molds in these schools, I conjecture that an education, based on critical thinking and research, is provided. I would like to stress that we never conceive education as dressing the students in uniforms; on the contrary, individual differences are paid attention and a great importance is place on them, and I would like to express that these differences are even encouraged. However, we have to qualify that never because of the structure or regulations of the schools, but due to the circumstances of our time, today's student is more

interested in the physical sciences, he or she has a tendency toward that field. The student cannot find an opportunity and possibility to display the individual differences through art and literature. The reason for this is not the schools and the education they impart, but the circumstances dictated by this age. Nevertheless, when these students are contacted, I am sure; it can be observed that there are among them many different ideas, tastes, and shades of colors and tones in the fields of art and literature.[429]

84. What is the main language of instruction in the schools? Are other languages taught? Is Arabic one of those?

It is primarily in the local language of a particular country. The courses of Mathematics, Physics, Chemistry, Biology, and Computer Sciences are taught in English. In addition, as a second language Turkish, too, is taught. No Arabic education is provided in countries other than the ones in which Arabic is the mother tongue. These are the countries like Algeria, Morocco, and Sudan. In these schools both Turkish as well as English is taught in good quality. In some places, Turkish is the second language; in some others, it is an elective course.[430]

85. What is the benefit of teaching Turkish abroad?

I carry the conviction that teaching Turkish and thinking in this language would earn for Turkey friendship, in a rather large circle. ... We have to make Turkish a language of the world in the future. Turkey's meeting with a new Turkic world and mix with them, the existence of new Turkish generations in Europe, the USA, and Australia, could be considered as a sign that Turkish will become a world language. For this reason, the development of Turkish is very important in terms of our future. On the other hand, realization of integration with the West, for instance, to become aware of the innovations obtained through the development of technology, namely with the transfer of knowledge and technology, adoption of all the fruitful outcomes of the age, [in a Turkified form], would serve the purpose of Turkish to become a common language.[431]

One becomes the owner of a system of thought through the knowledge he has and the words one knows through the books he reads. Those who are familiar with the languages like French or English, if they do not know their mother tongues very well, over time through the ideas passing, through the filters of print or audio material, comes under the impact of

---

[429] The interview given to Hakan Yavuz, *Milliyet*, 11 August 1997.
[430] Exclusive answer delivered to Doğu Ergil.
[431] Gülen 2007c, 170.

those ideas. They start thinking, sensing, hearing, and understanding like French or British people. Therefore, one of the conditions for preserving our essence and remain as ourselves is to learn our language with its particular attributes to use it properly and protect it. Along with our religion, we have to protect our tongue, as well. We are disseminating our national and religious values through our language, and we are telling the virtues of our religion through it. In that case, each one of us has to be sensitive on this issue, and we have to try to use this language everywhere and always in the proper manner.[432]

Gülen not only mentions language as a vehicle of communication, but he also discusses language as an essential part of a civilizational project. If we are to experience a Turkish renaissance, beginning with the 21st century, and if we are to produce a new civilization Gülen believes that the Turkish language has to be both a crane and a carrier, lifting that civilization and carrying it beyond its borders. But for this to be realized, first the Turkish language has to be developed and brought to the proper degree of maturity, able to comprehend and accommodate all the developments in science and technology. His suggestions on this matter are the following:

> Today, there is an enormously vast Turkic world, in order to actualize all these functions, to work with our insufficient and broken language like Persian, or Arabic or English and then to reach some goals seems to be rather difficult. When we look at it from this perspective, the importance of the Turkish language would place responsibilities on everyone, particularly the specialists of literature. For this reason, not satisfied with only learning and teaching what is already available, we should raise great talents and we should burden them with great responsibilities, so that we can make sure that our language would be represented at a very high level. For this, while inventing new words in accordance with its own rules, I believe in the necessity of retaining the words adapted into our language, and became part of the nature of this nation from other languages through their usage over the centuries. Yes, these words which became the property of this nation are now ours and form another dimension of the enrichment of our language. ...
>
> In order for our nation to explain itself to the whole world, to be able to prove itself one more time depends, in one sense, on the Turkish language becoming a world language.
>
> Lastly, I would like to present one subjective assessment of my own: Since the time past, I have had a different kind of love for the Turkish lan-

---

[432] Gülen 2010d, 33.

guage; and even a longing for it. For instance, if I was given the equal talent to be able to write in both either in Turkish or Arabic, that it is the language of the Qur'an, I would have chosen the Turkish language. ... In summary, Turkey and the Central Asia marching on to the future have to make Turkish the language of the world at any cost.[433]

86. How are the need for teachers and administrators in the schools met?

The firms, to which the schools belong, announce the teacher vacancies through the internet and the media, and among those who look with sympathy to this movement are selected through an interview. Another way is to select among those who are suggested and advised by those who are familiar with them since education years in the colleges. In addition, from among the graduates of these private high schools, those who have completed their university studies and have teacher certificates, return to these schools to teach, as a sign of their fidelity. The senior teachers in these schools hold seminars to train the newcomers to prepare them for the new job.[434]

The salaries of the teachers who are employed in these schools are always at a modest level.

87. What are the qualifications required of teachers and administrators in these schools?

The appointments of the teachers and administrators are carried out by the executive boards and board of trusties of the educational firms. One representative person from every firm has the task of supervising the educational activities of the schools; and in each respective school, there is a room to accommodate that representative.

With the proposal of the officer of the firm who acts as a founding representative, the principal is determined. Afterwards, as a result of the research and investigations of the principal, the prospective teachers are determined from among those who applied for teaching positions. The primary criteria looked for in a teacher are the values like achievements, self-sacrificing, honesty, good morals, the avoidance of bad habits.[435]

---

[433] Gülen 2007c, 171–173.

[434] Exclusive answer delivered to Doğu Ergil.

[435] *Ibid.*

According to Gülen, desiring the duty and applying for a teaching or administrative position is a sign of fidelity, and their going off to the duty is seen as a kind of Hijra. In order to be successful, they should have strong national and religious feelings. These characteristics play an important role in the assignment process of teachers.

88. What kind of extracurricular activities are offered outside the formal education in the schools?

> In the schools outside the regular education in the classes, whatever are fixed by the Ministry of National Education are approved as club activities, have been carried out by the specialist teachers. These activities vary somewhat, show some differences from primary schools to high schools.
>
> Sports activities are taken seriously. Through the clubs established by both school teams and the schools themselves, a vast amount of sports activities are being carried out. The sportive activities [swimming, soccer, basketball, and volleyball], cultural activities [theatre, cinema, photography, literature, publishing newspapers and magazines, and sightseeing], social projects, and studies for the Science Olympiads have been performed.[436]

An outside observer watching one or more Turkish Olympiads, held annually by the Gülen Movement in Turkey, could not help but take a note of these facts: Students coming from different racial, religious, and national backgrounds speak the Turkish language so well that they can even imitate some of theatre and vocal artists whose songs they are singing to the minute details, even the gestures and voice tones. They display many different artistic talents. This demonstrates that these schools are not behind in their club activities, compared to their successful counterparts in Turkey.

89. In countries where the majority of the population is are Muslim, how are religious and ethical courses that are not taught in these schools provided? How is religious education provided in non-Muslim countries?

The answer of Gülen to this question is short and categorical: "In the schools, no religious education is provided."

---

[436] *Ibid.*

This answer is provided with the expression of a person who is tired of repeating that the schools, attributed to his name, do not constitute an alternative model to the existing educational system in Turkey:

> In all of these institutions, entirely the same curriculum and programs which are carried out in similar official educational institutions are being implemented. For it to be otherwise is not possible, anyway. The schools that we are talking about are constantly under the official supervision. Those abroad, since their inception up until today, in terms of some for 9 or 10 years, it is for sure, they are constantly both under the gaze of respective intelligence services and also under the control and supervision of the educational ministries.
>
> Furthermore, all of these nations, on the issue of *irtica* [literally, the "old coming back," but in Turkish political parlance, it meant the "display of any Islamic sentiment." The term was invented by power elite in Turkey; the closest approximation is its rendering as "obscurantism"], are as sensitive as Turkey is. Besides, many people from all walks of life from Turkey went to see these schools; and many journalists wrote their impressions of them for days. As of today, was there any concrete evidence of the "education of *irtica*" found in any of these schools?
>
> Apart from the inspections, in these schools there are students from every segment of the society. Now, if there was no complaint from any of these on this issue, if no complaints came from the parents, within what kind of excuse, an *irtica* is attributed to these schools?
>
> As for the claim that through conducts, a kind of religion is inspired in these students: There are universal ethical criteria, there are forms of behavior required of the teachers by the educational institutions. Why should it be considered to be a religious education to behave within the framework of moral standards? Isn't it true that there are many ethical criteria, some of which are: treating the pupil well, to have a smiling face, respect for the elders, love for the minors, to be helpful to people in every matter, generosity, and forgiveness. Should they behave otherwise, should an unethical conduct be encouraged? We have never had a cause or mission implying political Islam. On the contrary, the expression I always use, "the Muslim identity from Turkey" was identified by the specialists of the related fields as "cultural Islam."[437]

This assessment implies that the state should not enter into the field of faith. This was not intentionally done by Gülen, but the widespread discussion in the world about it is along this line. As a consequence of the state's interference in the religious affairs, the following could result:

---

[437] The interview given to *Aksiyon*, nr. 183, 6 June 1998.

1. The religion, being an important component of the cultural field, is losing its organic tie with the society and is going into a mechanical relationship with a political institution, where it can be manipulated. This is aptly called the "politicization of religion."

2. The state, being the main institution of the politics, is entering into a relationship of tension with politicized religion.

3. If the religion (in broader sense, culture) is able to retain its autonomy, in the process of the society's adaptation to the age, it can establish more healthy relationships with and through new interpretations; it can respond more positively to the realities of the day. Whereas, when it comes under the influence of the politics (in other words the state), religion itself is frozen, becoming static. Its relationship with the change in the society and the world is broken. It is squeezed between its own precepts and the state's norms and rules. It cannot develop and it cannot be developed. It must assume a role that defends the existing political order, which is against its nature, or religion is made into an ideological vehicle for rebelling against the established political order by the state or forces outside the state.

90. Do the schools charge tuition fees?

Yes, in general the schools charge tuition fees. In every province, according to the economic level of that province, students are enrolled with a tuition fee, fixed, and announced by the executive committees and board members. In fixing the prices, the inflation rate is taken into account. As for the tuition fees of the schools abroad, it is arranged according to the conditions of the respective countries. While in Kenya, with the standards of Africa, 1500 US dollars are required for the high school level education, in Malawi, a poorer country, 700 US dollars are charged annually.

While at the stage of the establishment of these schools, a lot of support comes at the local and national level. In some places the host countries are giving the buildings. In some others, they do the restoration themselves. In Saint Petersburg, the building was donated by them. To an extent they supported, too, and one or two wealthy men in İstanbul said, "Let us finance them." While these schools are being opened, in some places [sometimes in older buildings] the men of religion, the clergymen are doing the restoration. ...

Those schools starting off without any tuition fees at the beginning are reaching a level where they try to stand on their own feet. They, on the other hand, become ready to accept it. They say: "These schools should not remain a burden on Turkey anymore. ... Since they provide good quality education, our children were able to capture some important spots in the Science Olympiads."[438]

91. How are the financial needs of students met?

In general, the schools charge tuition fees. The financial needs of the schools are met through the income coming from the students. When there is a financial deficit, these deficits are closed by the founding corporations, by additional help. The expenditures of the schools opened in partnership with the home country, are met by the local authorities. In addition, a help is sought from the families who can afford. Further, if there is a financial deficit that is met by the philanthropic businessmen there, who feel sympathy for the Gülen Movement, and philanthropic activities in general.[439]

Of course, it is not an easy matter to establish schools in foreign countries. Another issue is the question of to whom these schools belong? To this question, this is the answer Gülen gives:

The schools do not belong to certain individuals; these educational institutions belong to this nation. We have no love and passion other than seeking the pleasure of God and share our historical gains with the people of the world, and establish islands of peace in this bloody geography. We believe as a nation, we have a lot of beautiful things to offer. It is both our right and duty to display these beautiful things in an exhibition. Now in our age, these exhibitions are the educational institutions, the schools, and cultural centers, and even the business places established by those who went there with a consideration of trading and business. Because the things pouring out of their conducts and behaviors would again be our past, our good tastes, our religious and ethical considerations, and these values of our world mean a lot of worthy things in the eyes of the members of other civilizations.

If you still have doubts, go look, and ask the people involved. If you sincerely would like to learn from where the water for this mill comes, follow it from where it originates; in its channels, at the place it turns the wheel. If you are not biased, you would also see it. Whatever the power force was gaining independence to our nation, it is the same power and force behind these educational activities. These are the services, displayed

---

[438] Exclusive answer delivered to Doğu Ergil.
[439] *Ibid.*

in another way which was displayed through sacrifices during the War of Independence and the sources are in the hearts.[440]

Primarily through the dedication, help, and support of individuals (some wealthy, some middle class who believe that they are performing a religious and ethical duty) and through the efforts and sacrifices of the teachers, these schools increasingly stand on their own. It carries significance that nearly everything is accomplished by the volunteers, without expecting anything from the state. This state of affairs has resulted in the independence of both the movement and the schools. The movement which values independence has not sought outside resources, in order not to owe anything to anyone. The effort to produce its own resources has built an industrial and business empire, which is increasingly growing.

92. What is the relationship of the schools with national and local administrators?

The schools have been operating, bound by the laws of the respective countries and are inspected. To the extent that they allow, Ministry of National Education, Anadolu Lisesi curriculum is implemented. In every country they receive approval and encouragements by the administrators of the educational institutions and other organizations. Even these administrators desire their relatives to attend these schools.[441]

In order to gain trust, teachers and other staff members of the Gülen schools introduce themselves in positive ways to the government officials of the countries in which they had no previous familiarity. After passing this stage, again it became indispensable to get to know the people in positions of power, in order to acquire the school buildings, to prepare the school programs, to recruit local teachers, and to develop a structure that is in conformity with domestic laws, rules, and regulations. When this is accomplished, the schools are ready for operation.

After the establishment of the schools, the teachers and the administrators acquire a large circle of friendship with a view to introduce the investors arriving from Turkey with dignitaries of the host countries and the prominent members of the business community there. Success in business and trade increase the trust and the desire to cooperate. This

---

[440] Gülen 2010f, 221–222.
[441] Exclusive answer delivered to Doğu Ergil.

state of affairs has brought the Gülen schools into a central position. Indeed, some teachers and administrators in these schools have received awards, including honorary titles, by the leaders and other government officials of respective countries and continue to do so.

93. In general, what sectors of the society are enrolling their children in these schools?

> From every sector applying, from every level of achievements, the pupils are accepted into these schools. In selecting the students, no sector, class, or levels are taken into account.[442]

Elsewhere, Gülen states that their doors are open to every sector to avoid discrimination and prejudices. In turn, this helps their faith and the philosophy of the movement to be "progressive and inclusive."

Additionally, a diverse student body is utilitarian: Imagine that after 15 or 20 years, Central Asia will be governed by the leaders who have graduated from the schools established by the participants of the Gülen Movement, who speak Turkish and English well and who are well educated in the Western sense and Western standards. One does not have force oneself to see that this vision will be reality tomorrow. It is so clear because children graduating from these schools are the cream of the crop.

Some of the African government officials are also enrolling their children in these schools. Their interest was formed when the schools were established. For example, Ali Tambwe, one of the leading public figures of the country and a colleague of Julius Kambarage Nyerere, who pioneered Tanzania's independence movement. Ali Hassan Mwingi, who served as President of the country in the first half of the 1990s, invited members of the Gülen Movement to Tanzania, in order to establish a school in his country. One of the closest names to Sezai Kara, who established a Gülen school in Mozambique, was one of the leading figures in the country, Amade Camal.

94. How is the curriculum of these schools decided?

> The schools have been operating according to the rules of the curriculum of respective countries. To the extent that the native country's laws permit,

---

[442] *Ibid.*

the curriculum of the Anadolu Lisesi of the Ministry of National Education is being implemented, with a mutual agreement. In the "International Schools," in addition to the local curriculum, the curriculum determined by the chain of schools or the network, to which that particular school belongs, is implemented [e.g. ECIS].

The books, which got the approval from the related departments of the Ministry of National Education in Turkey, are being studied. These are the things to facilitate the demonstration of our own values. Other than this, there are no special curricula, determined by the schools themselves. There is this much that, in order to better the quality, some schools, of course, obtaining the permission of the National Education departments might increase the number of hours of certain courses.[443]

95. Are there mandatory projects required of the students, either during the academic year or during the summer holiday? If so, what are they?

There is no such an obligation. But there is, especially in primary schools, something called "summer bag" prepared by the home class teachers. Through that, a program is assigned to the students so that they will not be alienated from studying.

Without a forced orientation, according to the desire and talent of the students, some projects are prepared in conformity with the curriculum, like environmental projects, computer projects, sports teams, science fairs, urban culture, and the culture of coexistence.[444]

96. Where do the students that graduate from the secondary schools (i.e., high schools), continue their education?

It is not possible to make a generalization on this issue. But of course, in terms of majority, the graduating students have been enrolled in universities in various cities; some others prefer the universities abroad. Starting with their countries, having undergraduate studies in Turkey and the prestigious universities of the world, those who could finish the graduate studies, later return to their own countries.[445]

An implicit aim is detected in Gülen's mention that students "later return to their own countries." It is known that many of the students, who study

---

[443] *Ibid.*
[444] *Ibid.*
[445] *Ibid.*

abroad, prefer to remain in the country where they studies, if the circumstances warrant it. But it is reasonable to assume that the movement encourages the students to have a fondness for their own country and return to it, in order serve their own society. Some of those returning are employed in the movement's schools, the number of which is steadily increasing, or in businesses and the fields of investments. It is possible to say that the power and strength of the movement comes from the fact that it gives support to talented students from childhood until they have a career and, in turn, they remain with the movement.

97. How do officials of the Turkish Foreign Ministry (ambassadors and counselors) and the Turkish government view these schools? Is there any contribution they make? If so, to what extent?

There is supervision and monitoring everywhere. Both our government and the respective governments and their officials are constantly inspecting them. Then, there is the Turkish Ministry of National Education, calling to Turkey the principals and the directors of these schools and giving them seminars.[446]

Furthermore, there are various kinds of civilian establishments, the cultural, political, and economic organizations. They came and see whether they are trying to form an alternative to the state. I tell them this: "Send some teachers to the four corners of the world, open up schools in every part of the world, open up cultural centers, make the Turkish language into a world language, let everyone love Turkish, let everyone love the Turks and when they play their own role in the future, let it find the support. You do it."

I would even take a step further, despite the friends who do these services, despite those self-sacrificing people, those who are the rep of these institutions, the financiers, the businessmen; if I have the power, if my fame could reach, I would say to the whole nation: If some are saying, "Give those institutions to us, let us manage them," then you give them, surrender them, let them manage everything, let us see whether it is managed or not managed. It depends on some sacrifice. It depends on giving service while being hungry. It is related to giving without receiving anything in return. It is not something which could be done by someone who, as long as alive, during a duty, living like the kings, and when retired grasping the villa of retirement to pass the rest of life.

---

[446] The interview given to Nicole Pope, *Le Monde*, 28 April 1998.

It is not a question of anyone producing an alternative to the state, being in a struggle with it. On the contrary, there is the effort of supporting the state. No matter who is on the head of that state, they will comfortably have certain things they could use, and they would advance these possibilities further. This is another aspect of the matter.

In my opinion, there is a way discovered. There is a setting to which God Almighty mobilized our people to. If God wills, this service will continue forever. We will die, but those who come after us will own up the responsibility with more passion and love, they will further things if God wills. All of these are the things necessary to be done on behalf of our nation and the state.

Another issue is this: There are certain beautiful, great things that our state does which we cannot. But there are certain other things that the state might not be able to do it. For instance the state opens in some places schools or cultural centers ... these are the things, to a certain extent, bound by the international relations. For a period of time, your relationship with a certain country might be very good. Your commercial, industrial, and cultural relations with it might be very good. But there is a constant change in the world, in the social geography. You see France is with you, you see later that she is against you. You see that your relations with the Netherlands are fine. After a while you observe that she is opposed to you. Let us say, the government opens a university in a place; it opens a high school or a language course in another place. When your act of this kind depends on the relations of the states, and if the relations of our nation go sour with those nations, they would also close down that school or the course. To me, a clever government would act in this matter with alternatives. It would activate the civil society organizations. It could do certain things at the governmental level, suiting the honor and dignity of the government. But meanwhile, it would have alternative plans. It would say to the civic organizations, "You do also certain other things. If our governmental relations do not go well, you could at least continue yours." In fact, that is what happened. In some places, forgive me, experience of fiascos were the result of the decline in the relationships between the governments. In one of the Asian countries, due to the breakdown in the relationships between the governments was the cause of cessation of educational activities. In my opinion, an intelligent government would have many alternatives. It would not even think of only education, the schools, colleges, the language courses, cultural centers; but would establish there certain other things which would be appropriated by the populace like artistic activities, a theatre group, and a movie house. When they tell someone "go back," those people who are settled there would remain there, would continue the cause, and would retain the movement. One has to be with many alternatives. Just like many different shoots from different channels, we have to spread around the four corners of the world.

But we should never forget that whatever we do, we are doing it for the sake of the people, on behalf of our government. If the government comes and says to us, civilians and soldiers alike, for the time being you take your hands of this matter, we are taking care of it from now on. We would say, "ay ay," we would leave quietly. We would think that business is taken care; somehow it is being carried out. Heroically, with honor and dignity our friends can declare this everywhere they go.

No civil formation, no team, no movement, or group should think of itself in the place of the state; on the contrary, it should support the state; it should try to fill the vacuum somehow left by the state. While doing that it should never have a distance from the thinking that, "here I am an element or component of the state, I am doing these on behalf of it." It should always behind the state, it should lean on it, and it should do everything for the state.[447]

This extreme statist or state-dependent discourse might make one to think that Gülen or his followers to be statist without conditions or reservations. However, this would be an incorrect interpretation. Gülen and his movement do not seek to be in opposition to the state. The state's understanding, which is presented as a "foundational philosophy" and which legitimizes state control of religions and faiths, unilaterally has a problematic relationship with the Gülen Movement and other faith-based formations. It perceives all of them as a threat to secularism.

On the other hand, the Gülen Movement is a civic organization. It is voluntary and it moves with a sentiment of a mission, that believes in and that it considers a kind of calling of itself. In Turkey's political culture there is no such tradition. Until now, what was essential was the omnipotence of the state. The view that the state is not a servant of the people, but their master, was prevalent and predominant. As such, the civic society and its activities were viewed with doubt. For that reason, Gülen has stated repeatedly that he does not have any objection to handing over all the institutions that he and the members of his community have established to the "state," that is, of course, with one condition: The state would continue the work with the same enthusiasm, sacrifice, and productivity.

---

[447] Bu Hareket Devlete Alternatif mi? (Is this movement an alternative of the state?), *http://tr.fgulen.com/content/view/12134/9/*

98. Is there any criterion followed in order to choose the countries in which to establish schools?

No particular criteria are considered. Because of the absence of appropriate legal regulations, in some countries no school can be opened. In order for a school to be established in a particular country, certain conditions have to be present together. First of all, some people and firms have to be found to act as sponsors, in order to initiate the establishment of a school abroad. Then is required the permission of Turkish Ministry of National Education. After that, the administration of the country concerned has to show the green light. While the building is assigned by the host country, some of the teachers are appointed from Turkey, and some others are provided by the host country.[448]

99. Are there any countries which do not allow the schools to be opened? If so, which ones? Have schools been established in countries experiencing social or political problems, such as Afghanistan, Iraq, Philippines, and Bosnia Herzegovina? If so, have the schools made any positive contributions in terms of peace and prosperity?

There are schools in Afghanistan, Iraq, Philippines, and Bosnia Herzegovina. The most concrete example of these schools' contribution in terms of peace is that the children, whose fathers were fighting outside against each other, were receiving education on the same desks. The countries which do not allow the schools to be opened are the countries like Iran and Saudi Arabia. At this moment these countries do not allow them.[449]

At this stage, Gülen feels the need to touch upon the adversarial and negative conduct of Iran:

Iranians never wanted us. We have friends who did their doctorates there. They are teaching faculties in our universities. We have even sent a friend for the last time, in the latest period, when Turkey was developing a policy of good neighborliness. We said: "We would like to open up some schools." We said, "Let us together raise the architects of tomorrow." They said in reply: "If you would like to undertake some educational activities, then support us financially, let us do it ourselves." Yes, from their perspective, it is something prudent and wise.[450]

---

[448] Exclusive answer delivered to Doğu Ergil.
[449] *Ibid.*
[450] *Ibid.*

But in the final analysis Iran, since it always carries a doubt and worry that the prevailing theocratic regime will fall through outside interference, considers opening the way for a movement which has another interpretation of Islam objectionable:

> In our surroundings, there are several places where we could not enter. Syria did not give that chance to us; Saudi Arabia did not act with reasonableness at all. They were not fair. ... But since there are Turks in Northern Iraq, we said, "Let us open a school for the Turks there..." What are the considerations of our state regarding this matter? I requested the President to be asked about this matter. I said through the intermediaries: "If we do not do something like this, others would do it. Some secret agents set local people against one another. They start quarreling. If we enter there, we would be setting the balance. ... The Northern Iraq is our neighbor. We have to enter there so that there would not be problems. We have to enter with our own culture and conceptions. Let us not go into the future as two strangers. Let them know us and let us know them..." Dear President ... had said we could open up schools. Then, we opened a school in Erbil. They asked us for a second one. Neither Talabani nor Barzani made a serious objection. ... But Iran did not give us the opportunity in that matter.[451]

These words make it inevitable to reconsider the proposition that Islam is a religion of tolerance and open to every kind of ideas, as Gülen describes. The problem is not in the faith, but with those who carry that faith in relation to losing their power.

The authorities, who had already apprehended the administration of Iran, act out of their anxiety to continue their rule, rather than for their religion. When the matter is approached from this perspective, it becomes clear that the respect for the tolerance, understanding, and the differences, which are implicit in the religious principles, should be strengthened and consolidated by the legal regulations of a political regime. Even the most tolerant faith, which is not supported by the separation of powers, democratic participation, and the rule of law, in a regime ruled by religious leaders, could become a setting for legitimacy of fundamentalism and a regime of dictatorship. Gülen is aware of this fact, in terms of displaying the difference between the Islam of Turkey and other Islamic understandings and interpretations.

---

[451] *Ibid.*

100. Have the schools opened by the Gülen Movement made achievements on the national and international levels?

Gülen and his assistants have a long list of successes, ranging from sports to the Scientific Olympiads.

> The students of our schools abroad, in addition to winning the first places in the tests and contests held at the national level in their respective countries, and in many International Olympiads held at different times they had innumerable awards. For the first time in their history, Iraq and Afghanistan, in the Scientific Olympiads, had won the medals through these schools. The attraction of the people to these schools is very high. In Kyrgyzstan, in 2006, for the opening of 900 seats, 55,000 had applied.[452]

The schools are, in general, among the best in the towns in which they are located. For that reason, the public is extremely attracted to these schools. Teachers understand that they must be accessible to their students. Thus, they constantly provide help and support to the students in their daily work and homework. Parents are extremely appreciative of the teachers' dedication to their children. The teachers treat every pupil as if they were their own children and desire for them to have the best careers; they also feel the responsibility to prepare them for life. The teachers inculcate this sense of responsibility in their students, which increases their success. In short, the schools achieve both at national and international levels. However, it is only when these successes are assessed through the human yardstick, do academic achievements acquire meaning. It is understood that this is exactly the aim of the Gülen schools.

The Gülen Movement has an interesting and an important picture, a Turkish reality which is internationalized. This reality cannot be understood only through questions and answers. It has to be enriched by a sociological analysis at both, the scale of our country, and the world. The "Epilogue" was penned with this aim in mind.

---

[452] *Ibid.*

EPILOGUE

The *Jamaat*, the Process of its Formation, and the Assessment of the Gülen Movement in a Historical Context

The impact of Gülen and his followers, as well as the ideas and interpretations that they hold, are no longer a theoretical curiosity, but have grown to become a tangible and measurable international presence. Despite the movement's ability to distinguish itself from the pack of typical social movements, it has not yet been made the subject of a serious comprehensive analysis in Turkey. It has barely been able to transcend the daily storm of petty political attacks, which surround any group that holds to a strong and principled position.

What would be an effective method of studying the section of Turkish society known as the Gülen Movement? One potential avenue was to enter the group and live with them for a sufficient period of time. This is called a participant observation. Another way was to perform a systematic and thorough analysis from the outside, to observe the group's activities and evaluate them and to meet and talk with people within the movement. All of these were undertaken, but without meeting with the person in the center of the movement, a satisfactory investigation would have been impossible. For this reason, the author of this book interviewed Mr. Gülen twice in his residence in the upper Pennsylvania region of the United States, where he has been living for the last several years. He was asked questions about his opinions, aims, hopes and what types of people and societies share his ideals. The answers received make up the contents of this book.

Today, the Gülen Movement is the most valuable export of Turkey. The movement also holds considerable weight inside the country, through its ventures into education, finance, industry, trade, and media. How is it that an *imam* of the humblest of rural origins could inspire such a comprehensive movement that would grow into such an influential and powerful international network? The answers to these questions lie in

Gülen's ideas, and this book has been assembled so that the readers may judge them for themselves.

Let us start our analysis with a definition of the *jamaat* or religious community. The *jamaat* can be broadly defined as being a sub-group of society. *Jamaat*s exist in both modern and traditional societies. In traditional *jamaat*s, relationships are shaped by the values, habits, and conventions that have been handed down from previous generations. In this kind of society, what holds together the individuals are either habits or the activities that the members undertake and accomplish together. Here we are talking about traditional *jamaat*s, a space in which one is born, rather than a voluntary association.

Looked at from another perspective, the traditional *jamaat* is shaped in the natural flow of social life. It is a group that people join without any coercion because it satisfies some of our basic necessities. It derives its legitimacy from tradition, where the communication is face-to-face and much of the teaching is transmitted orally. These definitions, even if they take different structural forms depending on historical flow and social processes, still imply that the *jamaat* somehow retains its existence. People were driven to despair in the face of modernity and the extreme secularization that lead to irreligiosity and the loss of the sense of solidarity. There were already some *jamaat*s, but new ones were needed in order to face the new social and cultural needs. In this way, this new formation of the *jamaat* is not the consequence of traditionalism, but a product of modernity.

When we compare the various *jamaat*s, we must assess them, not only as historical events, but also as socio-cultural ones as well. Seen from this perspective, trying to understand the *jamaat*s becomes parallel to trying to understand the society and the human relationships of a given period. The *jamaat*s, which come into being through the preferences of many people, have to be studied seriously with all the dynamics they contain and the relationships that they establish within the societies in which they are located. The approach must be the result of a scholarly curiosity, independent of the researcher's attitude toward the *jamaat* under consideration. The topic deserves a sociological language and methodology, aiming at deconstruction, rather than working through cheap clichés, daily political concerns, and bias judgments.

Modernization and its economic infra-structure, the free-market economy, has torn people from existing traditional structures to the extent that they cannot be compared to previous generations in the same way. These new structures need a long time to evolve, and the social values which gave meaning to them, legitimizing them, took time to develop. The feeling of human loss was deepened to the extent that this process was forced and not allowed to mature. This attempt to synthetically push the process of a maturing society is repeated frequently in the changing modern world, to more or less the same dismal ends.

Structures blurred by the change, relationships that have lost their influence, fading values, and even physical space seemed to people to be a meaningless ambiguity that they could not transcend. It was all a vacuum, a vast emptiness that they could not fill. In this case, people look for a societal shell to seek refuge in, to protect them. The desire to seek such protection is not bound by time. It is a timeless fact. It is a human situation and independent of the normative evaluation of good and bad. In this new protective shell, they could find a value system and a form of relationship, which was similar to those they had known in the past. It is a shell to embrace, a shell which offered both understanding and support. It is a shell in which the power of the powerless is augmented, because it is multiplied by that of the other members.

In Turkey, the *jamaat* structure observed today is filling the void which once was formed by official institutions. It is replacing the loss of the old influence of kin relationship and accelerating the transformation of the extended family into a nuclear one. Those people who do not see enough support from their families and relatives to meet their changing needs in a different social and physical space (such as an urban center) have oriented themselves to larger and more functional networks of relationships. This transition, which takes place as belonging to a *jamaat*, has caused, and is causing at this moment, new forms of belongingness, solidarity, shared works, and protection. These have impacted the general structure of society and the system of values.

Formation of *jamaat* is not necessarily a phenomenon related to religion. But since religion has widely adopted and accepted common rules, implementation, rituals, and traditions, it facilitates the formation of *jamaat*. For this reason, it could be said that in Turkey "religious life" is maintained primarily through *jamaat*s. Even though the dervish lodges and retreat centers were closed down, the human need for belonging to a group is indifferent to bureaucratic dictation and, therefore, people took to rural areas to maintain their activities. Since they went underground, they distanced themselves and separated themselves from Sufism which had provided their legitimacy and attractiveness in the eyes of the public. These groups have remained as traditional structures, but their quality of teaching was not controlled by relatively more educated sectors.

In Turkey today, there are hundreds of Sufi orders under various names. Among them are groups with a larger number of followers, who have been able to maintain a relationship with the populace of the cities, because they were able to renew themselves by adapting to the social changes of the cities. To the extent that they are able to renew, they carry their visibility in cities to the public sphere and turn it into effectiveness. Thus, they are transforming the public sphere as well. Now, what the old guard sees as "dangerous for the regime" is this visibility and effectiveness in the public sphere.

One of the main themes in this concern is the desire to avoid sharing or losing power. The other is the individuals being swallowed by the *jamaats*. This is a rightful concern. However, one of the most important traits of the new *jamaats* is that they give identity to individuals who cannot find the means to individualize. The ethnic, religious, and cultural identities, which individuals cannot express because of having been banned, have become visible in the public sphere through the formation of *jamaats*. In this sense, the *jamaat* is not a structure one is born into, as in other groupings, but something joined and left voluntarily, formed over time, broken and revised or rebuilt. It is an arena of activities and maneuvers. The new *jamaats* and the old ones influence each other, and during the new *jamaats*' formation, a transition between old and new takes place. The identities of individual members are shaped and constructed partially or completely by the new *jamaats*.

Like the rest of Turkey, the *jamaats* also are impacted by the dynamics of the process of modernization and, of course, by its contradictions. In this process of change, we see secularization and metaphysical perception, the secular and the sacred, not in opposition, but juxtaposed side by side, one inside another, one overlapping the other. The same way it is possible for a group to gather around a spiritual idea and perceive the world through a unified lens, though the people may have little or nothing in common, secular *jamaats* are able to form through certain codes, symbols, and perceptions, such as historical interpretations or political preferences.

In this context, while a tendency toward spiritualism is observed in those who are secular, religious *jamaats* also have a tendency towards secularization and worldliness, especially if they are socially and economically independent. This proves that just like the whole society, the *jamaats* are not static and though their roots lie in the past, they are open to change. We have to accept that these micro and macro changes, impacting each other, generate dynamics which are quite different from what we see when look at either of these sets of changes individually. In the process of change (urbanization, industrialization, elevation of educational level, and modernization), both national factors (such as economic transformations and fundamentalist ideologies) and global factors (such as free flow of capital and new technologies) played a crucial role in the practical experience of those who are from the countryside and who experienced the fastest changes. Things that were discovered and experienced had not been previously known and thought to be impossible came into being. Further, the traditional sectors (or rather, the formerly traditional sectors) were able to embrace change rather than fear it. Set against this oceanic shift were those sectors which, in past decades had been pioneers of authoritative change from the top down, rather than organic change from the bottom up.

In this state of affairs, an interesting contradiction emerged: The established ruling elite resisted change and those who demand change (the rising and urbanizing sectors) were not yet in power. For this reason, there not only is a tremendous political tension, but also in the field of values, a profound cultural conflict.

In modern *jamaats*, voluntary relationships are predominant. Hence, the community is oriented and directed by universally accepted rules. In both the traditional, as well as the modern *jamaats*, relationships are closer. In traditional *jamaats*, there is a cultural homogeneity. In modern *jamaats*, the members come from different segments of society. What is important are the goals that bring them together and the activities derived from these goals. The Gülen Movement appears to display both. But in fact, the movement falls under the moderate and transitional category. It is not bound by a specific space or limited function. Though religious sources lie at the center of its value system, the Gülen movement is able to build a bridge between traditional values and the lifestyle of the modern world by subjecting these traditional sources to a new interpretation which fits it properly. It is exactly this style of interpretation which distinguishes the Gülen Movement from its contemporaries.

Society is a whole, consisting of the socioeconomic sectors whose functions are differentiated through a developed division of labor. The most important difference between society (*jamiyyah*) and community (*jamaat*) is the process by which social norms become institutionalized. In the case of society, it is done by the crystallization of rules into laws, which are enforced by a central administrative unit. Gülen's *jamaat* is a structure located in a shared area where community and society over-lap. It has been integrating previously traditional social sectors into a modern society. The vehicles making this integration possible are educa-tion, solidarity, capital, and initiative, both individual and communal. The close relationships and the common values maintaining them, which are to be found in every *jamaat*, also are in the Gülen *jamaat*, harmonized interpretations that Gülen derives from religion in conformity with modernity. These interpretations allow its members to flow with the pace of change, as they are in conformity with universal human values.

On the other hand, the Gülen group, which is included in the defini-tion of modern *jamaat*s, has been vocal in their stance against official demands and expectations. The group is one of the civic formations that defend sustainable economic welfare, as well as more liberal, social, and cultural rights and freedoms. The widespread membership of the move-ment increases its effectiveness.

That the Gülen group not only is called a *jamaat*, but also a "move-ment," can be explained by the fact that its traits transcend the localized nature of classical *jamaat*s and by its vivaciousness, in terms of activities and space. This vivaciousness, at the same time, prevents the group from blindly obeying a central authority.

Its autonomy, which today appears to be against the official political center, will tomorrow trigger a resistance against any tendency towards centralization that may arise within the movement. The reason for this judgment is not the peculiar traits of the Gülen *Jamaat*, but because its structure has spread throughout the world and the wide variety of its activities. It is very difficult for the participants, whose level and quality of education is increasingly better, to remain frozen in one kind of identity, or kept under tight control. However, there will always be something to bind them together. Otherwise, they cannot be a *jamaat*. These are the spiritual ties, which will hold them together in their ideals and bring about a sense of unity. Religion is the source of these ties and Gülen is its carrier. It is the Islam to be found in Gülen's interpretations which is congruent, and not in conflict, with the contemporary, modern world.

Today, most social scientists in Turkey describe modern society as a place where the individual feels powerless and without security in the face of giant organizations seeking ever greater control over their lives. For this reason, some social scientists defend the necessity to provide a new identity to an atomized society. Some factions have been defending the thesis of "*jamaat* of *jamaats*" as a remedy. They believe that this will break the centralist character of today's modern society.

For example, Amitai Etzioni, a German-Israeli-American sociologist who is one of the proponents of the *jamaat* (community) paradigm, defends that a good society is a federation of *jamaats*. The founding communities (*jamaats*) come together as carriers of various cultures, values, and sometimes even languages, and make up the *jamiyya*, or the society. What hold them together are shared laws (the kernel values of societal partnership), economy, and humane and democratic political values. This model reminds us of the Ottoman *millet* system. The Ottoman State had not asked for anything from its subjects, or *millets*, other than tax revenues and loyalty to the sultanate or its laws. These are also the characteristics of the modern society. The important difference that separates modern society from past societies is democracy. Everyone is equal before the law. Citizens participate in politics and they have the right to be treated well. They are able to oversee the central authority, which uses the power given to it by the people, to benefit the people.

Like every other system, democracy has a legal framework. This framework is provided by the constitution. As the societies change, the laws change in order to meet the new needs. In democratizing and developing societies, the new and the traditional are mixed together, and the constitutions, which are normative frameworks, are revised and amended. As civil society develops, some autonomous areas come into existence between the social-cultural units that make up that civil society. The sole, authoritarian, central administration determining everything yields its place to a more flexible, more sensitive form of administration that has already accepted the separation of powers and can work in better harmony with the local volunteer units.

Individuals are equalized before the law by the civil society gaining strength against the central government. Then these individuals participate in politics and political life under the identity umbrella of the group that they belong to. This is the way the unity of diversity is established. Otherwise, individuals in the population become indistinguishable from each other as the state works to shape the population to fit a mold which suits its needs. This process of synthesizing a population contradicts the spirit of democracy.

Citizens of a democracy are protected by law in their efforts to associate with like-minded people, even with the intention of using these associations to participate in local and national politics. Among these associations, competition and controlled conflict arises, as well as consensus. The conflicts are kept under control through laws and legal systems, which take a new shape in every period. As for competition, it can be channeled into its more positive counterpart, cooperation. Societal ethics is formed by the mixing of principles, born out of reconciliation between religion and the practices of daily life. We can call this consensus and the reconciliation reached among religious, racial, and cultural groups a "megalog." This is possible only when the entities are protected, against both the state and each other, through civil, volunteer, and autonomous social organizations. If those volunteer associations do not exist between the state and the individual, the official society swallows up the individual, and democracy is deprived of its organized infrastructure.

The Gülen group is this sort of civil society organization. But since it is thought by the elite in Turkey that this kind of organization can be established only by secular individuals and groups, civil organizations established by religious and traditional people are accused of having subversive political aims. For that reason, some have difficulty understanding the structure and the evolution of the Gülen Movement. But we have to remember that a similar movement arose in the West and was made the subject of a profound analysis.

In his writings, Max Weber discusses the religious orders of some Protestant denominations such as the Quakers, the Baptists, and the Methodists and how they applied their religious values and the principles that they had derived from them to their daily lives and their business and trade activities. He explained his views in his famous book *The Protestant Ethic and the Spirit of Capitalism*. In the same way, the Gülen group, by bringing the business activities of its members in line with the principles of religion, does not see any conflict between their economic activities and their faith.

As a consequence of these efforts, and in a short period of time, the ethical center and trust that has been lost in the business dealings of these earlier Protestant societies were to a great extent regained. It facilitated trade and made the society stronger, economically at the very least, and ethically and spiritually at best.

It is obvious that these religious orders are not the kind of organizations with which to face the challenges of modern times. The developments of freedom of expression and organization, petitioning for the redress of grievances to the government, and legal avenues for the opposition to the established order through legal channels outside the protective shield of religion have limited the need for religious orders in the West. However, the conservative, religious, and "rural" social sectors were excluded by the modernizing-centralist authority through their method of ruling by change from top to bottom. These excluded segments of society developed a growing hunger for an organizational means of obtaining status, influence, and the economic opportunities that they sought. For this reason, they showed a tendency to form a parallel society against the "official society" which used to hold all the power and necessary means for controlling. They discovered that they could obtain what they were looking for through the *jamaat*s that they had formed, by sharing and mutually helping each other.

There are many examples of this kind of organization. For instance, the best illustration is the use of the guild system by the pioneers of the so-called Turkish-Islamic colonization, the dervish *tariqa*s. The majority of the guild conventions are derived from Sufism as a religious foundation or a source. According to Ömer Lütfi Barkan, a historian of Turkish economic history, dervishes, along with the *Akıncılar* (frontier warriors), functioned to transform the military campaigns into an activity with a religious aim in mind rather than simply conquest.

Today's rising, rural middle class in Turkey and the members of the traditional sectors, who move to the cities from the countryside and seek a place in the static city social structure, bring a great dynamism to social life. This process of participation adds depths and complexity to the foundations on which politics and the economy have been standing. It has also been perceived by those who have been living in the cities for generations (and are, in general, bureaucrats) as a disturbing interference by the middle class. Seeing aspects of life in Turkey over which they have total control narrowing has provoked predictably severe reactions. They declare that the republic is under threat and that the unity of the country is on its way out, but also, and first and foremost, that the country's modern character is on the brink of annihilation. They have interpreted the Gülen Movement's effectiveness in the fields of education, trade, and societal life, not as a domestic dynamic, but as the result of a conspiracy aimed at Turkey from abroad.

In actual fact, what is happening is that the excluded and despised periphery has acquired vivaciousness and the control of the omniscient bureaucrats and the wealthy city dwellers who got rich through their support, has diminished. The segments that are disturbed by the growth of the Gülen movement include other slices of society as well, such as the former middle class who believes that at the center of culture, politics, and the economy, is a good administration. To the extent that the old middle class lost its effectiveness and its relationship with the world, it began to see the world as the "executor" of destructive change and turned its back on all Western values and processes.

There is one more thing that is not understood: While the former elite, which is increasingly losing influence and control, hardens its discourse and intensifies its activities, the religious *jamaats* like the Gülen Movement gladly shoulder the responsibility of social democracy, which is otherwise neglected. Their discourses are not adversarial, but soft. And the social help and support that they provide to the needy sectors of society, as well as to their members, fulfill the need of social solidarity and mutual help where the state has shortcomings. The position of the left, which cannot get organized, and the social democrats who cannot develop a modern program are taken over by the religious *jamaats*, which they see as a threat. What is interesting is that the needs which are met by the *jamaats* are more material than religious. While religiosity is important in the relationship within the *jamaat*, the relationship with outside groups, especially those abroad, are worldly and pragmatic.

It may seem to be a contradiction at first, but the *Adalet ve Kalkınma Partisi* (the Justice and Development Party), which is in government now, has weakened the function of mutual help and the sense of solidarity provided by the religious *jamaats*. This is because the party has put every kind of governmental means available at the disposal of the people, subsequently limited the need for, and narrowed the area of effectiveness, of the *jamaats*. The primary evidence of this proposition is the implementation of the "green card"—the health-care service provided to the bearers, virtually everyone who cannot afford insurance. No *jamaat* is in a position of enough power to compete with the things government can provide in the field of health.

In summary, after the establishment of the republic, various communities (both ethnic and religious) were targeted for liquidation, through the conception of creating a singular nation and a singular national identity that would not accommodate any difference. After the failure of this project due to its detachment from historical and social reality, every dormant group re-emerged in the public sphere. What is more, they re-emerged as "objectionable ghosts." Officially, they were not supposed to exist. In the educational system, for generations, the children were taught that they did not exist. This process of re-emergence was called *irtica* and Turkey was plunged into civil unrest and infighting, especially in the 1980s. The irreconcilable difference between reality and what was supposed to be has turned the country's political and cultural institutions into battlefields.

The groups, which were not within the official definition of citizen and nation, for the most part did not desire to separate or segregate, as is often assumed. They would have liked to join and be counted. But this perfectly human request was targeted as divisiveness and mischief. In addition to the only official identity, which was imposed vertically, from top down, the existence of many horizontal civic identities was confusing and demanded a new philosophy, as well as a new institutional and legal framework for society.

In a new legal and cultural structure, which have become obviously urgent, it is necessary for the political, cultural, and economic arenas to separate from each other and become autonomous, so that they do not trespass into each other's area; they need to develop concurrently on a parallel line. That is to say, let each cultural group be able to develop itself autonomously. Neither should it interfere with others nor should others interfere with it. As for the state, let it generate the necessary conditions for them to develop by keeping impartiality.

Only then, the cultural sphere can escape from the interference of politics; the cultural groups would not feel the need to give a struggle in the political arena for their existence and development; the culture would be freed from being an area of political fighting. Unfortunately, because the system of administration in Turkey makes an order of preference among the cultural groups and registers some of them as objectionable, the culture is always evaluated from a political perspective. No peace can be achieved among the cultural groups. The energy and the resources of the country are exhausted in vain, through these internal conflicts. As long as this continues, our democracy cannot be elevated to the level of modern standards.

The segments, which made up the religious, conservative "periphery," have established religious *jamaats* or sought asylum in them, in order to gather and unite their powers, along with the purpose of protection, establishment of solidarity, and mutual help. That is to say, the authoritarian-centralist political system, which was trying to impose secularization from above, without being aware of it, has produced its antithesis through the segments it had excluded. When it noticed this development, it tried to spread the belief of how Turkey was encircled by domestic and outside circles of treason, the enemies. And in this effort, it succeeded to a great extent. At this moment, Turkish society is in serious ambiguity and has concern for the future. What is ironic is that this situation makes the religious *jamaats* a more peaceful, quite, and trustworthy anchorage or causes them to be perceived as such. It is because the sense of belongingness, solidarity, security, and mutual help (e.g., food, jobs), which cannot be provided by the modern society/system, are being provided by the *jamaats*.

On the other hand, what is observed in some Sunni *jamaats* is the tendency to have a monopoly on the interpretation of religion. The notion that it is possible to reach the "truth" and the "salvation" only by way of this particular interpretation of the religion has various objectionable consequences. First, the religion itself is harmed by this and the original, fundamental sources are distanced. Second, people are confined within the borders of the *jamaat*, imprisoned in the *jamaat*, and their relationship with other sectors of the society is cut off, to a great extent. And lastly, the members of other *jamaats*, or those who are left altogether outside any of them, are considered "lost people," to be guided to the truth. However, if one forms one's identity, not from the society to which he belongs and the relationships and features of his daily life, but from membership in a particular *jamaat*, and if he uses this identity to further his own interests, to gain fame and position, or to take revenge or settle the accounts, then there can be no consensus or agreement in the society nor the principle of shared living or the setting for it. The difficult thing is to make personal choices, in the face of the crossfire of the time and the society, to be able to bear the consequences of the decisions made, and to race for success. In traditional societies and communities, instead of those values, a habit (cultural) is dominant that emphasizes bringing to the fore the *jamaat*, not the individuals, exalting obedience and bowing one's head to the authority, in order to maintain self-interest and protection. The *jamaats* derive benefits from this cultural infrastructure.

Not only for *jamaats*, it also is valid for the political parties in Turkey, which would be expected to be modern and democratic and obedient to authority and restraining tendencies towards individualism (with a logic of the adage in Turkish, "One who separates from the flock will be snatched away by wolfs."). The party membership is transformed into a sort of *jamaat* membership. The political parties, whether they are the carriers of religious or secular ideologies, have increasingly closed down on themselves and have cut off every kind of relationship with others, closing the door for reconciliation. This is the scene today. For this reason, while some religious *jamaats* develop organic ties with some political parties that they feel are close to themselves, the secular sector, which broke away from the whole society, by forming a *jamaat* within their group, have positioned themselves at a place where they have problems with other political parties and the rest of the world. In this kind of organization of *jamaats* (whether secular or religious), the leadership is not questioned or discussed, because that person has the right to determine how to perceive the world or to interpret the "truth" (the sacred for that group). This phenomenon is valid to the extent of the *jamaat's* hierarchical structure. Since the organization of the members is more horizontal in the *jamaats*, which opens up a space for individuals and encourages individual initiatives, this drawback is less visible.

As the society modernizes, as the division of labor develops, as the professionalism increases, the question arises whether the formation and influence of the *jamaat*s decrease? Perhaps, the traditional *jamaat*s will regress and lose their utility. But they would be replaced by voluntary group formations, whose members would face the challenges of the modern world, trying to find a place to seek refuge and desiring to augment their personal power with those of others. The most densely populated places with these formations would be the cities. Sociologically, it is an understandable and explicable phenomenon for people, who are squeezed between the modern and the traditional, between the urban and the rural, between the rich and the poor, between the cultures of the East and the West, to look for new *jamaat*s.

It is only normal for people in these civil and voluntary associations, whose value judgments, world views, and social-cultural-economic needs are similar, to seek and find each other. In this sense, *jamaat*s are safe shells for those in similar situations, who do not want to be lost and forgotten in the mazes of the modern world, where they have mutual help and support, running the affairs shoulder-to-shoulder in these safe shells.

There also is the issue of reward and sin. A society's maturity to reach a level to differentiate between right and wrong is possible only through development, education, and professionalism. The categories of "good" and "bad" are relative conceptions and subjective. But the categories of "good deed" and "sinful act" are value judgments, based on the sacred texts and internalized by a religious faith which had a long running tradition. It is a lot easier for people to orient their choices and conducts by means of these categories. And especially, if there is a *jamaat* to make this definition for the members, orienting and directing them is even easier. The belief that this "course of action," presented to them in a silver spoon, can keep away the participants from committing sins is important. Since the tight control and observation of each other by the *jamaat* members can prevent members from committing what they believe are sins, the membership in a *jamaat* is meaningful for many people. The purpose of many parents in sending their children to Qur'anic courses, *jamaat* dorms, or schools is to prevent them falling into the hands of the centers of evil. To the extent that the state is unable to carry out this function, the *jamaat*s gain in the same proportion to their effectiveness and diffusion.

Until now, *jamaat*s have been discussed, in general, and the Gülen Movement, in particular. Among the similar movements (*jamaat*s), the "Gülen *Jamaat*" is the one which is in best harmony with the world and an example of a civic organization which has gained an international character. With these features, the attention was drawn to the fact that the movement has opened an area for the individual within the identity and the spirit of the movement, has transcended the locality, and has gained a flexibility to be open to the world, originating from the national. It was emphasized that what is effective here is that, as much as the thoughts and interpretations of the movement's leader are followed, members, who are from dynamic social segments and are looking for a respectful and effective place in the world for themselves, are "on the rising."

However, it is important to note that every religious *jamaat* might not carry these features. The *jamaat*s, which melt individualism within the group psychology, evaluate its members through the abstinence from sins and a fear of guilt and not through their successes and works, thereby preventing the development of a conception of worldly ethics, are more widespread. In this type of entity, every word or behavior that goes beyond the interpretation or admonishing of the leader or the practices of the *jamaat* is treated as if they are outside the boundaries of the religion itself. New ideas and propositions are considered a deviation and approved interpretations and implementations are accepted as wisdom and the very truth itself. The individuals are encouraged to be obedient and static. This state of affairs neither prepares a possibility to meet with other individuals or groups on a common ground, nor does it allow the development of a democratic culture. Instead of a central authority, being criticized because it is authoritarian, the formation of civil centers which were voluntary to begin with, but became authoritarian over time, is an unfortunate development for democracy, as well as for the process of becoming civic. Moreover, this tendency toward authoritarianism is rather difficult to break, because the culture of religious *jamaat*s is oral culture. Therefore, since the interpretations of the *jamaat* leader or the prominent figures are taken as already given, it almost is impossible to compare them with the main sources and criticize what is stated.

In the formation of *jamaat*s, faith often is positioned as if it is an alternative or in opposition to reason and science. In this situation, it is possible that reason and science might be excluded from life. Additionally, when the reason and faith are positioned in opposition to each other, an absolute obedience is demanded of the *jamaat* members since faith does not require a proof. The acceptance of many things, which do not belong to the essentials of the faith, might result in an anti-religion stance. But in Islam, with the exception of the Qur'an, everything can be questioned. It is because their interpretations belong to this world and have no sanctity whatsoever. Only those, who ask questions and make criticisms, those who can transcend the social limitations through their reasoning, can elevate their own quality of lives, as well as the society and their fellow believers. Otherwise, for those who are conditioned to absolute obedience consider questioning as a sin, see his *jamaat* shell as a shield against the demands of the society, consider passivity as "good behavior." It is impossible for them "to save" themselves or the social and religious groups to which they belong.

The individual in the Gülen Movement is the one who makes the choice, in terms of faith, responsibility, and "good conduct." He makes the decision because God has given him will and reason. As long as this door is left open, the "crowd psychology" cannot have a dominant character. Only when this door (individual choice and the capacity to reason) is closed, the difference between the Gülen Movement and other religious formations might not remain. This interpretation is corroborated by the Qur'an: "*As long as a society does not change itself, God would not change their state of affairs.*" (Ar-Ra'd 13:11). As it is seen, instead of a passive waiting, the Qur'an praises humans whose acts are beneficial to themselves and others.

The *jamaat*s and the formation of *jamaat*s also are related to the identity crises the world is experiencing, under the impact of rapid change and globalization. The old relationships, established social structures, and the values which legitimize them are fading away. In their place, either new ones are forming or a vacuum exists. People sense psychologically this "falling into emptiness." In such a time of crises, if the social-economic-political system cannot quickly produce new values and structures/institutions, people experience anxiety and enter into tense relationships with the system. The groups in crises or in conflict with a system in the process of formation are being crystallized into pure forms. Two different camps take place: those who are trying to bring back and maintain the old system and those who are looking for and defend a new one. This is what is happening in Turkey today.

If this setting of crises and conflicts cannot be terminated, and an agreement cannot be reached on the common denominators, which would allow different social sectors to coexist without conflict, the weakening of the nation, which is a political and a legal phenomenon, will be inevitable. It is highly likely that we will not be able to transcend becoming an instable society, made up by the parallel *jamaats*. The only way out of this crisis is to transition from being a state that orders the society what it should be, into a state structure that is in harmony with the social realities of the society and acts in accordance with its will and choice. In short, closing the era of the "society of the state" and going into the stage of the "state of the society." Only a state with these features can envelope, with a political and legal sense of belonging, the fragmented structure of a society consisting of parallel groups.

Otherwise, in a society of conflicts and where the sense of unity is lost, the *jamaats* will take their places in the social fault lines and be a party to the conflict. If this happens, they will neither be able to contribute to the formation of a working law nor to the societal ethics. If they appropriate the philosophy of "Each sheep will be hanged by its own leg," forget preventing social atomization, they will negatively contribute to it. Indeed, various *jamaats* have been defending nationalism, along religious lines, and to an extent that it can be considered racism, they have been siding with ethnic groups; such discrimination is opposed to the spirit of Islam. The spread of these ideas through the *jamaats* have been harming the religion itself and blackening its unifying character.

When we think under the light of these assessments, the question we encounter is the following: How is it that, as Turkey became more and more modern, instead of diminishing, the *jamaats* got stronger and emerged as a social reality to be taken seriously? For some, this question is tantamount to, "Where did we make a mistake?"

The founders of the republic thought of two remedies in order to develop their country which was backward and their nation which was uneducated. The first was to educate the peasants, who made up almost 90 percent of the population at the beginning of the 1920s. The boy Hasan and the girl Fadik were supposed to be educated in the schools that were brought to the village; they were going to be more conscientious and productive; development was to begin in the villages. Decades later, Mao would try the same method in China, almost liquidating the middle class, which was the carrier of a higher civilization than a rural one, under the rubric and pretext of a "Cultural Revolution." He sought to nearly annihilate the country's accumulation of arts and sciences. His aim was to equalize the level of knowledge and the development of the society in general with the level of the countryside. The plan was to begin the development in the densely populated areas of the country-side and then spread it at the same pace to the rest of the country.

In Turkey, never such a radical and cruel development model was tried. But it was assumed that the villagers, who would become more knowledgeable and more productive through education in the country-side, could remain where they were living and develop their villages. The "Village Institutes" were the product of such an idea. However, there was a shortcoming of this enterprise: The education of the villagers had begun before launching a societal development, namely before creating a milieu in which these villagers could become productive and creative.

They were supposed to be raised in the environment of the village and remain there, but if the expression is proper, there were neither universities nor factories nor the concert halls where these future Einsteins and Mozarts could apply to life what they had already learned as knowledge and acquired as artistry. The sector that was educated in the village and was left in the village were lost and evaporated in the poverty and incapability of the countryside. The majority of those who found a place for themselves in the cities were monitored closely and persecuted because, before the society woke up, they did.

What about the educated city population? They were expected in official discourse to have "free conscience, free thoughts" and to become entrepreneurs. But the freedom which was necessary was never provided. As for the individual entrepreneurship, it was imprisoned and confined within the iron cage of statism. The "civilizing breath" of the statism and the economic value it produced was only enough for the city-living. The rural society maintained its life, deprived and poor, in isolation from the city and the world.

The republican rule also feared the "free citizen." With the claim, "We are a classless, integrated mass without any privileged segment," it tried to disseminate the belief that the state and the society are one whole and the same. All educational institutions taught that the society is undifferentiated, classless, a corporate structure, consisting of the groups which have among themselves solidarity and a division of labor. The laws banned the contrary discourse. Today's discourse, "We are a military nation," is the continuation of this discourse, and it is the greatest barrier in front of the society which is trying to become free, democratic, and civilized.

That cognitive and socio-economic inertia situation continued until the 1950's. The political intelligence has not supported the societal vivaciousness, which started after that date and the rapid social and economic change. The political intelligence tried to slow them down and they were taken under control by *coups d'état*. Not only could the state and the society not get along, but also a gap came into existence between those segments of society approved by the state and those that were deemed objectionable. This is the area that the formation of *jamaat* found as a blessed, fertile ground where it could flourish.

Like similar structures, the "Gülen Jamaat" was born in this milieu and opposed the corporatism. Because of its nature, it was civil and it did not need the state; it was a movement of volunteers. Like the society itself, it was unable to fit into the official narrow world of the official rules. But alas! Both the state and the sectors, as carriers of the centralist mentality of the state, claiming that only they represent the modernity, perceived the Gülen Movement and the similar movements as the *jamaats* of the rural/backward society.

Whereas, what was standing before their eyes was a new type of a community, made up of groups seeking a new place (status and function) for themselves in the society, and increasingly becoming modern.

What the official society (the state) should have done was to incorporate these structures/communities and generate a different kind of union. By excluding them and fighting against them, it lost the chance of creating a union based on societal differences. But the Ottoman model was exactly that.

The empire, by definition, was a conglomerate of *jamaats*. It was a functional tradition to give autonomy to the *jamaats*, in order to hold together such a fragmented structure and keep them under control. The state used to rule the communities, who were living in their own respective cultures, through the leaders of these *jamaats*. By contrast the republic neither recognized the right to exist, nor the cultural autonomy, nor the right to their organic leadership for the communities that it inherited from the empire. It believed that by grinding them all and assimilating them to resemble each other, uniformity could be achieved, which was supposed to do be done through law and politics. For this reason, the republic always fought with its own historical heritage and the sociological realities.

At the point we have arrived today, uniformity and the authoritarian conception of administration, which is the reason for the gap between the state and the society, must change. And this only is possible by acknowledgement and settlement of the accounts with our historical and sociological realities and by appropriating a philosophy of a pluralist and democratic administration. Otherwise, the central authority, by insisting on the corporatism, will have increasing difficulty in managing the affairs of the society.

Although it is a *jamaat* inspired by religion, the Gülen Movement has transcended long ago the formation of a traditional community and does not fit into the narrow formats of it. They are acquiring the characteristics that do not deserve the worry that "They are going to bring about a backward regime." The participants of the Gülen Movement, for over 20 years now, are intermingling with the population and the cultures of 100 or so countries. They are settling down, marrying, and establishing businesses. It is no longer possible to place those tens of thousands of people into the old local narrow molds of thought and conduct. While the participants of the Gülen Movement, by the passage of every day, resist against the cast of one-type citizenry, the central authority finds objectionable any changes in the relationship between the state and the society and resists it. If the modern *jamaats*, like the Gülen Movement, could develop the conscience of social responsibility, which does not enslave the soul and mind of the individual, that is pluralistic and tolerant against the differences, they can pioneer a new socialization by balancing the impact of the globalized modern society in destroying the traditional values and institutions. The avant-garde of this process must be an ethical understanding which includes the "other," a spirit of solidarity which does not exclude individual freedom and initiative, a civic area of responsibility and organization outside the official sphere of the state, democracy and law (culture of agreement) which are based on the reconciliation with different groups.

Do these aspirations enumerated so far consist only of an ideal fiction or is there a case similar to the Gülen Movement in our history? This is an appropriate question, inviting our minds to answer. Even though the historical period and the conditions of its emergence are different, the answer is yes, there is an organization similar to the Gülen Movement: *Ahilik*[453].

Ahilik is a guild or corporate organization brought into Anatolia from Central Asia. It is an organization of shopkeepers and artisans the rules of which are clearly stipulated in the by-laws called *futuwwatnamas*, which can be understood as the book of chivalry. It is usually claimed that the first *futuwwatnamas* penned were the *futuwwatnamas* of Abdullah al-Suhrawardi in the 12th century. It is clearly pointed out in historical studies that the philosophy that blew life into this document is Sufism.

The author of the first extant Turkish *futuwwatnamas* is registered as Çobanoğlu. According to this document, in order to enter to the *Ahilik* organization, it was necessary to have an art or trade or other than these, a profession. There was no place for idles and those who had no good morality in the organization. In the *dargahs* (convents) of the "brotherhood," history, literature, Sufism, the biographies of important figures, and the Turkish, Arabic, and Persian languages were taught. Later, with the exception of the obligation to work, in order to join the brotherhood, the limitations for the types of professions or vocations were lifted.

What we understand from the *futuwwatnamas* of Çobanoğlu, "entering the road," that is to say joining the *futuwwa* (by tying the girdle), used to be with the permission of the organization's leader. Those who would cause the organization to receive a bad image were not allowed to join. In order to demonstrate the significance that they attached to "life," those who kill humans or animals, thieves, those about whom the charges of adultery were proven, could not become members. The unbelievers were not admitted, nor were those who practiced an extreme form of austerity and abstinence from world.

The *Ahi* philosophy has six cardinal rules:

---

[453] Literally, "brotherhood." Since it denotes at the same time, the institution, its members and its particular philosophy, this inclusive Turkish word will be retained in translation from now onwards. Simply, the individual member is *ahi*.

1. Keep your hands open (share)
2. Keep your food-table open (be generous)
3. Keep your door open (be hospitable)
4. Keep your eyes shut (overlook others' faults, forgive)
5. Protect your waist (have chastity)
6. Keep your tongue (do not slander, do not curse, be well mannered)

With this ethical understanding and individual manners and upbringing, it is inevitable for these people to awaken a sense of security in their environments. On the other hand, the trust felt towards them is not based on only individual, isolated reasons. Their respect for what they were doing, doing everything properly according to the requirement of the jobs they performed (deserving their profession) and considering the societal benefits have a role in the trust they gained.

Ahilik does not only contain a philosophy of living, but also has a role in social organization and in the matter of arranging the social relationships. In the age *Ahilik* came out, the Turcoman tribes migrating into Anatolia were passing from a nomadic to a sedentary life. But the cities were the places where native and, in general, non-Muslim people were living. Turkish and Muslim populations could hold onto life in the cities they settled, only by solidarity among themselves and establishing economic security. To that end, they had to compete with the settled city-dwellers. In this competition, *Ahilik*, came in to meet the needs of organization, professional preparation, and principled life. Thus, both trade and artisanship developed and, at the same time, the Turks living in the cities, through their activities in these fields, adjusted to the city setting and became a power unto themselves. In this sense, *Ahilik* is a city culture, or rather, a culture of integration with the city.

In the Gülen Movement we also observe the effectiveness of educational and economical enterprises to help those who migrate from the rural areas to adjust t to the city culture. *Ahi* Guilds, along with this similarity, demonstrate closeness to Gülen thought, in terms of its philosophy and cardinal principles. *Ahilik*, which is a phenomenon of Turkish Anatolian, would not be encountered in the Arabian Peninsula or Iran. *Ahis*, which is a group of solidarity embracing Sufism, has accomplished a great civil organization in Anatolia, through their economic power, the sense of security that they spread around, and a professional organization which brings forth ethical norms. The interesting aspect of the matter is that this organization was realized outside the state and without any support from it. In terms of these attributes, as well, *Ahis* and the Gülen Movement resemble each other.

Another common characteristic of both organizations is that although they have rituals to abide by, rules not to be violated, and stages one has to go through in order to reach perfection, they are not hierarchical organizations with a bureaucratic character. Both are horizontal organizations where, rather than a central authority, the influence of spiritual authority is effective. Even in this matter, the *Ahi* Guild is much more formal. It has a program of perfection and elevation with three stages and nine doors. Of course, in that age this was necessary in order to hold the organization together and to provide the professional formation. Today, not much is demanded of the participants in the Gülen Movement other than to internalize a certain understanding regarding the worldly and other-worldly matters, to know basic religious sources, and to accept the interpretations of Gülen.

The professional education undertaken in *Ahi* Guilds within the organization is provided in Gülen Movement outside the organization. The members of the group take on various duties in the four corners of the world. Some of them take on educational tasks and some economical. But there are frequent transitions between the two. There also is a group of administrators who coordinate the activities. Other than the way in which they spread across the world, the Gülen Movement and the organization of *Ahi* Guilds resemble each other in many other ways.

The *Ahi baba*, who is the counterpart of the *jamaat* leader in the *Ahi* Guilds, used to be elected. His orders were absolutely obeyed since they were in conformity with the principles enumerated in the *futuwwatnamas*. If there were no orders coming from the sultan or a local administrator or, as it was the case during wars, when the central authorities were dissolved or took flight (as in the case of Mongolian invasions), *Ahis* used to shoulder the administration of the local works. The duty even included defending the locality, if occupation by a foreign force was threatened.

Ahis penetrated even into the villages, through the support of institutions called *yaran odaları* (rooms for friends). By establishing philanthropic foundations, they would help the poor and needy and become a vehicle for their children to be educated and find jobs. We see exactly the same things being accomplished by the members of the Gülen Movement.

It is also interesting to observe the similarities between what was said during the promotion ceremonies in the *Ahi* Guilds and Gülen's advice quoted throughout this book: the trustworthiness and truthfulness in trade, respect for the customer and the merchants, not mixing goods with tricks, informing the customer of the defects or faults in goods and services, not trying to harm anyone, helping those who are needy or in distress, respect for the scholars, love for the minors, compassion for the public, mercy for the powerless, not oppressing or injuring anyone, treating the apprentices and the foremen as if they were one's own children, and lastly obeying the sultan in the *Ahi* Guilds and the state in the Gülen Movement.

Obeying the administrative authorities, in principle, is the rule in both organizations. But, neither one needed a central authority from the perspective of their activities and their existence and retained their existence outside its umbrella scheme. Nevertheless, since they find societal stability important, they took extra precautions not to be in conflict with the central authority.

In summary, both *Ahi* Guilds and the Gülen Movement have provided groups "left outside, at the periphery" the possibility of obtaining a status and a place in society, to have a place at the center, to have self-confidence, and social upward mobility. *Ahi* Guilds brought out to the front the Muslim Turks *vis-à-vis* powerful Byzantine professional organizations or settled non-Muslim artisans and merchants, protected them and gave them the means through which they could compete. The Gülen Movement also gives youth, who come from villages and small towns of Anatolia and whose means of gaining status are very limited, as well as modest businessmen who are looking for an opportunity in the cities, the educational and trade opportunities to be able to compete in their country and the world and through which they can gain respect.

Just like the *Ahi* Guilds, the Gülen Movement is a "periphery" movement. It functions to integrate the "periphery groups" with the center and expand the center. By virtue of this, and by making part of the center those social segments that otherwise would display an anti-stance position against the system and thus the center, it has been transforming the system in the direction of pluralism and also has been providing a dynamism to it.

BIBLIOGRAPHY

Akademi Araştırma Heyeti (The Study Group of Akademi). 2006. *Sağduyu Çağrısı* (The Call for Common Sense). İstanbul: Işık.

Akman, Nuriye. 2004. *Gurbette Fethullah Gülen* (Fethullah Gülen in a Foreign Land). İstanbul: Zaman Kitap.

Akman, Nuriye. 1995. "Demokrasiden Dönülmez" (No way to leave democracy). *Sabah*. 27 Ocak.

Beşer, Faruk. 2006. *Fethullah Gülen Hocaefendi'nin Fıkhını Anlamak* (Understanding the *Fiqh* of Fethullah Gülen Hocaefendi). İstanbul: Ufuk.

Can, Eyüp. 1997. *Fethullah Gülen Hocaefendi ile Ufuk Turu* (Comtemplations with Fethullah Gülen Hocaefendi). İstanbul: Ad.

Dinçkol, Bihterin. 1992. *1982 Anayasası Çerçevesinde ve Anayasa Mahkemesi Kararlarında Laiklik* (Laicism in the Framework of 1982 Constitution and in the Decisions of the Constitutional Court). İstanbul: Kazancı.

Erdoğan, Latif. 2006. *Küçük Dünyam* (My Little World). İstanbul: Ufuk.

Ergene, M. Enes. 2005. *Gülen Hareketinin Analizi: Geleneğin Modern Çağa Tanıklığı* (The Analysis of the Gülen Movement: Tradition Witnessing the Modern Age). İstanbul: Yeni Akademi.

Gülen, Fethullah. 2010a. *Kırık Testi–3: Gurbet Ufukları* (Broken Pitcher, vol. 3: Horizons from Foreign Lands). İstanbul: Nil.

Gülen, Fethullah. 2010b. *Çağ ve Nesil–9: Sükutun Çığlıkları* (The Modern Age and the Contemporary Generation, vol. 9: The Screams of Silence). İstanbul: Nil.

Gülen, Fethullah. 2010c. *Asrın Getirdiği Tereddütler–4* (Questions and Answers about Islam, vol. 4). İstanbul: Nil.

Gülen, Fethullah. 2010d. *Kırık Testi–5: İkindi Yağmurları* (Broken Pitcher, vol. 5: The Afternoon Rains). İstanbul: Nil.

Gülen, Fethullah. 2010e. *Çağ ve Nesil–7: Işığın Göründüğü Ufuk* (The Modern Age and the Contemporary Generation, vol. 7: The Horizon Manifesting the Light). İstanbul: Nil.

Gülen, Fethullah. 2010f. *Kırık Testi–4: Ümit Burcu* (Broken Pitcher, vol. 4: The Constellation of Hope). İstanbul: Nil.

Gülen, Fethullah. 2010g. *Ruhumuzun Heykelini Dikerken–2* (The Statue of Our Souls, vol. 2). İstanbul: Nil.

Gülen, Fethullah. 2010h. *Kırık Testi–6: Diriliş Çağrısı* (Broken Pitcher, vol. 6: Call for Renewal). İstanbul: Nil.

Gülen, Fethullah. 2010i. *Speech and Power of Expression. On Language, Esthetics, and Belief.* New Jersey: Tughra.

Gülen, Fethullah. 2010j. *Prizma–4* (Prism, vol. 4). İstanbul: Nil.

Gülen, Fethullah. 2010k. *Kırık Mızrap* (Broken Plectrum). İstanbul: Nil.

Gülen, Fethullah. 2009a. *Kırık Testi–2: Sohbet-i Canan* (Broken Pitcher, vol. 2: Talks of the Beloved). İstanbul: Nil.

Gülen, Fethullah. 2009b. *Fasıldan Fasıla–4* (From Time to Time, vol. 4). İstanbul: Nil.

Gülen, Fethullah. 2009c. *Kırık Testi–1* (Broken Pitcher, vol. 1). İstanbul: Nil.

Gülen, Fethullah. 2008a. *İrşad Ekseni* (The Pivot of Enlightenment). İstanbul: Nil.

Gülen, Fethullah. 2008b. *Çağ ve Nesil–2: Buhranlar Anaforunda İnsan* (The Modern Age and the Contemporary Generation, vol. 2: Man in the Swirl of Crises). İzmir: Nil.

Gülen, Fethullah. 2008c. *Çağ ve Nesil–1* (The Modern Age and the Contemporary Generation, vol. 1). İzmir: Nil.

Gülen, Fethullah. 2008d. *Prizma–3* (Prism, vol. 3). İstanbul: Nil.

Gülen, Fethullah. 2008e. *Çağ ve Nesil–6: Yeşeren Düşünceler* (The Modern Age and the Contemporary Generation, vol. 6: Blossoming Thoughts). İzmir: Nil.

Gülen, Fethullah. 2007a. *Ölçü veya Yoldaki Işıklar* (Pearls of Wisdom). İstanbul: Nil.

Gülen, Fethullah. 2007b. *The Statue of Our Souls.* New Jersey: The Light.

Gülen, Fethullah. 2007c. *Prizma–2* (Prism, vol. 2). İstanbul: Nil.

Gülen, Fethullah. 2006a. *Çağ ve Nesil–8: Örnekleri Kendinden Bir Hareket* (The Modern Age and the Contemporary Generation, vol. 8: The Movement with its Own Samples). İstanbul: Nil.

Gülen, Fethullah. 2006b. *İnsanın Özündeki Sevgi* (Love in the Essence of Human Beings). İstanbul: Ufuk.

Gülen, Fethullah. 2006c. *Fasıldan Fasıla–5: Fikir Atlası* (From Time to Time, vol. 5: The Atlas of Thought). İstanbul: Nil.

Gülen, Fethullah. 2006d. *İnsanın Özündeki Sevgi* (Love in the Essence of Man). İstanbul. Ufuk.

Gülen, Fethullah. 2005a. *Pearls of Wisdom.* New Jersey: The Light.

Gülen, Fethullah. 2005b. *Kırık Testi 4: Ümit Burcu* (Broken Pitcher, vol. 4: The Constellation of Hope). İstanbul: Gazeteciler ve Yazarlar Vakfı.

Gülen, Fethullah. 2004a. "Paranoya İhtiyacı" (The Need for Paranoia). *Sızıntı*, nr. 300.

Gülen, Fethullah. 2004b. "Hak Kelimesi ve Ötesi" (The Word Justice and the Beyond). *Yeni Ümit*, nr. 63.

Gülen, Fethullah. 2003. "Işık Karanlık, Devr i Dâimi" (The Cycle of Light and Darkness). *Sızıntı*, nr. 298.

Gülen, Fethullah. 2002a. *Çağ ve Nesil–4: Zamanın Altın Dilimi* (The Modern Age and the Contemporary Generation, vol. 4: The Golden Period of Time). İzmir: Nil.

Gülen, Fethullah. 2002b. *Çağ ve Nesil–5: Günler Baharı Soluklarken* (The Modern Age and the Contemporary Generation, vol. 5: Days Feeling the Spring). İzmir: Nil.

Gülen, Fethullah. 2000. "Dar Bir Çerçevede Kadın" (The woman in a narrow framework). *Yağmur*, vol. 1, nr. 7.

Gülen, Fethullah. 1999. "İslam Düşüncesinin Ana Karakteristiği" (The Main Characteristics of the Islamic Thought). *Yeni Ümit*, nr. 44.

Gülen, Fethullah. 1998a. "Kültür Problemimiz ya da Kendimiz Olma–2" (Our Cultural Problem or Finding our Idendity–2). *Yeni Ümit*, nr. 42.

Gülen, Fethullah. 1998b. *Mefkûre İnsanı* (Man of Ideal). *Sızıntı*, nr. 237.

Gülen, Fethullah. 1998c. *Asrın Getirdiği Tereddütler–3* (Questions and Answers about Islam, vol. 3). İzmir: Nil.

Gülen, Fethullah. 1997a. "Orta Asya'da Eğitim Hizmetleri" (Educational Services in the Central Asia). *Yeni Türkiye Dergisi*, nr. 15. pp. 685–692.

Gülen, Fethullah. 1997b. *Fasıldan Fasıla–3* (From Time to Time, vol. 3). İzmir: Nil.

Gülen, Fethullah. 1996. *Fasıldan Fasıla–2* (From Time to Time, vol. 2). İzmir: Nil.

Gülen, Fethullah. 1985. "Izdırapla Bütünleşen Ruhlar" (The Souls Unified with Grief). *Sızıntı*, nr. 73.

Gündem, Mehmet. 2005. *Fethullah Gülen'le 11 Gün* (11 Days with Fethullah Gülen). İstanbul: Alfa.

Ilıcak, Nazlı. 1998. "21. Yüzyıla Yeni Bir Ses: Fethullah Gülen" (Fethullah Gülen: A New Voice for the 21st Century). *Akşam*. 12 Mart.

Özsoy, Osman. 1998. *Fethullah Gülen Hocaefendi ile Canlı Yayında Gündem* (Agenda with Fethullah Gülen Hocaefendi). İstanbul: Alfa.

Sarıtoprak, Zeki and Ali Ünal. 2005. "An Interview with Fethullah Gülen." *The Muslim World*. 95:3.

Sevindi, Nevval. 2002. Fethullah Gülen'le Global Hoşgörü ve New York Sohbetleri. İstanbul: Timaş.

Turgut, Hulusi. 1998. "Fethullah Gülen ve Okullar" (Fethullah Gülen and the Schools). *Yeni Yüzyıl*. 15 Ocak

Ünal, Ali. 2002. *M. Fethullah Gülen: Bir Portre Denemesi* (An Essay of Gülen's Portrait). İstanbul: Nil.

INDEX